perspectives

Technology and Society

D1244723

Academic Editor

Dianne Fallon

York County Technical College

coursewise
publishing
inc.

Bellevue • Boulder • Dubuque • Madison • St. Paul

Our mission at **Coursewise** is to help students make connections—linking theory to practice and the classroom to the outside world. Learners are motivated to synthesize ideas when course materials are placed in a context they recognize. By providing gateways to contemporary and enduring issues, **Coursewise** publications will expand students' awareness of and context for the course subject.

For more information on **Coursewise,** visit us at our web site: http://www.coursewise.com

To order an examination copy: Houghton Mifflin Sixth Floor Media 800-565-6247 (voice); 800-565-6236 (fax)

Coursewise Publishing Editorial Staff

Thomas Doran, ceo/publisher: Environmental Science/Geography/Journalism/Marketing/Speech
Edgar Laube, publisher: Political Science/Psychology/Sociology
Linda Meehan Avenarius, publisher: **Courselinks™**
Sue Pulvermacher-Alt, publisher: Education/Health/Gender Studies
Victoria Putman, publisher: Anthropology/Philosophy/Religion
Tom Romaniak, publisher: Business/Criminal Justice/Economics
Kathleen Schmitt, publishing assistant

Coursewise Publishing Production Staff

Lori A. Blosch, permissions coordinator
Mary Monner, production coordinator
Victoria Putman, production manager

Note: Readings in this book appear exactly as they were published.
Thus, inconsistencies in style and usage among the different
readings are likely.

Cover photo: Copyright © 1997 T. Teshigawara/Panoramic Images, Chicago, IL. All Rights Reserved.

Interior design and cover design by Jeff Storm

Library of Congress Catalog Card Number: 99-62218

ISBN 0-618-01238-9

Printed in the United States of America by Coursewise Publishing, Inc.
7 North Pinckney Street, Suite 346, Madison, WI 53703

10 9 8 7 6 5 4 3 2 1

from the
Publisher

Edgar Laube

Coursewise Publishing

One of my best friends in college came back very excited from a spring break trip to Florida. He had gone alone, driven straight through from Minnesota, and had camped out on a beach somewhere. What excited him, though, was that he had managed not to utter a word for seven days. It turned out that, after two days of the trip, he realized that he hadn't spoken to anyone, so at that point he decided to make an effort to extend the silence. I never found out what prompted him to start talking again.

I'm pretty sure that this would not be everybody's idea of a good time. However, I was struck by the fact that my friend had stepped back, and stepped away, from an activity that we all take for granted. In the process of doing so, he clearly developed a new perspective on what it means to communicate verbally. I'm sure that someone has stated this notion much more grandly: It's in changing a habit or routine that we begin to see the habit or routine in a new light. Or, the closer we are to something (a person, an idea, a behavior), the harder it is to see it objectively.

I mention this episode from thirty years ago because the lesson learned might apply to our current use of information and communications technology—the subject of this reader. We're surrounded by this technology, but we don't often step away from it to think about its effects and its implications for how we act and think, *and even for who we are.* These are huge questions, and they're not going to go away anytime soon.

Dianne Fallon has done a marvelous job of constructing a reader that helps us grapple with this large topic. Here you'll find the subject broken into eight sections. Each section is relevant and important in its own way, and offers differing perspectives. The result is a reader that helps you make sense of this thing—technology—that seems to have found its way into almost every aspect of our lives. It isn't always easy to live with it, and we can't live without it, so the smart thing is to try to understand it. And so, Dianne, thank you for your thoughtful presentation of these readings and your attention to the needs of students. You've helped us all step away and consider these issues in a coherent way.

Students, I hope that this reader will help you form your own opinions on the role of technology in your lives and in our society. Be sure to check out the rich resources at the accompanying **Courselinks**™ site for Technology and Society (http://www.courselinks.com). While you're there, please let Dianne and me know what you think of this reader and the site. We'd really like to hear from you.

Dianne Fallon is the Department Chair for English/Humanities at York County Technical College in Wells, Maine. She teaches a research and writing course called "Critical Thinking via the Internet," which focuses on social and ethical issues related to technology and the Internet. She also teaches composition, literature, and other writing and communications courses.

Her research interests include literacy acquisition and the teaching and learning of writing. She is especially interested in exploring how the integration of technology in the classroom influences student motivation. She also writes fiction and essays.

Dianne completed a bachelor's degree in English from Bowdoin College in 1984. She earned a master's degree in creative writing in 1993 from S.U.N.Y. Binghamton and a doctorate in English/creative writing from the same institution in 1996.

In her spare time, Dianne is either reading, drinking coffee, or planning some kind of outdoor adventure (or doing all of the above). In the summer of 1998, she completed a cross-country bicycle trip with her husband. They visited thirty-eight public libraries in fourteen states and happily discovered an email connection at most of them.

from the
Academic Editor

Dianne Fallon
York County Technical College

Technology is changing the ways we live, work, and communicate, and it's also changing us—at a dizzying pace. As a college student in the early 1980s, I typed all of my papers, conducted research by thumbing through the library card catalogue, and used the pen and the telephone to communicate with distant friends and family. For a long time, I purposely resisted adopting new technologies into my life. Technology, I believed, might automate my life, accelerate its pace, and alienate me from the human community. I had chosen to live in a small Maine town because I wanted a sense of community in my life: face-to-face interactions with real people. When my bank issued ATM cards, I stuck with my teller and supermarket check-cashing clerks. As answering machines became more common, I refused to give into a talking box that might replace conversations with family and friends.

In the late 1980s, I had the opportunity to teach overseas in Morocco. In the city of Safi, I lived comfortably but without many everyday modern conveniences like the telephone, the refrigerator, and the microwave oven. Communicating often required physical effort: a walk to the public phone at the post office or a bike ride across town to check in with friends. Lack of technology definitely slowed the pace of my life, a change that sometimes felt liberating and at other times frustrating.

When I returned to the United States in 1990, I was amazed at the extent to which once-scarce technologies—fax machines, pagers, personal computers—were now commonplace. Everyone had an answering machine, an ATM card, and a cellular phone, and now I wanted them, too. In the aftermath of life overseas, I willingly embraced these new technologies that promised to make the daily business of life smoother. It wasn't long before I'd invested in a computer, signed up for my first email account, and set my new answering machine to screen unwanted calls. With my ATM card, I could get money when I needed it, although I was disturbed to learn that a bank denied me a credit card because of erroneous information on my credit report. I loved communicating by email, but soon was overwhelmed by messages and annoyed by junk mail spamming. And I was glad to read student papers prepared, revised, and spell-checked on computer, but troubled by the fact that many of my students were at an academic disadvantage because they couldn't afford to buy their own computers.

Today I use email, listservs, and chat forums as a regular tool for communicating with students and professional colleagues. In the classroom, we harness the resources of the World Wide Web to conduct research, and my students build web pages to share their findings with the world. I can conveniently work at home because I can retrieve my voice mail from the office and log into my email account via the Internet.

I am a technology convert, but I remain a technology critic. As such, I critically examine technology at the same time as I embrace it. It is inevitable that technology will continue to change and that it will continue to change us, but that doesn't mean we can't make informed decisions about how we use and respond to technology's evolution. I designed *Perspectives: Technology and Society* to help you to develop an informed perspective for thinking through important issues related to technology and society.

The readings in this volume invite you to consider the social aspects, impacts, and implications of computers, the Internet, and related technologies. You will find a blend of theoretical articles, book excerpts, and journalistic pieces intended to stimulate your thinking about current controversies and issues related to technology, the Internet, and society. How do people evolve with technology? Is technology simply a "tool," or is it laden with values that shape our thoughts and actions? What ethical issues arise as new technologies are integrated into communities, schools, businesses, and the home?

These questions defy easy answers. The readings in *Perspectives: Technology and Society,* the resources at the accompanying **Courselinks**™ site for Technology and Society, and the R.E.A.L. web sites listed in this book and at the **Courselinks** site will provide you with a framework for becoming an effective and informed user of technology—a person who can raise questions and make judgments about the uses of technology in your classrooms, your community, and your workplace.

New technologies are introduced almost daily. The resources available on the Internet and World Wide Web are exploding at an exponential rate. Therefore, consider this volume a starting point for your exploration of the ideas, themes, and questions these new technologies raise. One of the most wonderful outcomes of the communications revolution is that it has broken down the wall between editors and readers. I look forward to hearing your thoughts about this book, its features, and your experiences in exploring the vast territory of cyberspace. What do you like about *Perspectives: Technology and Society?* Which readings are most intriguing? What would you like to see changed? Let me know what you think by writing to me at ydfallon@yctc.net.

I'd like to thank several people who helped me develop this reader: Ed Laube, my editor at **Coursewise,** who believed in this project; York County Technical College student Michelle Cote, who checked the accuracy of web addresses; Sarah Campbell, college librarian, who tracked down many articles and books for me; and my students in "Critical Thinking via the Internet," who help me to learn more about the Internet each time I teach. Finally, I'd like to thank my husband, Jeff Clifford, for his careful reading and his support along the way.

Editorial Board

WiseGuide Introduction

Critical Thinking and Bumper Stickers

The bumper sticker said: Question Authority. This is a simple directive that goes straight to the heart of critical thinking. The issue is not whether the authority is right or wrong; it's the questioning process that's important. Questioning helps you develop awareness and a clearer sense of what you think. That's critical thinking.

Critical thinking is a new label for an old approach to learning—that of challenging all ideas, hypotheses, and assumptions. In the physical and life sciences, systematic questioning and testing methods (known as the scientific method) help verify information, and objectivity is the benchmark on which all knowledge is pursued. In the social sciences, however, where the goal is to study people and their behavior, things get fuzzy. It's one thing for the chemistry experiment to work out as predicted, or for the petri dish to yield a certain result. It's quite another matter, however, in the social sciences, where the subject is ourselves. Objectivity is harder to achieve.

Although you'll hear critical thinking defined in many different ways, it really boils down to analyzing the ideas and messages that you receive. What are you being asked to think or believe? Does it make sense, objectively? Using the same facts and considerations, could you reasonably come up with a different conclusion? And, why does this matter in the first place? As the bumper sticker urged, question authority. Authority can be a textbook, a politician, a boss, a big sister, or an ad on television. Whatever the message, learning to question it appropriately is a habit that will serve you well for a lifetime. And in the meantime, thinking critically will certainly help you be course wise.

Question Authority

Getting Connected

This reader is a tool for connected learning. This means that the readings and other learning aids explained here will help you to link classroom theory to real-world issues. They will help you to think critically and to make long-lasting learning connections. Feedback from both instructors and students has helped us to develop some suggestions on how you can wisely use this connected learning tool.

WiseGuide Pedagogy

A wise reader is better able to be a critical reader. Therefore, we want to help you get wise about the articles in this reader. Each section of *Perspectives* has three tools to help you: the WiseGuide Intro, the WiseGuide Wrap-Up, and the Putting It in *Perspectives* review form.

WiseGuide Intro

In the WiseGuide Intro, the Academic Editor introduces the section, gives you an overview of the topics covered, and explains why particular articles were selected and what's important about them.

Also in the WiseGuide Intro, you'll find several key points or learning objectives that highlight the most important things to remember from this section. These will help you to focus your study of section topics.

WiseGuide Intro

At the end of the WiseGuide Intro, you'll find questions designed to stimulate critical thinking. Wise students will keep these questions in mind as they read an article (we repeat the questions at the start of the articles as a reminder). When you finish each article, check your understanding. Can you answer the questions? If not, go back and reread the article. The Academic Editor has written sample responses for many of the questions, and you'll find these online at the **Courselinks**™ site for this course. More about **Courselinks** in a minute. . . .

WiseGuide Wrap-Up

Be course wise and develop a thorough understanding of the topics covered in this course. The WiseGuide Wrap-Up at the end of each section will help you do just that with concluding comments or summary points that repeat what's most important to understand from the section you just read.

In addition, we try to get you wired up by providing a list of select Internet resources—what we call R.E.A.L. web sites because they're **R**elevant, **E**xciting, **A**pproved, and **L**inked. The information at these web sites will enhance your understanding of a topic. (Remember to use your Passport and start at http://www.courselinks.com so that if any of these sites have changed, you'll have the latest link.)

Putting It in *Perspectives* Review Form

At the end of the book is the Putting It in *Perspectives* review form. Your instructor may ask you to complete this form as an assignment or for extra credit. If nothing else, consider doing it on your own to help you critically think about the reading.

Prompts at the end of each article encourage you to complete this review form. Feel free to copy the form and use it as needed.

The Courselinks™ Site

The **Courselinks** Passport is your ticket to a wonderful world of integrated web resources designed to help you with your course work. These resources are found at the **Courselinks** site for your course area. This is where the readings in this book and the key topics of your course are linked to an exciting array of online learning tools. Here you will find carefully selected readings, web links, quizzes, worksheets, and more, tailored to your course and approved as connected learning tools. The ever-changing, always interesting **Courselinks** site features a number of carefully integrated resources designed to help you be course wise. These include:

- **R.E.A.L. Sites** At the core of a **Courselinks** site is the list of R.E.A.L. sites. This is a select group of web sites for studying, not surfing. Like the readings in this book, these sites have been selected, reviewed, and approved by the Academic Editor and the Editorial Board. The R.E.A.L. sites are arranged by topic and are annotated with short descriptions and key words to make them easier for you to use for reference or research. With R.E.A.L. sites, you're studying approved resources within seconds—and not wasting precious time surfing unproven sites.

- **Editor's Choice** Here you'll find updates on news related to your course, with links to the actual online sources. This is also where we'll tell you about changes to the site and about online events.

- **Course Overview** This is a general description of the typical course in this area of study. While your instructor will provide specific course objectives, this overview helps you place the course in a generic context and offers you an additional reference point.

- **www.orksheet** Focus your trip to a R.E.A.L. site with the www.orksheet. Each of the 10 to 15 questions will prompt you to take in the best that site has to offer. Use this tool for self-study, or if required, email it to your instructor.

- **Course Quiz** The questions on this self-scoring quiz are related to articles in the reader, information at R.E.A.L. sites, and other course topics, and will help you pinpoint areas you need to study. Only you will know your score—it's an easy, risk-free way to keep pace!

- **Topic Key** The online Topic Key is a listing of the main topics in your course, and it correlates with the Topic Key that appears in this reader. This handy reference tool also links directly to those R.E.A.L. sites that are especially appropriate to each topic, bringing you integrated online resources within seconds!

- **Web Savvy Student Site** If you're new to the Internet or want to brush up, stop by the Web Savvy Student site. This unique supplement is a complete **Courselinks** site unto itself. Here, you'll find basic information on using the Internet, creating a web page, communicating on the web, and more. Quizzes and Web Savvy Worksheets test your web knowledge, and the R.E.A.L. sites listed here will further enhance your understanding of the web.

- **Student Lounge** Drop by the Student Lounge to chat with other students taking the same course or to learn more about careers in your major. You'll find links to resources for scholarships, financial aid, internships, professional associations, and jobs. Take a look around the Student Lounge and give us your feedback. We're open to remodeling the Lounge per your suggestions.

Building Better Perspectives!

Please tell us what you think of this *Perspectives* volume so we can improve the next one. Here's how you can help:

1. Visit our **Coursewise** site at: http://www.coursewise.com

2. Click on *Perspectives*. Then select the Building Better *Perspectives* Form for your book.

3. Forms and instructions for submission are available online.

Tell us what you think—did the readings and online materials help you make some learning connections? Were some materials more helpful than others? Thanks in advance for helping us build better *Perspectives*.

Student Internships

If you enjoy evaluating these articles or would like to help us evaluate the **Courselinks** site for this course, check out the **Coursewise** Student Internship Program. For more information, visit:

http://www.coursewise.com/intern.html

Contents

At **Coursewise**, we're publishing connected learning tools. That means that the book you are holding is only a part of this publication. You'll also want to harness the integrated resources that **Coursewise** has developed at the fun and highly useful **Courselinks**™ web site for *Perspectives: Technology and Society.* If you purchased this book new, use the Passport that was shrink-wrapped to this volume to obtain site access. If you purchased a used copy of this book, then you need to buy a stand-alone Passport. If your bookstore doesn't stock Passports to **Courselinks** sites, visit http://www.courselinks.com for ordering information.

section 1

Critical Perspectives on Technology and Society

section 2

Computers Transforming Work, Home, and Family

section 3

Computers, Schools, and Learning

section 4

Men, Women and the Virtual Androgyne: Gender, Identity, and Social Relationships in Cyberspace

section

5

Censorship, Privacy, and Security in Cyberspace: Is Big Brother Watching You?

section 6

Truth, Lies, and the Creation of Knowledge

section 7

The Internet, Democracy, and the Silent Majority

section

8

**Future Trends:
Computers,
Information,
and Society**

Topic Key

This Topic Key is an important tool for learning. It will help you integrate this reader into your course studies. Listed below, in alphabetical order, are important topics covered in this volume. Below each topic you'll find the reading numbers and titles, and R.E.A.L. web site addresses, relating to that topic. Note that the Topic Key might not include every topic your instructor chooses to emphasize. If you don't find the topic you're looking for in the Topic Key, check the index or the online topic key at the **Courselinks**™ site.

Censorship
18   Cyber-Rape: How Virtual Is It?
22   Sex, Kids, and the Public Library
23   Free Speech on the Electronic Frontier
24   Two-Edged Sword: Asian Regimes
      on the Internet
25   On the Net, Anything Goes
26   What's Left of the Communications
      Decency Act?
30   As Hate Spills onto the Web,
      a Struggle Over Whether, and How,
      to Control It

Center for Democracy & Technology
http://www.cdt.org/

Electronic Frontier Foundation
http://www.eff.org/

Electronic Privacy Information Center
http://www.epic.org/

Computer-Mediated Communication
17   The Strange Case of the Electronic
      Lover
19   Gender and Democracy in Computer-
      Mediated Communication
20   Sad, Lonely World Discovered
      in Cyberspace
21   Technology: Critics Are Picking Apart
      a Professor's Study That Linked
      Internet Use to Loneliness and
      Depression
35   A Rape in Cyberspace: Or How an
      Evil Clown, a Haitian Trickster Spirit,
      Two Wizards, and a Cast of Dozens
      Turned a Database into a Society

Loebner Prize Home Page
http://www.loebner.net/Prizef/
      loebner-prize.html

Carnegie Mellon Human-Computer
      Interaction Institute
http://www.cs.cmu.edu/~hcii/

Computers and Society
1   The Medium Is the Message
2   Technology Makes Us Better:
      Our Oldest Computer, Upgraded
3   Out There in the Middle of the Buzz
4   Taking the Message Back
      from the Medium

Computers & Society
http://www.engr.csulb.edu/~sigcas/

The New York Times
http://www.nytimes.com/

Technology Review
http://www.techreview.com/

Cyberculture
15   Is the Net Redefining Our Identity?
16   Gender Swapping on the Internet
17   The Strange Case of the Electronic
      Lover
35   A Rape in Cyberspace: Or How an
      Evil Clown, a Haitian Trickster Spirit,
      Two Wizards, and a Cast of Dozens
      Turned a Database into a Society

Sexuality and Cyberspace
http://www.echonyc.com/~women/Issue17/
      index.html

Texts by Julian Dibbell
http://www.levity.com/julian/
      indexvanilla.html

Cyberdemocracy
24   Two-Edged Sword: Asian Regimes
      on the Internet
35   A Rape in Cyberspace: Or How an
      Evil Clown, a Haitian Trickster Spirit,
      Two Wizards, and a Cast of Dozens
      Turned a Database into a Society
36   Cyberdemocracy: Tip O'Neill, Meet
      Alvin Toffler
37   The Promise and Perils
      of Cyberdemocracy
38   Digital Democracy in Action

Center for Civic Networking
http://www.civicnet.org/

Center for Responsive Politics
http://www.crp.org/

National Budget Simulation
http://garnet.berkeley.edu:3333/budget/
      budget.html

Project Vote Smart
http://www.vote-smart.org/

Cyberlaw
25   On the Net, Anything Goes
26   What's Left of the Communications
      Decency Act?
32   Simulations on Trial

The New York Times
http://www.nytimes.com/

E-Commerce
40   From Internet to Information
      Superhighway
41   Seven Thinkers in Search
      of an Information Highway

The New York Times
http://www.nytimes.com/

Education
11   N-Gen Learning
12   The Computer Delusion
13   Computers, Thinking, and Schools
      in the "New World Economic Order"
14   Where Computers Do Work
41   Seven Thinkers in Search
      of an Information Superhighway

Computers and Classrooms: The Status
      of Technology in U.S. Schools
http://www.ets.org/research/pic/
      compclass.html

The New York Times
http://www.nytimes.com/

Planet Papert
http://sbm-www.pepperdine.edu/
      ~gstager/planetpapert.html

T.H.E. Journal
http://www.thejournal.com/

section 1

Learning Objectives

- Explain McLuhan's concept that "the medium is the message."

- Provide five examples of how computer technology improves the quality of life.

- Evaluate McKibben's concern about the erosion of opportunities for solitude.

- Explain Spindler's perspective on computers and society.

Critical Perspectives on Technology and Society

Remember the typewriter? Do you know how to use one? Less than fifteen years ago, the personal desktop computer was a novelty, reserved for consumers on the cutting edge. In most offices, IBM Selectrics far outnumbered computers.

Today, an estimated 50 percent of American households own one or more computers. According to a recent Nielsen Media Research survey, 70 million American adults are connected to the Internet. These figures surely will increase.

We are living in the Information Age. Everyone, it seems, is connected—or are they? If 70 million people represent a third of American adults, as the Nielsen survey surmises, then the majority of Americans remain unconnected. If the world is home to 6 billion people, as the United Nations Population Division estimates, then we see that the vast majority of global citizens are not part of the Information Age. While a significant number of people in several countries are living in a connected, digital world, we are far from the "global village" envisioned by Marshall McLuhan in 1964.

I point out these statistics because they highlight the need to maintain a critical stance on computers and technology. The trumpeting of statistics on Internet growth tends to obscure the fact that most people are not connected. The rush to computerize every aspect of life suggests that computers are the means to a more efficient, problem-free society. In many poor countries, providing clean water to villagers will remain a priority over connecting to the Internet, since clean water has a far greater impact on health and well-being than does a modem connection.

But I can anticipate arguments to the contrary—that the Internet, for example, will provide easy access to information about how to install and maintain modern water systems. Never mind that most villagers won't be able to read such information, especially if it's printed in English, or that they may lack the funds to purchase the pumps needed for cleaner water. The mantra "Information is power!" tends to discount the reality that access to information isn't necessarily access to power.

This example may seem far-fetched, but, in 1995, former Speaker of the House Newt Gingrich proposed a special tax credit to help poor people buy laptop computers. Laptop computers, he argued, would help reduce poverty because they would promote children's success in school and would allow poor people to start their own computer-related businesses.

While probably no family would object to receiving a discounted computer, Gingrich's proposal ignored the fact that owning a computer isn't necessarily a means to self-empowerment. You can debate this point in class—here, I will point out that the Gingrich proposal flows from a way of looking at the world called "technocratism." A technocrat enthusiastically endorses technology as the primary means to progress. Computers, technocrats assert, have made life better in many respects and will continue to improve the quality of life.

1

If you come to this text with a technocratic bias, you already may be thinking that I am taking a position against technology—that I am a modern-day Luddite. A Luddite is someone who is generally suspicious of technology and opposed to changes that involve new technologies. The term comes from the history of the Industrial Revolution in England. In the early nineteenth century, bands of workers newly displaced by machinery broke into factories and destroyed equipment, with the hope of saving their jobs. Today, the term has come to mean anyone who is opposed to technology, as well as opposed to accepting the inevitable nature of progress.

People who are critical about the uses of technology are often accused of being Luddites, as if there is always an either/or position. However, a third perspective is that of the technology critic. A technology critic uses critical thinking to examine technology and its appropriateness for a given situation. A technology critic may enthusiastically use technology yet refuse to accept the assumption that new technology is always superior to the old.

In this section, the readings present a variety of perspectives on technology as a means of helping you frame questions about the impact of technology on society and culture. The first reading, "The Medium Is the Message," by Marshall McLuhan, was published in 1964 in his book *Understanding Media*. Often we assume that information and ideas about technology are not valuable unless they are current, but McLuhan's ground-breaking work is more relevant today than ever. Technology, he asserts, is always an extension of ourselves, and new technologies affect how we think and live in unexpected ways.

In the next reading, "Technology Makes Us Better: Our Oldest Computer, Upgraded," by John Tierney, a technology enthusiast, asserts that the Internet, computers, and other technologies have improved the quality of life for many people.

Environmentalist Bill McKibben explores the theme of information overload in his short piece, "Out There in the Middle of the Buzz." Where is the line, he asks, between technology as our tool and technology as our master?

The last selection points again to the need for a critical stance on technology. "Taking the Message Back from the Medium," authored by Michael Spindler, CEO and president of Apple Computer, takes us back to McLuhan as he offers a critical perspective on technology and its impact. The fact that Spindler's livelihood is derived from technology adds an interesting dimension to his comments.

The companion web sites to this unit offer additional resources for exploring issues related to technology and society. The Special Interest Group on Computers and Society publishes a journal called *Computers and Society* and offers an outstanding collection of links related to this theme at the journal's web site. For news and developments related to technology, there may be no better resource than the online version of *The New York Times*. The online edition includes CyberTimes, a special section published expressly for the online audience. Every week it offers interesting commentary, information, and columns on computers and their impact on society.

As you explore the issues and questions raised in this unit, consider the messages of the media or technology with which you interface on a daily basis. What messages are contained in the word processing program with which you write your papers? How has the automobile impacted the design of your city or your college campus? How does your use of e-mail influence your relationships with distant family and friends? The readings in this chapter won't answer these questions, but they will help you develop your own answers!

Questions

Reading 1. Is technology simply a tool, or does it come laden with values? How does technology affect the way we think and act?

Reading 2. Does technology make life better? How might technology create a greater sense of community?

Reading 3. Is it possible today to "get away from it all"? Is it necessary?

Reading 4. Why does this computer company executive endorse a critical approach to technology? What are his concerns about the use of computers in society?

Is technology simply a tool, or does it come laden with values? How does technology affect the way we think and act?

The Medium Is the Message

Marshall McLuhan

In a culture like ours, long accustomed to splitting and dividing all things as a means of control, it is sometimes a bit of a shock to be reminded that, in operational and practical fact, the medium is the message. This is merely to say that the personal and social consequences of any medium—that is, of any extension of ourselves—result from the new scale that is introduced into our affairs by each extension of ourselves, or by any new technology. Thus, with automation, for example, the new patterns of human association tend to eliminate jobs, it is true. That is the negative result. Positively, automation creates roles for people, which is to say depth of involvement in their work and human association that our preceding mechanical technology had destroyed. Many people would be disposed to say that it was not the machine, but what one did with the machine, that was its meaning or message. In terms of the ways in which the machine altered our relations to one another and to ourselves, it mattered not in the least whether it turned out cornflakes or Cadillacs. The restructuring of human work and association was shaped by the technique of fragmentation that is the essence of machine technology. The essence of automation technology is the opposite. It is integral and decentralist in depth, just as the machine was fragmentary, centralist, and superficial in its patterning of human relationships.

The instance of the electric light may prove illuminating in this connection. The electric light is pure information. It is a medium without a message, as it were, unless it is used to spell out some verbal ad or name. This fact, characteristic of all media, means that the "content" of any medium is always another medium. The content of writing is speech, just as the written word is the content of print, and print is the content of the telegraph. If it is asked, "What is the content of speech?," it is necessary to say, "It is an actual process of thought, which is in itself nonverbal." An abstract painting represents direct manifestation of creative thought processes as they might appear in computer designs. What we are considering here, however, are the psychic and social consequences of the designs or patterns as they amplify or accelerate existing processes. For the "message" of any medium or technology is the change of scale or pace or pattern that it introduces into human affairs. The railway did not introduce movement or transportation or wheel or road into human society, but it accelerated and enlarged the scale of previous human functions, creating totally new kinds of cities and new kinds of work and leisure. This happened whether the railway functioned in a tropical or a northern environment, and is quite independent of the freight or content of the railway medium. The airplane, on the other hand, by accelerating the rate of transportation, tends to dissolve the railway form of city, politics, and association, quite independently of what the airplane is used for.

Let us return to the electric light. Whether the light is being used for brain surgery or night baseball is a matter of indifference. It could be argued that these activities are in some way the "content" of the electric light, since they could not exist without the electric light. This fact merely underlines the point that "the medium is the message" because it is the medium that shapes and controls the scale and form of human association and action.

Marshall McLuhan, "The Medium Is the Message," from *Understanding Media: The Extensions of Man*, MIT Press.

The content or uses of such media are as diverse as they are ineffectual in shaping the form of human association. Indeed, it is only too typical that the "content" of any medium blinds us to the character of the medium. It is only today that industries have become aware of the various kinds of business in which they are engaged. When IBM discovered that it was not in the business of making office equipment or business machines, but that it was in the business of processing information, then it began to navigate with clear vision. The General Electric Company makes a considerable portion of its profits from electric light bulbs and lighting systems. It has not yet discovered that, quite as much as A.T.&T., it is in the business of moving information.

The electric light escapes attention as a communication medium just because it has no "content." And this makes it an invaluable instance of how people fail to study media at all. For it is not till the electric light is used to spell out some brand name that it is noticed as a medium. Then it is not the light but the "content" (or what is really another medium) that is noticed. The message of the electric light is like the message of electric power in industry, totally radical, pervasive, and decentralized. For electric light and power are separate from their uses, yet they eliminate time and space factors in human association exactly as do radio, telegraph, telephone, and TV, creating involvement in depth.

A fairly complete handbook for studying the extensions of man could be made up from selections from Shakespeare. Some might quibble about whether or not he was referring to TV in these familiar lines from *Romeo and Juliet:*

But soft! what light through yonder window breaks?
It speaks, and yet says nothing.

In *Othello,* which, as much as *King Lear,* is concerned with the torment of people transformed by illusions, there are these lines that bespeak Shakespeare's intuition of the transforming powers of new media:

Is there not charms
By which the property of youth and maidhood
May be abus'd? Have you not read Roderigo,
Of some such thing?

In Shakespeare's *Troilus and Cressida,* which is almost completely devoted to both a psychic and social study of communication, Shakespeare states his awareness that true social and political navigation depend upon anticipating the consequences of innovation:

The providence that's in a watchful state
Knows almost every grain of Plutus' gold,
Finds bottom in the uncomprehensive deeps,
Keeps place with thought, and almost like the gods
Does thoughts unveil in their dumb cradles.

The increasing awareness of the action of media, quite independently of their "content" or programming, was indicated in the annoyed and anonymous stanza:

In modern thought, (if not in fact)
Nothing is that doesn't act,
So that is reckoned wisdom which
Describes the scratch but not the itch.

The same kind of total, configurational awareness that reveals why the medium is socially the message has occurred in the most recent and radical medical theories. In his *Stress of Life,* Hans Selye tells of the dismay of a research colleague on hearing of Selye's theory:

When he saw me thus launched on yet another enraptured description of what I had observed in animals treated with this or that impure, toxic material, he looked at me with desperately sad eyes and said in obvious despair: "But Selye, try to realize what you are doing before it is too late! You have now decided to spend your entire life studying the pharmacology of dirt!"

(Hans Selye, *The Stress of Life*)

As Selye deals with the total environmental situation in his "stress" theory of disease, so the latest approach to media study considers not only the "content" but the medium and the cultural matrix within which the particular medium operates. The older unawareness of the psychic and social effects of media can be illustrated from almost any of the conventional pronouncements.

In accepting an honorary degree from the University of Notre Dame a few years ago, General David Sarnoff made this statement: "We are too prone to make technological instruments the scapegoats for the sins of those who wield them. The products of modern science are not in themselves good or bad; it is the way they are used that determines their value." That is the voice of the current somnambulism. Suppose we were to say, "Apple pie is in itself neither good nor bad; it is the way it is used that determines its value." Or, "The smallpox virus is in itself neither good nor bad; it is the way it is used that determines its value." Again, "Firearms are in themselves neither good nor bad; it is the way they are used that determines their value." That is, if the slugs reach the right people firearms are good. If the TV tube fires the right ammunition at the right people it is good. I am not being perverse. There is simply nothing in the Sarnoff statement that will bear scrutiny, for it ignores the·nature of the medium, of any and all media, in the true Narcissus style of one hypnotized by the amputation and extension of his own being in a new technical form. General Sarnoff went on to explain his attitude to the technology of print, saying that it was true that print caused much trash to circulate, but it had also disseminated the Bible and the thoughts of seers and philosophers. It has never occurred to General Sarnoff that any technology could do anything but *add* itself on to what we already are.

Such economists as Robert Theobald, W. W. Rostow, and John Kenneth Galbraith have been explaining for years how it is that "classical economics" cannot explain change or growth. And the paradox of mechanization is that although it is itself the cause of maximal growth and change, the principle of mechanization excludes the very possibility of growth or the understanding of change. For mechanization is achieved by fragmentation of any process and by putting the fragmented parts in a series. Yet, as David Hume showed in the eighteenth century, there is no principle of causality in a mere sequence. That one thing follows another accounts for nothing. Nothing follows from following, except change. So the greatest of all reversals occurred with electricity, that ended sequence by making things instant. With instant speed the causes of things began to emerge to awareness again, as they had not done with things in sequence and in concatenation accordingly. Instead of asking which came first, the chicken or the egg, it

suddenly seemed that a chicken was an egg's idea for getting more eggs.

Just before an airplane breaks the sound barrier, sound waves become visible on the wings of the plane. The sudden visibility of sound just as sound ends is an apt instance of that great pattern of being that reveals new and opposite forms just as the earlier forms reach their peak performance. Mechanization was never so vividly fragmented or sequential as in the birth of the movies, the moment that translated us beyond mechanism into the world of growth and organic interrelation. The movie, by sheer speeding up the mechanical, carried us from the world of sequence and connections into the world of creative configuration and structure. The message of the movie medium is that of transition from lineal connections to configurations. It is the transition that produced the now quite correct observation: "If it works, it's obsolete." When electric speed further takes over from mechanical movie sequences, then the lines of force in structures and in media become loud and clear. We return to the inclusive form of the icon.

To a highly literate and mechanized culture the movie appeared as a world of triumphant illusions and dreams that money could buy. It was at this moment of the movie that cubism occurred, and it has been described by E. H. Gombrich (*Art and Illusion*) as "the most radical attempt to stamp out ambiguity and to enforce one reading of the picture—that of a man-made construction, a colored canvas." For cubism substitutes all facets of an object simultaneously for the "point of view" or facet of perspective illusion. Instead of the specialized illusion of the third dimension on canvas, cubism sets

up an interplay of planes and contradiction or dramatic conflict of patterns, lights, textures that "drives home the message" by involvement. This is held by many to be an exercise in painting, not in illusion.

In other words, cubism, by giving the inside and outside, the top, bottom, back, and front and the rest, in two dimensions, drops the illusion of perspective in favor of instant sensory awareness of the whole. Cubism, by seizing on instant total awareness, suddenly announced that *the medium is the message.* Is it not evident that the moment that sequence yields to the simultaneous, one is in the world of the structure and of configuration? Is that not what has happened in physics as in painting, poetry, and in communication? Specialized segments of attention have shifted to total field, and we can now say, "The medium is the message" quite naturally. Before the electric speed and total field, it was not obvious that the medium is the message. The message, it seemed, was the "content," as people used to ask what a painting was *about.* Yet they never thought to ask what a melody was about, nor what a house or a dress was about. In such matters, people retained some sense of the whole pattern, of form and function as a unity. But in the electric age this integral idea of structure and configuration has become so prevalent that educational theory has taken up the matter. Instead of working with specialized "problems" in arithmetic, the structural approach now follows the linea of force in the field of number and has small children meditating about number theory and "sets."

Cardinal Newman said of Napoleon, "He understood the grammar of gunpowder."

Napoleon had paid some attention to other media as well, especially the semaphore telegraph that gave him a great advantage over his enemies. He is on record for saying that "Three hostile newspapers are more to be feared than a thousand bayonets."

Alexis de Tocqueville was the first to master the grammar of print and typography. He was thus able to read off the message of coming change in France and America as if he were Reading aloud from a text that had been handed to him. In fact, the nineteenth century in France and in America was just such an open book to de Tocqueville because he had learned the grammar of print. So he, also, knew when that grammar did not apply. He was asked why he did not write a book on England, since he knew and admired England. He replied:

One would have to have an unusual degree of philosophical folly to believe oneself able to judge England in six months. A year always seemed to me too short a time in which to appreciate the United States properly, and it is much easier to acquire clear and precise notions about the American Union than about Great Britain. In America all laws derive in a sense from the same line of thought. The whole of society, so to speak, is founded upon a single fact; everything springs from a simple principle. One could compare America to a forest pierced by a multitude of straight roads all converging on the same point. One has only to find the center and everything is revealed at a glance. But in England the paths run criss-cross, and it is only by travelling down each one of them that one can build up a picture of the whole.

De Tocqueville, in earlier work on the French Revolution, had explained how it was the printed word that, achieving cultural saturation in the eighteenth century, had homogenized the French nation. Frenchmen were the same kind of people from north to south. The typographic principles of uniformity, continuity, and linearity had overlaid the complexities of ancient feudal and oral society. The Revolution was carried out by the new literati and lawyers.

In England, however, such was the power of the ancient oral traditions of common law, backed by the medieval institution of Parliament, that no uniformity or continuity of the new visual print culture could take complete hold. The result was that the most important event in English history has never taken place; namely, the English Revolution on the lines of the French Revolution. The American Revolution had no medieval legal institutions to discard or to root out, apart from monarchy. And many have held that the American Presidency has become very much more personal and monarchical than any European monarch ever could be.

De Tocqueville's contrast between England and America is clearly based on the fact of typography and of print culture creating uniformity and continuity. England, he says, has rejected this principle and clung to the dynamic or oral common-law tradition. Hence the discontinuity and unpredictable quality of English culture. The grammar of print cannot help to construe the message of oral and nonwritten culture and institutions. The English aristocracy was properly classified as barbarian by Matthew Arnold because its power and status had nothing to do with literacy or with the cultural forms of typography. Said the Duke of Gloucester to Edward Gibbon upon the publication of his *Decline and Fall*: "Another damned fat book, eh, Mr. Gibbon? Scribble, scribble, scribble, eh, Mr. Gibbon?" De Tocqueville was a highly literate aristocrat who was quite able to be detached from the values and assumptions of typography. That is why he alone understood the grammar of typography. And it is only on those terms, standing aside from any structure or medium, that its principles and lines of force can be discerned. For any medium has the power of imposing its own assumption on the unwary. Prediction and control consist in avoiding this subliminal state of Narcissus trance. But the greatest aid to this end is simply in knowing that the spell can occur immediately upon contact, as in the first bars of a melody.

A Passage to India by E. M. Forster is a dramatic study of the inability of oral and intuitive oriental culture to meet with the rational, visual European patterns of experience. "Rational," of course, has for the West long meant "uniform and continuous and sequential." In other words, we have confused reason with literacy, and rationalism with a single technology. Thus in the electric age man seems to the conventional West to become irrational. In Forster's novel the moment of truth and dislocation from the typographic trance of the West comes in the Marabar Caves. Adela Quested's reasoning powers cannot cope with the total inclusive field of resonance that is India. After the Caves: "Life went on as usual, but had no consequences, that is to say, sounds did not echo nor thought develop. Everything seemed cut off at its root and therefore infected with illusion."

A Passage to India (the phrase is from Whitman, who saw America headed Eastward) is a parable of Western man in the electric age, and is only incidentally related to Europe or the Orient. The ultimate conflict between sight and sound, between written and oral kinds of perception and organization of existence is upon us. Since understanding stops action, as Nietzsche observed, we can moderate the fierceness of this conflict by understanding the media that extend us and raise these wars within and without us.

Detribalization by literacy and its traumatic effects on tribal man is the theme of a book by the psychiatrist J. C. Carothers, *The African Mind in Health and Disease* (World Health Organization, Geneva, 1953). Much of his material appeared in an article in *Psychiatry* magazine, November, 1959: "The Culture, Psychiatry, and the Written Word." Again, it is electric speed that has revealed the lines of force operating from Western technology in the remotest areas of bush, savannah, and desert. One example is the Bedouin with his battery radio on board the camel. Submerging natives with floods of concepts for which nothing has prepared them is the normal action of all of our technology. But with electric media Western man himself experiences exactly the same inundation as the remote native. We are no more prepared to encounter radio and TV in our literate milieu than the native of Ghana is able to cope with the literacy that takes him out of his collective tribal world and beaches him in individual isolation. We are as numb in our new electric world as the native involved in our literate and mechanical culture.

Electric speed mingles the cultures of prehistory with the dregs of industrial marketeers, the nonliterate with the semiliterate and the postliterate. Mental breakdown of varying degrees is the very common result of uprooting and inundation with new information and endless new patterns of information. Wyndham Lewis made this a theme of his group of novels called *The Human Age*. The first of these, *The Childermass*, is concerned precisely with accelerated media change as a kind of massacre of the innocents. In our own world as we become more aware of the effects of technology on psychic formation and manifestation, we are losing all confidence in our right to assign guilt. Ancient prehistoric societies regard violent crime as pathetic. The killer is regarded as we do a cancer victim. "How terrible it must be to feel like that," they say. J. M. Synge took up this idea very effectively in his *Playboy of the Western World*.

If the criminal appears as a nonconformist who is unable to meet the demand of technology that we behave in uniform and continuous patterns, literate man is quite inclined to see others who cannot conform as somewhat pathetic. Especially the child, the cripple, the woman, and the colored person appear in a world of visual and typographic technology as victims of injustice. On the other hand, in a culture that assigns roles instead of jobs to people—the dwarf, the skew, the child create their own spaces. They are not expected to fit into some uniform and repeatable niche that is not their size anyway. Consider the phrase "It's a man's world." As a quantitative observation endlessly repeated from within a homogenized culture, this phrase refers to the men in such a culture who have to be homogenized Dagwoods in order to belong at all. It is in our I.Q. testing that we have produced the greatest flood of misbegotten standards. Unaware of our typographic cultural bias, our testers assume that uniform and continuous habits are a sign of intelligence, thus eliminating the ear man and the tactile man.

C. P. Snow, reviewing a book of A. L. Rowse (*The New York Times Book Review*, December 24, 1961) on *Appeasement* and the road to Munich, describes the top level of British brains and experience in the 1930s. "Their I.Q.'s were much higher than usual among political bosses. Why were they such a disaster?" The view of Rowse, Snow approves: "They would not listen to warnings because they did not wish to hear." Being anti-Red made it impossible for them to read the message of Hitler. But their failure was as nothing compared to our present one. The American stake in literacy as a technology or uniformity applied to every level of education, government, industry, and social life is totally threatened by the electric technology. The threat of Stalin or Hitler was external. The electric technology is within the gates, and we are numb, deaf, blind, and mute about its encounter with the Gutenberg technology, on and through which the American way of life was formed. It is, however, no time to suggest strategies when the threat has not even been acknowledged to exist. I am in the position of Louis Pasteur telling doctors that their greatest enemy was quite invisible, and quite unrecognized by them. Our conventional response to all media, namely that it is how they are used that counts, is the numb stance of the technological idiot. For the "content" of a medium is like the juicy piece of meat carried by the burglar to distract the watchdog of the mind. The effect of the medium is made strong and intense just because it is given another medium as "content." The content of a movie is a novel or a play or an opera. The effect of the movie form is not related to its program content. The "content" of writing or print is speech, but the reader is almost entirely unaware either of print or of speech.

Arnold Toynbee is innocent of any understanding of media as they have shaped history, but he is full of examples that the student of media can use. At one moment he can seriously suggest that adult education, such as the Workers Educational Association in Britain, is a useful counterforce to the popular press. Toynbee considers that although all of the oriental societies have in our time accepted the industrial technology and its political consequences: "On the cultural plane, however, there is no uniform corresponding tendency." (Somervell, I. 267) This is like the voice of the literate man, floundering in a milieu of ads, who boasts, "Personally, I pay no attention to ads." The spiritual and cultural reservations that the oriental peoples may have toward our technology will avail them not at all. The effects of technology do not occur at the level of opinions or concepts, but alter sense ratios or patterns of perception steadily and without any resistance. The serious artist is the only person able to encounter technology with impunity, just because he is an expert aware of the changes in sense perception.

The operation of the money medium in seventeenth-century Japan had effects not unlike the operation of typography in the West. The penetration of the money economy, wrote G. B. Sansom (in *Japan*, Cresset Press, London, 1931) "caused a slow but irresistible revolution, culminat-

ing in the breakdown of feudal government and the resumption of intercourse with foreign countries after more than two hundred years of seclusion." Money has reorganized the sense life of peoples just because it is an *extension* of our sense lives. This change does not depend upon approval or disapproval of those living in the society.

Arnold Toynbee made one approach to the transforming power of media in his concept of "etherialization," which he holds to be the principle of progressive simplification and efficiency in any organization or technology. Typically, he is ignoring the *effect* of the challenge of these forms upon the response of our senses. He imagines that it is the response of our opinions that is relevant to the effect of media and technology in society, a "point of view" that is plainly the result of the typographic spell. For the man in a literate and homogenized society ceases to be sensitive to the diverse and discontinuous life of forms. He acquires the illusion of the third dimension and the "private point of view" as part of his Narcissus fixation, and is quite shut off from Blake's awareness or that of the Psalmist, that we become what we behold.

Today when we want to get our bearings in our own culture, and have need to stand aside from the bias and pressure exerted by any technical form of human expression, we have only to visit a society where that particular form has not been felt, or a historical period in which it was unknown. Professor Wilbur Schramm made such a tactical move in studying *Television in the Lives of Our Children*. He found areas where TV had not penetrated at all and ran some tests. Since he had made no study of

the peculiar nature of the TV image, his tests were of "content" preferences, viewing time, and vocabulary counts. In a word, his approach to the problem was a literary one, albeit unconsciously so. Consequently, he had nothing to report. Had his methods been employed in 1500 A.D. to discover the effects of the printed book in the lives of children or adults, he could have found out nothing of the changes in human and social psychology resulting from typography. Print created individualism and nationalism in the sixteenth century. Program and "content" analysis offer no clues to the magic of these media or to their subliminal charge.

Leonard Doob, in his report *Communication in Africa*, tells of one African who took great pains to listen each evening to the BBC news, even though he could understand nothing of it. Just to be in the presence of those sounds at 7 P.M. each day was important for him. His attitude to speech was like ours to melody—the resonant intonation was meaning enough. In the seventeenth century our ancestors still shared this native's attitude to the forms of media, as is plain in the following sentiment of the Frenchman Bernard Lam expressed in *The Art of Speaking* (London, 1696):

'Tis an effect of the Wisdom of God, who created Man to be happy, that whatever is useful to his conversation (way of life) is agreeable to him . . . because all victual that conduces to nourishment is relishable, whereas other things that cannot be assimilated and be turned into our substance are insipid. A Discourse cannot be pleasant to the Hearer that is not easier to the Speaker; nor can it be easily pronounced unless it be heard with delight.

Here is an equilibrium theory of human diet and expression such as even now we are only striving to work out again for media after centuries of fragmentation and specialism.

Pope Pius XII was deeply concerned that there be serious study of the media today. On February 17, 1950, he said:

It is not an exaggeration to say that the future of modern society and the stability of its inner life depend in large part on the maintenance of an equilibrium between the strength of the techniques of communication and the capacity of the individual's own reaction.

Failure in this respect has for centuries been typical and total for mankind. Subliminal and docile acceptance of media impact has made them prisons without walls for their human users. As A. J. Liebling remarked in his book *The Press*, a man is not free if he cannot see where he is going, even if he has a gun to help him get there. For each of the media is also a powerful weapon with which to clobber other media and other groups. The result is that the present age has been one of multiple civil wars that are not limited to the world of art and entertainment. In *War and Human Progress*, Professor J. U. Nef declared: "The total wars of our time have been the result of a series of intellectual mistakes . . ."

If the formative power in the media are the media themselves, that raises a host of large matters that can only be mentioned here, although they deserve volumes. Namely, that technological media are staples or natural resources, exactly as are coal and cotton and oil. Anybody will concede that society whose economy is dependent upon one or two major staples like cotton, or grain, or lumber, or fish, or cattle is going to have some obvious social patterns of organization as a result. Stress on a few major staples creates extreme instability in the economy but great endurance in the population. The pathos and humor of the American South are embedded in such an economy of limited staples. For a society configured by reliance on a few commodities accepts them as a social bond quite as much as the metropolis does the press. Cotton and oil, like radio and TV, become "fixed charges" on the entire psychic life of the community. And this pervasive fact creates the unique cultural flavor of any society. It pays through the nose and all its other senses for each staple that shapes its life.

That our human senses, of which all media are extensions, are also fixed charges on our personal energies, and that they also configure the awareness and experience of each one of us, may be perceived in another connection mentioned by the psychologist C. G. Jung:

Every Roman was surrounded by slaves. The slave and his psychology flooded ancient Italy, and every Roman became inwardly, and of course unwittingly, a slave. Because living constantly in the atmosphere of slaves, he became infected through the unconscious with their psychology. No one can shield himself from such an influence (*Contributions to Analytical Psychology*, London, 1928).

References

Carothers, J.C.: "Culture, Psychiatry and the Written Word," *Psychiatry*, November, 1959.

Doob, Leonard W.: *Communication in Africa* (New Haven, Conn.: Yale University Press, 1961).

Gombrich, E.H.: *Art and Illusion*, A discovery of integral awareness amidst art illusions based on isolated visual sense. (New York: Pantheon Books, a Division of Random House, Inc., 1960.)

Selye, Hans: *The Stress of Life*, "The pharmacology of dirt" or an ecological approach to human stress. (New York: McGraw-Hill Book Company, 1956.)

 Article Review Form at end of book.

Does technology make life better? How might technology create a greater sense of community?

Technology Makes Us Better:

Our oldest computer, upgraded

John Tierney

When the Sojourner's tiny wheels rolled over the Martian surface on July 5, it was in some ways a bigger leap for mankind than Neil Armstrong's first step on the Moon. You may not have realized that if you were watching network television, which gave the Mars landing relatively short shrift. But that was the beauty of this extraterrestrial event: you didn't need a television to follow it.

Anyone in the world with a computer and an Internet connection could see pictures from the spacecraft. You could study Martian sunsets or put on cardboard 3-D glasses to take in a 360-degree view of the landscape. With a few clicks of the mouse, you could read a treatise on Martian geology, check out the latest weather conditions on the planet, sit in on a news conference or watch scientists issuing commands from the mission-control room. One Web site provided a recipe for throwing a Mars Madness Celebration—red and brown M & M's were recommended—and gave directions to dozens of such gatherings

across America. Other sites let you participate in on-line chats with planetary scientists as well as religious fundamentalists convinced that the mission was a hoax being staged in the Arizona desert. During the week of the landing, the various Mars Web sites were visited more than 200 million times.

It was easily the most popular event in the history of the Internet, proof at last that humanity could use this new medium for something loftier than viewing pictures of a naked Pamela Anderson Lee. The Moon landing was the apotheosis of the old technological order: a big-budget achievement of central planning, a cold-war triumph of the military-industrial complex packaged by politicians and presented to the masses by the media establishment. The Mars visit was a low-budget operation with a charming quirkiness to it, a peaceful scientific exercise instead of a propaganda victory over an enemy nation. In 1969, Communist authorities suppressed coverage of the Moon landing; this year, Russians followed the Mars mission on the World Wide Web,

using the very machines that helped end the cold war.

Is this a better world? Has technology made us better? Tools can't change human nature, but they can encourage or suppress certain qualities, and most people would probably agree on what constitutes "better": wiser, happier, kinder, more equitable and cooperative, less duplicitous and belligerent. The tricky part is defining "us."

In the two centuries after the Industrial Revolution, individuals reaped enormous personal benefits that were accompanied by some social liabilities. As people abandoned farms and small towns, they lost communal bonds; as personal incomes rose, public air and water got dirtier; as power became concentrated in capital cities, elites controlled new tools of mass communication and mass destruction. Indoor plumbing and washing machines freed women of onerous work, but there was less socializing at wells. Trains and cars enabled workers to move away from industrial neighborhoods, but these suburbanites spent more time alone in their cars and backyards, lapping up the wisdom of distant publishers and broadcasters instead of chatting with relatives and neighbors. Although new technology is often described as a Faustian bargain, historically it has involved a trade-off not between materialism and spirituality—lugging water from the well was not a spiritually uplifting exercise for most people, no matter how much it might appeal to the Unabomber—but between individual freedom and social virtue.

Today's technologies offer a better deal for everyone. Individuals are acquiring more control over their lives, their minds and their bodies, even their genes, thanks to the transformations in medicine, communications, transportation and industry. At the same time, these technologies are providing social benefits and undoing some of the damage of the past. Technology helps to conserve natural resources and diminish pollution. Today's farmers are so efficient that unneeded cropland is reverting to forests and parks; the most high-tech countries have the cleanest air and water. The Information Revolution, besides enabling people to visit Mars at will, is fostering peaceful cooperation on Earth by decentralizing power. Political tyrants and demagogic warmongers are losing control now that their subjects have tools to communicate directly with one another. People are using the tools to do their jobs without leaving their families. They're forming new communities in cyberspace and forming new bonds with their neighbors in real space. Technology has the potential to increase individual freedom and strengthen community—even

though at the moment, so many people complain it does neither.

Technology's victims have become familiar images in the media: on-line addicts who don't know their next-door neighbors; satellite-dish owners who have stopped reading; computer users overwhelmed by E-mail, infuriated by software glitches and baffled by incomprehensible manuals; workers displaced by machines or forced to put in longer hours; frazzled parents, especially working mothers, too exhausted and busy to spend time with their children. We contrast these pathetic figures with images of a happier past, of families quietly relaxing in a pre-machine age when people still had time to read, contemplate the meaning of life, visit with their relatives and neighbors.

But when exactly were those halcyon days? If premachine means before the Industrial Revolution, the average person then was short-lived, illiterate and oblivious to most culture beyond the village. Women's lives were consumed with domestic chores and continual pregnancies, and women were especially unlikely to be educated. Marriage records from a region of 1750's England, then one of the world's most literate societies, show that two-thirds of the bridegrooms could sign their names, but only one-third of the brides could. It would be hard to call that a better world.

Living conditions and educational opportunities certainly improved after the Industrial Revolution, but people still didn't have much time to sit around discussing the classics or communing with nature. In the middle of the last century, the typical man in Britain worked more than 60 hours a week, with no annual vacation, from age 10

until he died at about 50. That left him with about 90,000 hours of free time over the course of his adult life—barely a third of the free time enjoyed by today's workers. This trend shows no sign of abating, says Jesse H. Ausubel, director of the Program for the Human Environment at Rockefeller University. He projects that by the middle of the next century, the average workweek in America will be shorter than 28 hours.

Since 1965, Americans have gained an average of almost one hour of leisure each day, according to social scientists at the University of Maryland who have been studying people's "time diaries" over the past three decades. Americans are now spending a little more time reading books and magazines, exercising, pursuing hobbies and attending adult-education courses. Evidence from the diaries and other research shows that in recent decades, people have been going more frequently to art museums, the theater and the opera.

Contrary to popular stereotypes, the diaries show that the workweek has been shortening, that women have as much leisure time as men and that parents are spending as much time with their children as they did in the 1960's. These children, unfortunately, are less likely to live with two parents, which may be partly a consequence of technology that has made divorce and single parenthood less of an economic burden: men and women are presumably more inclined to live separately now that they can both support themselves outside the home, relying on machines to make clothes, clean house and do most food preparation. But new technology is hardly the only cause of the traditional family's decline, and in any case it's hard to get too nostalgic for the days when women had no choice but to stay in the kitchen.

Why, if men and women have more time and opportunity than ever to pursue their dreams, do they grouse so much about modern technology? One reason is that new technologies like computers usually are more trouble than they're worth—at first. They're hard to learn and create resentment among workers, particularly the unskilled ones who fear displacement and are jealous of higher-paid experts in the new technology. The introduction last century of electricity to factories did not immediately increase workers' pay and productivity; the widespread benefits came only after several decades, when factory managers and workers finally learned how to use the new motors efficiently. Then wages increased for everyone, raising the standard of living and creating new kinds of jobs. Luddites have been warning for two centuries that technology destroys jobs, but the overall effect of automation is to free workers to concentrate on other, less-tedious tasks. Today's workers are richer and more cultured than their Luddite ancestors (and better dressed, thanks to mechanical looms). While they may have fewer jobs in the textile industry, they have more opportunities to work as teachers, social workers, travel agents, personal trainers, writers and museum curators.

As much discomfort as the personal computer has caused, there's no reason to assume that the machines will remain complicated. Gadgets become simpler as technologies mature and marketers appeal to the masses. George Orwell's despair over cars, gramophones and tele-

phones was at least partly due to the crude state of those technologies in his day. The automobile was a relatively unreliable, high-maintenance machine until a couple of decades ago. Gramophones were cumbersome and yielded tinny sounds. Telephones were forever disturbing the peace of people trying to eat, converse or read. The phone didn't become wholly civilized until people were freed to ignore it by the invention of the answering machine—a contraption that was despised before coming to be regarded as a necessity. Today, E-mail is a novelty that can be disruptive, but pioneers are developing techniques for coping, like automated responses when there's no time to deal with an overloaded mailbox and filters to sift out the junk mail.

Another reason we grouse about modernity is that our expectations are higher. The middle class wants perquisites once limited to the rich, from material luxuries to cultural experiences to intellectual fulfillment. Our ancestors may have been content to pass the time on the porch chatting with neighbors about the weather and crop prices, but they didn't have many other choices. Today most people—including those academics who rhapsodize about traditional communities while working in offices far from their hometowns—demand more stimulation than their relatives and neighbors can provide. We feel more rushed because we have more possibilities.

"Free time is increasing, but not as fast as our sense of the necessary," says Geoffrey Godbey, a co-author of "Time for Life," a report on the time-diary research project. "With technology we've upped the ante. Instead of corresponding with 6 or 7 people, we have 150 E-mail partners. Thirty

years ago most people didn't bother shampooing their carpets or blow-drying their hair or making their own bread, but now that they have the equipment, they have higher standards."

The most dispiriting trend discovered by Godbey and his colleagues is the couch-potato paradox: people have been watching more television even though they rate it among their least-favorite forms of leisure. Americans average more than 16 hours a week, an increase of 4 hours since 1965, which means that most of our recently acquired free time has gone to the tube. A die-hard optimist could argue that television has been improving, that people are deriving joy and enlightenment from all those new cable channels, but it would be just as easy to argue that they're staring at cubic zirconium rings. The increase in tube-watching seems especially perverse considering that it coincides with a decline of two hours a week in the amount of time people spend socializing, an activity they consider much more enjoyable than television. A society of solitary people sitting at home enviously watching the camaraderie on "Friends" does not seem like a triumph of the communications revolution.

The good news is that people with computers are watching less television, and they've increased the amount of time spent socializing with family and friends (partly because they get together to play computer games). At the moment only about 40 percent of American households have computers, but the percentage is rising as the machines become cheaper and easier to use. Over the past year, home computers have begun outselling televisions in the United States, a statistic that cheers George Gilder, who in 1990 wrote a book titled *Life After Television*. Now the editor of the *Gilder Technology Report*, he expects the broadcast-television empires to collapse—and an intellectual culture to flourish—once the masses can easily receive video and text from a computer network as diverse as the Internet.

"When I debate network television executives," Gilder says, "they come up to me afterward and say: 'Look, you don't understand. People like the stuff we put on. We've done market surveys and we've found that people are boobs.' Well, I'm a boob when faced with conventional TV. It's too much work to find something good, and if you do, it probably won't accord with your particular interests. Television is a lowest-common-denominator medium even with 50 or 500 channels. You'd never go to a bookstore with only 500 titles. In the book or the magazine industries, 99.7 percent of the stuff is by definition not for you, and that's what the Internet is like. It's a first-choice medium with a bias toward each individual's area of excellence instead of the few commonly shared interests, which are mostly prurient and sensational."

Now that the computer is combining the television with the telephone, it's clear that George Orwell got things precisely wrong in *1984*. He was remarkably prescient to envision society's being transformed by a two-way communication device called the telescreen, but he didn't foresee that these telescreens would promote freedom. One-way television is useful to Big Brother, but two-way communication devices undermine central authority by communicating with one another. Totalitarian countries have fewer telephones than

televisions; democracies have more telephones.

Why was Orwell so technophobic, so sure that telescreens would promote tyranny and war? Peter Huber, a senior fellow at the Manhattan Institute who analyzes the mistakes of *1984* in his recent book, *Orwell's Revenge*, finds the answer in an essay Orwell wrote imagining how humans could free themselves of the drudgery of washing dishes. In this 1945 essay, Orwell considers the possibility of paper plates but settles on another solution: "Every morning the municipal van will stop at your door and carry off a box of dirty crocks, handing you a box of clean ones (marked with your initial, of course) in return." Orwell envisions a dishwashing factory run by a public agency—Big Brother's Ministry of Crockery, as Huber calls it.

"The thought of private, automatic dishwashing machines never even surfaces," Huber writes. "For Orwell, the centralization of powerful machines is inescapable economic destiny in the industrial age." The most graphic refutation of Orwell was the famous Apple commercial broadcast during the 1984 Super Bowl, in which the enslaved masses were liberated by a lone woman hurling a sledgehammer at a demagogue on a huge telescreen.

At the time it was a wonderful image of the home computer's revolutionary potential. In hindsight, it's even more apt, because the target of the attack, IBM, which then seemed to be the omnipotent Big Blue, was about to be humbled. It was more Wizard of Oz than Big Brother. The company had dominated the era of mainframe computers, but it floundered in the late 1980's when it faced competition from

upstarts offering cheaper, decentralized machines.

As these personal devices proliferate, it's becoming impossible for political leaders to censor information. Africa's leaders can control newspapers, but citizens in remote villages are now getting uncensored news from Africa Online. And as information becomes central to economies, the incentives for tyrants to wage war are diminishing. Military conquest of foreign lands made a certain amount of sense when the victors acquired manpower and resources from farms, mines and factories. Access to scarce natural resources was vital—in the Middle Ages, armies fought wars over salt. Today wealth is based more and more on information, not natural resources, which is why the Congo is poor despite its vast mineral reserves, and why Hong Kong is rich even though it must import food and drinking water. The Beijing autocrats may have acquired title to Hong Kong's real estate, but they haven't conquered it. They can't seal its borders or appropriate its wealth. If they try to stop Hong Kong's telescreens from communicating, computer keyboards around the world will respond, and Hong Kong's money will start to flow away, followed shortly by its populace.

Now that the specter of Big Brother is receding, today's critics of technology have been focusing on the opposite danger: too much freedom. Conservatives worry that traditional values are threatened by on-line crudity; liberals worry that social injustice and selfishness will prevail in the unregulated realm of cyberspace. The critics correctly see that governments are losing some of their power to impose laws and moral standards, but that doesn't mean we're doomed to chaos and cruelty. Humans developed sociable rules and moral codes long before the era of centralized governments. The Internet may look like a dangerously anarchic world, but it's actually fairly similar to the ancient environment in which humans evolved to become the most cooperative, virtuous creatures on earth.

The original Information Revolution occurred during the Pleistocene, a decentralized era if there ever was one, when hunter-gatherers on the African savanna developed a powerful new computer: the human brain. The brain evolved to its large size because its information-processing capacity enabled humans to band together and increase their chances of survival. The size of a primate's brain correlates directly with the size of its social group, and the formula worked out by scientists indicates that the human brain is sized for a group of about 150, which by no coincidence is the number in a typical band of hunter-gatherers.

The large brain enabled our ancestors to work together because they had so much information about one another. They knew whom to trust because they could store memories of past behavior and obtain news about others' reputations. They developed instincts and customs that stigmatized selfishness and encouraged voluntary cooperation, especially within the band but also with outsiders. Other animals make sacrifices for the common good of their immediate kin, performing acts of altruism that insure the survival of their mutual genes, but humans go further. "We are just about the only animals who act altruistically to-

ward nonrelatives," says Matt Ridley, a zoologist and the author of *The Origins of Virtue*, a new book analyzing the evolution and economics of cooperative behavior. "Humans can be selfish, of course, but what makes us special is our instinct to be nice to one another. Every culture defines virtue almost exclusively as pro-social behavior, and vice as anti-social behavior."

This cooperative spirit has made possible the division of labor, which has been the source of all wealth, technology and culture. Just as Stone Age toolmakers independently developed complex trading networks for obtaining rock blades from distant tribes, 11th-century merchants established a trading system across Europe without any central guidance or enforcement authority. The merchants traveling among disparate kingdoms developed their own legal code and observed it voluntarily because they knew that a violator would be ostracized and unable to conduct business. The mere communication of information was enough to make them behave honorably.

"The Information Revolution is taking us back toward our better social instincts," Ridley says."The Industrial Revolution helped centralize authority, creating hierarchical bureaucracies that tried to coerce cooperation but often brought out the most selfish instincts in both the rulers and their subjects. The way to regain community spirit is to have small institutions and horizontal networks of equals who voluntarily cooperate, like the people you see chatting on the Internet today. These virtual communities formed spontaneously because our brains are naturally inclined to this sort of information

exchange. It's what we spent most of our time doing in the Pleistocene."

The Pleistocene savanna makes a good image for the Internet: a wide-open frontier being settled without any central planning. A few sociopaths are out there spreading computer viruses, and encounters among strangers can provoke viciously uncivil "flame" wars. But rules of etiquette are evolving as people coalesce into communities and networks. By trading information, they're discovering whom to trust and whom to avoid. They're writing E-mail letters to relatives and scheduling meetings with friends. Some, like merchants, are cooperating for profit, but a surprising number seem to be acting out of pure goodwill. They're freely providing information, from software to consumer advice to counsel for the lovelorn.

Most of the information is of no interest to most people, which is why the Internet can seem so pointless. My first few forays persuaded me that it was the world's most effective way to waste time. But in researching this article, I decided to give it another try. I had just read a good review of *Data Smog,* a book by David Shenk about the dangers of the Information Revolution, so I looked for it among the 2.5 million books at the Amazon.com Web site. I found it right away, along with an assortment of reviews from newspapers and magazines. Some of the most succinct analysis ("Excellent at describing info glut, not so hot at solutions") came from laypeople who had volunteered their own comments.

There was also an area—"Check out these titles!"—listing other books ordered by buyers of this one, an extraordinarily useful cross-referencing feature. I began clicking from book to book, each time benefiting from the expertise of previous buyers to discover new related titles. It was like going from one Pleistocene water hole to another, at each stop picking up advice and directions to the next one.

Within a couple of hours I had found enough technophobic literature to keep George Orwell happy for years—hundreds of books ranging from old scholarly critiques of the Industrial Revolution to titles like *Surviving the Media Jungle* and *Under Technology's Thumb.* I discovered *Technolopoly,* by Neil Postman, revealing that America has become the world's "totalitarian technocracy," a place with no "transcendent sense of purpose or meaning."

Within a week, Amazon.com had graciously delivered to my door a small library assailing its own electronic technology. I read *Data Smog*—which decried the Internet's "fragmented, asynchronous, decentralized 'free-market' culture where the public good is sacrificed"—as well as Clifford Stoll's *Silicon Snake Oil* and *Amusing Ourselves to Death,* another lament by Postman. I went through treatises on information have-nots and spiritually deprived Internet surfers. I learned about a degraded electronic culture that is rendering books obsolete—an ominous trend revealed in books purchased on line at the largest, most helpful bookstore in history. I tried to take the warnings seriously, but as the experts described the terrible plight of Americans drowning in data, there was something I couldn't get out of my mind.

It was the line spoken by Emperor Joseph II after the premiere of "The Abduction from the Seraglio": "Too many notes, my dear Mozart." He was expressing the feeling common among the day's elite that Mozart's complex music was too fast-paced and stimulating for the average listener.

Like new music, new technology is always disturbing, especially to the establishment, and it always causes unforeseen problems. The agricultural and industrial revolutions were accompanied by new plagues, pollutants and weapons of destruction. Today's revolution will bring troubles and trade-offs, but we can cope with them. Transmitting information from one willing individual to another is hardly a new menace.

Like Mozart's music, this is something our brains are equipped to handle. This is what we're good at, and what makes us better.

 **Article Review Form at end of book.**

Is it possible to "get away from it all"? Is it necessary?

Out There in the Middle of the Buzz

Bill McKibben

Bill McKibben, a former staff writer for The New Yorker, *is the author of* The End of Nature *and* The Age of Missing Information. *He lives with his wife and daughter in the Adirondack Mountains of upstate New York.*

Out on a recent hike, I stopped for lunch at the edge of a high mountain pond. I could see another solitary hiker on the other side of the water, stretched out on a shelving rock about a hundred yards away. And I could hear him talking (sound carries extremely well across water; never negotiate a deal in a canoe). "It's so beautiful up here," he was saying. "It's so peaceful. What's happening with you?"

What I couldn't figure out was who he was talking to. Until I pulled out my binoculars and saw, of course, that he had a cell phone. For a moment I felt vastly superior—and then I reflected a bit. It's true I wouldn't carry a phone with me up a mountain. But I had carried my world with me nonetheless, marched right up there with my eyes fixed on the same vague middle distance that you see when you drive. My mind was abuzz with images, opinions; my mind was its own Bloom-berg box, happily chatter-ing away with a thousand dispatches an hour.

We live in the middle of the Buzz. Those billions of micro-processors that have spawned like springtime frogs in the last quarter century are constantly sending us information, data, images. Our minds marinate in it, till we're worried when it shuts off. What do you do first when you walk into an empty hotel room? Savor the silence? Or turn on the TV? And even when we get away from the machines for a while—even when we leave the phone at home—the Buzz comes with us. Quiet, solitude, calm: These are no longer automatic parts of the human experience. You have to fight as hard for them as a farm boy had to fight for novelty and thrill a century ago. How many minutes can you watch a sunset before your mind grows hungry for some faster di-version? How long can you stare up into the night sky?

This constant whispering in our ears, this constant dancing in front of our eyes—that's how technology changes us, weaning us away from ourselves. How can you figure out what you really want when someone's always talking to you, when there's al-ways another home page to click through? When you can't warm yourself by a mountain lake with-out checking in at home? Electronic communication, for the first time, makes culture ubiqui-tous. Almost nobody read books five hours a day, or went to the theater every night. We live in the first moment when humans re-ceive more of their information secondhand than first; instead of relying primarily on contact with nature and with each other, we rely primarily on the prechewed, on someone else's experience. Our life is, quite literally, mediated.

Maybe that's a good thing; maybe it's the direction in which we need to evolve on an ever more crowded planet. But I think it may be breeding a kind of des-peration in us, too, a frantic, reac-tive nervousness. That low, rumbling broadcast that comes constantly from ourselves, the broadcast that tells us who we are, what we want from life—that broadcast is jammed by all the other none around us, the lush static of our electronic age. We look for solitude in our (expen-sively silent) cars, but first the radio, then the phone, then the computer and the fax intrude. We look for peace in the mountains, but we drag the world along on a tether.

To quote Thoreau is to risk rejection as a romantic. But here goes. "Let us spend one day as deliberately as Nature, and not be thrown off the track by every nutshell and mosquito's wing that falls on the rails," he writes. Now that we've built a technosphere to amplify the sound of every nutshell and to broadcast high-quality pictures of each mosquito's wing, it's even better advice, albeit harder than ever to follow. Solitude, silence, darkness—these are the rarest commodities after a half century of electronics. The incredible economics of the information age mean that almost anyone can afford a large-screen television, a 28.8 modem. But how many can afford peace and quiet?

 Article Review Form at end of book.

Why does this computer company executive endorse a critical approach to technology? What are his concerns about the use of computers in society?

Taking the Message Back from the Medium

Michael Spindler

Michael Spindler, the former president and CEO of Apple Computer, has been one of the more visionary leaders of the computer industry.

What will this highly touted, globalized, fully interactive, multimedia future be like? Since we cannot predict the future all we can really point to today are the promises, obstacles and uncertainties. And, as with every major societal transformation, we can say that technology, competition and political and social forces will drive change, none of them moving ahead independently, but impacting each other.

The most important impact has to do with the media as the metaphor. If technology has the means of delivering information, then the medium has the impact. Each medium makes possible distinct modes of discourse by providing complete orientations of thought, expression and sensibility. Speech remains our primary and indispensable medium. It made us human; it keeps us human. It certainly defines what it is to be human. The speech medium was amplified through the telephone revolution. The

written word created the typographic society, from the Greek's invention of the alphabet to Gutenberg's movable type. This was enhanced through telegraphy. Photography added image to the ability to express experience much as music enriches it.

Television is the medium that has so far made the most dramatic impact on our social structure. Cultures and even nations appear defenseless to its influence. Television, however, is a discrete event separated in content, context and emotional texture. Television sells time in minutes and seconds in part because it uses images instead of words. It is thus the first medium bound by time dependence.

In the 19th century, the media was under the influence of politics, often under direct government influence. Today the situation is the opposite: Both politics and business turn into show business. Due to the power of television, politicians are most concerned about images or sound bites and sizzle. Politics has become based on polls instead of rational discourse. The pollster is the king and leadership follow polls. In other words, marketing has replaced politics and the prin-

ciple of reality has been replaced by the principle of pleasure.

Books and other media such as film are expected to deliver a consistent tone and continuity of content, not so with television, even television news. Television news nearly abandons logic, reason and sequence. Bite-size is best, complexity must be avoided, nuance is dispensable. Visual stimulation is a substitute for thought.

By substituting images for language, the TV commercial makes emotional appeal, not the test of truth, the basis of consumer decisions. Business expenditures as a result shift from product research market research, and TV commercials today have become the main method of presenting political ideas.

Perhaps most importantly, television has changed the nature of information packaging of other media so that the total information environment now begins to mirror more and more the television format. *USA Today* is a good case in point: It looks like a TV screen; stories are uncommonly short and design relies heavily on pictures and charts and color.

In fact sometimes television becomes vaudeville, where the

"Taking the Message Back from the Medium," by Michael Spindler, *New Perspectives Quarterly*, Spring 1995. Reprinted with permission of Blackwell Publishers.

public adjusts to incoherence and is amused into indifference. Television has become somewhat of a paradigm for our conception of how we consume public information. Aldous Huxley predicted some time ago that it would be more likely that democracies would rather dance and dream themselves into oblivion than march into it. The more contemporary version of this same critique can be found in Neal Postman's 1985 book, entitled *Amusing Ourselves to Death*. Contrary to Orwell, Huxley understood that the media, not central government, would take over control of society.

The medium should not overtake the message, and that is the promise of fully interactive multi-media. In this technological onslaught, we need to revisit the societal question of how to achieve technological pervasiveness while resisting the potential negative social consequences of what we have already witnessed with television.

Technology has always been the root cause of economic and social change. This time around it is no different. When Gutenberg invented the moveable type in Europe, the pessimists said it was bad because all the scribes would lose their jobs. The optimists said it was great because it would enable the distribution of books in libraries. The politicians said we can't have anything unless we create a law. And who was right? Well, the scribes did lose their jobs, but they were the ones who started the European wine industry. So, you cannot stop technology from moving forward.

The main trends shaping the shifting technology landscape in this new information age are profound:

- The complete shift from analog to digital technology in everything from telephone-switching systems to transmission to content creation and packaging and the end-user information devices;

- The impact of miniaturization technology on the size of products and the pervasiveness of mobile products;

- The continuous change and pace of technological deployment.

The new information appliances will be varied—smart communicators, multimedia PCs, receptor-boxes, game consoles, TV sets and smart-phones. Already in the 1960s, foresightful people realized that the destiny of the computer was to be an interactive, complimentary amplifier of human thought rather than remaining a mere transaction machine. They understood that if we could only pervasively network human beings and information appliances through computers we would create the universal information utility to which most human commerce, both intellectual and commercial, would flow.

Today, it is clear that the access to networking is not a problem at all—the Internet experience has shown that.

Information appliances for business organizations as well as residential use will continue to fragment because of different consumer constraints, such as the amount of discretionary income, and preferences for viewing and accessing multimedia information. This is particularly so for residential use because of varying life-style choices such as working at home. All this will lead to a fragmentation of application, rather than one

"killer" application that applies to all circumstances.

How many information appliances will we have at home and which one will be in highest use? Will it still be the television set? The television set has not acquired much intelligence in the past 10 years. It has remained a passive receiver for broadcast media. The basic multimedia architecture and versatility of a personal computer may provide a much better platform for a variety of end use appliances.

The phenomenal, instantaneous global access both to other people and, in the end, to the totality of mankind's knowledge, will have a profound impact on humanity. More and more people will possess personal information access. People will have universal e-mail phones and fax numbers that will stay with them for life and be usable no matter where in the world they are.

Massive cultural shifts will occur as they did around paper based information publishing, the invention of the telephone or television. We will shift from a pure broadcast-mat culture to a much more interactive society, developing ever more diverse communities of interests where people who otherwise had no contact can interact.

We do not yet understand the real impact of the global information society. The critical element for individuals moving into the future is not to obtain a Ph.D in information science, but to acquire a point of view of how information can best be useful to them.

Information, or more accurately, being informed, can be both a blessing and a curse. We crave more information; at the same time we feel inundated, intruded upon and lacking control.

The key concern as we move forward is to ensure that the real end-user remain in control of the outcome. The consumer, not some techno-buffs, must remain the sole judge of demand and consumption in this media-rich world coming into being.

I sincerely and personally hope that all of this doesn't mean we are moving into an information environment which more and more resembles the game "Trivial Pursuit." We need to have a culture that sustains the emotions, friendships and interpersonal connections necessary so that this technology does not become intimidating. As has been demonstrated many times over, a culture can survive misinformation and false information. It has not yet been proven, however, whether a culture can survive by taking the measure of the world in 30 second sound-bites.

My hope is that we do not end up with a societal model where five percent of the nation's population is well-educated, well-informed and earning good wages while the rest simply amuse themselves to death.

 Article Review Form at end of book.

WiseGuide Wrap-Up

In everyday life, we're usually more concerned with using a computer to accomplish tasks, rather than with reflecting on the messages and metaphors that the machine conveys. Understanding varied critical perspectives on technology provides us with a framework for asking better questions about how and why we use it. Which of these readings did you find most compelling, and why? Where would you place yourself on the scale between extreme technocratism and die-hard Luddite-ism?

R.E.A.L. Sites

This list provides a print preview of typical **Coursewise** R.E.A.L. sites. There are over 100 such sites at the **Courselinks**™ site. The danger in printing URLs is that web sites can change overnight. As we went to press, these sites were functional using the URLs provided. If you come across one that isn't, please let us know via email to: webmaster@coursewise.com. Use your Passport to access the most current list of R.E.A.L. sites at the **Courselinks**™ site.

Site name: Computers & Society

URL: http://www.engr.csulb.edu/~sigcas/

Why is it R.E.A.L.? This is the web site for the quarterly journal *Computers and Society,* published by the Special Interest Group for Computers and Society. Indexes to past journals are available, but not articles. The site includes an amazing set of links to organizations, publications, and research centers devoted to the study of the social and cultural impact of computers and technology.

Key topics: computers and society, ethics

Try this: Explore the index for past issues of the journal, select an article you'd like to present to your class, and consult your librarian about how to obtain a copy.

Site name: The New York Times

URL: http://www.nytimes.com/

Why is it R.E.A.L.? All the news that's fit to print, and then some, including CyberTimes, a special feature produced expressly for the online edition that covers news on the latest social, political, and technical developments related to the Internet and computer technology. CyberTimes also carries regular columns devoted to technology in education, cyberlaw, and e-commerce.

Key topics: computers and society, education, e-commerce

Try this: Browse through a current issue of CyberTimes and provide an update to your class on a current issue related to technology.

section

Computers Transforming Work, Home, and Family

Learning Objectives

- Describe the "ripple effect" created by computer networks in the workplace.

- Evaluate Horowitz's argument about how computers hinder worker morale.

- Imagine what the home of the future might look like.

- Brainstorm a list of lifestyle changes brought about by cell phones and pagers.

- Evaluate the measures proposed by Montgomery for protecting children online.

- Evaluate the dangers posed to children by pedophiles on the Internet.

WiseGuide Intro

Imagine that it's 10 P.M. and you've just put the kids to bed and settled down to relax after a long day of work, family activities, and chores. You're getting into the first chapter of a good book when your pager beeps. You check the message, reach for your office cell phone, and call your boss. She's just finished reading your proposal and needs a revised version early the next morning. She's sending her notes via e-mail, and you promise to fax the changes to her by 10 A.M. the next day.

Would you want to be paged at home on a regular basis for work-related reasons? Communication technologies such as pagers, faxes, and cell phones blur the boundary between the office and the home. These technologies make telecommuting more viable for many employees who welcome the flexibility of working from a home office. But cell phones and pagers also can create unwanted and stressful intrusions into the private world of family.

Either way, the situation you've imagined illustrates how technology is changing the way we work and live. Technology enthusiasts promote these changes as both liberating and efficient. When computers free employees from detailed hand work or manual labor, people become "knowledge workers," whose jobs allow them to exercise creative and critical thinking: to use their minds instead of their hands. Tools such as e-mail and computer networks promote the free exchange of information, thus promoting a more democratic workplace. Computers also make some tasks more efficient or contribute to efficiency in other ways: the telecommuting employee saves driving time when she spends two days a week working from home.

But technology critics remind us that the workplace transformed by computers also creates a new set of problems. Workers displaced by technology require more education and training to use new technology effectively and may not always be in a position to benefit from such training. Regular software and system upgrades create a need for frequent retraining if employees are to use computers efficiently. Computers can have as many adverse affects on health as any assembly line, with computer-related ailments now the fastest growing source of job-related health problems. And when computers are used to monitor employee efficiency and conversations, some chilling scenarios follow.

Technology also promises to deliver an array of consumer products designed to make the daily business of living easier. The Internet, for example, provides information at your fingertips, making it easy to check an investment portfolio, research a vacation, or help a child with a school report. Kids love to surf the Net and participate in chat rooms. But time spent on the Internet is time spent away from family or away from other activities, such as playing outdoors. Television viewing among children has decreased in recent years, and researchers speculate that, instead, kids are spending more of their free time online.

Many parents greet this news positively, because they view the Internet as inherently more educational and interactive than TV. But is it? Do parents always know how and why children are using the Internet? Can virtual reality replace authentic social relationships with real people? Does the Internet allow children to become easy psychological prey for advertisers, or for strangers seeking to exploit them?

The articles in this section invite you to consider these questions as you explore the impact of computers in the workplace and the home. In the first article, Bob Filipczak, editor of a human resources magazine called *Training,* reviews recent research which suggests that computer networks in the workplace can promote positive changes that improve communications and empower employees in the decision-making process.

But, in the article that follows, Tony Horowitz asks you to reconsider computers as democracy-enhancing tools. In "Mr. Edens Profits from Watching His Workers' Every Move," he argues that computer technology can adversely affect the morale and productivity of employees when it is used to monitor their work, especially in the case of low-skill jobs such as data entry.

How will computers affect our homes and family life in the future? Compaq Computer president and CEO Eckhard Pfeiffer presents his thoughts on the latest and greatest consumer technologies in an excerpt from his speech, "The PC Platform."

Is the picture painted by Pfeiffer too rosy? In "Too Many Gadgets Turn Working Parents into 'Virtual Parents,'" Sue Shellenbarger, a professor and researcher on computers in education, argues that the proliferation of cell phones, pagers, and other devices may make it more acceptable for parents to become "virtual parents," communicating with their children from work or other remote settings. Kathryn Montgomery also is concerned about the impact of technology on children. In "Children in the Digital Age," she outlines why we need to protect children from the commercial messages aimed at them on the World Wide Web. In the final article in the section, "Child Molesters on the Internet: Are They in Your Home?" journalist Bob Trebilock explores the real and imagined dangers to children from Internet pedophiles.

The companion web sites at the conclusion of this section invite you to investigate further how computers are changing the nature of work and family. Visit the site for the MIT Media Lab to explore the frontiers of research and development for communications and consumer technologies. The site Enough Is Enough offers information and advice on how to protect children as they surf the Net. MaMaMedia, a site aimed at children, is an excellent place to learn more about how kids are using the Internet.

You probably already can assess some changes in your own home and family brought about by technology over the years. Perhaps you or a sibling became addicted to a computer game such as Nintendo. Perhaps your parents ask you to carry a pager to keep in touch, or you may ask your children to do so. This section, I hope, will help you identify or predict other changes and to decide for yourself if they are mostly beneficial, or not.

How might computer networks promote a more democratic workplace? What other factors are necessary for such an environment to flourish?

The Ripple Effect of Computer Networking

The computer network your company installed is more than a simple change in the way employees communicate. The impact may dramatically affect the way they work and think.

Bob Filipczak

Bob Filipczak is staff editor of Training Magazine. *His e-mail address via MCI Mail is Sproskin.*

In the beginning, it was a simple concept. You have a computer and your co-worker has one, too. Both are useful tools, but what if you could share information between the two? What if you could get these computers to talk to each other across distances? What if. . . .

. . . and then there was light!

Without further notice, we were networked. Companies began to connect computers with cables, using network software to help the machines send information across the lines. Later, the networks connected PC's with file servers, essentially big hard drives that could be a central storehouse for programs everyone in the company used.

What business needs drove all this networking? There are probably as many rationales as there are organizations, but the simple desire to be more effective and get more work out of fewer people is the best all-purpose explanation. Others include the need to preserve the consistency of data and improve information sharing among headquarters and field-office employees.

One of the first byproducts of computer networking has been an increase in the speed of communications. Electronic mail (e-mail), document sharing, central data bases of information, and computer forums where people can discuss topics with each other in real time have all resulted from connecting computers to networks. All change the way people communicate, and changing the way people communicate within a company produces reverberations we are just beginning to understand.

Lee Sproull, a professor of management at Boston University, and Sara Kiesler, a professor of so-cial and decision sciences at Carnegie Mellon University in Pittsburgh, recognized some of the ripple effects of computer communications two years ago. In *Connections: New Ways of Working in the Networked Organization,* a book that examines some of the cultural implications of the computer-network revolution, Sproull and Kiesler write:

"Communication can't be separated from who is in charge of the giving, receiving, content, and use of what is communicated. Information control is tied to other forms of power and influence. When we change information control using technology, we also change the conditions for other control relationships in the organization."

So aside from the increase in efficiency, we're now beginning to see ramifications of those changes in communication and information control. These changes are what Sproull and Kiesler call "second level" effects of computer networks—the unforeseen ways people use the technology.

The Wall Street Journal and *Fortune* magazine use terms like "flattened hierarchies," "empowerment" and "teamwork" to describe the second-level effects of computer networks. Because employees are using networked computers to get access to important information, and sometimes important people, they start to ask questions about their limits. If, for example, your department can gather and crunch its own budget numbers because of the network, is there any reason to wait for the accounting department to do it? Or, if your employees don't like the new vacation policy, is there any reason they can't send the CEO electronic mail saying so?

Some of these changes appear to be no big deal. Others appear to have far-reaching implications, especially in a traditional corporate hierarchy. Either way, your computer network is making its mark on your corporate culture. And some of the changes may not be what the company had in mind when it invested in networking technology.

If You've Got the Time

So what are we really talking about here? In the future, computer videoconferencing may become a reality, but right now networks simply allow users to send files to other people and exchange e-mail. Even by using computer networks for those simple tasks, however, employees have begun to alter the way they accomplish their work.

For example, a friend who works for a computer company in Minneapolis used to make multiple journeys each month to Des Moines, IA, to help another division of the company work out its computer problems. When the Iowa division "got on" the network, my friend could go to Des Moines every morning if he had to and never leave his office.

On its face, that looks like a simple first-level efficiency outcome: It reduces travel time, for instance. But the immediacy of his consulting over the network also improved his service to the Des Moines division. He is available *all the time*. His availability to other divisions and co-workers is just one of the ripples that will translate to changes in work styles across the company. It seems obvious that this kind of change in work styles is bound to have some impact on an organization's culture, although there is considerable disagreement over whether computer networks will produce dramatic cultural change.

At the heart of the discussion about the ripple effects of e-mail and computer networks is what computer techies call "asynchronous communication." In practical terms, it means you don't need all the people involved in the communication to be available at the same time. In a phone conversation, for example, two or more people must be on the line at the same time to achieve communication. (With voicemail and answering machines, even this condition is becoming superfluous, but that's another story.)

With e-mail, communication is sent by one party at a time, usually at the convenience of both parties, and it's sent instantaneously. Since there's no time lag in sending and receiving

Subordinates, real experts, women and minorities are less reticent in a computer discussion.

e-mail, the only time-dependent factor is the convenience of the e-mail recipient. Clearly, a conversation over e-mail takes longer than face-to-face discussion, so urgent communication probably will remain the province of meetings or phone calls. But how much of our interoffice communication is *that* urgent? Assuming time and communication are among the scarcest resources in most organizations, e-mail addresses both shortages.

It's also important to take convenience into account in the e-mail equation. Say, for example, you need to ask your boss a question but it doesn't demand an urgent reply. If you send it over e-mail you won't forget to ask it when she gets back from her battery of meetings. Because she can answer it at her convenience, she may be able to give you a more complete answer and consider it more carefully. In this case, the communication of information is improved because it is asynchronous.

So far, the same could be said of putting a Post-it Note on her door or dropping a memo into her in-basket. But what if others might be able to address the question or benefit from the answer? An electronic distribution list can be an effective way to broadcast a question or concern to scores of people or even the whole company. In the hands of a CEO, this potential for immediate and widespread distribution becomes a new tool for communicating to employees.

Of course, in the hands of a front-line employee with a chip on his shoulder, the same tool can create problems.

A Force for Democracy?

E-mail and computer networking have the potential to flatten traditional hierarchies, but the impact depends on the company. Most experts agree that, in a hierarchical company with rigid chains of command, a network is not going to do much to make the company more egalitarian—at least in the short term.

"You don't stand up and announce, 'We're going to install a network and henceforth everyone will communicate openly and democratically across the organization,'" Sproull tells *Training*. On the other hand, she says, the democratization of computer-networked workplaces is inevitable.

In *Connections*, Sproull and Kiesler make a powerful case for the long-term, hierarchy-flattening power of e-mail conversation. In most cases, they examine the impact on meetings of conducting business electronically vs. face to face. Their findings might be a little scary—if you're a command-and-control type.

First off, status tends to be negated in an electronic meeting, whether it's conducted over e-mail or in real time (with everyone meeting simultaneously on the network and typing their suggestions and responses). In face-to-face meetings, people with higher status tend to dominate the discussion—whether or not they are the most knowledgeable on the subject. In electronic meetings, according to Sproull and Kiesler's research, contributions to the discussion tend to be more equal. Moreover, subordinates, real experts, women and minorities are less reticent in a computer discussion.

Sproull and Kiesler describe the democratizing effect of the technology in a study they conducted with some executives: "When groups of executives met face to face, the men in the groups were five times as likely as the women to make the first decision proposal. When those same groups met via computer, the women made the first proposal as often as the men did."

The authors traced similar results among graduate students teamed up with undergraduates to solve problems. Even when the undergraduate clearly knew more about a subject, face-to-face communication negated that expertise. Electronic meetings leveled the playing field between the two groups.

An outcome-focused person might rightfully ask whether the quality of the solutions was any better when the discussion was more democratic. Sproull and Kiesler say yes. The quality of decisions, solutions and products produced by a group communicating through computer networks was significantly better, according to their findings.

Yet many disagree that computer networks are going to change corporate cultures or knock executives out of their ivory towers. John Mueller, a technical writer in San Diego and co-author of *A Hands-On Guide to Network Management*, has set up networks for a lot of companies. He disagrees that a network will tend to flatten a company that isn't already evolving toward more open communications.

The contention that e-mail gives line employees more access to top executives is a fallacy, he says. If the company doesn't have a culture of open communication, few employees are going to bypass official lines of communication and go straight to the top. Even if they do, top managers will often stop reading their e-mail if they're inundated with gripe mail. When they stop reading and responding to e-mail, it sends a pretty clear message to the rest of the company that certain kinds of communication are not welcome.

Mueller also has seen some companies try to use a network to monitor individuals' work and reinforce the hierarchy. When that happens, he says, employees who think Big Brother is watching will likely avoid the network altogether, a reaction that defeats the purpose for investing in the network in the first place. "In companies where the Big Brother approach is used," he says, "the network doesn't work."

Paul Breo, owner of Chicago-based Infochi, a computer-network consulting company, agrees. "If [companies] use it as a whip or to harden a structure that might not have been good in the first place, then the whole networking process is going to be a failure, at least in terms of the human element," he says.

Sproull, however, stresses the long-term effects of computer communications. She and Kiesler outline four principles that a company should establish to make a network effective.

- The network should be available to everyone, not just the techies.

- There should be a spirit of open communication and flowing information so everyone can offer something and get something from it.

- The company should provide diverse computer forums to enable people to work together.

- The company should establish incentives and policies that encourage the exchange of information.

The Electronic Watercooler

The communication taking place on the computer networks in your company—people discussing movies and exchanging recipes using electronic mail—is really nothing new. Since before the first watercooler appeared in the first office, social interaction at work has been a fact of life. But when watercooler conversations move onto the computer network, all kinds of interesting things can happen.

First, and most important, informal conversations among employees are no longer limited to just a few people. Only so many people fit around a watercooler, but an e-mail distribution list is practically limitless.

"What happens invariably when I install a network is that the break room starts emptying out. And management gets super happy for at least a month or two until they figure out what's going on," says consultant John Mueller, author of *A Hands-On Guide to Network Management*. What's going on, of course, is that those dedicated employees sitting at their desks are assembled around an electronic watercooler. You'll be hard-pressed to figure it out by looking, however. When

they're working they're sitting in front of the computer and tapping on the keyboard. And when they're talking to each other about going out after work, they're doing exactly the same thing.

Some companies are less concerned about informal conversations than others; some even encourage the free exchange of ideas (and chitchat) via company-sponsored electronic bulletin board systems (BBSs). A BBS is similar to e-mail, but messages are available to everyone who has access to the system. When you write something on a BBS, it can be read by anyone who logs on to that area of the network.

Companies set up BBSs for a variety of purposes. IBM, for instance, has had a BBS for software developers for years. It gives programmers a place to discuss problems where peers can chime in with solutions. At Lotus Development, an informal BBS called Soapbox allows employees to post anything they want. Russ Campanello, vice president of human resources, says discussions range from "what to do with leftover cafeteria food" to searching for a good computer dealer in Cambridge, MA, to speculation

about why Digital Electronics Corp. used pentium chips in its new computer.

Some BBSs dedicated to a specific subject wither as employees' interest in the topic declines, says Steve Riley, a systems analyst for Ashland Chemical in Columbus, OH. He advises putting a termination date on most BBSs so people know they have a limited time to contribute. A BBS dedicated to discussion of your new corporate vision, for example, should terminate by the date the vision is supposed to be completed.

Lee Sproull, a professor of management at Boston University and co-author of *Connections*, says some internal BBSs can thrive for longer than three months, but they must be dedicated to topics that attract lasting attention. The one topic that stands the test of time, she says, is food. A BBS dedicated to restaurant reviews and recipes can keep employees' attention longer than just about anything, although systems dedicated to information about a company's competitors can last just as long.

—B.F.

In this kind of climate, write Sproull and Kiesler, the long-term effects of democratization through computer networks will unfold. In the absence of these principles, the changes will take longer, Sproull says, but they will still evolve.

David Daniels, a senior consultant with Metropolitan life, a New York-based insurance company, agrees with Sproull's prediction of the long-term effects. We are just beginning to see the impact of computer communications, he says, but it will include a gradual opening of the corporate culture.

Sheldon Laube, national director of information and technology for Price Waterhouse, the New York-based accounting and consulting firm, puts a different

spin on the debate. A computer network will definitely change a corporate culture, he says, but not the underlying corporate values. His argument goes like this: The corporate culture is a reflection of the way people in a company work. Groupware (software that allows document sharing and electronic meetings) and e-mail undeniably change work styles, but company values are deeper than the surface culture. And values are very difficult to change, assuming you want to change them at all. For example, your company may value customers above all else, and a computer network probably won't change that. But if front-line employees have better access to accounts and can answer customer questions faster and with more confi-

dence, then the employees' sense of enpowerment (in other words, the culture) could change.

Flame Mail

Sproull and Kiesler are not unequivocal boosters of electronic communications, despite some of the evidence they cite. Other experiments they've done reveal some of the disadvantages of e-mail in terms of communication, reaching consensus and information overload.

The first drawback they mention is that as an informal mode of communication, e-mail is a double-edged sword. For some reason, e-mail feels more casual to users than either written or face-to-face communication. It encourages people to write short, concise and pointed communiqués that tend to cut through bureaucratic mumblings and the ambiguities of business jargon. You may not consider that a problem, but this informality has also given birth to the phenomenon of "flame mail."

Flame mail or flaming are terms that were coined to describe the terse, angry, insulting or threatening tone of many e-mail messages. Flame mail occurs on public electronic bulletin board systems (BBS) or between employees on e-mail systems within a company. Sproull and Kiesler pinpoint a variety of reasons for the incendiary nature of flame-mail messages, and many of them are inherent disadvantages of e-mail and computer communications.

Because computer communication is primarily text-based—i.e., written words—people don't have any of the additional clues that make up a face-to-face or telephone conversation. There's no tone of voice, gesture or facial expression to fill in communication gaps, so people often use more expressive language. That crescendo of expressive language can be interpreted as an indication of strong emotions, something generally frowned on in a business environment. In other words, some "flame mail" isn't really very flame-like at all. It's just perceived as unusually blunt in relation to the more formal tone of traditional business correspondence.

The cause of more aggressive flame mail can be traced partly to what Sproull and Kiesler refer to as the ephemeral nature of computer communications. It's generally agreed that the written word is more formal than the spoken word, but because there is no physical record of e-mail (i.e., paper) people seem to attach less importance to it. Consequently, they are more likely to "flame."

Mistakes in e-mail etiquette are easy to make because it's a new medium and the rules are still being written. Daniels tells of the time he wrote an e-mail message to a co-worker and, by mistake, used the caps lock on his keyboard. Because the whole message was in capital letters, the recipient thought Daniels was angry. He got back a response asking, "Why are you shouting at me?"

Rick Rabideau, an Atlanta-based consultant and expert on computer collaboration in work groups, says flame mail tends to generate more flaming unless someone breaks the cycle. "When you get a zinger, sit back and let it age a day or two before you zing them back," advises Rabideau. This computer equivalent of counting to 10 should take some of the venom out of responses.

"When you get a zinger, sit back and let it age a day or two before you zing them back."

Oddly enough, consensus building may be another casualty of computer communications. In face-to-face meetings, the 80–20 rule often applies: 80 percent of all the talking and input comes from 20 percent of the participants. Precisely because electronic meetings tend to level the playing field in terms of hierarchy, you get more input from more people. Moreover, the participants are less likely to back down from their opinions if they don't see their bosses glaring at their suggestions. Consequently, reaching a consensus via e-mail can be a laborious and frustrating process. When Sproull and Kiesler tried to test the consensus-building properties of elec-

tronic communication, they had to abandon the experiment when participants got so caught up in arguing that no consensus was reached.

Information overload may be the most productivity-busting aspect of computer-network communications. Once a network is installed, line workers may have immediate access to almost anyone in the company. That's when a kind of volcano effect can spew out over managers and top executives. Without social barriers to upward communication, the CEO of a good-sized company might receive 50 e-mail messages a day. E-mail usually just lands in a manager's desktop computer in a lump. Everything from recipes for a new dessert to someone interested in selling a concert ticket to notification that his performance appraisal forms are due in two days can pile up in a manager's e-mail in-box, with no way to separate the important from the fluff.

Sure, managers can just stop reading all e-mail to avoid this pitfall. One professional confessed that the CEO of his company has a computer on his desk but never turns it on; there's not much chance that anyone sends that executive electronic mail. On the other hand, if people don't read their e-mail in the interests of saving time or preventing information overload, they defeat the purpose of using a computer network to improve communications.

A better solution is the use of computer-network filters, what *The Wall Street Journal* terms "bozo filters." If you want to eliminate e-mail correspondence from known "bozos," you can program the software so mail originating from certain individuals never gets delivered to your mailbox. In a kinder, gentler work environment, however, filters can also prioritize your e-mail so it doesn't arrive in one enormous lump. A filter, for example, can ensure all mail with your supervisor's name on it lands at the top of your list.

Lotus Notes, a popular groupware program that lets people share all kinds of information and e-mail correspondence, has a sophisticated filter, or "agent," that organizes e-mail into folders. Therefore, computer tips from the training department land in one folder and missives from the board of directors land in another. Notes can even search your mail for strings of words and prioritize them that way. If, for example. you're working on a project to develop an aperture flywheel gramis with a vacuum gasket, you can have all e-mail that contains that string of words sent to the same folder.

An easier way to prevent important mail from getting buried in an information avalanche is to train employees in how to use e-mail effectively. Russ Campanello, vice president of human resources for Lotus Development, says his company not only built Notes, it also uses the software on a day-to-day basis. His simple solution to losing important mail within a pile of random e-mail deposits is to tell employees to include the words "action request" on the subject line. That way, he separates information that's nice to know from the stuff asking him to do something.

If you're going to use a filter to screen out mail, instead of just prioritizing it, you also run the risk of losing any important information a bozo might send you. Rabideau says we are still a few years away from a truly intelligent filter that can read your messages and make a judgment call on whether you need it or not. He also suggests that employees should be informed if you're using a filter to screen mail. "On one hand you're telling them 'I'm open, please send me messages,' but on the other hand, 'I have my bozo filter and am screening them out.' It's a little contradictory," admits Rabideau.

Out in the Boondocks

Some advantages to computer-networked communication go deeper than just better communication, not the least of which is the ability to connect with "peripheral" employees—those who are located away from company headquarters. Sproull and Kiesler cite several studies that indicate that computer communication boosts the morale of these employees and helps them feel more in touch with the rest of the company.

This is precisely what General American Life Insurance, a St. Louis-based insurance provider, had in mind when it decided to upgrade its computer communication to Notes, says Larry Connor, group administration vice president. General American's sale reps around the country could access headquarters via a network set up years ago, but it was a cumbersome, inefficient system and field reps hated to use it.

Consequently, Connor's department was constantly dealing with field employees who didn't send policies to headquarters in a timely manner. Using Notes not only cut in half the time it took reps to enter the information into the computer network, it also decreased the number of clarifying questions Connor's employees had to ask reps.

How's that again? Employees who use e-mail are more loyal?

Connor's group has just five new-business coordinators and, under the old system, they were continually swamped with phone messages from sales reps. Because these coordinators now spend less time clearing up ambiguities, they are more available—by phone and computer—to help sales reps with more important issues. Moreover, the scarce new business coordinators can broadcast answers to frequently asked questions throughout the network.

Price Waterhouse's Laube, a peripheral employee himself, agrees that a good computer network is a morale builder. Because the chairman of the company uses e-mail to deliver messages to employees, everyone gets important information at the same time. In the past, Laube's California office workers might wait a week before a memo from headquarters got to them. Now the chairman can send instantaneous messages—whether important policy changes or wishes for a happy new year—to every Price Waterhouse office in the world.

The worldwide computer network also creates another advantage for Price Waterhouse's peripheral employees: virtual teams. Now, through electronic document sharing and videoconferencing over the network, a team can include the best people for the job no matter where they are located, says Laube.

Nevertheless, he cautions, computer networks do not obviate the need for face-to-face communication. "I live in California, and the senior executives are in New York. When it comes time to review my budget, we don't do it over e-mail," says Laube.

His warning is echoed by others: E-mail cannot replace

face-to-face meetings. It can, however, make meetings more efficient because all participants can arrive completely informed about the agenda and updated on any new developments.

Another effect that Sproull and Kiesler discovered as they researched computer communication was an increase in company loyalty among employees. How's that again? Employees who use e-mail are more loyal? In a study of employees of a city government, they found that over 90 percent routinely used electronic mail. Furthermore, Sproull and Kiesler write: "We discovered that the more [employees] used it, the more committed they were to their employer—measured by how willing they were to work beyond the requirements and hours of their jobs, how attached they felt to the city government, and how strongly they planned to continue working for the city." The researchers also discovered that the relationship between workplace loyalty and computer communication was stronger in employees who worked later shifts, another finding that bolsters the argument that e-mail strengthens the commitment of peripheral workers.

Sproull and Kiesler's analysis of computer-network communication uncovers many "second-level" effects on organizations. But they posit that any new technology has at least three levels of impact on society—and that with computer communication, we've only just begun to see the effects of Level 2.

What happens when organizations go from LANs (local area networks) to WANs (wide area networks) like Compuserve, America On-line, MCI Mail or the Internet? According to the newly formed Internation Internet Association (IIA), the Internet adds a million users to its ranks every month. Max Robbins, IIA's executive director, says about 99 percent of the additions to the user base in the last three years have come from the business sector.

It's one thing when employees can access top executives via e-mail. What happens when employees can access professional peers over the Internet? And what happens to a company's trade secrets when these discussions heat up? No one has answers to these questions yet, but a little forethought about the costs, benefits, and far-reaching implications of computer networks is probably in order. Clearly, the networks set up in companies all over the country are more than a tangle of cables and software. These computer networks are changing the way employees communicate, and that changes everything.

 Article Review Form at end of book.

Would you like to be monitored by a computer while on the job? When is the use of such technology appropriate for ensuring productivity?

Mr. Edens Profits from Watching His Workers' Every Move

Tony Horowitz

Control is one of Ron Edens's favorite words. "This is a controlled environment," he says of the blank brick building that houses his company, Electronic Banking System Inc.

Inside, long lines of women sit at spartan desks, slitting envelopes, sorting contents, and filling out "control cards" that record how many letters they have opened and how long it has taken them. Workers here in "the cage," must process three envelopes a minute. Nearby, other women tap keyboards, keeping pace with a quota that demands 8500 strokes an hour.

The room is silent. Talking is forbidden. The windows are covered. Coffee mugs, religious pictures, and other adornments are barred from workers' desks.

In his office upstairs, Mr. Edens sits before a TV monitor that flashes images from eight cameras posted through the plant. "There's a little bit of Sneaky Pete to it," he says, using a remote control to zoom in on a document atop a worker's desk. "I can basically read that and figure out how someone's day is going."

This day, like most others, is going smoothly, and Mr. Edens's business has boomed as a result. "We maintain a lot of control," he says. "Order and control are everything in this business."

Mr. Edens's business belongs to a small but expanding financial service known as "lockbox processing." Many companies and charities that once did their paperwork in-house now "out-source" clerical tasks to firms like EBS, which processes donations to groups such as Mothers Against Drunk Driving, the Doris Day Animal League, Greenpeace, and the National Organization for Women.

More broadly, EBS reflects the explosive growth of jobs in which workers perform low-wage and limited tasks in white-collar settings. This has transformed towns like Hagerstown—a blue-collar community hit hard by industrial layoffs in the 1970s—into sites for thousands of jobs in factory-sized offices.

Many of these jobs, though, are part-time and most pay far less than the manufacturing occupations they replaced. Some workers at EBS start at the minimum wage of $4.25 an hour and most earn about $6 an hour. The growth of such jobs—which often cluster outside major cities—also completes a curious historic circle. During the Industrial Revolution, farmers' daughters went to work in textile towns like Lowell, Massachusetts. In post-industrial America, many women of modest means and skills are entering clerical mills where they process paper instead of cloth (coincidentally, EBS occupies a former garment factory).

"The office of the future can look a lot like the factory of the past," says Barbara Garson, author of *The Electronic Sweatshop* and other books on the modern workplace. "Modern tools are being used to bring nineteenth-century working conditions into the white-collar world."

The time-motion philosophies of Frederick Taylor, for instance, have found a 1990s correlate in the phone, computer, and camera, which can be used to monitor workers more closely than a foreman with a stopwatch ever could. Also, the nature of the work often justifies a vigilant eye. At EBS, workers handle thousands of dollars in checks and cash, and Mr. Edens says cameras help deter would-be thieves. Tight security also reassures visiting clients. "If you're disorderly, they'll think we're out of control and that things could get lost," says Mr. Edens, who worked as a financial controller for the National Rifle Association before founding EBS in 1983.

But tight observation also helps EBS monitor productivity and weed out workers who don't keep up. "There's multiple uses," Mr. Edens says of surveillance. His desk is covered with computer printouts recording the precise toll of keystrokes tapped by each data-entry worker. He also keeps a day-to-day tally of errors.

The work floor itself resembles an enormous classroom in the throes of exam period. Desks point toward the front, where a manager keeps watch from a raised platform that workers call "the pedestal" or "the birdhouse." Other supervisors are positioned toward the back of the room. "If you want to watch someone," Mr. Edens explains, "it's easier from behind because they don't know you're watching." There also is a black globe hanging from the ceiling, in which cameras are positioned.

Mr. Edens sees nothing Orwellian about this omniscience. "It's not a Big Brother attitude," he says. "It's more of a calming attitude."

But studies of work place monitoring suggest otherwise. Experts say that surveillance can create a hostile environment in which workers feel pressured, paranoid, and prone to stress-related illness. Surveillance also can be used punitively, to intimidate workers or to justify their firing.

Following a failed union drive at EBS, the National Labor Relations Board filed a series of complaints against the company, including charges that EBS threatened, interrogated, and spied on workers. As part of an out-of-court settlement, EBS reinstated a fired worker and posted a notice that it would refrain from illegal practices during a second union vote, which also failed.

"It's all noise," Mr. Edens says of the unfair labor charges. As to the pressure that surveillance creates, Mr. Edens sees that simply as "the nature of the beast." He adds: "It's got to add stress when everyone knows their production is being monitored. I don't apologize for that."

Mr. Edens also is unapologetic about the Draconian work rules he maintains, including one that forbids all talk unrelated to the completion of each task. "I'm not paying people to chat. I'm paying them to open envelopes," he says. Of the blocked windows, Mr. Edens adds: "I don't want them looking out—it's distracting. They'll make mistakes."

This total focus may boost productivity, but it makes many workers feel lonely and trapped. Some try to circumvent the silence rule, like kids in a school library. "If you don't turn your head and sort of mumble out of the side of your mouth, supervisors won't hear you most of the time," Cindy Kesselring explains

during her lunch break. Even so, she feels isolated and often longs for her former job as a waitress. "Work is your social life, particularly if you've got kids," says the 27-year-old mother. "Here it's hard to get to know people because you can't talk."

During lunch, workers crowd in the parking lot outside, chatting nonstop. "Some of us don't eat much because the more you chew the less you can talk," Ms. Kesselring says. There aren't other scheduled breaks and workers aren't allowed to sip coffee or eat at their desks during the long stretches before and after lunch. Hard candy is the only permitted desk snack.

New technology, and the breaking down of labor into discrete, repetitive tasks, also have effectively stripped jobs such as those at EBS of whatever variety and skills clerical work once possessed. Workers in the cage (an antiquated banking term for a money-handling area) only open envelopes and sort contents; those in the audit department compute figures; and data-entry clerks punch in the information that the others have collected. If they make a mistake, the computer buzzes and a message such as "check digit error" flashes on the screen.

"We don't ask these people to think—the machines think for them," Mr. Edens says. "They don't have to make any decisions."

This makes the work simpler but also deepens its monotony. In the cage, Carol Smith says she looks forward to envelopes that contain anything out of the ordinary, such as letters reporting that the donor is deceased. Or she plays mental games. "I think to myself, A goes in this pile, B goes here, and C goes there—sort of like Bingo." She says she sometimes feels "like a machine," particularly when she fills out the "control card" on which she lists "time in" and "time out" for each tray of envelopes. In a slot marked "cage operator," Ms. Smith writes her code number, 3173. "That's me," she says.

Barbara Ann Wiles, a keyboard operator, also plays mind games to break up the boredom. Tapping in the names and addresses of new donors, she tries to imagine the faces behind the names, particularly the odd ones. "Like this one, Mrs. Fittizzi," she chuckles. "I can picture her as a very stout lady with a strong accent, hollering on a street corner." She picks out another: "Doris Angelroth—she's very sophisticated, a monocle maybe, drinking tea on an overstuffed mohair couch."

It is a world remote from the one Ms. Wiles inhabits. Like most EBS employees, she must juggle her low-paying job with child care. On this Friday, for instance, Ms. Wiles will finish her eight-hour shift at about 4 P.M., go home for a few hours, then return for a second shift from midnight to 8 A.M. Otherwise, she would have to come in on Saturday to finish the week's work. "This way I can be home on the weekend to look after my kids," she says.

Others find the work harder to leave behind at the end of the day. In the cage, Ms. Smith says her husband used to complain because she often woke him in the middle of the night. "I'd be shuffling my hands in my sleep," she says, mimicking the motion of opening envelopes.

Her cage colleague, Ms. Kesselring, says her fiance has a different gripe. "He dodges me for a couple of hours after work because I don't shut up—I need to talk, talk, talk," she says. And there is one household task she can no longer abide.

"I won't pay bills because I can't stand to open another envelope," she says. "I'll leave letters sitting in the mailbox for days."

 Article Review Form at end of book.

Will emerging consumer technologies improve the quality of life? Will they be adopted by most consumers?

The PC Platform

Eckhard Pfeiffer

Eckhard Pfeiffer is president and CEO of Compaq Computer Corporation.

Today's PC has evolved to the point of fundamentally redefining experience for people of all ages.

In fact, the PC has progressed so far and so fast along the inventive continuum that it now defines the computer industry. And it will come to define the consumer electronics industry as well.

The Evolution and Growth of Computer Use

As computing and communications have fused, we've seen the PC evolve from a stand-alone personal productivity device to a communications tool—a connector and coordinator. And when combined with the Internet, the PC can radically transform personal and business communication, commerce, education, healthcare delivery, home automation, entertainment and play, and perhaps even government.

The PC's life-changing power is not lost on people. While personal computers are in just one-third of American homes today, many, many more people aspire to owning a PC, mostly because of its educational value. A recent survey found that more than 80 percent of people who plan to buy one soon say it's mainly for their children's education. We know that a majority of all computer purchases are influenced by a child in the household.

So by 1998, we expect half of American homes to have at least one PC. In fact, households with more than one computer will become as common as households with more than one TV, VCR, or phone.

According to market researcher Link Resources, 11 million U.S. homes already have two or more working PCs. New users tend to spend more time on the PC than in front of the TV.

Why is this happening?

Well, the PC's become so versatile and such a magnet for more and more functionality that the entire family wants to use it at the same time. And who can blame them? Can you think of any other mass market product that has proved so adaptable, so multiform,

> **"The PC's become so versatile and such a magnet for more and more functionality that the entire family wants to use it at the same time."**

so elastic in function, definition, and price?

The same PC can be used today as a telephone, a fax machine, a modem, a scanner, copier, and TV. It can be used as a connection to the increasingly commercialized and ubiquitous Internet. It can be used as a node on the office network. A tool for managing personal finance or educating and entertaining children. A vehicle for telecommuting and videoconferencing. A place to play audio and video CD-ROMs. As well as an intelligent command center for controlling your major appliances and monitoring your home's energy use and security systems.

What's more, the PC can connect to nearly every kind of communications infrastructure. You can hook it up to analog and ISDN (integrated switched digital network) lines, to Ethernet, cable, infrared, and wireless communications of all kinds.

And that's essential because people want to connect—to one another, to the Internet, to on-line services, to businesses, to the

Keynote address by Eckhard Pfeiffer, January 5, 1996. Winter Consumer Electronics Show, Las Vegas, Nevada.

ocean of information in cyberspace. Little surprise then that in 1995 the two-phone-line household became a common fact of life. The connection machine par excellence is the PC. And this gateway device keeps getting more and more powerful.

Computers in Every Room

I see the PC as a universal tool for home and business. By universal tool I mean it does many things well. And its features, form factor, and price can be tailored to suit the activities that go on in the different rooms of your home. I believe the PC now has a place in nearly every room of your home. And yet it won't be the same kind of computer in each room.

We've put this idea into practice by helping design what we call the Information Highway House. It's a real four-bedroom house located just north of San Francisco in Corte Madera. Inside are five different Compaq PCs linked in an Ethernet-based local area network.

With these PCs, family members can schedule a doctor's appointment, buy stocks, or pay bills electronically from the den. They can research a school project or listen to interactive books from the bedroom. They can look up a recipe on the kitchen PC, and laugh at comedy routines in the living room. This cyberspace house represents just the earliest stages of what will be possible before the turn of the century.

I say that because today's PC has only just entered its adolescence. Its hormones are just kicking in. Its major growth and the realization of its full potential lie ahead. In fact, it's as far from a commodity as a product can be.

To know that's true, just consider how many really different versions of the PC are emerging. Everything from high-end clustered multiprocessor servers for the datacenter, to room-specific devices for the home, to lightweight, mobile PC companions that combine data transmission and voice recognition capabilities.

No single commodity motherboard can meet all these form factors or all customer needs cost effectively. I think the PC is about where the automobile was back in the 1920s. While we're past the equivalent of drivers needing to crank and choke their cars by hand, we're not yet to the point of automatic transmission—let alone antilock brakes and air bags. In short, PC advances in the next two decades will dwarf those of the past two.

Now, there are other reasons for my optimism. Given the momentum behind the Internet, we're going to see a major increase in communications bandwidth to the home. This bandwidth will be delivered by ISDN, broadband over copper wires, cable modems, direct digital satellite services, and ultimately all-optical networks.

The Computerized Home of the Future

What's more, we at Compaq are convinced there's enormous opportunity to integrate the PC far more completely into the home. Your home can have far more diverse and interactive links to the outside world. That way you can pull in digital content on demand along with a wealth of information and services. And you can engage in full-blown electronic

commerce, telemedicine, and distance learning.

Equally important, I believe your home itself can become a far more intelligent and automated environment and as programmable as a PC.

These developments are pulling us toward the Intelligent Networked Home of the very near future. I know the idea of a "smart home" has been around for decades. Back in the 1950s, science fiction writer Ray Bradbury offered a memorable vision.

In one of his short stories, he described a 21st century house where the front door recognizes visitors and lets them in, the kitchen ceiling "speaks," reminding you which bills are due today. And tiny robot mice roam the floors collecting dust.

In another story, we read about a family whose house has a special room built just for the kids. It's a virtual reality nursery that brings to life in three dimensions whatever scene the kids are thinking about, whether it's the cow jumping over a very realistic moon, lions prowling an African plain, or more to the point, parents turning over their car keys and credit cards to their kids.

Compaq's vision of the intelligent home is a bit more down to earth and it's available this century!

Home Computers of the Very Near Future

With that in mind, let's consider the following scenario. Suppose it's January 5th in the year 2000. It's a weekday, 6:30 in the morning. You shuffle to the kitchen in

> "The PC now has a place in nearly every room of your home."

search of coffee and turn on your voice- and touchscreen-activated kitchen PC-TV.

With its advanced digital display system, this PC can handle the spectrum of bandwidths, aspect ratios, and scan rates depending on the content you've selected. And it's linked to a multi-channel, multi-point distribution system whether wireless digital broadcast, wireless cable, or digital satellite video and data.

> "Your home itself can become a far more intelligent and automated environment and as programmable as a PC."

You select CNN *Headline News*, which reports that the Winter Consumer Electronics Show is under way. You notice a live satellite feed of CES is available and watch a few minutes of the opening keynote. With a touch of the PC's keypad, you check for any pressing phone, fax, or E-mail messages delivered overnight.

Software agents that act on your behalf by knowing your interests prioritize your messages and point out a conflict in your schedule for the day. These agents interact with you on your monitor through animated facial expressions.

While this is happening, your wife is in the bedroom seated by a large-screen PC connected to wide-area ATM-based, broadband services. She's flying to China this afternoon for an extended business trip. But before leaving the country, she wants to consult with her doctor to make sure her vaccinations are up to date.

While waiting for her scheduled 7:00 A.M. telemedicine appointment, she reads her personalized electronic newspaper, which was compiled overnight by her software agents scanning the network. This morn-ing's lead stories notify her of a delay in her flight's departure, Beijing restaurant reviews, and an acquisition just undertaken by the Chinese customer she's visiting.

At 7:00 sharp a chime sounds, and her doctor's face appears in a high-quality video tile on her PC. She touches the tile with her finger, causing it to fill the screen. During this personal videoconference, her doctor reviews her medical record and the latest health advisories from China.

Meanwhile, your teenage daughter starts her day as she always does, by jumping on the I-phone (the Internet phone) to talk to a friend in Germany. She also logs into a video rental store on the Net, looks at a dozen movie trailers, and selects the one she'll watch that evening on the living room PC-TV, which has a 60-inch screen.

After your wife leaves for the airport, and the kids head off to day care and school, you drive to the office for a quick meeting. Your house, sensing it's now empty, automatically switches to "away mode," turning off lights, closing drapes, dialing back the thermostat, and resetting the security system. In fact, your home network is con-

> "With a touch of the PC's keypad, you check for any pressing phone, fax, or E-mail messages delivered overnight."

stantly monitoring its subsystems, ready to page you if there's any change from the normal settings.

Later that morning while you're at work, your home security system sends you an urgent page with the message: "Front window broken. Security com-pany called." With voice commands directed at your desktop PC, you dial into your home remotely. You speak your personal ID code and then say: "Activate control console. Activate security camera."

You take a quick pan of your front yard and notice a tree limb leaning against your house, and a crack running the length of your living room window. Relieved that no one has broken in, you send an "all-clear" signal to your security company. And then you say to your computer: "Find a nearby glass repair service and dial the number."

Two hours later, a technician from "Window Doktor" arrives in your driveway. Your security system senses someone approaching your front door and pages you again. The technician holds his badge up to the security camera for verification, and you remotely unlock the front door.

A couple of hours later, he sends a page that the window has been replaced and the bill comes to $485. And over the Web, you send a secure electronic payment to "WindowDoktor.com."

When you get home that evening, you decide to call up the energy management program on your PC. This gives you an up-to-the-minute look at your phone and utility bills. It also lets you save money by shifting your peak power consumption to times of day when rates are significantly lower.

Now I could continue with this scenario, but you get a sense of the wealth of convenience offered by an intelligent Networked Home. Perhaps you're thinking if this is not complete fantasy, then it must require the resources of a Warren Buffett [as of 1995, the wealthiest man in America]. Well, we believe this scenario is not only feasible but affordable. Most of the technology needed to fully implement home automation and provide valuable services is here today.

Through the centuries, the focal point of the house has changed several times. Early on, it was the fireplace. People gathered around it to keep warm and cook their meals. Over time, that focal point switched to the kitchen. And then it seemed to switch to the TV. But now, I believe the home's new focal point is becoming the PC.

 Article Review Form at end of book.

Will you become a "virtual parent" someday? How might this phenomenon impact children?

Too Many Gadgets Turn Working Parents into "Virtual Parents"

Sue Shellenbarger

Working parents note: From the folks who brought you virtual reality and the virtual office, now comes a new kind of altered state: virtual parenting.

No one is pushing a virtual-reality headgear as a substitute for parents—yet. But if Martians landed tomorrow and sampled a few high-tech ad campaigns, they might think we were close.

Many marketers are promoting cellular phones, faxes, computers and pagers to working parents as a way of bridging separations from their kids. A recent promotion by AT&T and Residence Inns suggests that business travelers with young children use video and audiotapes, voice mail, videophones and e-mail to stay connected, including kissing the kids goodnight by phone.

A joint promotion by three companies aimed at business travelers urges faxing homework back and forth or arranging family conference calls—"a virtual family reunion." Kinko's, the business-services chain, promotes videoconferencing, and Motorola pushes pagers for families.

These ideas can work well, of course. Family use of all kinds of high-tech gear is booming, and the trend is meeting a real need for working parents, who often wish they could be in two places at once. When Mark Vanderbilt, a network systems engineer, was planning a scientific expedition to Antarctica, he taught his wife and three children to send and receive live video feeds over the Internet.

Philip Mirvis, a consultant and University of Michigan management professor, e-mails his nine- and ten-year-olds when he travels or works late. And flight attendant Marianne Bradley-Kopec of St. Petersburg, Fla., made a video of herself singing lullabies for her baby; her sitter used it to calm him, she says.

But at the risk of sounding cranky, I think some marketers are pushing a good thing too far. One joint brochure by AT&T and others suggests to parents that if they must miss a child's Little League game, they call the field for a play-by-play account by cellular phone. ("All it's going to do is bother everybody!" says Susan Ginsberg, a New York educational consultant who advised MCI on another family-oriented campaign.)

More advice from adland: Business travelers can dine with their kids by speakerphone or "tuck them in" by cordless phone. (If anyone suggested to my kids that they cuddle up with a cordless phone, they'd probably throw it across the room.)

Separately, a management newsletter recommends faxing your child when you have to break a promise to be home, or giving a young child a beeper to make him feel more secure when left alone.

The man who apparently coined the term "virtual parenting"—Gil Gordon, a Monmouth Junction, N.J., management consultant—sees a risk in such excesses. Mr. Gordon, a telecommuting expert, was among the first to warn against burnout among high-tech workers who overuse their gadgets. He uses faxes and e-mail with his own kids, ages 12 and 16. But again he sees a hazard in overusing technology, with working parents' using it "instead of being there."

High-tech gear fails families when they try to use it:

1. **As a substitute for warm human contact.** A New York banker raised the ire of family members by calling them only from his car phone when stuck in traffic. His family knew he was reaching out only during time he couldn't spend doing anything else, says Wayne Myers, a psychiatrist and professor at Cornell Medical School.

2. **As a Band-Aid for too much absence.** At one East Coast company that pressures employees to stay at work late every evening, working parents try to compensate by secretly sending e-mail home, says Deborah Swiss, a Boston author and gender-equity consultant. In that setup, she adds, no one wins—the kids, their distracted parents or the employer.

3. **As a stand-in for adults.** Sharon Maltagliati, an Ellicott City, Md., entrepreneur, tested a computerized calling system with 50 families to check on children home alone after school.

But so many parents failed to provide adequate backup, in the form of adults who would step in when needed, that she dropped it. "People were using it like a babysitting service," she says.

As a working parent who grew up on "Star Trek," it's easy for me to harbor unrealistic wishes about technology. During years of missing my young children while traveling on business, I looked forward to sharing long talks from the road by phone. So when my daughter reached first grade, I called her one night from a hotel room 2,900 miles away and eagerly questioned her about her day. A pause ensued. "Mom, when are you coming home?" she finally asked. After mulling my answer, she reminded me that her favorite TV show was on and hung up. (Sometimes, I guess, you just have to be there.)

The trick for working parents is to find the middle ground—where technology enriches our ties with children, rather than underscoring separations. People already are drawing those lines on work matters. When AT&T tested an ad campaign for a fax machine that could be used to get work done on the beach, consumers told researchers they didn't *want* to work on the beach, an AT&T executive told a recent conference.

We might do well, it seems to me, to be just as thoughtful about using technology in family life.

 Article Review Form at end of book.

Why is Montgomery concerned about the commercialization of the Internet? Does children's contact with advertising via the Internet differ from contact via television?

Children in the Digital Age

Kathryn C. Montgomery

After 50 years of controversy over the impact of television on children, a new world of online media is emerging that may have even greater impact on them. Almost one million children in the United States are now using the World Wide Web, according to a research and consulting firm specializing in interactive technology, and 3.8 million have Web access—figure that will grow rapidly in coming years. Like adults, children will increasingly be connected to a vast digital universe that transcends the family, the local community, and even the nation. Education will expand beyond the classroom and other traditional settings, as more interactive "edutainment" becomes available. New personal and portable technologies will enable children to inhabit their own separate electronic worlds.

The dazzling graphics and engaging interactivity of the new multimedia technologies will make them potent forces in the lives of children. If harnessed properly, the new media could enhance their drive to learn, provide them with access to a rich diversity of information and ideas, and enable them to reach across community and national borders. But there is also peril: Video game channels, virtual shopping malls, and manipulative forms of advertising targeted at children could further compound the problems in the existing media that have troubled parents, educators, and child advocates for decades.

We are in the midst of the formative stage of this new digital age. Government policies are being debated and enacted, marketing and programming strategies are being developed, and services for children are being designed. If we are to believe some hyperbolic visions of cyberspace, the information superhighway will be a great equalizing force that will bring unprecedented opportunity for all. Improvements in education and other benefits for children are often at the center of these visions. But history offers us cautionary lessons. In this century enthusiasts have hailed every new medium—from radio to FM to television to cable to satellites—with claims that it would reinvigorate our culture, expand educational opportunities, and enhance the democratic process. None has lived up to these claims. In each case, powerful commercial forces have used civic values to gain support for the new medium—and then squelched the very policies necessary to serve the public good.

In this recent phase, powerful media companies have already poured vast amounts of money into lobbying to shape the 1996 Telecommunications Act. From the beginning, corporations were able to frame the debate. While some political leaders, such as Al Gore as a senator, compared the new information superhighway to the interstate highway system, the Clinton administration's vision quickly became a privately built and operated national information infrastructure (NII). The Telecommunications Act is designed to encourage competition by deregulating the telecommunications market. Public interest advocates, though pitifully underfinanced, were able to win only a few positive provisions for consumers. The interests of children were not central to the legislative debate, and the little attention paid to children was misdirected at indecent content on the Internet. As a result, the law ignores or inadequately addresses critical issues that will have a significant long-term effect. In the wake of the legislation, we need a new strategic understanding of what needs to be done to make the best of the new media—and to avoid the worst.

Electronic Inclusion

While traditional media are sometimes viewed as unnecessary diversions, digital media will soon become an integral part of daily life. Those without access to the communications system are likely to fall behind in education and be unable to compete in a highly selective job market. Yet just as access is becoming imperative, the number of children living in poverty, with little or no access to technology, is growing at an alarming rate. According to a 1994 survey, 11 percent of families with incomes of less than $20,000 have a computer, compared to 56 percent of families with incomes above $50,000. One out of ten children under the age of six lives in a home without a telephone.

To its credit, the Clinton administration has raised the issue of disparities between the information rich and information poor. In its 1993 Agenda for Action, the White House called for all schools, libraries, and hospitals to be connected to the national information infrastructure by the year 2000. The idea was to provide equitable access through these institutions, even if it couldn't be assured for all homes. At present, there are a handful of government programs intended to encourage innovation and pay for pilot projects, but the administration has mostly relied on private, voluntary efforts to meet this goal.

Some promising projects have emerged, such as California's NetDay, a one-day effort in March 1996, spearheaded by Sun Microsystems, in which volunteers across the state strung miles of wire to connect elementary and secondary schools to the Internet. Relying heavily on such voluntary efforts, however, will likely leave many communities and schools unconnected. The vast majority of public schools, particularly for minority and low-income children, lack the basic technology and training to provide students access to computer networks.

Even if more children are able to use the new media through schools and libraries, they will still be at a disadvantage relative to children with access at home. An hour or two of computer laboratory time in school is not enough to acquire the technological competence that colleges and many jobs will require. Some argue that the costs of the equipment will go down dramatically in the next few years, making computer communications as affordable as televisions and VCRs. But monthly service charges are another barrier, and communications services that are now free or very inexpensive may become unaffordable. While some form of over-the-air television is likely to remain free, most other video services will require payment. For families in poverty, either the upfront cost of equipment or service charges may be insurmountable barriers.

The Telecommunications Act could have created comprehensive policies for ensuring equitable access to the national information infrastructure. But because of the conservative political climate, the federal deficit, and unprecedented lobbying expenditures and campaign contributions by the telecommunications industries, the legislation dealt very narrowly with the issue. The education and library communities were able to win a provision that requires telecommunications companies to offer less expensive connection and service charges to schools and libraries than to homes and businesses. But the Federal Communications Commission (FCC) must define what "affordable" means. In consultation with the states, the FCC is now supposed to develop a universal service policy for the new digital era that includes the provisions for schools and libraries.

A New Media Environment

Access isn't the only challenge; the quality of the new media culture for children also raises concern. Unlike TV, online media are dynamic and two-way. This participatory quality makes them particularly compelling to children. Such technological breakthroughs as real-time audio, real-time video, and virtual reality modeling language (which allows programmers to turn Web sites into three-dimensional environments) are transforming online media. Eventually, this interactive online world could supplant traditional television as the most powerful and influential medium in children's lives.

Many online services are now available that seek to challenge children by exposing them to places, people, and ideas far outside their everyday experiences. For example, Plugged In, a Web site created by a community computing center in Palo Alto,

> Access isn't the only challenge; the quality of the new media culture for children also raises concern.

California, allows poor children to explore the Internet, produce their own art, and display it to other children around the world. [See the article in this issue by Mitchel Resnick and Natalie Rusk, "Computer Clubhouses in the Inner City," page 60.]* Another Web site, CyberKids, enables children to write and share their own stories in an online magazine. Special networks have been established to foster online communities for children. With help from a federal grant from the National Telecommunications and Information Agency, the National Youth Center Network is addressing such problems as violent crime and unemployment by electronically linking youth centers in low-income neighborhoods.

These educational and civic services, however, are in danger of being overshadowed by a powerful interactive commercial culture with an unprecedented ability to capture children's attention. Marketing to children has become a multibillion dollar business. The direct spending power of children, almost all of it discretionary, has risen rapidly in recent years. In 1995, according to *Interactive Marketing News* and *Youth Markets Alert,* children under 12 spent $14 billion, teenagers another $67 billion, and together they influenced $160 billion of their parents' annual spending. As an executive for Turner Home Entertainment recently explained: "Probably for the first time in the consumer business, kids are now being recognized as a truly gigantic part of the consumer purchasing block." In the last decade, these trends triggered a proliferation of new

*Does not appear in this publication. Refers to the July–August 1996 issue of *The American Prospect.*

TV networks aimed at capturing a segment of the hot children's market, including the controversial classroom news service Channel One, the highly profitable Nickelodeon cable channel, CNN's Cartoon Channel, and the Fox Children's Network.

With the FCC's deregulation of children's television in the mid-1980s, toy manufacturers began the wholesale creation of "kidvid" series that served as half-hour commercials for a line of licensed products—from He-Man to the Care Bears to the Transformers. Character licensing has become the driving force not only in children's television, but also in much of the rest of children's culture. Cross-promotion of licensed products through TV, movies, magazines, discount stores, and fast food restaurants has produced a proliferation of licensed characters that permeate every facet of a child's life.

The new online services for children are being developed in the context of this highly commercialized children's media culture. Children are a disproportionately important market for the new interactive media because they are early adopters of high-tech products. Marketers who view children as the "lucrative cyber-tot category" see the emerging media as a fertile new frontier for targeting children. As an executive from Saatchi and Saatchi, a leader in the online kids' marketing field, recently proclaimed, "There is nothing else that exists like it for advertisers to build relationships with kids."

Advertisers are already aggressively moving into cyberspace. A new Coalition for Advertising Supported Information and Entertainment (CASIE),

Federal regulations limit TV advertising to children, but no such rules exist in cyberspace.

led jointly by the American Association of Advertising Agencies and the Association of National Advertisers, is spearheading lobbying efforts to ensure that advertising becomes the dominant mode for funding online content and to ward off government restrictions. The coalition claims that advertiser support for online services is the only way to make information services affordable to all.

But the consequences of making advertising the key to universal access for children are troubling. Advertisers are not just supporting online content; they are shaping much of the virtual landscape for children. At Saatchi and Saatchi, psychologists and cultural anthropologists have perfected a variety of techniques—including play groups, art, and games—to probe children's feelings and behavior when they go online. They are also studying the nature of "kids' culture" as a separate set of experiences and values from that of adults. Knowing that children often use computers alone, marketers are carefully cultivating this separateness in the design of online services that circumvent parental authority. One online children's service recently published results from a survey that asked children whom they trusted more—their parents or their computers. The majority of respondents said they put more trust in their computers.

According to advertising researchers, going online quickly puts children into a "flow state," that "highly pleasurable experience of total absorption in a challenging activity." This is an optimal condition for advertisers to reach children. Traditional commercials will not work online. "Anything that is perceived as an interruption of the flow state," explained a Saatchi and Saatchi executive, "whether it's artwork being downloaded or an ad that is obtrusively splattered on a screen, is going to get a negative reaction." So the solution is the seamless integration of content and advertising in "branded environments." The goal of these environments is to "get kids involved with brands"—including "brand characters, brand logos, brand jingles, and brand video."

Major children's advertisers have Web sites where children are encouraged to come and play for extended periods of time with such product "spokescharacters" as Ronald McDonald, Kellogg's Snap, Crackle, and Pop, and Chester Cheetah. The aim is to encourage children to develop ongoing relationships with the characters—and the products. Within days of visiting the Kellogg's Web site recently, for example, one child received unsolicited e-mail from Snap, Crackle, and Pop, urging her to return for more fun.

The new interactive media are being designed to compile personal profiles on each child to help in developing individually tailored advertising known as "microtargeting" or "one-to-one marketing." The sites get children to volunteer such personal data as e-mail address, street address, the identity of other family members, and purchasing behavior and preferences. Sophisticated computer software can track every move a child makes online and give marketers "clickstream data" or, in the vernacular of the business, "mouse droppings."

Federal regulations limit TV advertising to children, but no such rules exist in cyberspace. Marketers can pursue children with few restraints. Nothing prevents them from collecting personal information from children and selling it to third parties. The lines among advertising, entertainment, and information—already dangerously blurred in television and other media—are likely to disappear entirely in the new online environment. "What is really happening [on the Web]," explains one industry expert, "is what will ultimately happen on interactive television: the infomercialization of all programming." Adds another: "The blending of entertainment with advertising will work if packaged correctly: just look at how the toy industry has taken over production of Saturday morning cartoons."

Even traditionally noncommercial services are likely to be shaped by the norms of this new unregulated media environment. While PBS is prohibited from most forms of advertising on television, there are no restrictions on its use of advertising online. Children's Television Workshop, producer of such highly acclaimed noncommercial programs as *Sesame Street* and *Ghostwriter*, has recently begun developing advertiser-supported cable and online services for children.

An Agenda for Reform

Although the 1996 Telecommunications Act established a broad framework for federal policy, there are still opportunities to influence the shape of the new electronic media. Three key goals should guide public and private voluntary efforts.

Ensuring Universal Access

Every child, regardless of income, should have access to the advanced communications technologies and services necessary for their education and full participation in society. Providing access to telecommunications can in no way be a technological quick fix for more complex social and political problems. But those problems will only intensify unless we adopt policies—and invest significant resources—to ensure access for all segments of society.

Political participation needs to be expanded beyond those groups that have traditionally been involved in telecommunications policy. Child advocacy, parent, health, and other constituencies need to understand what may seem to be a highly technical subject. Targeted strategic interventions at the state level could have a positive influence on local communications services. In such states as Ohio, coalitions of education, consumer, and low-income advocates have succeeded in obtaining substantial resources for community computing centers, educational technology, and training. Public interest groups need to monitor the plans of telecommunications companies to prevent "electronic redlining"—omitting low-income neighborhood from new initiatives. Public hearings can help raise the level of the debate and create a forum for articulating a public vision for how the new telecommunications can serve children. Such organizing efforts could lay the groundwork for a national movement on behalf of children's interests in the national information infrastructure.

Developing Safeguards

Preventing the commercialization of online media for children may be impossible, but there is an important opportunity to influence the design of new interactive services. A report issued in late March by the Center for Media Education, the organization of which I am president, documented the emerging patterns of online advertising and marketing to children. In response, a few companies have stopped some of the most egregious practices, and industry trade associations have promised to adopt guidelines to regulate their own conduct. As past experience has shown, however, self-regulation is likely to have little impact unless there is effective government oversight and enforcement. New screening software programs, such as Net Nanny, Cyber Patrol, and SafeSurf, may enable parents to screen out certain content areas or restrict the information that children can give out, but these tools are unlikely to be sufficient. Because children are a particularly vulnerable audience, effective legal safeguards will be necessary to prevent manipulation by advertisers and to protect children and their families from invasions of privacy.

The Center for Media Education and Consumer Federation of America have jointly urged the Federal Trade Commission to develop guidelines for advertising to children in cyberspace. These rules would restrict the collection of personally identifiable information from children and require disclosures of data collection practices on all Web sites and online content areas directed at children. In addition, we are calling on the FTC to require clear separation between content and advertising in online services targeted at children. These rules should also apply to the interactive television services under development. Although the U.S. district court decision on June 12 restricts government regulation of indecent content on the Internet,

it does not prohibit either regulation of commercial speech or government safeguards to protect online privacy.

The global nature of the Internet also calls for international efforts to develop standards for new media programs and services targeted at children. Since many countries already have stricter policies for protecting children than we do, international guidelines could raise the standards for children's interactive media in the United States.

Creating a Noncommercial Children's Civic Sector

The emerging media environment should serve children not only as consumers, but also as citizens. While a number of exciting services for children are available on the Internet, they may disappear or be overshadowed by an all-pervasive commercial culture that will capture and dominate children's attention. If, as current trends suggest, the dominant method of financing the new media is likely to be advertising, we need to assure the availability of noncommercial educational and informational services for children. Just as we have public spaces, playgrounds, and parks in our natural environment, so we should have public spaces in the electronic environment, where children will be able to play and learn without being subject to advertising, manipulation, or exploitation.

New models for producing and distributing noncommercial services need to be explored. For example, an alliance of nonprofits, artists, film makers, and educators might create a new

children's service that combined the traditions of public television with the innovative potential of the Internet. Public and private funds might help launch a children's version of C-SPAN— "Kidspan." A consortium of government and private program suppliers from various countries might create an international children's programming service.

To ensure long-term survival, noncommercial programs and services need a dependable source of funds. One untapped revenue source could be the sale of broadcast spectrum, valued at as much as $70 billion. Other possibilities include the creation of a trust fund exclusively for children's services, using a combination of public and private money.

There is also a need for more civic-minded research to think through these issues. The telecommunications industries have enormous resources for sophisticated economic analysis, but the public interest community has been ill-equipped to compete. New models for financing universal access and achieving other reform objectives need to be explored.

This is the ideal time for efforts to insure this new media system serves the needs of children. Once the new media institutions are firmly entrenched, it will be almost impossible to change them. The system is still fluid enough for those who care about the character of our culture and our children to create a rich electronic legacy for future generations.

 Article Review Form at end of book.

Why has the amount of child pornography exploded on the Internet?
Is this phenomenon harmful to children?

Child Molesters on the Internet:

Are they in your home?

Bob Trebilock

Bob Trebilock writes frequently for Redbook *on news and social issues.*

Like many parents of young children, I'd read the headlines about pedophiles trying to seduce kids and swapping pornography on the Internet. This sort of deviant behavior, I assumed, must lurk in deep, all-but-impenetrable recesses of cyberspace. But when I got this assignment to report on the 'Net's red-light district, I decided to see what an on-line novice like myself could find.

Armed with a hint or two from a computer consultant, I turned on the standard-issue computer in my family room and clicked on Usenet, a section of the World Wide Web where anyone can post or access messages and photographs related to a specific topic, and typed in the words "alt.sex.incest." In less than a minute, I was scrolling through hundreds of brief text messages from guys who offered to swap photographs or described their sexual fantasies with children. One message was repeated four times: "Subject: Re: z9x7 I lookin' 4 cindys series. . . ." I clicked my mouse.

The text came up quickly, a request for a series of photos. "I only have cindy 1, 2, 8, 15, 17 . . . if someone can repost 'em all . . . thanx."

Underneath was a reply from another user: "Here's 3, 4, and 5. Enjoy! Rick." Below the text, a color image appeared on my screen, slowly unrolling from top to bottom like a window blind. As the first image formed, I took a sharp, deep breath. At the top of the photo, a pair of chubby, dimpled knees was spread apart. Naked from the waist down, Cindy was lying on her back, legs apart. It was a typical centerfold pose, but Cindy was no typical centerfold model. She was not much older than 6.

Eleven more shots formed on my screen, the same little girl performing oral sex on an adult male. As I exited the file, my hands were shaking and my stomach was churning.

I looked at my watch. In less than 15 minutes, without any special software or expert knowledge, I'd found a deviant world without sexual boundaries, one that could be located by curious teenagers and potential child molesters alike. Though I called the police to report what I'd seen, I still didn't sleep well that night. Who was Cindy? Who was forc-ing her to do those things? And, given the rash of recent headlines about computer-related sex crimes, is any child safe from sexual exploitation in the age of the mouse and the modem?

Make no mistake about it: The Internet is a powerful tool that levels the information playing field. On-line in your home, you can view the Louvre's art collection, chat with David Bowie on his fiftieth birthday, and access research from top academic institutions across the country. No wonder the 'Net is growing so explosively. In just three years, America Online, the largest commercial service provider, has expanded from 1 million to 8 million households, and, globally, 30 million people are estimated to be logging on-line.

Granted, the vast majority of what's on the Internet is entertaining, informative, if not educational. But the 'Net does have a dark side. "I call the Internet the playground of the nineties for pedophiles," says Donna Rice Hughes, director of marketing and communications for Enough Is Enough, a Fairfax, Virginia, nonprofit group that campaigns to make the Internet safe for children.

Hughes may have a point. In addition to housing pictures of dozens of children, like the ones of Cindy, the Internet has spawned sites featuring snapshots of children—unwittingly photographed while at play in parks and at the beach—who serve as pedophiles' love objects; kids-only chat rooms where child molesters prowl; and electronic support groups in which "boy-lovers" validate each other's most disturbed impulses.

Could these pedophiles be reaching right into your home via the family PC? What are authorities doing to regulate this booming and, at times, unsettling new forum? And what can you, as a parent, do to protect your children?

Can We Talk? The Danger of Chat Rooms

"How old are u?"

The words appeared simultaneously on screens in New Hampshire and California.

"I am 14," the user in California replied.

"love to do u then," the man in New Hampshire typed.

"I would like that," the boy replied.

The man's name was Alan Hicks. A 46-year-old mechanical engineer and one-time Big Brother, Hicks was also a convicted pedophile who had served time for molesting young boys. After his release on parole, Hicks joined a treatment group and agreed to make a training film about his life for the benefit of law enforcement officials.

He also discovered the Internet. During one year on-line,

he befriended numerous boys in chat rooms. When the boys were willing, Hicks took the conversations private, where he talked graphically about sex and E-mailed pornographic photos. In return, he asked for favors—a pair of underwear, even samples of boys' urine and semen.

Hicks would probably still be on-line today if he hadn't sent a nude photo of himself to a police informant who turned it over to James McLaughlin, a Keene, New Hampshire, police detective currently working with federal authorities on a nationwide probe of child exploitation on the Internet. By coincidence, Detective McLaughlin recognized Hicks from that training film he made, and helped return him to jail last November.

The Hicks case illustrates the most palpable danger to children on-line: child molesters lurking in chat rooms devoted to innocent subjects like sports and music. "Ultimately," McLaughlin says, "pedophiles will try to get the kids to agree to phone or mail contact, and then arrange for a meeting." The scary truth is, some succeed. Last November, Cary Bodenheimer, a 30-year-old engineer for a major aircraft manufacturer in the Philadelphia area, pled guilty to having had sex in an Illinois motel room with a 13-year old girl he had met over the Internet. A year earlier, James Heigh, 29, of Keizer, Oregon, was convicted of third-degree rape after he met a 14-year-old girl on-line, engaged her in lengthy phone calls, and then had sex with her.

Granted, the number of cases is relatively small, and only 23 incidents involving chat rooms were reported between 1994 and 1996, according to the National Center for Missing and Exploited

Children. But, warns J. Robert Flores, senior trial attorney with the Department of Justice Child Exploitation and Obscenity Section, "This is a new crime that's just three or four years old. Not all law enforcement agencies are reporting their numbers."

Insidiously, these overtures by pedophiles are often made while mom and dad are in the next room, pleased that their child is learning to use the computer rather than watching mindless TV. Teens, for their part, are often bolder on-line than they would be in the real world. "Sex is on the minds of a lot of 12- and 13-year-olds," says Gary Hewitt, a psychotherapist in Rochester, New York, who has worked with children who were abducted and exploited by strangers. "They'll go on-line and open up. A pedophile will then tell that child whatever he or she wants to hear to bond with them."

To safeguard children from these anonymous predators, America Online has added guards to monitor the kids-only chat rooms for suspicious dialogue. A good first step, but private messages—invisible to the rest of the chat room—cannot be screened, and that's where a pedophile is likely to begin forging a relationship with a child.

Experts agree that the best way to keep your child safe in cyberspace is the same as keeping your child safe in the real world: parental involvement. Says Sergeant Nick Battaglia, former supervisor of the child exploitation unit of the San Jose Police Department, and an expert on computer-related sex crimes, "Just like you wouldn't let your child play alone in an urban park for three hours, you shouldn't let them play alone on the Internet."

Battaglia urges parents to keep the computer in a central location, limit how much time your child spends on-line, and educate yourself about the technology so you can monitor what your child is doing. Most critically, go on-line with your child as often as possible to help her identify inappropriate requests, and emphasize that people encountered in chat rooms are strangers, just like the ones you've warned them about in the real world. Finally, insist that your child never give out personal information—home address, phone number, school name—on-line without first asking your permission, and never agree to meet someone in person without a parent being present.

Kiddie Porn's New Life On-line

While on-line chat rooms pose a new threat to our children, authorities also credit the Internet with reviving an old foe: child pornography. The problem is pressing enough that the FBI formed the "Innocent Images" task force, a three-year undercover investigation focusing on the use of on-line computer services to distribute kiddie porn which has led to about 70 felony convictions. But to be candid, FBI spokesperson Larry Foust admits, they have only scratched the surface.

Indeed, it's never been a better time to be a pedophile: The Internet has opened up a new, anonymous way for pedophiles to exchange and expand their collections of porn, says Don Huycke, program manager of the Child Pornography Enforcement Program for the U.S. Customs Service, the long-standing experts in kiddie porn, since so much of it has been produced overseas. "They'll say: I

want two little girls age 6 to 9 having sex. We find guys making 40 to 50 downloads per night of child pornography."

The resurgence of kiddie porn marks an end to one of law enforcement's success stories. In 1982, a Supreme Court decision approved the ban on the distribution of material depicting children engaged in sexual conduct, virtually shutting down the U.S. kiddie porn industry by the end of the decade. By 1993, all that had changed with the mushrooming popularity of the Internet: In the last fiscal year, the number of search warrants issued by Customs involving child pornography increased by 220 percent, with the majority of those cases involving the use of computers. Though most child pornography online has been culled from magazines produced in the seventies and early eighties, some experts hint that the Internet encourages new images to be created. Thanks to new technology, like digital cameras, porn can be produced directly on-line, without leaving the literal paper trail that photos do when developed and published.

Child porn is dangerous, the experts say, not just because kids are molested during the production but because pedophiles use the images to convince children that sex with adults is enjoyable and natural. What's more, mental health professionals worry about the long-term impact of child pornography on the Internet. Says David N. Greenfield, Ph.D., a Hartford, Connecticut, psychologist who has studied the phenomenon of Internet addiction, "I'm concerned about kids being exposed to this material when they are too young to realize it's an unrealistic portrayal of sexual behavior. Seeing child pornography on the 'Net legitimizes it, which is dangerous."

Can anything be done to wipe this sort of material off the Internet? Authorities hope so. Last year, Congress passed the Communications Decency Act, which prohibits the knowing distribution of indecent material to minors by computer. A bill introduced by Senator Orrin G. Hatch, which passed in September 1996, makes it illegal to produce "morphed" child pornography, in which perfectly innocent pictures of children are altered by computer to show them engaged in sex acts, say, by grafting the head of a child onto the body of a nude, slender adult.

Enforcing the law, however, is the real challenge. Given the millions of web sites—and the ability of pedophiles to encrypt photos, or put them in a code that can only be translated with special software—most police departments are ill-equipped to find such pornography. Until the police catch up with the child pornographers, parents can rely on "net nanny" software programs (similar to the V-chip for your television set) to control the sites a child can browse on the web. Some service providers, such as America Online, perform the same function.

Could My Child's Photo Be on the 'Net?

More alarmingly, authorities are finding that even children with absolutely no connection to child pornography are turning up on-line as love objects for pedophiles. Consider the case of George Chamberlain, a 56-year-old pedophile serving a 35-year sentence in Minnesota for child sexual assault. In 1995, authorities seized a prison computer used by Chamberlain as part of a computer programming and telemarketing business run by prison inmates. Connected to the information superhighway, he also swapped child pornography and e-mail messages with other pedophiles on the Internet.

Worse still, investigators discovered a list stored on computer with the names, ages, and addresses of 3,000 children, culled from seemingly harmless listings in local newspapers. Though Chamberlain denied compiling the names, to investigators, they looked like a virtual catalog of potential abuse victims. The list's mere existence raises the question: Could my child be on the Internet without my knowledge?

Though unlikely, the answer is yes. Circulating in Usenet groups are photos of fully clothed cheerleaders, gymnasts, and little girls at play, snapped by pedophiles' cameras and posted in files labeled "erotica"—clearly, someone's fantasy material. On the World Wide Web, some sites created by self-described "boylovers"—men infatuated with young or teenage boys—receive almost a quarter-million visitors in a given four-month period. Visit the "Boys in the Real World" site to see photos of prepubescent boys at play taken at Disneyland, Sea World, and the San Diego Zoo. At ComQuest Boys, a message by the web page's producer describes how he took his photos of boys frolicking on a Santa Monica beach: "I had to get within about 12 feet of my unsuspecting subjects in order to fill the frame, which is a challenge to say the least. If I . . . visit a beach . . . again, I hope to get beautiful boys to volunteer to be photographed and show their smiling faces and newly forming muscles."

Authorities stress that these photos serve solely as fantasy material for pedophiles who are un-

likely to try to find or make contact with the children depicted. Yet, as a cop and a parent, Nick Battaglia admits, "Those sites are very upsetting, because someone's taking your privacy and exploiting your child." Unfortunately, he adds, "there's nothing illegal about it." And there's very little you can do to protect your family, beyond confronting anyone who seems to be taking inappropriate photos of your—or anyone else's—child.

How Child Molesters Network in Cyberspace

Beyond trading fantasy material, pedophiles have even formed online support groups, in which they bolster one another's egos and share tips. "Boylovers with integrity and courage can use the resources of the Internet . . . to break through the boundaries that others would impose in this culture," asserts the NAMBLA Bulletin, the voice of the North American Man/Boy Love Association. In the past, pedophiles were fundamentally an isolated group. Thanks to the Internet, that's changing—and fast—as pedophile support groups spring up on-line. One site, alt.support.boylovers, provides answers to frequently asked questions like "What do boylovers feel?" and recommends literary works with a boy-lover theme, such as Thomas Mann's *Death in Venice*. The site's mission: to provide acceptance "for boy-lovers who do not consider themselves in need of conversion to an orientation other than their natural one."

The quest for acceptance is precisely what concerns law enforcement officers and mental health professionals. Chris Hatcher, Ph.D., a clinical professor of psychology at the

University of California in San Francisco who studies pedophiles and child abductors, has coined the phrase "virtual validation" to describe the burgeoning network of pedophiles on-line. "They're able to be in contact with sometimes hundreds of other people with similar beliefs," explains Dr. Hatcher. "That is a level of validation they were never able to obtain before."

Coupled with the availability of child pornography on the 'Net, Dr. Hatcher argues that the virtual validation pedophiles find on-line may encourage someone who has not yet molested a child to do so. "Pedophiles who make contact with children have a developmental pattern," says Dr. Hatcher. It begins with fantasy, moves to gratification through pornography, then voyeurism, and finally to contact. "The 'Net accelerates that pattern. It gives them a level of virtual validation that would have otherwise taken years to obtain." Adds Gary Hewitt, "The support group sites give pedophiles a real sense of power, and the impetus to go out and molest someone." Protected by First Amendment rights, these cyberspace support-group sites are difficult to restrict.

What's Next?

Last April, a 10-year-old girl was invited to a slumber party at the home of another little girl in Greenfield, California. What her parents didn't know: The friend's father, Ronald Riva, was a member of the Orchid Club, an on-line group of men who met in pedophile chat rooms and used the Internet to swap pornography and truelife stories of child molestation.

That night, Riva and another club member, who was visiting,

"Why Pedophiles Go On-Line": One Convict's Story

"Child pornography is pedophile's rock cocaine. It's a quick fix. It's cheap, and thanks to the Internet, it's everywhere."

The speaker's name is "Bob," and he's a computer expert in his forties. He's also a recovering pedophile who has spent 20 years on the wrong side of the law. Talking to me by phone from a southern state he will not identify, Bob says he's watched the explosive growth of pedophiles on the Internet from both sides of the fence.

Why is the Internet so enticing for pedophiles? "It's created easily accessible stimulation for child molesters," says Bob. "You can download pictures in complete anonymity. You do not have to make any kind of human contact."

Anonymity is so crucial, says Bob, because your average pedophile "is not the dirty old man in a trench coat, but a teacher at your local elementary school. The Internet becomes his outlet."

Bob acknowledges that chat rooms pose the greatest physical danger to your child on-line. However, he notes, "On the computer, the search for a victim is an arduous task that's fraught with danger due to the intensity of law enforcement."

"Besides," he adds, "victims are too easy to find in other places." Successful pedophiles, he explains, "are better with your children than you are. They give them more attention. They are your swim coach, your Sunday school teacher—people you trust to come into contact with your child every single day."

Which children, I ask, were safe from these predators? Kids who got a lot of love, attention, and time from their parents, Bob said, were least likely to be curious about what another adult might offer.

---

awoke the girl, then fondled her in front of a digital camera attached to a computer. The images of her molestation were broadcast to other members of the group, who watched the live event on their computers and responded interactively, typing in what they'd like to see happen next.

This shocking crime led to an investigation by U.S. Customs and other agencies, ending in the indictments of 16 members of the Orchid Club. The first known example of pedophiles using the Internet for real-life abuse of a child, the Orchid Club might be a barometer of where we are headed on the Internet.

Most experts agree that the Internet phenomenon is still too new to predict the future danger to children. As more people become familiar with the 'Net, and the potential dangers of this otherwise positive medium, kids may be safer than ever. Or the threat could snowball. Technology like digital cameras and video conferencing that download images directly into the computer may create more home-grown child pornography, as in the Orchid Club case.

Despite the high-tech wizardry employed by the Orchid Club members, the case serves as a cautionary reminder about how pedophiles always have—and probably always will—operate. The 10-year-old victim met her molesters in the neighborhood. Observes Burt G. Hollenbeck Jr., Ph.D., a New Hampshire psychologist who has treated around 400 pedophiles, "The focus on computers as a threat to our children obscures the fact that the real danger is in our backyards. As a society, we'd rather think the molester is some faceless guy at a computer terminal. But every guy at a PC has another identity. He's also grandpa, the teacher, or our next-door neighbor."

 **Article Review Form at end of book.**

WiseGuide Wrap-Up

Technology is changing the way we live and work in ways we have yet to fully understand or measure. To further explore the ideas presented in this section, you may want to interview an employee at your school or a local company to learn more about how computers and technology have changed his or her job during the past ten years. Or you could interview your parents or grandparents to learn more about how the introduction of new technologies in your home has impacted your family's lifestyle during the past years.

R.E.A.L. Sites

This list provides a print preview of typical **Coursewise** R.E.A.L. sites. There are over 100 such sites at the **Courselinks**™ site. The danger in printing URLs is that web sites can change overnight. As we went to press, these sites were functional using the URLs provided. If you come across one that isn't, please let us know via email to: webmaster@coursewise.com. Use your Passport to access the most current list of R.E.A.L. sites at the **Courselinks**™ site.

Site name: MIT Media Lab

URL: http://www.media.mit.edu/

Why is it R.E.A.L.? This is an excellent site for exploring the frontier of research and development in computer-mediated communication, educational technologies, and technologies for the home. Research groups include "Toys of Tomorrow," "Digital Life," "News of the Future," and "Things That Think."

Key topics: home and family, education, future trends

Try this: Explore one of the Research or Special Interest Groups at the Media Lab to learn more about a current project.

Site name: Enough Is Enough

URL: http://www.enough.org/

Why is it R.E.A.L.? This site provides tips and information on protecting children as they surf the Internet.

Key topics: home and family

Try this: Evaluate the tips on protecting children. Are they likely to be effective? Why or why not?

Site name: MaMaMedia

URL: http://www.mamamedia.com/

Why is it R.E.A.L.? This is a commercial site for children that is dedicated to nurturing a love of learning. The site includes more than 100 activities for the "Digital Sandbox" and links to more than 2,000 children's web sites. Seymour Papert, MIT researcher on computers and education, serves on the advisory board.

Key topics: home and family, education

Try this: Explore one of the children's activities in the "Digital Sandbox." What messages, in McLuhan's sense, does the activity convey?

---

section

3

Learning Objectives

- Describe the constructivist approach to learning and how it differs from the traditional instructionist approach.

- Summarize the argument as to why programs in art, music, and physical education may be more important for children's development than instruction in computers.

- According to Neill, how do computers in the classroom reinforce societal inequalities?

- Describe several criteria that may be necessary to effectively integrate computers into the classroom.

- Summarize the advantages and disadvantages of integrating computers into the classroom.

Computers, Schools, and Learning

 **WiseGuide Intro**

Is your local high school connected to the Internet? Are computers readily available to students at your college? How are these tools used to enhance classroom instruction?

According to a 1996 Educational Testing Service study, 64 percent of U.S. schools had access to the Internet somewhere in the building, but only 14 percent of classrooms had Net access. While most schools surveyed had computers in the building, student–computer ratios varied greatly. School districts attended by poor and minority students had fewer computers than did other schools and were the least likely to be connected to the Internet.

In his 1996 re-election campaign, President Clinton pledged that all classrooms would be connected to the Internet by the year 2000. To that end, the federal government is providing millions of dollars to support the cost of buying computers and software, wiring classrooms for Internet access, and training teachers how to use this technology. While it remains unlikely that all classrooms will be connected to the Internet in the year 2000, Clinton's funding initiative will go a long way in assisting schools to become technology-rich. But absent from this initiative are some fundamental questions.

Do we need Internet access in every classroom? Is the computer always an effective means of enhancing instruction? Do computers promote or inhibit the development of basic skills? Will they enhance schools and learning, or will computers be used mostly as expensive flash cards for traditional drill-and-practice exercises? Who supports the cost of maintaining and upgrading computers once grant monies have been spent?

These are some of the questions we will examine in this section—questions that promoters of technology in education would be wise to ask more frequently. Technocratism seems to flourish more in education than in any other field, with politicians and administrators quick to jump on technology as a magic bullet solution to the problems that challenge our educational system today.

In the first article in this section, "N-Gen Learning," writer Don Tapscott presents his vision of the classroom as a place where computers promote "constructivist" learning, which builds on children's natural curiosity. Teachers, he suggests, will become more like coaches or facilitators, helping students use the information tools of the World Wide Web to carry out projects that develop higher-order thinking skills such as problem solving and critical thinking—skills on which society will place a premium in the twenty-first century.

Tapscott's classroom is an appealing place. But is it an illusion, or even a delusion? In "The Computer Delusion," *Atlantic Monthly* writer Todd Oppenheimer asserts that teachers are seldom prepared to design the type of classroom Tapscott envisions. More common, he suggests, is the use of the computer as a sort of glorified baby-sitter. Furthermore, he says, many schools may be sacrificing parts of the curriculum that are vital to children's psychosocial development in order to pay for expensive computer technology.

Monty Neill also paints a bleak picture of the computer classroom in his 1995 essay, "Computers, Thinking and Schools in the 'New World Economic Order.'" Neill suggests that, despite claims about the rise of the "knowledge worker," the controlling class of society wants no more problem solvers and critical thinkers today than it did in the assembly-line era. This neo-Marxist perspective on education argues that, instead of promoting critical thinking, computers in schools will be used to train students to sit in front of terminals and complete routine tasks.

Despite these critiques, examples abound of schools where creative teachers are using computers to motivate students and enhance the school curriculum. In their article "Where Computers Do Work," Betsy Wagner, Stephen Gregory, and associates describe six classrooms where teachers have successfully integrated computers into the curriculum.

The companion web sites at the end of this section offer a starting point for further research on technology and education. At the E.T.S. site, you can review the report that was cited in this introduction: "Computers and Classrooms: The Status of Technology in U.S. Schools." To find out more about specific applications of technology in education, check out *T.H.E. Journal: Technical Horizons in Education.* Another site, Planet Papert, is devoted to the work of Dr. Seymour Papert, a renowned educational researcher whose influence is apparent in the article by Don Tapscott. To learn more about constructivist learning and computers, review some of the articles, interviews, and other information at this site.

That computers will continue to be integrated into all levels of education, including college education, is a given. But that they will be integrated appropriately and to good purpose is far from certain. This section, I hope, will help you evaluate the use of technology in your classes, and in classrooms you may encounter as a parent, an employee, or a community member.

? Questions ?

Reading 11. Do you believe that computers transform classrooms? What are "higher-order" thinking skills, and how might computers enhance their development?

Reading 12. How much money can we afford to spend on technology-rich classrooms? Is instruction necessarily improved by the use of computers?

Reading 13. What is the "New World Economic Order" envisioned by Neill? How do computers in the schools contribute to its development?

Reading 14. Would you want to attend or teach in one of these schools? Are we likely to see more of them in the future?

Do you believe that computers transform classrooms? What are "higher-order" thinking skills, and how might computers enhance their development?

N-Gen Learning

Don Tapscott

Like millions of girls her age, 11-year-old Esra Korukcu of Avanos, Turkey, loves to skip rope and ride a bicycle. During the winter her understanding parents allow Esra and her sisters to roller skate in the living room, "but we have to take care not to break anything."

Esra's life is absolutely unremarkable, yet kids in thousands of American classrooms have read on the World Wide Web a detailed account of how Esra spends her day. They know her hobbies, what her school is like, what her parents do for a living, and that she has a scar on her knee from falling off her bike. This information is available on the Web because Esra has volunteered her story to GlobaLearn, an inspired company of young adults who travel the world and chronicle their journey through the eyes of children.

In 1997, the company organized a five-month trek across, Asia, following the same route as Marco Polo, and later in the year another expedition traveled through Brazil. In each community, the expedition spent a day with a young boy or girl, such as Esra, who are called *hosts*. A profile of the host is prepared, sharing the youngster's thoughts on subjects such as family, school, hobbies, local community, and life in general.

"On school days," Esra tells us, "my morning begins at 7:30 A.M. when I get up. I wash my face, get dressed, and then join my family for breakfast. I love milk and always have it for breakfast, along with bread, *pikmas* (Turkish jam), *sucuk* (soo-jook—a Turkish sausage), and cheese. If I am lucky, my mom lets me have chocolate spread on my bread."

The youngsters that GlobaLearn meets with are asked whether they have any special wishes for the thousands of kids who will be reading their stories. Fifteen-year-old Ufuk Sahin from Istanbul, Turkey, replied: "If I had to give a message to kids all over the world, I would have to say 'make peace and stay cool.' I do not like to give advice though, probably because I do not like being given advice."

GlobaLearn is one of the earliest and most elegant examples of how the Internet can bring the world into the classrooms of the nation. The company was founded by Murat Armbruster in 1993 with a mission "to prepare children for global citizenship and develop in them the skills, awareness, and determination to become responsible stewards of the earth."

To tell their story to the world, GlobaLearn's expedition team travels with state-of-the-art electronic equipment, including portable computers, digital photo and video recorders, high-speed modems, and a mobile satellite transmitter. The data is sent via satellite to GlobaLearn's New Haven, Connecticut headquarters, where it is edited and formatted for presentation on GlobaLearn's Web site—a process that takes about an hour each day. GlobaLearn also provides curriculum materials, including lesson plans and reproducible worksheets, on its Web site.

At noon each day the team takes a photo of what it is doing and puts this on the Net. Each of the five team members also submits a daily journal, often investigating some aspect of the local culture or economy, such as a visit to a cheese or pottery factory. The idea is to stimulate kids in the classrooms to conduct similar research into their own communities—making them active participants rather than just passive observers. Students use the field teams as extensions of themselves to investigate the historical, cultural, and physical features of the earth's environment. This supplements the data from the students' explorations of their own communities. Students are then able to make "dynamic comparisons between their experiences and the experiences of others in different countries."

Kids in the classrooms are encouraged to submit questions to GlobaLearn's New Haven headquarters and each week 10 questions are randomly picked and relayed to the expedition. Questions range from "do you get carsick?" to "how do the clothes in Turkey differ from the United States?"

There is also an area on GlobaLearn's Web site where kids and teachers from different classrooms can discuss issues among themselves or comment on the expedition. The feedback is very positive. One Oakland, California teacher concluded: "My students are most interested in the host profiles, but some of the investigations have also held their interest. They like hearing about different foods, too. Someone else said there is so much stuff, it's overwhelming, which is almost so, but it's good to be able to choose from the wealth. Thanks."

GlobaLearn promises that future expeditions will continue to focus on children while maintaining a commitment to its initial concept: "That learning must be engaging and exciting; that the world is the greatest resource for learning; and that technology has given education an invaluable medium by which to access the world and participate in it."

Learning in a Knowledge-Based Economy

The Net Generation children using GlobaLearn are beginning to process information and learn differently than the boomers before them. New media tools offer great promise for a new model of learning—one based on discovery and participation. This combination of a new generation and new digital tools will cause a rethinking of the nature of education—in both content and delivery. As the N-Gen enters the work force, it will also place profound demands on its employers to create new environments for lifelong learning.

Growing up is about learning. However, the economy and society these kids are growing into is very different than that of the boomers. The destination is different and so is the route the kids must take.

An economy is a system for the creation and distribution of wealth. As I explained in *The Digital Economy*, the new economy is based on human capital and networks. In this economy, knowledge permeates through everything important: people, products, organizations.

In the new economy, wealth is increasingly created by knowledge work—brain rather than brawn. There have always been people who have worked with their minds rather than their hands. In the new economy, they are the majority of the work force. Already, almost 60 percent of American workers are knowledge workers and 8 of 10 new jobs are in information-intensive sectors of the economy. In the past 25 years, the number of Americans with college degrees has tripled from 12 to 37 million. The per-

centage of adults who are college graduates has doubled from 11 to 22 percent.[1] The factory of today is as different from the industrial factory of the old economy as the latter was from the craft shop of the earlier agrarian economy. A typical AlliedSignal plant is full of robots and brimming with microprocessors, and many of the plant workers have engineering degrees. Some Nortel plants have a work force averaging a community college degree. The N-Gen is destined for a world of knowledge work.

Increasingly, key assets are human. Consider Netscape as a new-economy company. When evaluating the assets of a new-economy company like Netscape, you don't ask old-economy questions like "How much land does the company own?" or "What is the value of Netscape's manufacturing facilities—its plants?" Rather, the only meaningful assets are contained in the minds of the managers and employees of the company.

The dominant form of capital in the emerging economy can currently be examined in the computer room of your local school's library. More than any other generation, these children need—and want—to construct solutions to the growing problems that threaten this small and increasingly fragile planet. If this is true, there is no more critical challenge facing business and government than to understand how that capital can be nourished—for the betterment of the individual and for all.

More important, the N-Generation will not only become the means of production, it will become the dominant social force, shaping not only economic activity but our social structures, the environment, and human existence. What kind of education will equip the N-Generation for this task? How will it acquire the values, the critical thinking, the collaborative skills, the mastery of communication required to protect and advance society?

If we intend to answer these questions through our educational systems, we have to look at the kinds of students who are in our schools or will be entering them soon. One example of an N-Gen preschooler is four-year-old Ryan McNealy, whose parents decided to get him a computer because they felt that he was watching too much television. They bought Ryan several children's educational programs, which he installed on his Mac and taught himself how to use. He particularly liked *Reader Rabbit*, which reads stories while the text is on the screen. Says his father Brian, "It was like a video game to him, but we soon learned that he was actually not just playing, he was learning."

After a few months, Ryan asked his father to come to the computer to see something. He pulled up a digital story and proceeded to read it off the screen. His father thought he had simply memorized the story, but Ryan insisted that he was reading. His father handed Ryan a children's book and he read that too. Ryan, still four, now conducts science experiments which he learns from his computer. Recently he was in the fridge getting ice cubes and headed out the door. Dad was puzzled and followed him. Ryan placed the cubes on white and black construction paper in the sunlight. He was investigating the impact of color on heat absorption.

Now, imagine being Ryan's kindergarten teacher.

Broadcast Learning

Historically, the field of education has been oriented toward models of learning which focus on instruction—what we can call *broadcast learning*. The term *teacher* implies approaches to learning where an expert who has information transmits or broadcasts it to students. Those students who are "tuned in" take the information they are "taught"—i.e., which is transmitted to them—into active working memory. The field of educational psychology is rich with research, theories, and lessons regarding what impedes such information from being received and stored for subsequent replay. It has long been thought that through repetition, rehearsal, and practice, facts and information can be stored in longer-term memory, which can be integrated to form larger knowledge structures. The product of this is certain outcomes and behaviors—which, in turn, can be measured during testing.

The lecture, textbook, homework assignment, and school are all analogies for the broadcast media—one-way, centralized, and with an emphasis on predefined structures that will work best for the mass audience.

This approach has been the foundation of authoritarian, top-down, teacher-centered approaches to education which go back centuries. At the extreme, reinforcement and punishment were said to enhance learning. I remember my father describing how he was hit with a ruler for giving the wrong answer to a question. More recently, a school of psychology called behaviorism, popular in the 1960s and 1970s (and still in vogue in some circles), emphasized the importance of reinforcement in learn-

ing. Positive reinforcement is said to result in certain outcomes. Similarly, negative reinforcement, or the lack of positive reinforcement, leads to the extinguishing of certain behaviors. So when a rat exhibits desired behaviors in a cage (called a Skinner box, after the founder of behaviorism B. F. Skinner), the animal is reinforced through receiving a food pellet. The rat has been taught the relationship between doing something and being reinforced. Behaviorism extrapolated from the experience with rats to humans and was an important influence in education for many years.

Today, teaching methods and even many computer-based instruction programs are largely based on this broadcast view of learning. The teacher is primarily a transmitter. Curricula are designed by experts who presumably know the best sequencing of material and how children can best learn math, acquire a new language, or understand Mesopotamia. Programs are not customized to each student, but rather designed to meet the needs of a grade—one-size-fits-all, like a broadcast.

Of course, many teachers have worked hard to be more than just transmitters of information, measurers of retention, and judges of performance. Dating back to Sidney Poitier in *To Sir With Love*, Hollywood and the television networks have made a mini-industry of great teachers. Most of us can recall at least one teacher who inspired us to be our best; who jolted us into thinking differently; who enabled us to process and integrate information from different fields; who helped us acquire knowledge and values. I remember listening to my high-school music teacher take us through a vivid and passionate tale of Tchaikovsky's life. As a class, we imagined the anguish Tchaikovsky must have felt as we listened, enchanted, to the Symphony *Pathetique*. Not one of us stirred. We were enthralled and inspired to work hard on developing our musical abilities.

But, notwithstanding the noble and sometimes heroic efforts of teachers, working with large class sizes and limited resources, the delivery system of education is still very much designed around the broadcast model. This is especially true today, in a time of cutbacks in educational spending in many countries. When you have a class with 38 students and no technological tools for a different approach, broadcast not only makes sense, it is the only option.

The Crisis in Education

It has become cliché to say that the educational system in the United States and other developed countries is in crisis. True enough, some schools look more like war zones. Test results are not encouraging. Parents are not happy. There are cutbacks in funding in many advanced countries. And, overall, there is a feeling that, given all the improvements in technology and epistemology, we could be doing much better.

Further, the echo wave is crashing into a school system which is designed for fewer kids. (See Fig. 7.1.)* United States school enrollments will continue to increase at least until the year 2006, with 54.6 million school-age children. The previous peak was set by the boomers in 1971, with 51.3 million attending American schools. And, unlike the previous boom in student population, this

*Note: This figure is not included in this publication.

one is a "long, slow, rising wave and we see no immediate falloff," according to a U.S. Department of Education study entitled, *A Back to School Special Report: The Baby Boom Echo.* Between 1996 and 2006, public high school enrollment is expected to increase by 15 percent, the number of high school graduates will increase by 17 percent and college enrollment is projected to rise by 14 percent. The ethnic composition of the schools will continue to change as well, with Latino-Americans and Asian-Americans the fastest growing segments of the student population.[2]

The implications of student growth are jarring. Assuming the current broadcast teaching model (as the Department of Education report does), 190,000 new teachers will be required. Add to this the 175,000 teachers who retire or change professions each year and need to be replaced. The report calculates that 6000 new schools will be needed, not including the replacement of older, badly out-of-date schools and facilities. There will be approximately $15 billion in additional annual operating expenditures. A myriad of concerned parents and well-intentioned educators are working to address the problem. There is growing appreciation that the old approach is ill-suited to the intellectual, social, motivational, and emotional needs of the new generation.

Six Truisms and Corresponding False Conclusions

In our research we have been impressed and sometimes amazed by how the digital media enable a new view of education and, more broadly, learning. Yet we also heard every conceivable argu-

ment against using the digital media to transform the model of learning. Many of these arguments start off with a true statement and then draw a conclusion which is unwarranted.

Truism 1: *"The problems with the school system go far beyond the schools."* True enough. By the time kids get to the schools, many have already been significantly damaged. The most critical period of brain development is the first three years of life. Because of the breakdown of the traditional family, many children are lacking good parental attention during this formative period. The number of single-parent families has grown from 10 percent in 1965 to 28 percent in 1996. Most children come from families where there is no stay-at-home parent. (See Fig. 7.2.)* The percentage of families with both parents working has risen from 37 percent in 1975 to 62 percent in 1996. In most families, both parents must work to get by. This is a big change. Combine this with working single parents and we've got a whopping 64 percent of families where all parents are working. Overall, parents spend 40 percent less time with children than they did at the peak of boom families, and many of these hours are spent watching TV, where opportunities for meaningful interaction are reduced.[3]

When children come to school hungry or from dysfunctional family situations, lacking motivation and seeing no hope to better their lot in life, then the schools will be troubled places. It is true that to really fix the schools we must fix much of what ails us as a society.

*Note: This figure is not included in this publication.

False conclusion: *"We should not take dramatic steps to transform the schools."* Of course the problem of the schools cannot be addressed in isolation, but this is not to say that we shouldn't take steps now to rethink the education system—both what is done at schools and how it is done. There are numerous examples of teachers, administrators, and parents who work together to create a school of the future. In so doing they change the context. A good example is the River Oaks School in Oakville, Ontario, which I described in *The Digital Economy*. Most students have a desktop computer, used for interactive, self-paced learning. The curriculum has been changed significantly, as has the role of the teacher—all for the better according to everyone involved, including parents. The result was improved student learning and high student motivation. The River Oaks project didn't solve the problems of the community, but it has helped change the community by improving community involvement in the welfare of children. It not only changed the children, but the attitudes of parents and local businesses, for the better.

The old saw "everything is connected to everything else" cuts both ways. Schools are a product of economic, social, and values structures. But, conversely, change a school and you change the world.

Truism 2: *"We need to understand the purpose of the schools—the ends of education, not just the means."* The most articulate spokesman of this view is social critic and technology skeptic Neil Postman. "Should we privatize our schools? Should we have national standards of assessment? How should we use computers?

How shall we teach reading? And so on. . . . These questions evade the issue of what the schools are for. It is as if we are a nation of technicians, consumed by our expertise of how something should be done, afraid and incapable of thinking about why."[4]

Postman argues that the schools should serve several purposes: to help students understand that we are all stewards of the Earth, relying on each other and protecting our small planet; to cure the itch for absolute knowledge and certainty; to encourage critical thinking and the ability to disagree and argue; to encourage diversity while understanding that this does not negate standards; and to develop and use language, which is the basis of making us human, and which enables us to transform the world and in doing so to transform ourselves ("when we form a sentence we are creating a world").

False conclusion: *"We should table any discussion of means until we have agreement on the ends."* Let us accept Postman's aspirations for education. While Postman's discussion of the ends of education may be laudable, he misses an important point: the means have become the ends. The broadcast approach to learning (which Postman does not appear to support) is becoming antithetical to the ends he espouses. The schools are not producing the language-rich critics, arguers, collaborators, and stewards he seeks— in part because the broadcast model of learning is an obstacle to such development.

Conversely, in adopting the new interactive model of learning, N-Geners are already assimilating the learning goals Postman espouses. They aren't just discussing such goals—they're

achieving them. They rely on each other for learning. They debate everything online. They are critics. They are tolerant of diversity in their collaborations. And they communicate by forming sentences—they are creating their worlds. Through a new communications medium, N-Geners are already becoming what Postman aspires for them. McLuhan's words are ringing true through the N-Generation: Their medium has become the message. It's not a case of ends before means. The means are beginning to create new learning results. Postman's hostility toward technology is misdirected as he tilts at the windmills of the broadcast media.

What about the critics who say that e-mail and chatting are not improving communication skills because the spelling, punctuation and style are not proper? My observations tell me the critics are wrong. Time spent using these services is time spent reading. Time spent thinking about your response is time spent analyzing. And time spent composing a response is time spent writing. Such intense communications activity can be either very immediate with tight time pressures, such as on a chat line, or reflective, such as on a bulletin board or e-mail. Writing is like a muscle; it requires exercise. These kids are developing a powerful muscle that will serve them well in future work environments.

Says Allison Ellis of Free-Zone, "The more chances that kids have to read and write, the better." In fact, on FreeZone, if sentence structure, grammar, or spelling inhibits the child's ability to communicate effectively, the FreeZone moderator will correct them by saying, "Hey, I didn't understand your point because you didn't complete your sentence." Moreover, language is something which evolves. The N-Generation is using the characters of the ASCII alphanumeric keyboard to add rich nonverbal elements to written communications. Their creativity in doing so seems infinite.

Truism 3: *"The solution to the problem of education is not technology."* It seems that in every discussion I've had recently about United States government's efforts to get computers into the schools, someone will say that computers aren't the answer. "It won't help to just throw computers at the wall, hoping something will stick." "I've seen lots of computers sitting unused in classrooms. I've even seen them sitting for months in their packing boxes." "Isn't technology a solution in search of a problem?" Or, as David Shenk, author of the book *Data Smog*, says, "Let's be very skeptical when people like the President and Vice President say [computers and the Internet] are going to revolutionize education. I think that is absolute hogwash."[5]

Theodore Roszak, who wrote *The Cult of Information: A Neo-Luddite Treatise on High Tech, Artificial Intelligence and the True Art of Thinking*, said in a recent article, "People who recommend more computers for the schools are like doctors who prescribe more medicine. What medicine? How much medicine? For what reason? The same questions apply to computers."[6]

Of course, unloading millions of computers into school warehouses and classrooms will not cure what ails contemporary education, any more than dumping a random selection of books into schools 200 years ago or prescribing random medicine to a patient would. To rephrase an election slogan, "It's the curriculum, stupid."

False conclusion: *"We should abandon or delay efforts to infuse schools with the digital media."* Rather than "People who recommend more computers for the schools are like doctors who prescribe more medicine," it is more true that "People who oppose computers in the schools are like doctors who oppose the use of modern medicine." Unlike medicine, the use of the new media to transform education will not be determined or sanctioned in some educational equivalent of the FDA. Rather, it will grow from the rich experience of students working with teachers, researchers, business people, and educators to forge, through actual experience, a new model of learning.

This is not to say that children should be guinea pigs. There is plenty of experience already to show that the new media can be a stimulus for change.

The digital media are a necessary but insufficient condition for reinvention of education. Computers and the Net are simply preconditions for moving to a new paradigm in learning. However, every project we investigated that introduced the Net and computer technology to students has been a stimulus for more far-reaching change. Such initiatives raise issues for teachers, parents, educators, and students to address. They encourage curiosity and experimentation. They enable the natural leaders for change to come forward and debunk old stereotypes. They pose questions raised by Roszak—but in real life, not academic debate. What is this new technology about? How can we use it? How might this affect the way we teach and the role of the teacher?

Most importantly, such initiatives provide the children them-

selves with the tools they need to learn and to catalyze the rethinking of education. Changes to a century-old system will not come about because of some top-down decree from educators. The schools need to become learning organizations themselves. Teachers, administrators, and students need to learn as organizations together. And I have become convinced that the most revolutionary force for change is the students themselves. Give children the tools they need and they will be the single most important source of guidance on how to make the schools relevant and effective.

Truism 4: *"It's dumb to teach children how to use computers instead of teaching them math, science, reading, and writing."* This statement was made to me by Michael Bloomberg in the previously mentioned debate at a recent conference of business leaders in Switzerland. Or, as Julianne Malveaux writes in a *USA Today* column entitled "Make Basics a Higher Priority than Internet," "Computer literacy is no substitute for basic literacy."[7] We can certainly all agree that kids need to learn the basics, and if we must compare, then this is more important than learning the exec function in Windows 95. Furthermore, numerous studies have shown that teachers who approve of computers in the classroom seek, as a primary goal, to "teach computer literacy."[8]

False conclusion: *"We should abandon or delay efforts to get the digital media into the schools."* Bloomberg and those like him have it wrong on three counts. First, use of technology does not inhibit learning about math, science, reading, and writing. The opposite is true. The research to date shows that when appropriately integrated into a curriculum, the new media improve student performance, not to mention motivation, collaboration, and communication skills. Even when it is not part of the curriculum, use of the new technology helps in learning basic abilities. Chat groups involve reading and writing. Compare this to television.

Second, fluency with the new media is required for productive life in the new economy and effective citizenship in the digital age. It is important that children know not only how to keyboard, search the Net, participate in a virtual community, or use important software applications (all learned effortlessly by children), but that they understand the underlying assumptions behind technology. Children don't need to become geeks, but they do need to know about software and how it works and to feel empowered to change their online world and the rules of the game.

Third, children acquire fluency with the media not just by studying these media but by using them to do other things. Comments like Bloomberg's are ironic in that they paint a picture of a teacher explaining to students how to use computers. The opposite is more likely to be true in many classrooms because of the generation lap. The students teach themselves. While they're at it they can probably teach their teachers as well. This has been the experience to date.

These new-breed teachers know that they are not just teaching children about computers but rather using computers to help children learn. "I teach cyber arts, but I don't teach computer courses. I teach extended media. I teach video production. I teach imaging. I teach photography and a lot of it uses computers. . . . But it is not a computer class," says Kathy Yamashita, cyber arts teacher, Northview Heights Secondary School, North York, Ontario. While Yamashita's comment is insightful, in reality students are also acquiring computer fluency. Says Alliance for Converging Technologies president David Ticoll, commenting on this case, "If she's teaching techniques for image enhancement on a computer, she's teaching a computer skill, just like teaching photography involves camera and lighting skills." Learning about anything in the digital age should enhance fluency with the digital media as a by-product—just like learning in the age of the printing press also enhanced reading and writing skills.

Truism 5: "Learning is social." Most understanding is socially constructed. Through conversation and dialogue, children come to their own understanding of an experience. This is true for adults as well. Learning organization theorist Peter Senge argues forcefully that learning within organizations tends to occur in teams.[9]

False conclusion: "Computers are used individually, therefore they inhibit learning, which is done socially." The computer has shifted from a tool to automate and manage information to something broader—a communications tool. Anyone with experience using the Net, even in its current, relatively primitive form, can grasp this concept. E-mail, chat sessions, bulletin-board-type forums, video conferencing, and shared digital workspaces are all communications tools. This is true for Web sites, which increasingly involve interaction with people. For example, children's personal Web sites are used as a way to share information and opinions with others—interactively.

Furthermore, much Net-based activity in homes and schools involves face-to-face interaction. When children cluster around computers at River Oaks School, you can hear their excitement—literally—by the buzz and laughter in the room. The same was true when my son and I searched the Net for his project on fish. True, to get the photos he needed we had to look at a lot of snapshots taken of fish in personal aquariums around the world, not to mention the products of assorted trout-fishing expeditions. But the experience was a very social one.

Truism 6: "Teachers are skilled, motivated professionals dedicated to the advancement of their students." Both my parents were teachers. They cared deeply about their students. They took it personally when a student failed or could not learn. Society has made a huge investment in teachers—there are currently 3,092,000 teachers in the United States. Increasingly, teachers work under very difficult conditions. It would be wrong to place the blame for the crisis in education at the feet of teachers. Further, there are many examples of teachers who enthusiastically support the new view of learning and the role of the digital media.

False conclusion: "Teachers are not an obstacle." It shouldn't surprise us that many teachers resist change. When a shift like this occurs, leaders of the old are often the last to embrace the new. Old paradigms, if I may use that word, die hard. Teachers have been schooled in the broadcast mode of pedagogy. As evidence, a 1997 survey of 6000 United States teachers, computer coordinators, and school librarians found that 87 percent believe that Internet usage by students in grades 3 to 12 does not help improve classroom performance.[10] This is an amazing number, perhaps explained by the sad reality that most of these teachers have not attempted to use the Internet to change the way learning is imparted.

"Everything they learn from day one reinforces their role as the sage on the stage," says Michael Dore, director of the Hacienda/La Puente Unified School District in Southern California. "So when they get computers in the classroom they use them for drill and kill—practice and testing. By training, teachers reject the discovery model of learning." Education and technology specialist Bob Beatty is involved in a project to get 40,000 students wired in the city of London. Referring to the role of teachers as maintaining discipline and order, he says, "It's strange, but there are never discipline problems when the kids are using their computers. The only problem is peeling them off the screen."

Teachers have legitimate concerns about their role as the learning model changes to interactive from broadcast. The irony here is that if they don't change and transform their classrooms and themselves to the new model, they face even greater threats to their job security. Society will find other ways to deliver learning and bypass them. The huge rise in the number of home schooled students from 20,000 in the late 1970s to more than 600,000 today in the United States alone, is evidence of this.

From Broadcast Learning to Interactive Learning

Unfortunately, as mentioned above, computers in the schools today are used primarily for teaching basic computer skills, for traditional "drill and kill" instruction, for testing, and for record keeping.[11] The N-Gen experience to date with the digital media points to a new paradigm in learning. The new media enable—and the N-Gen needs for learning demand—a shift from broadcast learning to what I call Interactive Learning. . . .

The ultimate interactive learning environment will be the Web and the Net as a whole. It increasingly includes the vast repository of human knowledge, tools to manage this knowledge, access to people, and a growing galaxy of services ranging from sandbox environments for preschoolers to virtual laboratories for medical students studying neural psychiatry. Today's baby will learn about Michelangelo tomorrow by walking through the Sistine Chapel, watching the artist paint, and perhaps stopping for a conversation. Students will stroll on the moon. Petroleum engineers will penetrate the earth virtually. Doctors will navigate through your cardiovascular system. Researchers will browse through a library. Auto designers will sit in the back seat of a car they are designing to see how it feels and examine the external view.

Eight Shifts of Interactive Learning

By exploiting the digital media, educators and students can shift to a new, more powerful, and more effective learning paradigm.

1. From Linear to Hypermedia Learning

Traditional approaches to learning are linear. This dates back to the book, which is usually read from beginning to end, as a learning tool. Stories, novels, and other narratives are linear. Most textbooks are written to be tackled from beginning to end. Television shows and instructional videos are designed to be watched from beginning to end.

But N-Gen access to information is more interactive and nonsequential. Notice how a child channel surfs when watching television? I note that my kids go back and forth between various TV shows and video games when they're in the family room. No doubt this will be extended to surfing the Net as our TV becomes a Net appliance.

When we observed our N-Gen sample surfing the Net, they typically participated in several activities at once. When surfing some new material, they hyperlinked to servers and information sources all over the place. Seven-year-old Robert Huang and his sister Franny, eleven, came to our office to show us how they surf the Net. Robert looked up the movie *Independence Day*, followed links to fans' pages, and returned to the search engine. Interestingly, Robert entered three different searches, but he never went more than two pages away from the *Independence Day* site. If a download took too long or a page disappointed him, he hit the back key to return to the site.

Franny was a little more focused. Her pet hamster Bupsie was pregnant and she wanted to see sites about baby hamsters. After conducting a *Yahooligans* search, she followed several links to other hamster owners' pages. She traced the mouse over the length until she found a link to an online journal which, with text and photographs, traced the development of a baby hamster from its blind and hairless infancy to adulthood—a process that takes only a few weeks. Franny intentionally avoided a guinea pig link on one hamster page because, "I don't like guinea pigs, but some people in South America eat them and even I don't want to see a fried one."

2. *From Instruction to Construction and Discovery*

Seymour Papert says, "The scandal of education is that every time you teach something, you deprive a child of the pleasure and benefit of discovery."[16]

At the risk of sounding equally heretical, there is a shift away from pedagogy—the art, science, and profession of teaching—to the creation of learning partnerships and learning cultures. The schools can become a place to learn rather than a place to teach. According to John Seely Brown, head of the Xerox Palo Alto Research Center (PARC), "Pedagogy had to do with optimizing the transmission of the information. What we now find is that kids don't want optimized, predigested information. They want to learn by doing—where they synthesize their own understanding—usually based on trying things out." Learning becomes experiential.

This is not to say that learning environments or even curricula should not be designed. They can, however, be designed in partnership with the learners or by the learners themselves.

This approach is described by educators as the constructivist approach. Rather than assimilating the knowledge broadcast by an instructor, the learner constructs knowledge anew. Constructionism argues that people learn best by *doing* rather than simply being told: constructionism as opposed to instructionism. The evidence for constructionism is persuasive, but it shouldn't be too surprising. The enthusiasm youngsters have for a fact or concept they "discovered" on their own is much more likely to be meaningful and retained than the same fact simply written out on the teacher's blackboard.

Computers today are used to teach mathematics using the drill and kill narrative. "How dull that is!" says Coco Conn. "That's why we never learn math, because it's *all* about *math*." She describes the Cityspace project, where children from multiple locations collaborate to construct virtual cities, right down to the streets, buildings, and rooms in the buildings. "In projects such as this, you're dealing with a lot of math because the kids are sitting there thinking about the scaling of the model, how many polygons they can put in their object—all about thinking spatially and mathematically. They are doing it in a way that's fun and also relevant to something that they are creating." Conn explains that when the project was demonstrated in a four-day workshop, "We had the math teachers tell everyone what the kids were doing with math, and everyone was astounded."

3. *From Teacher-Centered to Learner-Centered Education*

The new media enable centering of the learning experience on the individual rather than on the transmitter. Further, it is clear that learner-centered education improves the child's motivation to learn. Learning and entertainment can then converge.

It is important to realize that shifting from teacher-centered to learner-centered education does not suggest the teacher is suddenly playing a less important role. A teacher is equally critical and valued in the learner-centered context, and is essential for creating and structuring the learning experience. Much of this depends on the subject; no one would suggest, for example, that the best way to learn the piano is the discovery mode.

In the past, education has tended to focus on the teacher, not the student. This is especially true in postsecondary education, where the specific interests and background of the teacher strongly influence the content. Much of the activity in the classroom involves the teacher speaking and the student listening.

Learner-centered education begins with an evaluation of the abilities, learning style, social context, and other important factors of the student that affect learning. It would extensively use software programs which can structure and tailor the learning experience for the child. It would be more active, with students discussing, debating, researching, and collaborating on projects.

4. *From Absorbing Material to Learning How to Navigate and How to Learn*

This includes learning how to synthesize, not just analyze. N-Geners assess and analyze facts—a formidable and ever-present challenge in a data galaxy of easily accessible information sources. But more important, they synthesize. They engage with information sources and other people on the Net and then build or construct higher-level structures and mental images.

"In our generation, we reach for the manuals—if we don't know how to do something, we ask," says Seely Brown. "We don't engage directly with the unknown and then do sense-making afterwards. Kids today engage and synthesize. Our generation is good at the analysis of things, as opposed to the synthesis of things."

Educom is a consortium of universities and colleges dedicated to the transformation of higher education through information technology. Carol Twigg, Educom vice president, notes how the knowledge explosion has an impact on the curriculum in postsecondary education. She notes that the cliché is that by the time a student studying to become an engineer graduates, half of his knowledge is already obsolete: "To use your broadcast metaphor, the professor says 'Here is your curriculum, I will broadcast it at you, you will somehow absorb it and then move on and be prepared for life.' This is literally a joke." She says we can no longer prepare students to live in a world of rapid change by 'shoveling' knowledge at them. "No one has yet come to grips with this whole concept of learning how to learn. No one is doing that in a full curricular sense."

5. From School to Lifelong Learning

For the young boomers looking forward to the world of work, life was divided into the period when you *learned* and the period when you *did*. You went to school and maybe university and learned a competency—trade or profession—and for the rest of your life your challenge was simply to keep up with develop-

ments in your field. But things changed. Today many boomers can expect to reinvent their knowledge base constantly. Learning has become a continuous, lifelong process. The N-Gen is entering a world of lifelong learning from day one, and, unlike the schools of the boomers, today's educational system can anticipate this.

Richard Soderberg of the National Technological University puts it well: "People mistakenly think that once they've graduated from university they are good for the next decade—when they're really good for the next ten seconds." This is a reflection of the knowledge explosion in which the knowledge base of humanity is now doubling annually.

6. From One-Size-Fits-All to Customized Learning

Mass education was a product of the industrial economy. It came along with mass production, mass marketing, and the mass media. Businesses everywhere are shifting to a molecular or individualized approach. We have markets of one, where a soccer club is treated as a market composed of individuals. There are production runs of one—highly customized—from bread to newspapers. We customize products with our own knowledge.

Schooling, says Howard Gardner of the Harvard Graduate School of Education, is a mass-production idea. "You teach the same thing to students in the same way and assess them all in the same way." Pedagogy is based on the questionable idea that "optimal learning experiences," as John Seely Brown describes them, can be constructed for groups of learners at the same age level. In this view, a curriculum is developed based on predi-

gested information and structured for optimal transmission. If the curriculum is well structured and interesting, then large proportions of students at any given grade level will "tune in" and be able to absorb the information.

The digital media enable students to be treated as individuals—to have highly customized learning experiences based on their background, individual talents, age level, cognitive style, interpersonal preferences, and so on.

As Papert puts it: "What I see as the real contribution of digital media to education is a flexibility that could allow every individual to discover their own personal paths to learning. This will make it possible for the dream of every progressive educator to come true: In the learning environment of the future, every learner will be 'special.'"[18]

In fact, Papert says of the one-age-classroom-fits-all-model "community of learning" shared by students and teachers: "Socialization is not best done by segregating children into classrooms with kids of the same age. The computer is a medium in which what you make lends itself to be modified and shared. When kids get together on a project, there is abundant discussion; they show it to other kids, other kids want to see it, kids learn to share knowledge with other people much more than in the classroom.[19]

7. From Learning as Torture to Learning as Fun

Maybe torture is an exaggeration, but for many kids class is not exactly the highlight of their day. Some educators have decried the fact that a generation schooled on *Sesame Street* expects to be entertained at school—to enjoy the learning experience.

These educators argue that the learning and entertainment should be clearly separated. As Neil Postman says, ". . . *Sesame Street* does not encourage children to love school or anything about school. It teaches them to love television."[20]

But doesn't that say more about today's schools—which are not exactly exciting places for many students—than it does about the integration of learning and entertainment? I'm convinced that one of the design goals of the New School should be to make learning fun! Learning math should be an enjoyable, challenging, and, yes, entertaining activity just like learning a video game is. And it can be! Besides, *Sesame Street* let the entertainment horse out of the barn. So did video games, the Web, FreeZone, MaMaMedia, and a thousand others.

It is said, however, that if learning is fun it can't be challenging. Wrong! Try getting through the seven levels of Crash Bandicoot or FIFA soccer on your kids' video game if you think entertainment and challenge are opposites. The challenge provides much of the entertainment value and vice versa.

Why shouldn't learning be entertaining? *Webster's Ninth College Dictionary* gives the third and fourth definitions of the verb "to entertain" as "to keep, hold, or maintain in the mind," and "to receive and take into consideration." In other words, entertainment has always been a profound part of the learning process and teachers have, throughout history, been asked to convince their students to entertain ideas. From this perspective, the best teachers were the entertainers. Using the new media, the teacher becomes the entertainer and in doing so builds enjoyment, motivation, and responsibility for learning.

8. From the Teacher as Transmitter to the Teacher as Facilitator

Learning is becoming a social activity facilitated by a new generation of educators.

The topic is saltwater fish. The teacher divides the grade 6 class into teams, asking each to prepare a presentation on a fish of its choice covering the topics of history, breathing, propulsion, reproduction, diet, predators, and "cool facts." The students have access to the Web and are allowed to use any resources they want. Questions should be addressed to others in their team or to others in the class, not the teacher.

Two weeks later, Melissa's group is up first. The students in the group have created a shark project home page with hot links for each of the topics. The presentation is projected onto a screen at the front of the class as the girls talk. They have video clips of different types of sharks and also a clip of Jacques Cousteau discussing the shark as an endangered species. They then go live to Aquarius—an underwater Web site located off the Florida keys. The class can ask questions of the Aquarius staff, but most inquiries are directed at the project team. One of the big discussions is about the dangers posed to humans by sharks versus the dangers to sharks posed by humans.

The class decides to hold an online forum on this and invite kids from their sister classes in other countries to participate. The team invites the classes to browse through its project at any time, from any location, as the site will be "up" for the rest of the school year. In fact, the team decides to maintain the site, adding new links and fresh information throughout the year. It becomes a living project. Other learners from other countries find the shark home page helpful in their projects and build links to it. The team has to resource the information, tools, and materials it needs.

The teacher acts as a resource and consultant to the teams. He is also a youth worker—as one of the students was having considerable problems at home and was not motivated to participate in a team. Although the teacher can't solve such problems, he takes them into account and also refers the student to the guidance counselor. The teacher also facilitates the learning process, among other things participating as a technical consultant on the new media. He learns much from Melissa's group, which actually knows more about sharks than he does (his background is art and literature, not science). The teacher doesn't compete with Jacques Cousteau, but rather is supported by him.

This scenario is not science fiction. It is currently occurring in advanced schools in several countries. The teacher is not an instructional transmitter. He is a facilitator to social learning whereby learners construct their own knowledge. The students will remember what they learned about sharks as the topic now interests them. More importantly, they have acquired collaborative, research, analytical, presentation, and resourcing skills. With the assistance of a teacher, they are constructing knowledge and their world.

Needless to say, a whole generation of teachers needs to learn new tools, new approaches, and new skills. This will be a challenge—not just because of resistance to change by some teachers, but also because of the current atmosphere of cutbacks, low teacher morale, lack of time due to the pressures of increased workloads, and reduced retraining budgets.

The Future of Schools and Colleges

A recent public broadcasting program discussed corporate influence in the schools. The big issue debated was the potential dangers of Coke machines in the school cafeterias. While we should be concerned about the idea of company-sponsored learning with everything from ads on the blackboard to company-sponsored teachers, the producers created a tempest in a teapot and missed the real issue. For those concerned about corporate influence in education, the issue is not corporations in the schools. Rather, unless there is a big change in direction, the corporation will become the school!

Some schools, colleges, and universities are working hard to reinvent themselves, but progress is slow. This is truest for public institutions, but now both are in peril. Add to this tardiness the fact that N-Geners will perform knowledge work requiring lifelong learning and you have a formula for the privatization of education. This does not mean simply that companies will take over public schools. Rather, the private sector is tending to shoulder a growing burden for learning. Evidence for this is articulated in the little-known but very stimulating book *The Monster Under the Bed* by Stan Davis and Jim Botkin. The book argues that education, once the province of the church, then the government, is increasingly falling to business since it is business that ends up having to train knowledge workers. Say Davis and Botkin, "With the move from an agrarian to an industrial economy, the small rural schoolhouse was supplanted by the big brick urban schoolhouse. Four decades ago we began to move to another economy, but we have yet to develop a new educational paradigm, let alone create the 'schoolhouse' of the future, which may be neither school nor house."[21]

Because the new economy is knowledge-based and learning is part of day-to-day economic activity and life, both companies and individuals have found that they need to take responsibility for learning simply to be effective. The enterprise becomes a school in order to compete. Motorola U now has formal accreditation for courses it provides to employees. Many larger companies such as Xerox, Andersen Worldwide, and IBM have huge university-like campuses.

David and Botkin present data to show that in 1992 the growth in formal budgeted employee education grew by 126 million additional hours. This represents the equivalent of almost a quarter of a million additional full-time college students— 13 new Harvards. This is more growth in just one year than the enrollment growth in all the new conventional college campuses built in the United States between 1960 and 1990. "Employee education is not growing 100 percent faster than academia, but 100 times—or 10,000 percent—faster,"[22] says Davis and Botkin.

And for Carol Twigg, this is just the beginning. "Once the business community takes the step to integrate themselves with education, there will be an explosion in learning products. They're all still trying to sell to the higher-education buyers instead of the end consumer. Once they get that piece, then I think we will see a real change."

Another factor is that sales and education are converging. Every spring the telecommunications company GTE has held seminars in over a dozen cities. The program, which is attended by the company's customers, is called "GTE University." The company understands that to sell in the new economy you need to educate your customers. The company cannot market sophisticated telecommunications services unless its customers understand the current innovations in networking and how these can be applied to the competitive success of their firms. The sessions are also strongly attended by local government executives who need to know how the new technologies can help them deliver better, less costly government.

A logical step for GTE would be to expand this program into full courses on various topics. Such courses would be unique—not currently offered by any traditional universities or private training companies. GTE could probably charge for attendance as the demand would be very strong. Further, they could seek formal university accreditation or partner with some institution which can already grant degrees.

All this spells trouble for the schools and colleges that don't transform themselves. Many parents who can afford it are turning to private schools, private tutors, home schooling, and extensive use of CD- and Net-based learning environments as an alternative to public education. There is the obvious danger of a two-tier education system—one public for the lower classes and one private for the upper classes. Similarly, nonproactive schools and public educators will find themselves losing control over curriculum as attractive interactive learning products such as *Bill Nye, the Science Guy* seep into the system. But unfortunately, many politicians seem more concerned with cutting educational budgets than attempting to address the fundamental problems of the education system.

As the N-Geners graduate from high school, we can see big changes coming in the nature of and the delivery system for post-secondary education as well. In *The Digital Economy,* I argued that the universities and colleges were in deep trouble. With tenured professors, teachers threatened by technology, a history of little competition, and teaching traditions dating back centuries—to name a few problems—many educational institutions have become mired in the past. If the universities don't reinvent themselves in terms of their delivery system and relationship with the private sector, many will be doomed. This view was controversial, to say the least.

Educators really took note when none other than Peter Drucker shocked the post-secondary world in the March 10, 1997 issue of *Forbes* magazine. Confirming leading educators' worst nightmare, he stated publicly: "Thirty years from now big university campuses will be relics." Referring to the impact of the digital revolution, Drucker said: "It is as large a change as when we first got the printed book." He continued: "It took more than 200 years for the printed book to create the modern school. It won't nearly take that long for the big change. . . ."

Already we are beginning to deliver more lectures and classes off campus via satellite or two-way video at a fraction of the cost. The college won't survive as a residential institution. Today's buildings are hopelessly unsuited and totally unneeded."[23]

But isn't there a role for face-to-face communication? What about learning as a social experience? Clearly, the undergraduate residential campus is a transition place for youth in moving from home and high school to the world of knowledge work—not to mention that many still remember the university experience as the greatest time of their life.

But graduate studies may be better handled through integration with companies, private and other research laboratories, field work with government agencies, and other organizations. One thing is guaranteed. The status quo will not survive. The centralized university will give way to more distributed molecular structures, just as the centralized corporation is becoming internetworked. The university as mainframe will be replaced by the university as network.

These ideas are increasingly coming into the mainstream. Carol Twigg notes that when faculty place their courses on the Web, students don't want face-to-face interaction or small groups. "They are organizing peer discussion groups on the Net. They like being able to participate in the middle of the night—you know how kids are," she says. "Even with the primitive technology of today you don't hear kids saying, 'Oh dear, I wish we could get together once a week so we can see and touch each other.'" Children get together for other reasons, primarily social, and have ways to do this beyond the school.

One of the strongest trends is a shift to part-time education. Many students need to work to fund university attendance. Many more in the workforce are registering in university courses as part of the trend in lifelong learning. According to the National Center for Educational Statistics, part-time students are now the new majority. Nearly half of college and university students attend on a part-time basis—6.6 million in 1993, up from 3 million in 1970. Over the same time period, the number of full-time students grew by only 38 percent. During 1994, 76 million adults (40 percent of the population) participated in one or more adult education activities. Those with more education are more likely to take additional courses. College graduates are nearly twice as likely to sign up for adult education courses, compared to those who have not attended college.[24]

The same trends are occurring at the graduate level—which has historically been primarily residential. According to Twigg, "Every time a company like AT&T hiccups and 40,000 people lose their jobs, thousands go back to school."

The academic calendar will be tossed out as well. The old view was, "Our calendar is based on an academic year with two semesters with courses on alternating days of the week." The new calendar does not belong to the university. It belongs to the student. Anticipate changes regarding faculty as we shift from the autonomous professor to teams which collaborate to create learning environments for students.

The New Teacher

As the digital media enter the schools and are instantly embraced by savvy and fearless N-Gen students, whither the teacher? Given the growing evidence that interactive media can dramatically improve the learning process, clearly teachers will need to change their role. Rather than fact repeaters, they can become motivators and facilitators. . . .

What is the new teacher like?

Small miracles have been occurring over the last three years at William Lyon Mackenzie Collegiate in North York, Ontario. The Emerging Technologies program mixes grades 10 to 12 to work on projects involving teams and the new media. The students learn by discovery. Through teams they source answers to their questions and resources to conduct their projects—from other students, outside parties, and the Net. The learning model is one of student-centered discovery enabled by emerging technologies.

When the program began, teacher Richard Ford told the students on their first day of class that their first project was for each to design their own Web page and present it to the group by Friday. When he asked how many knew how to design a Web page, 6 of the 32 kids in the class indicated they had some experience. Richard then suggested to the class that they should remember those faces, "because they are your mentors."

The students learn to cooperate, work in teams, solve problems, and take responsibility for their own learning—by doing. If there's something they don't understand, they must ask everyone else in the class before they can ask the teacher. Right after the first class, one girl asks, "What's a Web page?" Richard shrugs and says, "I don't know." Within a few days the kids have gotten the

message. "And who's the last person you ask for help?" says Richard. Everyone replies in unison, "You are."

The model is that everyone relies on everyone else, sharing their expertise. Richard told them that if everyone didn't present their Web page on Friday, then everyone would get a zero. On the second day of class some of the kids were going around asking others if they needed help. However, when the learners have exhausted all routes and cannot find a solution to something, they can approach the teacher (called the facilitator). He then will w⟋ with them as a team m⟋ find a solution which can ⸺

1
th⸺
ers

to gi⸺
got a⸺
class. C⸺
no Engl⸺
the other⸺ ⸺⸺ont of
the class. ⸺ ⸺ered up the
courage to ⸺proach the front of
the room, then, turning, stood there and said "My Web page. . . .First time. . . . Graphics. . . . See link. Thank you." All the other kids applauded. "It was a very emotional moment for everyone," says Richard. "Everyone knew what an accomplishment it was for this boy to speak in front of everyone else in another language, presenting his first Web page." Afterward, outside the classroom, he approached

Richard and said to him, smiling broadly, "I am proud."

For Richard, "There is something that happens when you decide for yourself that you're going to learn something and do something. This is much more powerful than when someone else says you have to do this."

"The kids not only learned about the new media and developed language and presentation skills, they learned about how to interact with clients and meet deadlines and most important they learned about how to share expertise and how to source it as well," says project coordinator ⸺cki Saunders. "The kids work ⸺ times longer because they are ⸺xcited about their projects."

After the first week the learn⸺ ⸺nched into Web design for ⸺ents. One group built the ⸺e for the Canadian ⸺ting Corporation movie ⸺ Another did the design ⸺ York-based artist ⸺r Kustera—who came ⸺ for a week to work ⸺ hired the group to ⸺bout a conference ⸺Meeting Media," ⸺ kids came together in ⸺onto to present their projects to other kids from across the city. Kids from grades 2 to 13 presented their animation and multimedia projects and all this was captured on a CD.

For their midterm "exam," the students had to create a three-page Web site or a three minute video. They were placed in groups of four, selected intentionally to help them overcome their obstacles to development. For example, all the "blockers" were put in one group. The project had to have a purpose. The students also had to discuss their own individual contributions and to assign marks to each other. The kids really had to wake up and work hard. A lot of buttons were pushed.

According to Vicki, "Richard is able to find the hook that turns kids on."

Richard has a radical view of the role of the teacher. "I don't teach. If I teach, who knows what they will learn. Teaching's out. I tell kids that there are no limits. You can create whatever you want to create. If it's impossible, it will just take a bit longer. My main function is to get kids excited, to consider things that they haven't done before. I'm working to create citizens in a global society."

He also deemphasizes his role as a judge. "We're trying to create a stage for them to present their ideas and their work to others. If a student hands something in to a teacher, she doesn't necessarily learn. The intention of the work becomes to satisfy the teacher's vision. We're not expanding the student's vision.

"For example, I whisper to a student who is doing a project on his home country, 'What about if you were to present this project on the Web?' The student realizes people will read it and see it. They might e-mail him back. They might set up a newsgroup. Maybe someone from their home town might join the conference. He may be able to share his ideas with others around the world."

Richard acts as a facilitator to set a hook. "If they grab hold, they're off on a voyage of discovery. We both discover. I learn through each of them—I learn about how people carry each other from village to village when he puts a photo on the Web. I learn about his culture when people begin to communicate with him from the other side of the globe.

"Everything you do affects others. We're asking kids to create their place in this global society. Whatever you want is possible. There are no limits. You create who you are in your space."

Notes

1. U.S. Census Bureau, Education and Social Stratification Branch.
2. "Investing in America's Future, a statement by U.S. Secretary of Education, Richard W. Riley" from "A Back to School Special Report: The Baby Boom Echo," August 1996, National Center for Education Statistics.
3. U.S. Bureau of Labor Statistics.
4. Postman, Neil. *The End of Education: Redefining the Value of School.* New York: Vintage Books, 1995.
5. As quoted in *Investor's Business Daily,* 30 April 1997.
6. Roszak, Theodore. "Internet as Teacher Makes Students Stupid," *New Internationalist,* 1997.
7. Malveaux, Julianne. "Make Basics a Higher Priority than Internet," *USA Today.*
8. Becker, H. J. "How Computers Are Used in United States Schools." Basic data from the 1989 I.E.A.
Computers in Education Survey, *Journal of Education Research,* pp. 407–420.
9. Senge, Peter. *The Fifth Discipline.* New York: Doubleday, 1990.
10. Market Data Retrieval cited in *USA Today,* 11 March 1997.
11. A study of 1,001 teachers conducted by Jostens Learning Corp. and the American Association of School Administrators found that while 94 percent of teachers and school superintendents believe computers have improved teaching and learning, they are most frequently used for "teaching computer skills, classroom instruction, and record keeping."

Footnotes 12–15 do not appear in this publication.

16. Papert, Seymour. Ibid., p. 68.

Footnote 17 does not appear in this publication.

18. Papert, Seymour, Ibid.
19. *Christian Science Monitor,* 21 April 1997.
20. Postman, Neil. *Amusing Ourselves to Death: Public Discourse in the Age of Show Business.* New York: Penguin Books, p. 144.
21. Davis, Stan, and Botkin, Jim. *The Monster Under the Bed: How Business Is Mastering the Opportunity of Knowledge for Profit.* New York: Simon & Schuster, 1994, p. 23.
22. Davis, Stan, and Botkin, Jim. Ibid., p. 88.
23. Drucker, Peter. *Forbes,* 10 March 1997, pp. 126–7.
24. Speer, Tibbett. "A Nation of Students." *American Demographics,* August 1996.

Article Review Form at end of book.

How much money can we afford to spend on technology-rich classrooms? Is instruction necessarily improved by the use of computers?

The Computer Delusion

Todd Oppenheimer

There is no good evidence that most uses of computers significantly improve teaching and learning, yet school districts are cutting programs—music, art, physical education—that enrich children's lives to make room for this dubious nostrum, and the Clinton Administration has embraced the goal of "computers in every classroom" with credulous and costly enthusiasm.

In 1922 Thomas Edison predicted that "the motion picture is destined to revolutionize our educational system and . . . in a few years it will supplant largely, if not entirely, the use of textbooks." Twenty-three years later, in 1945, William Levenson, the director of the Cleveland public schools' radio station, claimed that "the time may come when a portable radio receiver will be as common in the classroom as is the blackboard." Forty years after that the noted psychologist B. F. Skinner, referring to the first days of his "teaching machines," in the late 1950s and early 1960s, wrote, "I was soon saying that, with the help of teaching machines and programmed instruction, stu-

dents could learn twice as much in the same time and with the same effort as in a standard classroom." Ten years after Skinner's recollections were published, President Bill Clinton campaigned for "a bridge to the twenty-first century . . . where computers are as much a part of the classroom as blackboards." Clinton was not alone in his enthusiasm for a program estimated to cost somewhere between $40 billion and $100 billion over the next five years. Speaker of the House Newt Gingrich, talking about computers to the Republican National Committee early this year, said, "We could do so much to make education available twenty-four hours a day, seven days a week, that people could literally have a whole different attitude toward learning."

If history really is repeating itself, the schools are in serious trouble. In *Teachers and Machines: The Classroom Use of Technology Since 1920* (1986), Larry Cuban, a professor of education at Stanford University and a former school superintendent, observed that as successive rounds of new technology failed their promoters' expectations, a pattern emerged. The

cycle began with big promises backed by the technology developers' research. In the classroom, however, teachers never really embraced the new tools, and no significant academic improvement occurred. This provoked consistent responses: the problem was money, spokespeople argued, or teacher resistance, or the paralyzing school bureaucracy. Meanwhile, few people questioned the technology advocates' claims. As results continued to lag, the blame was finally laid on the machines. Soon schools were sold on the next generation of technology, and the lucrative cycle started all over again.

Today's technology evangels argue that we've learned our lesson from past mistakes. As in each previous round, they say that when our new hot technology—the computer—is compared with yesterday's, today's is better. "It can do the same things, plus," Richard Riley, the U.S. Secretary of Education, told me this spring.

How much better is it, really?

The promoters of computers in schools again offer prodigious research showing improved academic achievement after using their technology. The research has again come under occasional attack, but this time quite a number of teachers seem to be backing classroom technology. In a poll taken early last year U.S. teachers ranked computer skills and media technology as more "essential" than the study of European history, biology, chemistry, and physics; than dealing with social problems such as drugs and family breakdown; than learning practical job skills; and than reading modern American writers such as Steinbeck and Hemingway or classic ones such as Plato and Shakespeare.

In keeping with these views New Jersey cut state aid to a number of school districts this past year and then spent $10 million on classroom computers. In Union City, California, a single school district is spending $27 million to buy new gear for a mere eleven schools. The Kittridge Street Elementary School, in Los Angeles, killed its music program last year to hire a technology coordinator; in Mansfield, Massachusetts, administrators dropped proposed teaching positions in art, music, and physical education, and then spent $333,000 on computers; in one Virginia school the art room was turned into a computer laboratory. (Ironically, a half dozen preliminary studies recently suggested that music and art classes may build the physical size of a child's brain, and its powers for subjects such as language, math, science, and engineering—in one case far more than computer work did.) Meanwhile, months after a New Technology High School opened in Napa, California, where computers sit on every student's desk and all academic classes use com-

puters, some students were complaining of headaches, sore eyes, and wrist pain.

Throughout the country, as spending on technology increases, school book purchases are stagnant. Shop classes, with their tradition of teaching children building skills with wood and metal, have been almost entirely replaced by new "technology education programs." In San Francisco only one public school still offers a full shop program—the lone vocational high school. "We get kids who don't know the difference between a screwdriver and a ball peen hammer," James Dahlman, the school's vocational-department chair, told me recently. "How are they going to make a career choice? Administrators are stuck in this mindset that all kids will go to a four-year college and become a doctor or a lawyer, and that's not true. I know some who went to college, graduated, and then had to go back to technical school to get a job." Last year the school superintendent in Great Neck, Long Island, proposed replacing elementary school shop classes with computer classes and training the shop teachers as computer coaches. Rather than being greeted with enthusiasm, the proposal provoked a backlash.

Interestingly, shop classes and field trips are two programs that the National Information Infrastructure Advisory Council, the Clinton Administration's technology task force, suggests reducing in order to shift resources into computers. But are these results what technology promoters really intend? "You need to apply common sense," Esther Dyson, the president of EDventure Holdings and one of the task force's leading school advocates, told me recently. "Shop

with a good teacher probably is worth more than computers with a lousy teacher. But if it's a poor program, this may provide a good excuse for cutting it. There will be a lot of trials and errors with this. And I don't know how to prevent those errors."

The issue, perhaps, is the magnitude of the errors. Alan Lesgold, a professor of psychology and the associate director of the Learning Research and Development Center at the University of Pittsburgh, calls the computer an "amplifier," because it encourages both enlightened study practices and thoughtless ones. There's a real risk, though, that the thoughtless practices will dominate, slowly dumbing down huge numbers of tomorrow's adults. As Sherry Turkle, a professor of the sociology of science at the Massachusetts Institute of Technology and a longtime observer of children's use of computers, told me, "The possibilities of using this thing poorly so outweigh the chance of using it well, it makes people like us, who are fundamentally optimistic about computers, very reticent."

Perhaps the best way to separate fact from fantasy is to take supporters' claims about computerized learning one by one and compare them with the evidence in the academic literature and in the everyday experiences I have observed or heard about in a variety of classrooms.

Five main arguments underlie the campaign to computerize our nation's schools.

- Computers improve both teaching practices and student achievement.

- Computer literacy should be taught as early as possible; otherwise students will be left behind.

- To make tomorrow's work force competitive in an increasingly high-tech world, learning computer skills must be a priority.

- Technology programs leverage support from the business community—badly needed today because schools are increasingly starved for funds.

- Work with computers—particularly using the Internet—brings students valuable connections with teachers, other schools and students, and a wide network of professionals around the globe. These connections spice the school day with a sense of real-world relevance, and broaden the educational community.

"The Filmstrips of the 1990s"

Clinton's vision of computerized classrooms arose partly out of the findings of the presidential task force—thirty-six leaders from industry, education, and several interest groups who have guided the Administration's push to get computers into the schools. The report of the task force, "Connecting K–12 Schools to the Information Superhighway" (produced by the consulting firm McKinsey & Co.), begins by citing numerous studies that have apparently proved that computers enhance student achievement significantly. One "meta-analysis" (a study that reviews other studies—in this case 130 of them) reported that computers had improved performance in "a wide range of subjects, including language arts, math, social studies and science."

In a recent poll U.S. teachers ranked computer skills and media technology as more "essential" than European history, biology, chemistry, and physics.

Another found improved organization and focus in students' writing. A third cited twice the normal gains in math skills. Several schools boasted of greatly improved attendance.

Unfortunately, many of these studies are more anecdotal than conclusive. Some, including a giant, oft-cited meta-analysis of 254 studies, lack the necessary scientific controls to make solid conclusions possible. The circumstances are artificial and not easily repeated, results aren't statistically reliable, or, most frequently, the studies did not control for other influences, such as differences between teaching methods. This last factor is critical, because computerized learning inevitably forces teachers to adjust their style—only sometimes for the better. Some studies were industry-funded, and thus tended to publicize mostly positive findings. "The research is set up in a way to find benefits that aren't really there," Edward Miller, a former editor of the *Harvard Education Letter*, says. "Most knowledgeable people agree that most of the research isn't valid. It's so flawed it shouldn't even be called research. Essentially, it's just worthless." Once the, faulty studies are weeded out, Miller says, the ones that remain "are inconclusive"—that is, they show no significant change in either direction. Even Esther Dyson admits the studies are undependable. "I don't think those studies amount to much either way," she says. "In this area there is little proof."

Why are solid conclusions so elusive? Look at Apple Computer's "Classrooms of Tomorrow," perhaps the most widely studied effort to teach using computer technology. In the early 1980s Apple shrewdly realized that donating computers to schools might help not only students but also company sales, as Apple's ubiquity in classrooms turned legions of families into Apple loyalists. Last year, after the *San Jose Mercury News* (published in Apple's Silicon Valley home) ran a series questioning the effectiveness of computers in schools, the paper printed an opinion-page response from Terry Crane, an Apple vice-president. "Instead of isolating students," Crane wrote, "technology actually encouraged them to collaborate more than in traditional classrooms. Students also learned to explore and represent information dynamically and creatively, communicate effectively about complex processes, become independent learners and self-starters and become more socially aware and confident."

Crane didn't mention that after a decade of effort and the donation of equipment worth more than $25 million to thirteen schools, there is scant evidence of greater student achievement. To be fair, educators on both sides of the computer debate acknowledge that today's tests of student achievement are shockingly crude. They're especially weak in measuring intangibles such as enthusiasm and self-motivation, which do seem evident in Apple's classrooms and other computer-rich schools. In any event, what is fun and what is educational may frequently be at odds. "Computers in classrooms are the filmstrips of the 1990s," Clifford Stoll, the author of *Silicon Snake Oil: Second Thoughts on the Information Highway* (1995), told *The New York Times* last year, recalling his own school days in the 1960s. "We loved them because we didn't have to think for an hour, teachers loved them because they didn't have to teach, and parents loved them because it showed their schools were high-tech. But no learning happened."

Stoll somewhat overstates the case—obviously, benefits can come from strengthening a student's motivation. Still, Apple's computers may bear less responsibility for that change than Crane suggests. In the beginning, when Apple did little more than dump computers in classrooms and homes, this produced no real results, according to Jane David, a consultant Apple hired to study its classroom initiative. Apple quickly learned that teachers needed to change their classroom approach to what is commonly called "project-oriented learning." This is an increasingly popular teaching method, in which students learn through doing and teachers act as facilitators or partners rather than as didacts. (Teachers sometimes refer to this approach, which arrived in classrooms before computers did, as being "the guide on the side instead of the sage on the stage.") But what the students learned "had less to do with the computer and more to do with the teaching," David concluded. "If you took the computers out, there would still be good teaching there." This story is heard in school after school, including two impoverished schools—Clear View Elementary School, in southern California, and the Christopher Columbus middle school, in New Jersey—that the Clinton Administration has loudly celebrated for turning themselves around with computers. At Christopher Columbus, in fact, students' test scores rose before computers arrived, not after-

ward, because of relatively basic changes: longer class periods, new books, after-school programs, and greater emphasis on student projects and collaboration.

During recent visits to some San Francisco-area schools I could see what it takes for students to use computers properly, and why most don't.

On a bluff south of downtown San Francisco, in the middle of one of the city's lower-income neighborhoods, Claudia Schaffner, a tenth-grader, tapped away at a multimedia machine in a computer lab at Thurgood Marshall Academic High School, one of half a dozen special technology schools in the city. Schaffner was using a physics program to simulate the trajectory of a marble on a small roller coaster. "It helps to visualize it first, like 'A is for Apple' with kindergartners," Schaffner told me, while mousing up and down the virtual roller coaster. "I can see how the numbers go into action." This was lunch hour, and the students' excitement about what they can do in this lab was palpable. Schaffner could barely tear herself away. "I need to go eat some food," she finally said, returning within minutes to eat a rice dish at the keyboard.

Schaffner's teacher is Dennis Frezzo, an electrical-engineering graduate from the University of California at Berkeley. Despite his considerable knowledge of computer programming, Frezzo tries to keep classwork focused on physical projects. For a mere $8,000, for example, several teachers put together a multifaceted robotics lab, consisting of an advanced Lego engineering kit and twenty-four old 386-generation computers. Frezzo's students used these materials to build a tiny electric car, whose motion was to be triggered by a light sen-

sor. When the light sensor didn't work, the students figured out why. "That's a real problem—what you'd encounter in the real world," Frezzo told me. "I prefer they get stuck on small real-world problems instead of big fake problems"—like the simulated natural disasters that fill one popular educational game. "It's sort of the Zen approach to education," Frezzo said. "It's not the big problems. Isaac Newton already solved those. What come up in life are the little ones."

It's one thing to confront technology's complexity at a high school—especially one that's blessed with four different computer labs and some highly skilled teachers like Frezzo, who know enough, as he put it, "to keep computers in their place." It's quite another to grapple with a high-tech future in the lower grades, especially at everyday schools that lack special funding or technical support. As evidence, when *U.S. News & World Report* published a cover story last fall on schools that make computers work, five of the six were high schools—among them Thurgood Marshall. Although the sixth was an elementary school, the featured program involved children with disabilities—the one group that does show consistent benefits from computerized instruction.

Artificial Experience

Consider the scene at one elementary school. Sanchez, which sits on the edge of San Francisco's Latino community. For several years Sanchez, like many other schools, has made do with a roomful of basic Apple IIes. Last year, curious about what computers could do for youngsters, a local entrepreneur donated twenty costly Power Macintoshes—three for each of five classrooms, and one for each of the five lucky teachers to take home. The teachers who got the new machines were delighted. "It's the best thing we've ever done," Adela Najarro, a third-grade bilingual teacher, told me. She mentioned one boy, perhaps with a learning disability, who had started to hate school. Once he had a computer to play with, she said, "his whole attitude changed." Najarro is now a true believer, even when it comes to children without disabilities. "Every single child," she said, "will do more work for you and do better work with a computer. Just because it's on a monitor, kids pay more attention. There's this magic to the screen."

Down the hall from Najarro's classroom her colleague Rose Marie Ortiz had a more troubled relationship with computers. On the morning I visited, Ortiz took her bilingual special-education class of second-, third-, and fourth-graders into the lab filled with the old Apple IIes. The students look forward to this weekly expedition so much that Ortiz gets exceptional behavior from them all morning. Out of date though these machines are, they do offer a range of exercises, in subjects such as science, math, reading, social studies, and problem solving. But owing to this group's learning problems and limited English skills, math drills were all that Ortiz could give them. Nonetheless, within minutes the kids were excitedly navigating their way around screens depicting floating airplanes and trucks carrying varying numbers of eggs. As the children struggled, many resorted to counting in whatever way they knew how. Some squinted at the screen, painstakingly moving their fingers from one tiny egg symbol to

the next. "*Tres, cuatro, cinco, seis . . . ,*" one little girl said loudly, trying to hear herself above her counting neighbors. Another girl kept a piece of paper handy, on which she marked a line for each egg. Several others resorted to the slow but tried and true—their fingers. Some just guessed. Once the children arrived at answers, they frantically typed them onto the screen, hoping it would advance to something fun, the way Nintendos, Game Boys, and video-arcade games do. Sometimes their answers were right, and the screen did advance; sometimes they weren't; but the children were rarely discouraged. As schoolwork goes, this was a blast.

"It's highly motivating for them," Ortiz said as she rushed from machine to machine, attending not to math questions but to computer glitches. Those she couldn't fix she simply abandoned. "I don't know how practical it is. You see," she said, pointing to a girl counting on her fingers, "these kids still need the hands-on"—meaning the opportunity to manipulate physical objects such as beans or colored blocks. The value of hands-on learning, child-development experts believe, is that it deeply imprints knowledge into a young child's brain, by transmitting the lessons of experience through a variety of sensory pathways. "Curiously enough," the educational psychologist Jane Healy wrote in *Endangered Minds: Why Children Don't Think and What We Can Do About It* (1990), "visual stimulation is probably not the main access route to nonverbal reasoning. Body movements, the ability to touch, feel, manipulate, and build sensory awareness of relationships in the physical world, are its main foundations."

The problem, Healy wrote, is that "in schools, traditionally, the senses have had little status after kindergarten."

Ortiz believes that the computer-lab time, brief as it is, dilutes her students' attention to language. "These kids are all language-delayed," she said. Though only modest sums had so far been spent at her school, Ortiz and other local teachers felt that the push was on for technology over other scholastic priorities. The year before, Sanchez had let its librarian go, to be replaced by a part-timer.

When Ortiz finally got the students rounded up and out the door, the kids were still worked up. "They're never this wired after reading group," she said. "They're usually just exhausted, because I've been reading with them, making them write and talk." Back in homeroom Ortiz showed off the students' monthly handwritten writing samples. "Now, could you do that on the computer?" she asked. "No, because we'd be hung up on finding the keys." So why does Ortiz bother taking her students to the computer lab at all? "I guess I come in here for the computer literacy. If everyone else is getting it, I feel these kids should get it too."

Some computerized elementary school programs have avoided these pitfalls, but the record subject by subject is mixed at best. Take writing, where by all accounts and by my own observations the computer does encourage practice—changes are easier to make on a keyboard than with an eraser, and the lettering looks better. Diligent students use these conveniences to improve their writing, but the less committed frequently get seduced by electronic opportunities to make a school paper look snazzy. (The easy "cut and paste" function in today's word-processing programs, for example, is apparently encouraging many students to cobble together research materials without thinking them through.) Reading programs get particularly bad reviews. One small but carefully controlled study went so far as to claim that Reader Rabbit, a reading program now used in more than 100,000 schools, caused students to suffer a 50 percent drop in creativity. (Apparently, after forty-nine students used the program for seven months, they were no longer able to answer open-ended questions and showed a markedly diminished ability to brainstorm with fluency and originality.) What about hard sciences, which seem so well suited to computer study? Logo, the high-profile programming language refined by Seymour Papert and widely used in middle and high schools, fostered huge hopes of expanding children's cognitive skills. As students directed the computer to build things, such as geometric shapes, Papert believed, they would learn "procedural thinking," similar to the way a computer processes information. According to a number of studies, however, Logo has generally failed to deliver on its promises. Judah Schwartz, a professor of education at Harvard and a codirector of the school's Educational Technology Center, told me that a few newer applications, when used properly, can dramatically expand children's math and science thinking by giving them new tools to "make and explore conjectures." Still,

"Most knowledgeable people agree that most of the research isn't valid," says one observer about studies showing that computers enhance achievement.

Schwartz acknowledges that perhaps "ninety-nine percent" of the educational programs are "terrible, really terrible."

Even in success stories important caveats continually pop up. The best educational software is usually complex—most suited to older students and sophisticated teachers. In other cases the schools have been blessed with abundance—fancy equipment, generous financial support, or extra teachers—that is difficult if not impossible to duplicate in the average school. Even if it could be duplicated, the literature suggests, many teachers would still struggle with technology. Computers suffer frequent breakdowns; when they do work, their seductive images often distract students from the lessons at hand—which many teachers say makes it difficult to build meaningful rapport with their students.

With such a discouraging record of student and teacher performance with computers, why has the Clinton Administration focused so narrowly on the hopeful side of the story? Part of the answer may lie in the makeup of the Administration's technology task force. Judging from accounts of the task force's deliberations, all thirty-six members are unequivocal technology advocates. Two thirds of them work in the high-tech and entertainment industries. The effect of the group's tilt can be seen in its report. Its introduction adopts the authoritative posture of impartial fact-finder, stating that "this report does not attempt to lay out a national blueprint, nor does it recommend specific public policy goals." But it comes pretty close.

Each chapter describes various strategies for getting computers into classrooms, and the introduction acknowledges that "this report does not evaluate the relative merits of competing demands on educational funding (e.g., more computers versus smaller class sizes)."

When I spoke with Esther Dyson and other task-force members about what discussion the group had had about the potential downside of computerized education, they said there hadn't been any. And when I asked Linda Roberts, Clinton's lead technology adviser in the Department of Education, whether the task force was influenced by any self-interest, she said no, quite the opposite: the group's charter actually gave its members license to help the technology industry directly, but they concentrated on schools because that's where they saw the greatest need.

That sense of need seems to have been spreading outside Washington. Last summer a California task force urged the state to spend $11 billion on computers in California schools, which have struggled for years under funding cuts that have driven academic achievement down to among the lowest levels in the nation. This task force, composed of forty-six teachers, parents, technology experts, and business executives, concluded, "More than any other single measure, computers and network technologies, properly implemented, offer the greatest potential to right what's wrong with our public schools." Other options mentioned in the group's report—reducing class size, improving teachers' salaries and facilities, expanding hours of instruction—were considered less important than putting kids in front of computers.

"Hypertext Minds"

Today's parents, knowing first-hand how families were burned by television's false promises, may want some objective advice about the age at which their children should become computer literate. Although there are no real guidelines, computer boosters send continual messages that if children don't begin early, they'll be left behind. Linda Roberts thinks that there's no particular minimum age—and no maximum number of hours that children should spend at a terminal. Are there examples of excess? "I haven't seen it yet," Roberts told me with a laugh. In schools throughout the country administrators and teachers demonstrate the same excitement, boasting about the wondrous things that children of five or six can do on computers: drawing, typing, playing with elementary science simulations and other programs called "educational games."

The schools' enthusiasm for these activities is not universally shared by specialists in childhood development. The doubters' greatest concern is for the very young—preschool through third grade, when a child is most impressionable. Their apprehension involves two main issues.

First, they consider it important to give children a broad base—emotionally, intellectually, and in the five senses—before introducing something as technical and one-dimensional as a computer. Second, they believe that the human and physical world holds greater learning potential.

The importance of a broad base for a child may be most apparent when it's missing. In *Endangered Minds,* Jane Healy wrote of an English teacher who could readily tell which of her students' essays were conceived on a computer. "They don't link ideas," the teacher says. "They just write one thing, and then they write another one, and they don't seem to see or develop the relationships between them." The problem, Healy argued, is that the pizzazz of computerized schoolwork may hide these analytical gaps, which "won't become apparent until [the student] can't organize herself around a homework assignment or a job that requires initiative. More commonplace activities, such as figuring out how to nail two boards together, organizing a game . . . may actually form a better basis for real-world intelligence."

Others believe they have seen computer games expand children's imaginations. High-tech children "think differently from the rest of us," William D. Winn, the director of the Learning Center at the University of Washington's Human Interface Technology Laboratory, told *Business Week* in a recent cover story on the benefits of computer games. "They develop hypertext minds. They leap around. It's as though their cognitive strategies were parallel, not sequential." Healy argues the opposite. She and other psychologists think that the computer screen flattens information into narrow, sequential data. This kind of material, they believe, exercises mostly one half of the brain—the left hemisphere, where primarily sequential thinking occurs. The "right brain" meanwhile gets short shrift—yet this is the hemisphere that works on different kinds of information simultaneously. It shapes our multi-faceted impressions, and serves as the engine of creative analysis.

Opinions diverge in part because research on the brain is still so sketchy, and computers are so new, that the effect of computers on the brain remains a great mystery. "I don't think we know anything about it," Harry Chugani, a pediatric neurobiologist at Wayne State University, told me. This very ignorance makes skeptics wary. "Nobody knows how kids' internal wiring works," Clifford Stoll wrote in *Silicon Snake Oil,* "but anyone who's directed away from social interactions has a head start on turning out weird. . . . No computer can teach what a walk through a pine forest feels like. Sensation has no substitute."

This points to the conservative developmentalists' second concern: the danger that even if hours in front of the screen are limited, unabashed enthusiasm for the computer sends the wrong message: that the mediated world is more significant than the real one. "It's like TV commercials," Barbara Scales, the head teacher at the Child Study Center at the University of California at Berkeley, told me. "Kids get so hyped up, it can change their expectations about stimulation, versus what they generate themselves." In *Silicon Snake Oil,* Michael Fellows, a computer scientist at the University of Victoria, in British Columbia, was even blunter. "Most schools would probably be better off if they threw their computers into the Dumpster."

Faced with such sharply contrasting viewpoints, which are based on such uncertain ground, how is a responsible policymaker to proceed? "A prudent society controls its own infatuation with 'progress' when planning for its young," Healy argued in *Endangered Minds.*

Unproven technologies . . . may offer lively visions, but they can also be detrimental to the development of the young plastic brain. The cerebral cortex is a wondrously well-buffered mechanism that can withstand a good bit of well-intentioned bungling. Yet there is a point at which fundamental neural substrates for reasoning may be jeopardized for children who lack proper physical, intellectual, or emotional nurturance. Childhood—and the brain—have their own imperatives. In development, missed opportunities may be difficult to recapture.

The problem is that technology leaders rarely include these or other warnings in their recommendations. When I asked Dyson why the Clinton task force proceeded with such fervor, despite the classroom computer's shortcomings, she said, "It's so clear the world is changing."

Real Job Training

In the past decade, according to the presidential task force's report, the number of jobs requiring computer skills has increased from 25 percent of all jobs in 1983 to 47 percent in 1993. By 2000, the report estimates, 60 percent of the nation's jobs will demand these skills—and pay an average of 10 to 15 percent more than jobs involving no computer work. Although projections of this sort are far from reliable, it's a safe bet that computer skills will be needed for a growing proportion of tomorrow's work force. But what priority should these skills be given among other studies?

Listen to Tom Henning, a physics teacher at Thurgood Marshall, the San Francisco technology high school. Henning has a graduate degree in engineering, and helped to found a Silicon Valley company that manufactures electronic navigation equipment. "My bias is the physical

reality," Henning told me, as we sat outside a shop where he was helping students to rebuild an old motorcycle. "I'm no technophobe. I can program computers." What worries Henning is that computers at best engage only two senses, hearing and sight—and only two-dimensional sight at that. "Even if they're doing three-dimensional computer modeling, that's still a two-D replica of a three-D world. If you took a kid who grew up on Nintendo, he's not going to have the necessary skills. He needs to have done it first with Tinkertoys or clay, or carved it out of balsa wood." As David Elkind, a professor of child development at Tufts University, puts it, "A dean of the University of Iowa's school of engineering used to say the best engineers were the farm boys," because they knew how machinery really worked.

Surely many employers will disagree, and welcome the commercially applicable computer skills that today's high-tech training can bring them. What's striking is how easy it is to find other employers who share Henning's and Elkind's concerns.

Kris Meisling, a senior geological-research adviser for Mobil Oil, told me that "people who use computers a lot slowly grow rusty in their ability to think." Meisling's group creates charts and maps—some computerized, some not—to plot where to drill for oil. In large one-dimensional analyses, such as sorting volumes of seismic data, the computer saves vast amounts of time, sometimes making previously impossible tasks easy. This lures people in his field, Meisling believes, into using computers as much as possible. But when geologists turn to computers for "interpretive" projects, he finds, they

often miss information, and their oversights are further obscured by the computer's captivating automatic design functions. This is why Meisling still works regularly with a pencil and paper—tools that, ironically, he considers more interactive than the computer, because they force him to think implications through.

"You can't simultaneously get an overview and detail with a computer," he says. "It's linear. It gives you tunnel vision. What computers can do well is what can be calculated over and over. What they can't do is innovation. If you think of some new way to do or look at things and the software can't do it, you're stuck. So a lot of people think, 'Well, I guess it's a dumb idea, or it's unnecessary.'"

I have heard similar warnings from people in other businesses, including high-tech enterprises. A spokeswoman for Hewlett-Packard, the giant California computer-products company, told me the company rarely hires people who are predominantly computer experts, favoring instead those who have a talent for teamwork and are flexible and innovative. Hewlett-Packard is such a believer in hands-on experience that since 1992 it has spent $2.6 million helping forty-five school districts build math and science skills the old-fashioned way—using real materials, such as dirt, seeds, water, glass vials, and magnets. Much the same perspective came from several recruiters in film and computer-game animation. In work by artists who have spent a lot of time on computers "you'll see a stiffness or a flatness, a lack of richness and depth," Karen Chelini, the director of human resources for Lucas Arts Entertainment, George Lucas's interactive-games maker, told me recently. "With traditional art training, you train the eye to pay attention to body movement. You learn attitude, feeling, expression. The ones who are good are those who as kids couldn't be without their sketchbook."

Many jobs obviously will demand basic computer skills if not sophisticated knowledge. But that doesn't mean that the parents or the teachers of young students need to panic. Joseph Weizenbaum, a professor emeritus of computer science at MIT, told the *San Jose Mercury News* that even at his technology-heavy institution new students can learn all the computer skills they need "in a summer." This seems to hold in the business world, too. Patrick MacLeamy, an executive vice-president of Hellmuth Obata & Kassabaum, the country's largest architecture firm, recently gave me numerous examples to illustrate that computers pose no threat to his company's creative work. Although architecture professors are divided on the value of computerized design tools, in MacLeamy's opinion they generally enhance the process. But he still considers "knowledge of the hands" to be valuable—today's architects just have to develop it in other ways. (His firm's answer is through building models.) Nonetheless, as positive as MacLeamy is about computers, he has found the company's two-week computer training to be sufficient. In fact, when he's hiring, computer skills don't enter into his list of priorities. He looks for a strong character; an ability to speak, write, and comprehend; and a rich education in the history of architecture.

The Schools That Business Built

Newspaper financial sections carry almost daily pronouncements from the computer industry and other businesses about their high-tech hopes for America's schoolchildren. Many of these are joined to philanthropic commitments to helping schools make curriculum changes. This sometimes gets businesspeople involved in schools, where they've begun to understand and work with the many daunting problems that are unrelated to technology. But if business gains too much influence over the curriculum, the schools can become a kind of corporate training center—largely at taxpayer expense.

For more than a decade scholars and government commissions have criticized the increasing professionalization of the college years—frowning at the way traditional liberal arts are being edged out by hot topics of the moment or strictly business-oriented studies. The schools' real job, the technology critic Neil Postman argued in his book *The End of Education* (1995), is to focus on "how to make a life, which is quite different from how to make a living." Some see the arrival of boxes of computer hardware and software in the schools as taking the commercial trend one step further, down into high school and elementary grades. "Should you be choosing a career in kindergarten?" asks Helen Sloss Luey, a social worker and a former president of San Francisco's Parent Teacher Association. "People need to be trained to learn and change, while education seems to be getting more specific."

Enthusiasm for computer activities is not universally shared by specialists in childhood development. The greatest concern is for the very young.

Indeed it does. The New Technology High School in Napa (the school where a computer sits on every student's desk) was started by the school district and a consortium of more than forty businesses. "We want to be the school that business built," Robert Nolan, a founder of the school, told me last fall. "We wanted to create an environment that mimicked what exists in the high-tech business world." Increasingly, Nolan explained, business leaders want to hire people specifically trained in the skill they need. One of Nolan's partners, Ted Fujimoto, of the Landmark Consulting Group, told me that instead of just asking the business community for financial support, the school will now undertake a trade: in return for donating funds, businesses can specify what kinds of employees they want—"a two-way street." Sometimes the traffic is a bit heavy in one direction. In January, *The New York Times* published a lengthy education supplement describing numerous examples of how business is increasingly dominating school software and other curriculum materials, and not always toward purely educational goals.

People who like the idea that their taxes go to computer training might be surprised at what a poor investment it can be. Larry Cuban, the Stanford education professor, writes that changes in the classroom for which business lobbies rarely hold long-term value. Rather, they're often guided by labor-market needs that turn out to be transitory; when the economy shifts, workers are left unprepared for new jobs. In the economy as a whole, according to a recent story in *The New York Times*, performance trends in our schools have shown virtually no link to the rises and falls in the nation's measures of productivity and growth. This is one reason that school traditionalists push for broad liberal-arts curricula, which they feel develop students' values and intellect, instead of focusing on today's idea about what tomorrow's jobs will be.

High-tech proponents argue that the best education software does develop flexible business intellects. In the *Business Week* story on computer games, for example, academics and professionals expressed amazement at the speed, savvy, and facility that young computer jocks sometimes demonstrate. Several pointed in particular to computer simulations, which some business leaders believe are becoming increasingly important in fields ranging from engineering, manufacturing, and troubleshooting to the tracking of economic activity and geopolitical risk. The best of these simulations may be valuable, albeit for strengthening one form of thinking. But the average simulation program may be of questionable relevance.

Sherry Turkle, the sociology professor at MIT, has studied youngsters using computers for more than twenty years. In her book *Life on the Screen: Identity in the Age of the Internet* (1995) she described a disturbing experience with a simulation game called SimLife. After she sat down with a thirteen-year-old named Tim, she was stunned at the way

Tim can keep playing even when he has no idea what is driving events. For example, when his sea urchins become extinct, I ask him why.

Tim: "I don't know, it's just something that happens."

ST: "Do you know how to find out why it happened?"

Tim: "No."

ST: "Do you mind that you can't tell why?"

Tim: "No. I don't let things like that bother me. It's not what's important."

Anecdotes like this lead some educators to worry that as children concentrate on how to manipulate software instead of on the subject at hand, learning can diminish rather than grow. Simulations, for example, are built on hidden assumptions, many of which are oversimplified if not highly questionable. All too often, Turkle wrote recently in *The American Prospect,* "experiences with simulations do not open up questions but close them down." Turkle's concern is that software of this sort fosters passivity, ultimately dulling people's sense of what they can change in the world. There's a tendency, Turkle told me, "to take things at 'interface' value." Indeed, after mastering SimCity, a popular game about urban planning, a tenth-grade girl boasted to Turkle that she'd learned the following rule: "Raising taxes always leads to riots."

The business community also offers tangible financial support, usually by donating equipment. Welcome as this is, it can foster a high-tech habit. Once a school's computer system is set up, the companies often drop their support. This saddles the school with heavy long-term responsibilities: maintenance of the computer network and the need for constant software upgrades and constant teacher training—the full burden of which can cost far more than the initial hardware and software combined. Schools must then look for handouts from other companies, enter the grant-seeking game, or delicately go begging in their own communi-

ties. "We can go to the well only so often," Toni-Sue Passantino, the principal of the Bayside Middle School, in San Mateo, California, told me recently. Last year Bayside let a group of seventh- and eighth-graders spend eighteen months and countless hours creating a rudimentary virtual-reality program, with the support of several high-tech firms. The companies' support ended after that period, however—creating a financial speed bump of a kind that the Rand Corporation noted in a report to the Clinton Administration as a common obstacle.

School administrators may be outwardly excited about computerized instruction, but they're also shrewdly aware of these financial challenges. In March of last year, for instance, when California launched its highly promoted "NetDay '96" (a campaign to wire 12,000 California schools to the Internet in one day), school participation was far below expectations, even in technology-conscious San Francisco. In the city papers school officials wondered how they were supposed to support an Internet program when they didn't even have the money to repair crumbling buildings, install electrical outlets, and hire the dozens of new teachers recently required so as to reduce class size.

One way around the donation maze is to simplify: use inexpensive, basic software and hardware, much of which is available through recycling programs. Such frugality can offer real value in the elementary grades, especially since basic word-processing tools are most helpful to children just learning to write. Yet schools, like the rest of us, can't resist the latest toys. "A lot of people will spend all their money on fancy new equipment that can do great things, and sometimes it just gets used for typing classes," Ray Porter, a computer resource teacher for the San Francisco schools, told me recently. "Parents, school boards, and the reporters want to see only razzle-dazzle state-of-the-art."

Internet Isolation

It is hard to visit a high-tech school without being led by a teacher into a room where students are communicating with people hundreds or thousands of miles away—over the Internet or sometimes through video-conferencing systems (two-way TV sets that broadcast live from each room). Video conferences, although fun, are an expensive way to create classroom thrills. But the Internet, when used carefully, offers exciting academic prospects—most dependably, once again, for older students. In one case schools in different states have tracked bird migrations and then posted their findings on the World Wide Web, using it as their own national notebook. In San Francisco eighth-grade economics students have E-mailed Chinese and Japanese businessmen to fulfill an assignment on what it would take to build an industrial plant overseas. Schools frequently use the Web to publish student writing. While thousands of self-published materials like these have turned the Web into a worldwide vanity press, the network sometimes gives young writers their first real audience.

The free nature of Internet information also means that students are confronted with chaos, and real dangers. "The Net's

Reducing class size, improving teachers' salaries, expanding hours of instruction—all were considered less important than giving kids computers.

beauty is that it's uncontrolled," Stephen Kerr, a professor at the College of Education at the University of Washington and the editor of *Technology in the Future of Schooling* (1996), told me. "It's information by anyone, for anyone. There's racist stuff, bigoted, hate-group stuff, filled with paranoia; bomb recipes; how to engage in various kinds of crimes, electronic and otherwise; scams and swindles. It's all there. It's all available." Older students may be sophisticated enough to separate the Net's good food from its poisons, but even the savvy can be misled. On almost any subject the Net offers a plethora of seemingly sound "research." But under close inspection much of it proves to be ill informed, or just superficial. "That's the antithesis of what classroom kids should be exposed to," Kerr said.

This makes traditionalists emphasize the enduring value of printed books, vetted as most are by editing. In many schools, however, libraries are fairly limited. I now volunteer at a San Francisco high school where the library shelves are so bare that I can see how the Internet's ever-growing number of research documents, with all their shortcomings, can sometimes be a blessing.

Even computer enthusiasts give the Net tepid reviews. "Most of the content on the Net is total garbage," Esther Dyson acknowledges. "But if you find one good thing you can use it a million times." Kerr believes that Dyson is being unrealistic. "If you find a useful site one day, it may not be there the next day, or the information is different. Teachers are being asked to jump in and figure

out if what they find on the Net is worthwhile. They don't have the skill or time to do that." Especially when students rely on the Internet's much-vaunted search software. Although these tools deliver hundreds or thousands of sources within seconds, students may not realize that search engines, and the Net itself, miss important information all the time.

"We need *less* surfing in the schools, not more," David Gelernter, a professor of computer science at Yale, wrote last year in *The Weekly Standard*. "Couldn't we teach them to use what they've got before favoring them with three orders of magnitude *more*?" In my conversations with Larry Cuban, of Stanford, he argued, "Schooling is not about information. It's getting kids to think about information. It's about understanding and knowledge and wisdom."

It may be that youngsters' growing fascination with the Internet and other ways to use computers will distract from yet another of Clinton's education priorities: to build up the reading skills of American children. Sherry Dingman, an assistant professor of psychology at Marist College, in Poughkeepsie, New York, who is optimistic about many computer applications, believes that if children start using computers before they have a broad foundation in reading from books, they will be cheated out of opportunities to develop imagination. "If we think we're going to take kids who haven't been read to, and fix it by sitting them in front of a computer, we're fooling ourselves," Dingman told me not long ago. This doesn't mean that teachers or parents should resort to books on CD-ROM, which Dingman considers "a great waste of time," stuffing children's minds with "canned" images instead of stimulating youngsters to create their own. "Computers are lollipops that rot your teeth" is how Marilyn Darch, an English teacher at Poly High School, in Long Beach, California, put it in *Silicon Snake Oil*. "The kids love them. But once they get hooked. . . . It makes reading a book seem tedious. Books don't have sound effects, and their brains have to do all the work."

Computer advocates like to point out that the Internet allows for all kinds of intellectual challenges—especially when students use E-mail, or post notes in "newsgroup" discussions, to correspond with accomplished experts. Such experts, however, aren't consistently available. When they are, online "conversations" generally take place when correspondents are sitting alone, and the dialogue lacks the unpredictability and richness that occur in face-to-face discussions. In fact, when youngsters are put into groups for the "collaborative" learning that computer defenders celebrate, realistically only one child sits at the keyboard at a time. (During my school visits children tended to act quite possessive about the mouse and the keyboard, resulting in frustration and noisy disputes more often than collaboration.) In combination these constraints lead to yet another of the childhood developmentalists' concerns—that computers encourage social isolation.

Just a Glamorous Tool

It would be easy to characterize the battle over computers as merely another chapter in the world's oldest story: humanity's natural resistance to change. But that does an injustice to the forces at work in this transformation. This is not just the future versus the past, uncertainty versus nostalgia; it is about encouraging a fundamental shift in personal priorities—a minimizing of the real, physical world in favor of an unreal "virtual" world. It is about teaching youngsters that exploring what's on a two-dimensional screen is more important than playing with real objects, or sitting down to an attentive conversation with a friend, a parent, or a teacher. By extension, it means downplaying the importance of conversation, of careful listening, and of expressing oneself in person with acuity and individuality. In the process, it may also limit the development of children's imaginations.

Perhaps this is why Steven Jobs, one of the founders of Apple Computer and a man who claims to have "spearheaded giving away more computer equipment to schools than anybody else on the planet," has come to a grim conclusion: "What's wrong with education cannot be fixed with technology," he told *Wired* magazine last year. "No amount of technology will make a dent. . . . You're not going to solve the problems by putting all knowledge onto CD-ROMs. We can put a Web site in every school—none of this is bad. It's bad only if it lulls us into thinking we're doing something to solve the problem with education." Jane David, the consultant to Apple, concurs, with a commonly heard caveat. "There are real dangers," she told me, "in looking to technology to be the savior of education. But it won't survive without the technology."

Arguments like David's remind Clifford Stoll of yesteryear's promises about television. He wrote in *Silicon Snake Oil*,

"Sesame Street" . . . has been around for twenty years. Indeed, its idea of making learning relevant to all was as widely promoted in the seventies as the Internet is today.

So where's that demographic wave of creative and brilliant students now entering college? Did kids really need to learn how to watch television? Did we inflate their expectations that learning would always be colorful and fun?

Computer enthusiasts insist that the computer's "interactivity" and multimedia features make this machine far superior to television. Nonetheless, Stoll wrote,

I see a parallel between the goals of "Sesame Street" and those of children's computing. Both are pervasive, expensive and encourage children to sit still. Both display animated cartoons, gaudy numbers and weird, random noises. . . . Both give the sensation that by merely watching a screen, you can acquire information without work and without discipline.

As the technology critic Neil Postman put it to a Harvard electronic-media conference, "I thought that television would be the last great technology that people would go into with their eyes closed. Now you have the computer."

The solution is not to ban computers from classrooms altogether. But it may be to ban federal spending on what is fast becoming an overheated campaign. After all, the private sector, with its constant supply of used computers and the computer industry's vigorous competition for new customers, seems well equipped to handle the situation.

In fact, if schools can impose some limits—on technology donors and on themselves—rather than indulging in a consumer frenzy, most will probably find themselves with more electronic gear than they need. That could free the billions that Clinton wants to devote to technology and make it available for impoverished fundamentals: teaching solid skills in reading, thinking, listening, and talking; organizing inventive field trips and other rich hands-on experiences, and, of course, building up the nation's core of knowledgeable, inspiring teachers. These notions are considerably less glamorous than computers are, but their worth is firmly proved through a long history.

Last fall, after the school administrators in Mansfield, Massachusetts, had eliminated proposed art, music, and physical-education positions in favor of buying computers, Michael Bellino, an electrical engineer at Boston University's Center for Space Physics, appeared before the Massachusetts Board of Education to protest. "The purpose of the schools [is] to, as one teacher argues, 'Teach carpentry, not hammer,'" he testified. "We need to teach the whys and ways of the world. Tools come and tools go. Teaching our children tools limits their knowledge to these tools and hence limits their futures."

 Article Review Form at end of book.

What is the "New World Economic Order" envisioned by Neill?
How do computers in the schools contribute to its development?

Computers, Thinking, and Schools in the "New World Economic Order"

Monty Neill

Capitalism is the first productive system where the children of the exploited are disciplined and educated in institutions organized by the ruling class.

—Mariarosa Dalla Costa and Selma James

Two primary reasons are given for plugging schools into the National Information Infrastructure (NII; called "the information superhighway"). Plugging-in is required to prepare students to be highly skilled, highly paid workers in the economy of the future; and it is essential for reforming schools into institutions that will produce students who can think and solve problems.

The "double helix" of high-skill jobs and cognitively complex schooling is presented as liberatory (Berryman and Bailey 1992). But the use of computerization toward a distinctly nonliberatory end is the more likely consequence of the twinning of school and work in the emerging world capitalist economy.

Computers and the Jobs of the Future

Both conservatives and liberals argue that for the U.S. to "be number 1" in the world economy a more educated working class is needed, one that works harder *and* smarter. The claim is that then corporations will create jobs that utilize the workers' skills. These high-skill workers will be more productive than others and will therefore earn high wages. The alternative, they warn, is low skills and low wages. Schools must therefore educate "all" students to "world-class standards" so that the corporations will be competitive.

This argument is made in the report *America's Choice* by the National Center on Education and the Economy (NCEE 1990), probably the most influential piece on U.S. education since *A Nation at Risk* (fraudulently) maintained that falling school quality endangered national security. The NCEE view can be found in legislation, particularly the recently enacted Goals 2000 school reform bill; in numerous corporate education reform proposals (e.g., California Business Roundtable 1994); and various books and government reports (e.g., Carnevale and Porro 1994). It has become virtually unquestioned conventional wisdom.

The most obvious thing about this claim is that it presumes an uncontrollable and inevitable economy to which "we" must adapt. It demands that educators accept, not challenge—never mind reconstruct—the economy.

Yet two points about the emerging economy suggest that "we" should not accept it. First, continual lowering of wages is already fact and not likely to turn around; second, most new hires are not likely to be doing high-skill work. For U.S. workers, real wages have been declining nearly 1 percent per year for two decades, while the dispersion of the wage—the gap between high- and low-wage work—has simultaneously widened.

As Midnight Notes (1992) argues, this calculated intent of the capitalist system over the past twenty years to reduce working-class power and income around the globe has had substantial success. Its political and technical ability to move products and services rapidly around the world has weakened the capacity of working people to band together at the national level to push up or even maintain wages. Since the competition for jobs cannot be contained by national borders, wages are dropping toward the lowest levels among the competitors, even for many high-skill jobs such as computer programmer. This push is, if anything, intensifying. The North American Free Trade Agreement, for example, is organized as a one-way ratchet to continue the lowering of wages in Mexico, Canada, and the U.S. (Calvert and Kuehn 1993), to intensify what Kuehn terms "the race to the bottom." There is certainly no reason to believe that the capitalist system will create a worldwide high-wage system or that the U.S. will remain immune from wages within its borders falling to "world-class standards."

The fallacy that most jobs will be high-skill is also widely accepted. Yet even strong proponents of the claim, such as Bailey (1991), acknowledge that most new hires for at least a decade will be filling old slots that do not require the knowledge and skills that proponents of the "high-skills" argument point to. Moreover, the labor market fore-casts that project growth in the U.S. in medium- or high-skill jobs do not consider changes in the world economy that are dispersing skilled employment more widely while driving down wages. At most, the number of middle-level-skill jobs will grow slightly in the coming decade.

Even school reformers whose first interest is not in creating workers to serve the economy nonetheless buttress their reform proposals by pointing to the presumed high-skill information economy. But what are the implications of all this for schools? Lower wages coupled with continuous attacks on public services and increased class and race stratification—the actually existing U.S. conditions—strongly suggest continuation of the "savage inequalities" so eloquently described by Jonathan Kozol (1991): sharp class gradations with immiseration for many.

The way computers and paraphernalia have been distributed already indicates this (Piller 1992; Pearlman 1994; Ramirez and Bell 1994; SEDLetter 1993). Not only are rich kids more likely to have computers at school, but their schools' machines are more apt to be up to date, drive more sophisticated software, and be connected to the Internet. Most schools are barely wired—most classrooms don't have telephone jacks or the electric wiring to run more than a couple of computers. The less money a school or school district has, the less likely it will be able to ride on the information superhighway. Presuming that funding can be found for these essentials, schools still must raise money to stay on line and educate teachers in technology use: over a five-year period, the hardware is only 18 percent of the cost of using technology (Van Horn 1994).

Telecommunications corporations are eager to exploit the school market, sometimes offering to wire schools in exchange for controlling the wires that will hook the schools to the Internet and thus to corporate coffers (Coile 1994; Einstein 1994). Poor schools in particular are prey for technology profiteers such as Whittle Communications' now-defunct Channel One. Channel One provided satellite dishes, VCRs, and TV monitors to schools that agreed to force students to watch a ten-minute daily "newscast" that included two minutes of ads. Schools in poor neighborhoods or those with the lowest per student annual spending were respectively two or six times more likely to have Channel One than were schools with the wealthiest students or highest per student spending (Morgan 1993).

Health and safety issues of computer use are also most stark for poor schools. Children are more susceptible to radiation, including that from computers, and are also at risk for the same muscular and eye strains as adults (Miller 1992). Schools that can barely afford computers are least likely to shield them or purchase ergonomically correct furniture.

In sum, the savage inequalities of the past will extend into the wired savagery of the future. There is neither empirical nor theoretical reason to believe this scenario will change for the better so long as the capitalist system continues. In general, students from low-wage families and communities need more resources if they are to catch up in the kinds of skills (technical, academic, and cultural) sought for in high-wage occupations—yet they get substantially less. Why expect the capitalist system and its government to invest extra funds to develop low-income children into sophisticated problem-solving workers if the jobs don't and won't exist?

In any event, wherever the system does invest in schooling, its purpose is to intensify schoolwork by children and to prepare them for future work—while presenting this as in the students' interest. The call for students to work harder in school is as ubiquitous as the call for schools to produce high-skill workers—and usually comes from the same sources.

Computerization of schools will not contribute to "high wages" or "good jobs." The U.S. class hierarchy will not be ameliorated by computerization, but will be intensified. Indeed, computers have been a fundamental weapon in the capitalist war against the working class over the past two decades. If computer knowledge is required in the economy, it is not because of any capitalist desire for highly paid workers or any great need for highly skilled workers.

Thinking Machines for Thinking Students?

A strong claim is sometimes made that using computers and related high-tech machinery is *necessary* for a change to a mode of schooling that focuses on thinking. For example, Ramirez and Bell (1994) conclude

It is the position of this paper that if systemic school reform in this country is to succeed it will only do so with the application of telecommunications and information technologies at the classroom level with a simultaneous focus on sustained professional development for teachers.

The argument rests on the purported necessity of computers for enabling all students to engage in higher-order thinking activities such as understanding complex ideas, solving real-world problems, and analyzing critically.

There is an irony in this claim. The emphasis on higher-order thinking in schools rests substantially on the foundation of cognitive psychology. As Noble (1989) has shown, cognitive psychology evolved in large part because the U.S. military wanted to create artificial intelligence—but it had no useful understanding of the genuine thing. The military therefore funded extensive research in cognition, research that ended up largely confirming what progressive educators and psychologists had long maintained, that humans learn actively and by constructing and modifying mental models.

The dominant psychological theories in the U.S. have been behaviorist. In the version influencing schooling, humans supposedly learned by passively accumulating isolated bits of information. In time, the bits could be shaped into successively more complex patterns. The impact, however, was that schools presumed students could not think in a given area until they had accumulated enough bits. Those who did not sufficiently grasp the bits were condemned never to do anything interesting in school. This approach still dominates curriculum, instruction, and the ubiquitous standardized tests. Cognitive psychology, however, proposes learning as a fundamentally different process. Recognizing that students think, learn by thinking, and can learn to think better or differently, it calls for a "thinking curriculum" (cf. Resnick 1987).

The irony here is that having constructed cognitive psychology in order to develop "thinking machines," the machines are now presumed indispensable for helping students learn to think. But the very existence of thinking in schools without computers shows clearly that machines are not necessary for a thinking curriculum. The reason schools haven't encouraged thinking is not because they have lacked computers, but because the system did not want thinking workers.

A softer claim for the necessity of computers is that because of the way the economy relies on computerization, only via computers will it provide access to materials and knowledge that will facilitate higher-order thinking in academic areas for many more children. Presumably, the NII will enable access to teachers and learned people, data banks and libraries, analytical tools such as statistical packages, and other software.

Despite the absence of funds, it is claimed that teachers working in poor systems will be able to get this complex operation functioning. However, if teachers had the time, training, and support to do this, they could reorganize their classrooms for inquiry, dialogue, critical thinking, understanding, and problem-solving—with or without computers. They don't succeed for a number of reasons: too many students, lack of resources and knowledge, and standardized tests that militate against thinking. Somehow, though, the computer will be the means to make the instructional leap.

Still, the claim of the value of computers has some persuasive aspects, though with many caveats:

- The tools free up time. For example, because of

calculators, rather than spend time on arithmetical drill, students can spend time on learning mathematical reasoning and problem-solving.

- Access to information is enhanced. In many schools, the library is outdated or inadequate. The cost of some information will cheapen, making it more accessible— assuming that poor schools have the money to get and stay on line. Access, however, says nothing about the nature of the materials available on line. In seeking information, whether on networks or elsewhere, one is limited by one's inquiry framework. Without a strong frame, a student will simply be buried in tons of data. Access to information means little without guidance in learning to use information—which raises questions of whose guidance for what purposes.

- Access to people is expanded. You can use the Internet to dialogue with people all over the planet. (Of course people from all over the planet may now live in your neighborhood.) Computer advocates constantly tout examples of "real" scientists talking with kids from some school, but once millions of students are on line, how many scientists will spend time sorting through hundreds of on-line requests?

- Access to some kinds of computerized tools enable students to work on sophisticated problems rather than more basic and boring ones. Working on more realistic and complex tasks, doing so in collaboration with others, proceeding at one's own pace, even having a real-world use for the results, all can help motivate students. Again,

much of this does not require computers or the NII. Moreover, once the technology becomes old hat, deeper issues of the purpose for schooling will inevitably reappear for students, for whom lack of control often guarantees lack of interest (Herndon 1972).

The important issues are not ones of technology but of politics: will the funding be there? what kinds of guidance to what ends will students receive? who controls the technology? for whom will the computer ultimately be useful? Class relations that are played out in technology implementation are also implicated in technology construction. What is done with tools is not determined so much by those who use the tools as by those who construct them. Thus, the ways in which the makers design technology can largely control the structuring and solution of problems by users, to whom the control by the maker remains invisible (Madaus 1993). Computer use is then falsely promoted as a neutral yet liberatory tool.

Controlling School and Work

The controlling class no more wants problem-solvers and critical thinkers to do most jobs of the future than it did in the past, during the assembly-line era. Computer use in schools *will* fit the economy—not the mythical economy of "high skills and high wages," but the real economy of "the race to the bottom." While following orders, not questioning, being on time, and submitting one's personality to the dictates of the school all prepared workers for jobs in the mass-production era, the school-work form directly fit the actual

jobs for only a relatively few workers. With computerization, however, form can more closely resemble function.

The McDonald's level of familiarity with technology requires no actual knowledge of computers or much thought. Data-entry (with the computer monitoring your speed) and similar work does not require higher-order thinking. Schools will train students to sit in front of computers and do routine work in direct preparation for their jobs. For them, this will be their real-world learning connection.

Use of computers at the technician level sometimes does require decision making, but the parameters are usually specified carefully, meaning that the thinking done is not at the order of making definition but of application. (A look at the actual jobs described by Bailey (1990) or Zuboff (1988) reveals this.) These jobs do require more academic—school-based—knowledge and the ability to apply that knowledge, and the number of these kinds of medium-level-skill jobs probably will increase in the coming decade. Controlling the development and nature of the thinking of those who have limited-problem-solving jobs will be another task of schools.

Data-entry, monitoring, and limited problem-solving will continue to comprise most computer use by the great majority of employees in the U.S., barring an upheaval against the jobs system. Noble's (1991) critique of Zuboff points out that the "intellective" work she glorifies in fact includes two kinds of work that imply a corresponding schooling: one that is scientific and problem-solving and another that is primarily monitoring the process—a difference that "reflects a cavernous hierarchical division of labor." And, Noble adds, the latter is more "about attitudes and disposition than about 'knowledge' or intellectual abilities." The mind is reduced to the hand. For most, schooling, wired or not, is preparation for routine work, same now as it ever was. However, I suspect that though "the more things change" is still operative, there are yet some important changes in the offing. The changes have to do with capitalist control over thinking.

As Noble (1989) explains, behaviorism largely treated thinking as a black box. On the assembly line, it did not matter what, or if, the worker thought, as long as he or she behaved: came to work, did the job, didn't cause trouble. To the extent that thinking was an issue, the concern was how to manipulate the worker into working harder (i.e., to control behavior). Industrial psychology developed as a tool to help organize and ensure the functioning of the productive process. It developed a knowledge base that retains its usefulness for management, because traditional "good worker" characteristics are still those most desired by the bosses (NCEE 1990).

In a system that did not want workers to think too much but needed to control their actions, behaviorist psychology was useful. Thus, corporations, foundations, and government agencies funded research that provided ready tools for shaping schooling and controlling workers.

Cognitive psychology is more useful to today's system, which needs workers to think for the system and to think differently, manipulating abstract symbols. The schools are to provide these skills. Those who use computers to analyze, create, or con-

trol will be few in number but important to the system (Bailey 1991; Reich 1992). They too must be programmed, but with allowance for a greater degree of self-regulation.

The danger of progressive education that expects students to think and problem-solve is that it might get out of control, leading students to "unrealistic expectations" and a command of areas of knowledge useful for attacking the system. But as Dalla Costa and James (1975) note, as long as progressive schooling remains within control, it not only presents no danger, it may be a source of yet greater profits (see also Robins and Webster 1989, 218–25). The question for the owners of capital, then, is how to ensure control of the "thinking" curriculum. Revealingly, much of the proposed school reform that rests on cognitive science as the model for instruction still rests on behaviorism for motivation and discipline.

The plans of the New Standards Project are perhaps most illustrative. (The founders of New Standards are leading cognitive psychologist Lauren Resnick and Marc Tucker, head of the NCEE, which produced *America's Choice*, calling for "high skills and high wages.") New Standards, which has signed up sixteen states in its development program, proposes not only a new curriculum, instructional methods, assessments, and professional development for teachers, but also the use of performance levels and tests to measure student progress toward goals that are substantially about workforce preparation. Nonpromotion and nongraduation are the negative reinforcers to complement the presumably more interesting new curriculum.

So what's new? Surely not the drive for control or the use of behaviorism. What is potentially new are the means of control, the computer itself, and the target of control: thinking. On one level this is already quite visible in the use of the work tool to monitor the pace of the work. In schools, however, the issue is more subtle. For example, the application of computers to real-world problems will teach students how to solve problems on terms amenable to the controllers of the system and will sort out those who are most willing and able to do so. The "less able" will be funneled to less cognitively complex computer work to prepare them for lower-skill jobs (or lack thereof), while the less willing will be driven out.

The determination of "less able" is a matter of assessment. While assessment is a necessary part of learning, it is all too likely that emerging cognitive techniques will simply become a more sophisticated method for sorting students. Much of this may be done via computerized exams, enabling a high degree of standardization to "world-class" levels; currently, the same old tests used for sorting by class, race, and gender are being adapted for computer (FairTest 1992). Down the road, this could entail use of sophisticated means of analyzing everything from problem-solving ability to personality constructs to degrees of willingness to work (Raven 1991). This knowledge is used, however, not to help students but to control them (Robins and Webster 1989).

Moreover, the computer itself will be used to shape the personality. The model is the computer—the malleable, controllable, programmable "smart machine." Part of the information-technology agenda is to learn how better to control the thinking of humans. At the crudest level, schools will try to do what they have always tried to do, shape students into workers, but the more subtle strategy is to make the mind *want* to be computerized. Perhaps the child must be caught at a young enough age so that she is less able to resist effectively.

Thinking is redefined as what computers do or what humans do to interact with computers, eliminating the rest of the mind and body from thinking. Zuboff (1988) explains how paper workers historically used smell, touch, and direct sight on the job, and she understands this as a widely generalized use of intelligence, an intelligence destined to be replaced by more abstract modes, tied to symbols on computer screens. Thus, the alienation of the body, long a trend under capitalism (Midnight Notes 1982), leaps to a new qualitative level as the definition of thinking is reshaped to meet new capitalist needs.

Social alienation also intensifies as humans interact via the computer, a form of interaction virtually stripped of emotional and social cues. Already some hints are emerging that extended replacement of in-person interaction by virtual interaction decreases a person's ability to socialize comfortably with other people when in their physical presence. Programs in which students work collaboratively on computer projects will ameliorate this tendency, but the students will still be learning "skills" needed to desocialize themselves. Privatization of schooling will further desocialization because it will increasingly allow schooling at home; contact with others will be only via the wire. (Michigan State has already awarded "charter school" status, and thus funding, to a "school" that is basically an electronic hookup among home-schoolers; the "school" is organized around "Christian" fundamentalist ideology (Walsh 1994)).

In inducing physical and social isolation, the computer is the extension of the "white man." Devoid of emotion, disconnected from the body (except during a *work*out), nonnurturing and unmusical, the type of the "white man" excludes all the human traits capitalism has attached to women and people of color (particularly Africans). I am not talking genetics but about the historical hierarchical division of labor that associates human qualities with the work one is forced to do and then calculatedly reproduces those qualities in people in order to force them to do the work (James 1975). The "white man"—really, *bourgeois*—qualities are now to be extrapolated and intensified, abstracted into the computer and then used to school the child into being computerlike.

Complex problem-solving can itself be a form of mindlessness. The language of school reform pays some attention to the issue of "habits of mind." On the one side, it suggests that students learn to think about their thinking, learn not to just accept but to probe, question, challenge. Well and good if it happens, but it is more likely that "habits of mind"—that is, "critical thinking"—will be confined to areas defined and controlled by the system.

The computer thus will be used to control how one learns to think in order to subsequently control how one thinks. The trajectory of the capitalist use of computers goes from constructing cognitive science for planning artificial intelligence to using artificial intelligence to control thinking as defined through cognitive science. Salomon, Perkins, and Globerson (1991) argue that use of intelligent technologies will make humans themselves more intelligent, provided, however, that these advances are "cultivated through the appropriate design of technologies and their cultural surrounds." The definitions of intelligence, the uses to which intelligence will be put, who is to be made more intelligent and how, and the questions of purpose, design, and control are deferred for "people of different expertise"—academicians all—to debate and plan.

The idea that the capitalist system wants a good many critical thinkers is simply absurd—it can only spell trouble unless the thinkers are thinking for, not against, the boss. Thus the point is to produce the human as puzzle-solver, not really as critical thinker. Puzzles can be entertaining, challenging, require lots of thought, and yet be substantively mindless. The mind is thus habituated to thinking only in limited, even if complex, ways.

The beauty of the computer is not simply the speed with which it computes, nor even all the troublesome work-resistant workers it can replace, but that it can simultaneously powerfully shape the mind and the personality. Thus, if *successful*, computerization will enable the production of the human as computer.

The world has for centuries been dominated by capital, with its exploitation of a hierarchy of labor power starting with the unwaged (Dalla Costa and James 1975) and interwoven with factors of gender and race. While working-class resistance has pushed the capitalist system to crisis, the working class has not resolved the crisis in its favor (Midnight Notes 1992). Now, as capitalism appears on the advance and recomposes the working class—while incorporating all its old forms, from slavery on—we see the spread of fantastical illusions, from fundamentalist religion to computers, as liberation from the miseries of the world. More mundanely, the use of computers in schools is presented as opening up the possibility of schooling as exciting, powerful learning that leads to "better jobs." Yet the excitement and power will not be for the many—unless the many change society, its economy, politics, and social relations, and how it educates its children.

Only egalitarian, collective, working-class power can assure that any particular technology will be used for its benefit—if it should be used at all. Liberation is not a matter of technology but of social relations. A first step in the transformation of social relations is to refuse the inevitability of the economy.

References

Bailey, Thomas. 1990. "Jobs of the Future and the Skills They Will Require: New Thinking on an Old Debate." *American Educator* 14 (1).

———. 1991. "Jobs of the Future and the Education They Will Require: Evidence from Occupational Forecasts." *Educational Researcher* 20 (2).

Berryman, Sue E., and Thomas R. Bailey. 1992. *The Double Helix of Education and the Economy.* New York: Institute on Education and the Economy, Teachers College, Columbia University.

California Business Roundtable. 1994. *Mobilizing for Competitiveness: Linking Education and Training to Jobs.* San Francisco: CBR.

Calvert, John, and Keuhn, Larry. 1993. *Pandora's Box: Corporate Power, Free Trade, and Canadian Education.* Toronto: Our Schools/Our Selves Education Foundation.

Carnevale, Anthony P., and Jeffrey D. Porro. 1994. *Quality Education: School Reform for the New American Economy.* Washington: Office of Educational Research and Improvement, U.S. Department of Education.

Coile, Zachary. 1994. "'Free' Computer Revolution Now Has a Price Tag." *San Francisco Examiner* (January 30).

Dalla Costa, Mariarosa, and Selma, James. 1975. *The Power of Women and the Subversion of the Community.* 3d ed. Bristol, England: Falling Wall.

Einstein, David. 1994. "Pac Bell to Wire State's Schools for High Tech." *San Francisco Chronicle* (February 19).

FairTest. 1992. *Computerized Testing: More Questions than Answers.* Cambridge, Mass.: FairTest.

Herndon, James. 1972. *How to Survive in Your Native Land.* New York: Bantam.

James, Selma. 1975. *Race, Sex, and Class.* Bristol, England: Falling Wall.

Keuhn, Larry. 1994. "NAFTA and the Future of Education." Paper for the annual conference of the National Coalition of Education Activists (August). Portland, Oreg.

Kozol, Jonathan. 1991. *Savage Inequalities: Children in America's Schools.* New York: Crown.

Madaus, George. 1993. "A National Testing System: Manna from Above? An Historical/Technological Perspective." *Educational Assessment* 1 (1).

Miller, Norma L. 1992. "Are Computers Dangerous to Our Children's Health?" *PTA Today* (April).

Midnight Notes. 1982. "Mormons in Space." *Computer State Notes.* Boston: Midnight Notes.

———. 1992. *Midnight Oil.* New York: Autonomedia.

Morgan, Michael. 1993. "Channel One in the Public Schools: Widening the Gap." A research report prepared for UNPLUG. Amherst, Mass.: Author.

National Center on Education and the Economy (NCEE). 1990. *America's Choice: High Skills or Low Wages!* Rochester, N.Y.: NCEE.

The New Standards Project. 1992. *A Proposal.* Pittsburgh: Learning Research and Development Center & National Center on Education and the Economy.

Noble, Douglas D. 1989. "Mental Material: The Militarization of Learning and Intelligence in U.S. Education." In *Cyborg Worlds.* Edited by Les Levidow and Kevin Robins. London: Free Association.

———. 1991. "In the Cage with the Smart Machine." *Science as Culture* 10.

Pearlman, Robert. 1994. "Can K–12 Education Drive on the Information Highway?" *Education Week* (May 25).

Piller, Charles. 1992. "Separate Realities." *Macworld* (September).

Ramirez, Rafael, and Rosemary Bell. 1994. *Byting Back: Policies to Support the Use of Technology in Education.* Oak Brook, Ill.: North Central Regional Educational Laboratory.

Raven, John. 1991. *The Tragic Illusion: Educational Testing.* Unionville, N.Y.: Trillium.

Reich, Robert B. 1992. *The Work of Nations.* New York: Vintage.

Resnick, Lauren P. 1987. *Education and Learning to Think.* Washington: National Academy Press.

Robins, Kevin, and Frank Webster. 1989. *The Technical Fix: Education, Computers, and Industry.* New York: St. Martin's.

Salomon, Gavriel, David N. Perkins, and Tamar Globerson. 1991. "Partners in Cognition: Extending Human Intelligence with Intelligent Technologies." *Educational Researcher* 20 (3).

SEDLetter. 1993. "Cyberschooling: Fiber Optic Vision? Or Virtual Reality?" *Southwest Educational Development Laboratory Newsletter* 6 (1).

Van Horn, Royal. 1994. "Building High Tech Schools." *Phi Delta Kappan* (September).

Walsh, Mark. 1994. "Charter School Opponents Taking Cases to Court." *Education Week* (October 7).

Zuboff, Shoshana. 1988. *In the Age of the Smart Machine: the Future of Work and Power.* New York: Basic Books.

 Article Review Form at end of book.

Would you want to attend or teach in one of these schools? Are we likely to see more of them in the future?

Where Computers Do Work

In these six classrooms, PCs promote learning, excite students and free up teachers to teach.

Betsy Wagner, Stephen Gregory, Richard Bierck, Missy Daniel and Jonathan Sapers

Ever since Thomas Edison declared that his motion picture camera would revolutionize education, Americans have hoped the latest gizmo would inspire students to soar. Radio. Filmstrips. Television.

And, for more than a dozen years, computers. High-tech businesses will rake in some $4 billion this year from elementary, middle and high schools on instructional technology, twice as much as five years ago. President Clinton has proposed an additional $2 billion in federal money so that "every 12-year-old can log on to the Internet." Countless parents and private groups pour sweat equity and millions of dollars into bringing wires and computer wares into schools.

So where's the payoff? Few teachers are trained to use computers or to navigate the Internet. School boards don't know what to look for. Good software is rare. And nobody seems to have enough time to think up the best ways to harness the undeniable potential of these powerful machines.

Make that almost nobody. *U.S. News* has found six schools with lessons to teach all of us about computer technology. The most important is that technology is not magic. Money matters far less than the dedication and innovative spirit of the teachers in these classrooms.

Lesson 1

It's not the PCs That Matter. It's How They're Used

Thurgood Marshall High School, San Francisco

As computers go, the PCs in Dennis Frezzo's classroom in San Francisco's Thurgood Marshall Academic High School are Paleolithic. Some are 286 machines nearly as old as the 50 or so sophomores and juniors in Frezzo's robotics class. The creaky Compaq, Wyse and IBM systems, many of them well-intentioned castoffs from local banking and accounting firms, help teach the students how to program robots that are assembled from Lego blocks. And they do just fine.

"They let me pose very real electrical and mechanical prob-

lems," says Frezzo, who keeps track of time with a stopwatch slung round his neck. "If the students type in the wrong computer code, their robot does some stupid thing and they begin to see the logic in programming."

Getting with the program. Students first learn the rudiments of Lego Logo, a robotics language that orders robots to perform such functions as rotating and positioning a mechanical arm and picking up and dropping objects. Then Frezzo unleashes his charges to devise, assemble and program their creations. The students start out on paper, then hunker down in front of a computer to see if their laborious programming works.

Sometimes it doesn't, as 15-year-old Omar Khaliq discovers when his group's robot arm, instead of stopping as it was supposed to do to pick up a Lego block, overshoots it by several inches. As his group's code writer, Omar has to go back into the program so that the arm, tethered to the computer through a cable, will move for precisely 3.5 seconds. It takes him 30 minutes of trial and error, but Omar doesn't mind. "It was interesting to figure out," says the young engineer, whose test scores were mediocre at the beginning of the year. Now Omar is among the top programmers in his class.

Raphael Crawford-Marks, 16, finds Frezzo's class far more engaging than the basic programming course in Pascal he took last year. "We get to figure out how to use the computer to run something that affects the real world," says the sophomore, whose short blond locks sport a healthy splash of green. "It's a lot more satisfying to get a robot to work than to make the computer spit back pictures of little spaceships blowing up space aliens."

Marshall opened only three years ago, the result of a 1983 federal court consent decree requiring San Francisco schools to offer minority students greater educational opportunities. The student body is 21 percent Hispanic, 25 percent black and 38 percent Asian, none with significant prior exposure to math or science.

To Omar, the school's emphasis on computer-aided education is a boon to his personal future. "This world is going to be high tech, so it's better we know [computers] now," says the lanky teen as he rummages through a box of wires and robot parts.

Frezzo thinks too many educators are overly eager to use computers. "Computers have to be critically applied," he says. "We can't just put students in front of computers and say, 'OK, learn.'"

Lesson 2
Let Students Learn at Their Own Pace

Langley High School, Pittsburgh

Ninth grader William Kirchner regards the algebra problem on the glowing screen, punches in numbers and hesitates when they turn to italics—the signal that he did something wrong. The software posts a suggestion, and William glides toward the solution. "I like the computer," he says, calling up the next problem. "You don't always have to have a teacher."

But teacher Maura Moran is there if needed. A girl across the room is stumped. If she makes 50 cents for each snow cone she sells but has to pay a friend $50 to use his snow-cone machine, how does she calculate the profit on 200 snow cones? After two suggestions and a pat on the back from Moran, the student makes x the number of snow cones sold and figures out that her profit is equal to $.50x - \$50$. Moran walks away, and the now smiling student resumes her work.

The air fairly hums with high-intensity concentration. Some of the students mutter to themselves as they work; others talk at the screen, which offers neither color nor sound. All 22 students are doing algebra at their own speed, moving to more advanced problems as they master the skills. They can always call on Moran, who wanders from student to student.

Here math is no abstraction. Teachers instruct all ninth and 10th graders three days a week in such real-world problems as calculating wages, evaluating car-rental rates and comparing cellular phone plans. The other two days they do similar work on computers that track individual progress. The key is Intelligent Computer Tutor, software developed at Carnegie Mellon University that blends research into the psychology of learning with programming that lets the computer correct and coach at any point during the problem-solving process.

Clear thinkers. First tried in 1992, the program now is standard for all Langley first-year algebra and geometry classes and has spread to seven other Pittsburgh-area schools. In a Carnegie Mellon study covering school years 1993–94 and 1994–95, Langley algebra students scored about twice as high in problem-solving skills and ability to work with graphs, charts and equations as their traditionally taught schoolmates did. They also did 15 percent better on math questions from the Scholastic Assessment Test. The suburban students did just as well.

Teachers credit the independence fostered by the software, which doesn't penalize students for taking risks. Rather, it guides them, picks up weaknesses and helps students overcome them by posing new problems. "It knows what I have to work harder on," says Diane Schwenninger, a ninth grader at Hampton High School Pittsburgh's suburbs.

Students say they'd much rather calculate the life span of a threatened rain forest or how many trips a medevac helicopter can make on a set budget than slog through the contrived problems that haunt traditional textbooks. Hampton teacher Kathy Dickensheets rolls her eyes: "Those two trains that were always headed toward each other: Did we ever just let them crash?"

Lesson 3
E-Mail Can Be More Than Chatter

Windsor High School, Windsor, Conn.

Arms control diplomats from Russia generally don't wear flannel shirts, baseball hats and sneakers during work hours.

They probably don't bring Ring Dings and pretzels to international summits. But these six "Russian" weapons experts are role-playing students in a Global Education class at Windsor High. Since they conduct negotiations via modem, appearance and eating habits hardly matter.

On this rainy autumn afternoon, the six seniors huddle near their classroom windows in front of one of four PCs their teacher has begged from the school or snared through a grant. The students and their classmates are taking part in the University of Connecticut's CPIN program, for Connecticut Project in International Negotiation.

CPIN is a high-tech version of the Model United Nations programs, which bring high school students to spots all over the country to form mock committees and debate global issues. Each CPIN class adopts the identity of a different country. Over a six-week span, the teams discuss international arms control, the environment, drug trafficking and human rights by exchanging thousands of E-mail messages posted each day and in eight online chats that take place in real time after school. Before the students even sit down at the keyboards, they scour newspapers, magazines, encyclopedias—and, of course, the Internet—for data that support their country's position and undermine their opponent's.

As the students try to figure out the best way to get what they want, they begin to think the way diplomats do, sorting through the issues and reducing them to a manageable few. "I get the feeling we'll be doing a lot of damage control," says 17-year-old Jamie Durning as he burrows into a heap of background material about nuclear weapons, the specific topic of today's after-school summit on the broad question of arms control. Before they log on, the "Russians" settle on two main goals for today's agenda: to tell the world their country supports the principle of disarmament and to sweet-talk the United States into an alliance. They hope that an agreement will enhance both their stability and their global profile.

Keeping cool. Things don't go according to plan. Within the first 20 minutes, America proposes to tie each country's arms expenditures to a percentage of its gross national product. Such a limit, argue the U.S. delegates, would help nations conserve funds for "fundamental social needs." Among themselves, the Russians explode. The system unfairly favors America, they complain. But like good ambassadors, they hide their anger behind a dispassionate reply: "If cooperation is to be accomplished," reads their reply on the screen, "such self-interest must be avoided."

Making dry subjects absorbing and letting students learn by doing helps ensure the lessons stick. With Windsor High School's Global Education class a year behind him, University of Connecticut freshman Matt Wininger readily recalls the simulation in which he and his French arms control team united with China, figuring that "with 1.2 billion people on our side, we'd be stronger." The move brought condemnation from France's own human-rights team—and sanctions from CPIN's director, a University of Connecticut associate professor who broke up the union because he believed France would never actually pursue such a tactic. "We learned the phrase 'cause and effect,'" says Matt. "We didn't think the whole world would turn against us just because we allied ourselves with China. It was a gamble and we lost."

As they learn the unruly ways of the real world, Windsor students also get a hefty lesson in computers, which they rarely see in other classes. By the end of the six weeks, they know how to log on to the simulation server, send text files and conduct E-mail dialogues. Some even master the elusive art of finding useful information on the Internet. "At first computers feel intimidating," says senior Chris Ferrero. "But part of me realizes that this is the wave of the future. So latch on to it now or get left behind."

Lesson 4
Technology Can Help Special Kids, Too

Harvard Kent School, Charlestown, Mass.

Classmates Matthew Leung, 9, and Guerson Vincent, 11, have a tough time holding a No. 2 pencil or writing a legible sentence and get frustrated when they try to read their own writing or a book. It's understandable, since these are boys with Down's syndrome.

But settled in front of a Macintosh in Room 201 of the Harvard Kent School, a mouse at hand and teacher Jack McCauley, 33, hovering nearby, they happily take turns "reading" a CD-ROM version of Mercer Mayer's book *Just Grandma and Me*. They look at the pages on the screen while an animated female voice narrates, and turn to the next page by using the mouse to click on an arrow. With a program called My Words, they can retrieve familiar words from a vocabulary list and print out sentences using them—

in large, easy-to-read type. Or they can draw and paint on-screen with Kid Pix software.

This classroom is filled with children who have two or more disabilities—cerebral palsy, Down's syndrome, autism and severely impaired vision are just a few of them—and who generally cannot keep up with their peers. The computer helps them pick up academic skills—reading, writing, counting.

But just as important, says McCauley, it functions as "a vehicle for inclusion." Because his students use *WiggleWorks*, the same book on CD-ROM from Scholastic Inc. as Harvard Kent's regular classes use, the technology stamps them "as kids who can learn, as part of the community," says McCauley.

Children with multiple disabilities learn better, says McCauley, if each one gets a personally tailored education plan that appeals to as many senses as possible. Computer programs offer visual and sound cues and can be customized almost infinitely, from expanding the on-screen type to inserting photos of the children into a story. From the pace of voiceovers and spoken directions to the mouse clicks required to execute a command, timing, volume, speech and speed all can be varied. The computer, says McCauley, "has galvanized this population. It encourages exploration, because you can't make a mistake."

His students' growing self-confidence underscores his claim. When Matt clicks on the mouse and greets the image that appears on the screen with a triumphant thumbs up, it's as though he has just walked through a door he has learned to open. This year Guerson's social skills are strong enough to enable him to navigate the building on his own with a hall pass just like any other kid, and, according to McCauley, technology is the catalyst. "It promotes independence," he says, "so when Guerson can work confidently by himself at the computer, then I can say, 'Let's try this, too.'"

The entire neighborhood becomes a classroom. When McCauley's students go on a "community experience" outing to a nearby store, they use Apple's Quicktake camera to snap pictures of themselves and the people they meet, upload the digitized images and print them out on the classroom's one Macintosh. "It helps me bring the world to them," says McCauley. Technology means immediacy, and for these students, "immediacy is vital. This is real-time teaching; the learning experience becomes specifically about them and what they are doing, not Dick and Jane."

Lesson 5
Unleash Teachers to Be Creative

North East High School, North East, MD.

It's a warm October afternoon in this sleepy river town at the northern tip of the Chesapeake Bay. On the second floor of the local high school, girls in Don Shaffer's sophomore biology class shed their white cheerleader jackets and boys roll up their shirt sleeves. They have exactly seven minutes to feed and water the classroom plants, insects and rodents. As soon as the last mouse is secured in its tiny cage, the students scurry to form groups around seven computers to work with digital oysters.

Most of the school's students make little use of computers Shaffer's class is at them almost daily, creating complex models of global warming, poring over spreadsheets, entering data from field trips to a local stream. Last year, the students worked on eight-year-old Apple IIGS machines and four-year-old Macintosh LC II's in the computer lab next door. Now they use new Power Macs, thanks to two recent grants.

The students fire up the Chesapeake Bay Oyster, a CD-ROM program Shaffer wrote because his school couldn't afford to buy software. The students become scientists analyzing the decline in the bay's adult oysters. It is no hypothetical problem. While the bay is full of young oysters, it has yielded fewer and fewer adults. Some 200,000 bushels of oysters were harvested from the bay last year, compared with 1 million in 1987. Scientists are monitoring the oyster population closely, searching for ways to boost the falling numbers.

A map of the Chesapeake pops up on the screen, with a dozen real oyster beds labeled. A digitized voice (Shaffer's wife's) instructs students to select a bed for study. A four-girl group chooses the Swans Point bed, near the bay's eastern shore. A click of a mouse button sends an animated boat churning across the green water and reaching down with a dredge to bring up oysters. The catch mimics what scientists snagged there four years ago: 337 live adults, 279 "smalls"—oysters below the minimum market size of 3 inches across—and 13 dead. The students take a break for a narrated on-screen video of an actual oyster harvest, a slide of two oyster parasites and a close-up of an open oyster that inspires disgusted shrieks.

It's time to get serious. Armed with data about the water's oxygen levels, pollution, contamination by heavy metals and other variables, the students conduct experiments in four on-screen labs to elicit reasons for the oyster decline. They check their hypotheses with a click of the mouse. "This kind of data would be impossible for students to get themselves," says Shaffer, who spent the last two summers gathering statistics and building the program around them.

"I like this better than listening to Mr. Shaffer lecture," says 15-year-old Jessica Simmons. "It's more interesting." And it's far more challenging than note taking, since the real-life statistics are full of complications and contradictions. "When you look at real data, the numbers are 'dirty,'" Shaffer explains. "That's the way the scientific world is. It gives students a taste of reality."

After an hour at "their" bed, the girls turn to the other 11 for clues. Oxygen levels look normal, they conclude. So do figures for phosphates, a measure of fertilizer runoff and use of detergents. "Between all of us, we can figure out what's going on," insists Jessica. After some debate, they blame Dermo and MSX, parasitic diseases that have devastated several other oyster beds and infected 23 percent of the Swans Point oysters. To test the hypothesis, the girls recommend infecting healthy oysters and seeing what happens. As the bell rings signaling the end of the 90-minute class, Jessica lets out a sigh. "This really makes you think," she says.

Lesson 6
Use the Internet the Right Way

Dalton School, New York City

Malcolm Thompson teaches astronomy at this Upper East Side private school solely with seven Mac clones, $100 astronomy software and the World Wide Web. His students learn about eclipses with Voyager II, a program from Carina Software that can plot the movements of the heavens 5,000 years into the past—or the future. Students study the evolution of galactic clusters by downloading Hubble Space Telescope images from a National Aeronautics and Space Administration Web site [http://cossc.gsfc.nasa.gov/apod/lib/galaxyclusters.html].

"Most of the explanations in astronomy emerge from observations done over long periods," says Thompson, 58. "Now you can compress the motions during those periods into a few seconds so you can conceptualize them." Says senior Jon Rameau: "You see how it works rather than the idea being told to you."

Using hand-held calculators, students previously had time to test theories such as Hubble's Law only on a few examples. The law holds that because the universe is constantly expanding, the distance between an observer on Earth and a far-off galaxy can be determined from the rate of expansion. Computers let the students quickly verify the law on a dozen galaxies. "One of the things about kids is that they won't ask a question if it will take them a long time to answer it," says Thompson.

The students download Milky Way photos from another NASA site [http://cossc.gsfc.nasa.gov/apod/lib/aptree.html], check sunspots at a site maintained by the National Oceanic and Atmospheric Administration [http://www.sel.noaa.gov:80/images] and browse astronomy libraries from Australia to Japan. Naturally, the course outline, assignments and student work are on the Web [http://www.dalton.org/groups/astro].

Some 10 to 20 students got better jobs or internships partly because of their new-found Web skills, says Thompson. "Before this year, I didn't exactly consider myself a Web crawler," says senior Wei-San Tjong. "But if you want to find something out and [Thompson] doesn't want to help you and gets moody, you have to find it yourself."

And the results? A group of Thompson's students did 33 percent better than a group of their classmates on a 1993 test of their skill at analyzing and interpreting data. "In educational research, that's a big difference," says John Black, a professor at Columbia University's Teachers College who administered the test as part of an overall assessment of Dalton's technology program.

The night sky is still part of Thompson's course. Early in the course, the students prepare for an evening on a New York City rooftop by setting the Voyager II program to the date and time and predict the positions of various planets, stars and constellations. When they conduct their night-time observations, they check their findings against the program's predictions. "If you just had [Voyager II] and you never told the kids they were looking at the sky, it would be a video game," Thompson says. "This experience takes the kid from where he is in his experience of the world and says: 'Here is how this connects to the formal systems of science.'"

Rules to Compute By

Before committing to computers in their schools, educators and parents might take these guidelines to heart.

- Beware of flash. Much educational software is slick but flawed. "It's not enough just to have software that looks good," says Linda Roberts, director of the U.S. Department of Education's Office of Educational Technology. Avoid drill- or game-oriented programs. Spreadsheet programs are a better choice. Inherently flexible, they can help teach biology, chemistry and algebra concepts. For English and history teachers, basic word-processing programs can help students edit and improve their writing.

- Use computers only where they make sense. Good teachers boot up a computer only to help students in a way that otherwise would be difficult.

- Train teachers. A principal would never stick a science teacher at a piano and expect Mozart to emerge—but he just might put her at a computer and demand that she be the next Bill Gates. Educator after educator says training is the most crucial ingredient of an effective computer program and the one that is underfunded the most often. "I would rather not afford the technology than not afford the training," says Jeri Hodges, executive director of instructional technology applications for the Dallas public schools.

- Don't expect miracles. Computers don't always result in higher test scores, and they certainly can't turn a flailing school system around by themselves. Before investing, ask yourself what you expect computers to do for your school. If the answer is simply to teach keyboarding skills, a roomful of refurbished machines may be adequate. If you hope to weave software into the general curriculum, computers in each classroom work best. And if you want computers to overcome poor teaching, overcrowded classrooms or unmotivated students, forget the whole thing.

 Article Review Form at end of book.

WiseGuide Wrap-Up

Today computerized classrooms are commonplace at many schools and colleges. To further investigate how or if computers enhance education, visit a local elementary school or high school classroom that uses computers. Are the computers used as a tool in a constructivist classroom? Are they drill-and-practice baby-sitters? What messages are being conveyed to students as they work with the technology? You also might explore how computers are used in various courses at your college.

R.E.A.L. Sites

This list provides a print preview of typical **Coursewise** R.E.A.L. sites. There are over 100 such sites at the **Courselinks**™ site. The danger in printing URLs is that web sites can change overnight. As we went to press, these sites were functional using the URLs provided. If you come across one that isn't, please let us know via email to: webmaster@coursewise.com. Use your Passport to access the most current list of R.E.A.L. sites at the **Courselinks**™ site.

Site name: Computers and Classrooms: The Status of Technology in U.S. Schools.

URL: http://www.ets.org/research/pic/compclass.html

Why is it R.E.A.L.? This is an informative report authored by researchers at Educational Testing Service in Princeton, NJ.

Key topics: education

Try this: Review the report summary. How are students using computers in schools? Does this report tend to refute or deny Oppenheimer's critique? Why or why not?

Site name: T.H.E. Journal

URL: http://www.thejournal.com/

Why is it R.E.A.L.? Technical Horizons in Education (T.H.E.) Journal features articles on innovative uses of technology in education. The site includes a search engine for past issues and an amazing set of links to education resources (see "Road Map to the Internet").

Key topics: education

Try this: Search the journal archive to find a recent article on education and technology.

Site name: Planet Papert

URL: http://sbm-www.pepperdine.edu/~gstager/planetpapert.html

Why is it R.E.A.L.? This site is devoted to articles, interviews, and links related to Dr. Seymour Papert, renowned MIT researcher in computers and education.

Key topics: education

Try this: Visit the site and read the online interview with Seymour Papert to learn more about his influence on educational applications of technology.

section 4

Men, Women, and the Virtual Androgyne: Gender, Identity, and Social Relationships in Cyberspace

Learning Objectives

- Describe some effects that occur when people experiment with their identities in online forums.

- According to Bruckman, why do people "gender swap" online?

- Evaluate the ethics of the gender-swapping electronic lover.

- Describe how "cyber-rape" might desensitize people to violence against women.

- Describe the patterns of gender difference noted by Herring.

- Evaluate the conclusions of the Carnegie Mellon study.

What's the difference between LOL—"life on line"—and RL—"real life"? For many people, the world of cyberspace opens up new opportunities for developing social and professional relationships. Online, people exchange information, join support groups, and fall in love. For some, LOL becomes RL, as they decide that the relationships they've formed in the virtual world are more satisfying than those with their families, in their communities, and at work.

Are the relationships we form in cyberspace, in chat rooms, via e-mail, and in online forums such as MUDs and MOOs a mirror of those we form in face-to-face living, or is there a different quality to these relationships? An intriguing new field of research, computer-mediated communication (CMC), seeks to understand how we develop social relationships in electronic environments and how this computer-mediated communication affects our understanding of ourselves and those with whom we communicate. Human-computer interaction is a related field of study that investigates how humans interact with computers.

Some CMC researchers speculate that communication in online forums allows people to experiment with different aspects of their identity—to be more assertive if they usually are timid, to experience life as a man if they are a woman, or to experience life as gender-neutral. Experiments with identity, they suggest, may influence a person's "real-life" identity and relationships.

In "Is the Net Redefining Our Identity?" Paul Judge provides a journalistic account of the work of MIT social scientist Sherry Turkle and presents her ideas about how people use online forums to explore their identity. Georgia Tech researcher Amy Bruckman, a former graduate student at MIT and founder of MediaMoo, is especially interested in how children interact with computers. In this section, her article, "Gender Swapping on the Internet," focuses not on children but on the phenomenon of "gender swapping" in MUDs and MOOs, which are text-based multi-user virtual reality environments.

Lindsy Van Gelder's article, "The Strange Case of the Electronic Lover," first published in 1985, has become a classic piece for evaluating some of the ethical issues surrounding computer-mediated communication. The electronic lover of the story reconstructed his identity online, posing as a disabled woman and becoming one of the most beloved members of an online community—until he revealed his "true self." Was his behavior ethical? Do online forums represent a safe space for experimenting with identity, or can there be unpleasant real-life consequences when we participate in such experiments?

Have you ever been "flamed" via e-mail or been the victim of degrading insults in a chat room? How would you feel if you opened your mailbox to find a letter threatening to kill or harm you? In "Cyber-rape: How Virtual Is It?" *Ms.* writer Debra Michals raises questions about the power of text in asking us to examine whether or not violence carried out in online forums can harm its victims in ways similar to real-life assault.

The next article, "Gender and Democracy in Computer-Mediated Communication," by linguist Susan Herring, looks at how gender influences communication in online forums. Herring evaluated a series of transcripts from online forums to analyze how men and women communicate in these environments. Her conclusions may surprise you.

Can you spend too much time online? According to a recent study conducted at Carnegie Mellon University, the answer is yes. The *New York Times* article, "Sad, Lonely World Discovered in Cyberspace," reports on this research, which concluded that spending time online can lead to loneliness, depression, and isolation. This study, which had been supported by grants from several major companies, including Apple Computer, Hewlett-Packard, and AT&T Research, was published amid much controversy. The second *Times* article, "Technology: Critics Are Picking Apart a Professor's Study That Linked Internet Use to Loneliness and Depression," reports on the criticism generated by the study.

The companion web sites listed at the end of this section provide you with more opportunities to explore human-computer interaction and the impact of cyberspace on identity and social relationships. At the Loebner Prize home page, you can learn more about the Turing Test and the world's most human-like computer programs. The site entitled Sexuality and Cyberspace offers some fascinating accounts of how people explore their identity and sexuality in online environments. The third site features a collection of texts by Julian Dibbell, a writer for the *Village Voice* who frequently explores topics related to cyberculture.

Perhaps the most exciting dimension of cyberspace is that it presents us with the opportunity to meet and form relationships with people from all over the world. How these relationships influence our lives and identity continues to evolve. This section will help you develop your own questions and answers about the difference, or not, between "LOL" and "RL."

Questions

Reading 15. Are you a different person online? How might life online influence identity in real life?

Reading 16. Would you gender-swap online? What does such posing suggest about gender identity?

Reading 17. What expectations do we develop about relationships we form online? Were the charges of ethical wrongdoing in this case justified?

Reading 18. Can words assault a victim as much as action? Should perpetrators of cyber-rape suffer criminal penalties?

Reading 19. Is life online a mirror of real life, or a different world? What differences does Herring observe in the communication styles of men and women?

Reading 20. How much time online is too much? Are relationships formed online an acceptable substitute for those formed in the physical world?

Reading 21. Why was the methodology of the Carnegie Mellon study criticized? What kind of methodological approach might satisfy the critics?

Are you a different person online? How might life online influence identity in real life?

Is the Net Redefining Our Identity?

Sociologist Sherry Turkle argues that online encounters are reshaping human relations.

Paul C. Judge

Lurking in the corners of the Internet, Sherry Turkle has become the Margaret Mead of cyberspace. The Massachusetts Institute of Technology sociologist and psychoanalyst is a celebrity in computer circles for her studies of seductions, gender-swapping, democratic uprisings, even virtual rape—all of it conducted online. But she was stopped cold when she stumbled across her online double a few years ago.

Turkle encountered "Dr. Sherry," a self-described "cyberpsychologist," in one of several virtual communities she frequents. Her doppelganger was passing out electronic questionnaires and conducting online interviews. "I told myself that surely one's books, one's intellectual identity, one's public persona are pieces of oneself that others may use as they please," Turkle recalls. Yet here was "a little piece of my history spinning out of control."

For Turkle, it was life imitating art—or research. Her 1995 book, *Life on the Screen*, argues that computers and the Internet are redefining human identity, as people explore the boundaries of their personalities, adopt multiple selves, and form online relationships that can be more intense than real ones. The World Wide Web is "redefining our sense of community and where we find our peers," she says.

"People Side"

Turkle has developed a following beyond academe. Consultants and executives at Xerox' Palo Alto Research Center (PARC), American Online, McKinsey, and other members of the business community have taken to quoting her books and discussing her ideas. McKinsey consultant John Hagel says Turkle is one of the few investigators "pushing the people side of research on virtual communities, as opposed to the technology."

It's an important distinction for the corporate world. Turkle's research on children who grow up with computers, for example, gives insights into what type of adult consumers they might become. She finds that children are developing new patterns of thinking by piecing together concepts from fragments they find scattered around the Web. "Children from the earliest age have been teaching themselves how to make the most of life on the screen," she says. As a result, today's children will likely buy more, work more, and socialize more in the virtual world.

Turkle gained widespread recognition with the publication of *The Second Self* in 1984. The book, a hot seller, was praised for the way it combined the tools of psychoanalysis with detailed observations of computer users. Since then, popular attention has focused on the more sensational aspects of her work: How people use the Internet to engage in online sex, or "tinysex," as she calls it, and the surprisingly large number of men who adopt female personae online.

But all of her work revolves around the same issue—the ways in which computer interfaces are

Turkle Talk

Sherry Turkle's provocative views hold that the Internet provides a radical departure in how we interact with one another.

Multiple Selves Communication in cyberspace lets people explore their personalities by creating new on-line personae.

Soft Mastery The Internet is turning computers from computational devices into tools for collaboration—playing to the way women approach machines.

Global to Local Ironically, the sweeping, global reach of the Internet is leading people back to local communities and resources.

Bricolage (tinkering) Those able to blend their virtual experience and "real life" are improvisational tinkerers—which includes many computer-using children.

blurring the psychological boundaries between people and machines. She is intrigued, for example, by virtual communities known as multi-user domains (MUDs). There, people interact through personae they have created, and they navigate through virtual cities. The online site Habitat, in fact, started as a MUD but evolved into a game with multiple players using guns and other weapons.

Soon, she recounts, the "citizens" of Habitat started the same debate over violence that obsesses the real world. Some proposed banning guns, but others liked the Wild West atmosphere. In the midst of the debate, a clergyman founded the "Order of the Walnut" within Habitat, whose members pledged never to use weapons. Eventually, guns were banned from Habitat's town but allowed in the surrounding wilds.

Boundaries

Turkle has also taken a hard look at how women use computers—"more as a harpsichord than a hammer," she says. Because the culture of technology has been largely male, Turkle says, its values have been hierarchy and control. With the rise of the Internet, a broad shift is under way to a culture that values collaboration and community—attributes more hospitable to women. Ted Leonsis, president of AOL's content division, says the numbers prove Turkle right: AOL's female membership has grown from 18% to 45% in the past two years.

Some of Turkle's ideas are old concepts dressed up in cyberclothing. She believes computers provide people with the means to explore the boundaries of self by shifting from one persona to another, even when they jump from writing a memo in one window to joining an online chat in another: Different roles are required for each task. But role-juggling didn't start with the PC. The telephone demands juggling, too, as does a switch from the workplace to parenting. John Seely Brown, research director at Xerox PARC, recalls the thrill of using Morse code to communicate with people around the world who had no idea he was only 12. "There are a lot of things in cyberspace that actually have much longer historical roots," says Brown.

The sensational aspects of Turkle's work: How people use the Internet to engage in "tinysex," as she calls it, and the large number of men who adopt female personae online

Nontechie

Turkle's own roots are in psychology, not technology. Her first book, published in 1975, was about the role of Freud in the French intellectual awakening of the 1960s. "It wasn't in the cards, given my training, that I would find the computer," she says. Soon after she landed at MIT in 1975, she became curious about the relationships between people and machines. When Apple Computer Inc.'s Macintoshes began turning up at MIT in the early 1980s, she saw people bonding with the machines, partly, she surmised, because the easy-to-use interface allowed nontechies to explore them.

Her observations gave rise to *The Second Self*, which was criticized by some for its lack of hard data. Turkle says her approach is designed only to reveal a range of behaviors, not assess their frequency. "You have to trust my intellectual taste," she admits. Mitchell Kapor, founder of Lotus Development Corp. and president of Kapor Enterprises Inc., defends Turkle as a pioneer in "investigating the new psychological realities—how people's experiences of themselves and others are different because of the way they interact on the Net."

What about the danger of addiction in the virtual realm? Turkle regards such fears as overblown, but some researchers disagree. New York psychologist Mark Stafford is generally supportive of Turkle's research but says she is overly optimistic about the beneficial impact computers can have on their users. "The technology allows for some very perverse behavior," Stafford says. Perhaps Turkle's mysterious online double, appropriating her life and work, is an example.

Article Review Form at end of book.

Would you gender-swap online? What does such posing suggest about gender identity?

Gender Swapping on the Internet

Amy Bruckman

Amy Bruckman[1] is the founder of MediaMOO, a MUD designed as a professional community for media researchers.

Gender Swapping on the Internet

On the television show *Saturday Night Live*, a series of skits concerned a character named Pat, who has no apparent gender. The audience is tempted with the promise of clues. In one episode, Pat gets his or her hair cut. A sign in the salon says that men's haircuts are $7, and women's haircuts are $9. The audience waits in suspense: when Pat goes to pay, his or her true gender will be revealed. The humor of the series lies in the fact that those hopes are constantly foiled; in this instance, Pat leaves $10 and says to keep the change.

Fundamental to human interactions that the idea of a person without gender is absurd. The audience thinks that surely some clue must reveal Pat's gender, but none ever does. Many who have never seen *Saturday Night Live* know about Pat.[2] The

character has become a kind of cultural icon. Pat's popularity is revealing.

On many MUDs, it is possible to create gender neutral characters. It is possible not only to meet Pat, but also to be Pat. When I[3] first met an ungendered character, I felt a profound sense of unease. How should I relate to this person? Most unsettling was my unease about my unease: why should this matter? I am having a casual conversation with a random stranger; why should I feel a need to know his or her gender?

The experience highlights two things: the ways in which gender structures human interactions, and, more importantly, the ways in which MUDs help people to understand these phenomena by experiencing them. This essay briefly introduces the technology called MUDs, and then analyzes a community discussion about the role of gender in human social interaction which was inspired by the participants' experiences in MUDs. Gender swapping is one example of how the Internet has the potential to change not just work practice but also culture and values.

What Are MUDs?

A MUD is a text-based multi-user virtual-reality environment. As of April 16th, 1993, there were 276 publicly announced MUDs based on twenty different kinds of software on the Internet. I will use the term "MUD," which stands for "Multi-User Dungeon," to refer to all the various kinds.[4] The original MUDs were adventure games; however, the technology has been adapted to a variety of purposes.

When a person first logs onto a MUD, he or she creates a character. The person selects the character's name and gender, and writes a description of what the character looks like. It is possible for a character to be male or female, regardless of the gender of the player. In many MUDs, a character can also be neuter or even plural. A plural character could, for example, be called swarm_of_bees or Laurel&Hardy.

MUDs are organized around the metaphor of physical space. You can "talk" to anyone in the same virtual room. When you connect to a MUD at the Media

The Internet Society, 1993.

Lab called MediaMOO,[5] you see the description:

>connect guest

Okay, . . . guest is in use. Logging you in as 'Green_Guest'

*** Connected ***

The LEGO Closet

It's dark in here, and there are little crunchy plastic things under your feet! Groping around, you discover what feels like a doorknob on one wall.

Obvious exits: out to The E&L Garden

MediaMOO is a virtual representation of the MIT Media Lab. Typing "out" gets you to the "E&L Garden," a central work area for the lab's Epistemology and Learning research group:

>out

The E&L Garden

The E&L Garden is a happy jumble of little and big computers, papers, coffee cups, and stray pieces of LEGO.

Obvious exits: hallway to E&L Hallway, closet to The LEGO Closet, and sts to STS Centre Lounge

You see a newspaper, a Warhol print, a Sun SPARCstation IPC, Projects Chalkboard, and Research Directory here. Amy is here.

>say hi

You say, "hi"

Amy says, "Hi Green_Guest! Welcome!"

The earliest MUDs such as "MUD1" and "Scepter of Goth" were based on the role-playing game Dungeons and Dragons, and were written in late 1978 to 1979.[6] They were also based on early single-user text adventure games, such as the original AD-VENT by Crowther and Woods [7]. In adventure-based MUDs, the object is to kill monsters and obtain treasure in order to gain "experience points." As a character gains experience, he/she/it becomes more powerful.

In 1989, a graduate student at Carnegie Mellon University named James Aspnes decided to see what would happen if the monsters and magic swords were removed. He created a new type of MUD, called "TinyMUD," which was not an adventure game. Instead of spending time killing virtual monsters, participants work together to help extend the virtual world using a simple programming language. Langdon Winner remarks that "social activity is an ongoing process of world-making" [9]. In MUDs, this is true in a literal sense.

In most MUDs, characters are anonymous. People who become friends can exchange real names and e-mail addresses, but many choose not to. Conventions about when it is acceptable to talk about "real life" vary between communities. In most MUDs, people begin to talk more about real life when they get to know someone better. However, in some communities such as those based on the *Dragonriders of Pern* series of books by Anne McCaffrey, talking about real life is taboo.

MUDs are increasingly being used for more "serious" purposes. Pavel Curtis of Xerox PARC has developed a MUD to enhance professional community among astrophysicists called AstroVR [4]. The MediaMOO project, which I began in fall of 1992, is designed to enhance professional community among media researchers [2]. Media-MOO currently has over 500 participants from fourteen countries and is growing rapidly.

MUDs also have an intriguing potential as an educational environment. Since 1990, Barry Kort has been running a MUD for children called MicroMUSE.[7] I am currently in the process of designing a MUD language and interface to make the technology more usable by children as part of my dissertation research. I hope to use this technology to encourage ten- to twelve-year-old girls to be more interested in computers.

A Public Debate about Gender

Gender pervades human interactions in such basic ways that its impact is often difficult to observe. Phenomena that are subtle in real life become obvious in MUDs, and are a frequent topic of discussion on Usenet newsgroups about MUDs. For example, men are often surprised at how they are treated when they log on as a female character. Andrew writes on the newsgroup rec.games.mud:[8]

Back when I had time for MUD, I, too, played female characters. I found it extraordinarily interesting. It gave me a slightly more concrete understanding of why some women say, "Men suck." It was both amusing and disturbing.

Female characters are often besieged with attention. By typing the Who command, it is possible to get a list of all characters logged on. The Page command allows one to talk to people not in the same room. Many male players will get a list of all present and then page characters with female names. Unwanted attention and sexual advances create an uncomfortable atmosphere for women in MUDs, just as they do in real life.

Many people, both male and female, enjoy the attention paid

to female characters. Male players will often log on as female characters and behave suggestively, further encouraging sexual advances. Pavel Curtis has noted that the most promiscuous and sexually aggressive women are usually played by men. If you meet a character named "FabulousHotBabe," she is almost certainly a he in real life [3].

Perhaps more damaging than unwanted sexual advances are unrequested offers of assistance. Carol, an experienced programmer who runs a MUD in Britain, writes on rec.games.mud:

What I *do* think is funny is this misconception that women can't play muds, can't work out puzzles, can't even type "kill monster" without help. (Okay, I admit we have it on this side of the Atlantic too . . .) Thanks, guys. . . . I log on, they work out I am female, and then the fun begins. Oh joy! After all, I don't log on to see whether people have found bugs with my little area, or to dispense arbitrary justice ("Please, Miss, he stole my sword!") or to find a friend. I call Aber-o-rama[9] (for this is the place) expressly to meet little spods who think (I assume) that because I am female I need help. People offering me help to solve puzzles *I* wrote are not going to get very far.

Do you think all women in real life too are the same? We don't squeak and look helpless *all* the time (in my case, only when I am tired and can't be bothered to wire the plug, change a fuse or remove the centipede from the bath (I really should move house . . .)).

The constant assumption that women need help can be damaging to a woman's sense of self-esteem and competence. If people treat you like an incompetent, you may begin to believe it. Carol here is honest and astute enough to admit that women as well as men help create this problem—sometimes she acts helpless when

she's simply "tired and can't be bothered" to complete an uninteresting or unpleasant task.

In the same netnews discussion, Dennis concurs with Carol:

I played a couple of muds as a female, one making up to wizard level. And the first thing I noticed was that the above was true. Other players start showering you with money to help you get started, and I had never once gotten a handout when playing a male player. And then they feel they should be allowed to tag along forever, and feel hurt when you leave them to go off and explore by yourself. Then when you give them the knee after they grope you, they wonder what your problem is, reciting that famous saying "What's your problem? It's only a game." Lest you get the wrong idea, there was nothing suggestive about my character, merely a female name and the appropriate pronouns in the bland description. Did I mention the friendly wizard who turned cold when he discovered I was male in real life? I guess some people are jerks in real life too.

Male characters often expect sexual favors in return for technical assistance. A male character once requested a kiss from me after answering a question. A gift always incurs an obligation. Offering technical help, like picking up the check at dinner, can be used to try to purchase rather than win a woman's favor. While this can be subtle and sometimes overlooked in real life, in MUDs it is blatant, directly experienced by most, and openly discussed in public forums such as this Usenet discussion.

Ellen provides an interesting counterpoint:

This is very odd. I played LPmud[10] once, just to find out what it was like. Since most LP's do something hideous with my preferred capitalization of my preferred name, I chose a different name, and thought,

what the heck, I'd try genderbending and find out if it was true that people would be nasty and kill me on sight and other stuff I'd heard about on r.g.m.[11] But, no, everyone was helpful (I was truly clueless and needed the assistance); someone gave me enough money to buy a weapon and armor and someone else showed me where the easy-to-kill newbie[12] monsters were. They definitely went out of their way to be nice to a male-presenting newbie . . . (These were all male-presenting players, btw.[13])

One theory is that my male character (Argyle, description "A short squat fellow who is looking for his socks") was pretty innocuous. Maybe people are only nasty if you are "A broad-shouldered perfect specimen of a man" or something of that nature, which can be taken as vaguely attacking. People are nice if they don't view you as a threat.

Ellen's point is intriguing, and takes the discussion to a new level of sophistication. In *Group Psychology and Analysis of the Ego*, Sigmund Freud suggests that "love relationships . . . constitute the essence of the group mind" [5]. Issues of sexual power structure interpersonal interactions, and are more complex than "boy chases girl." Argyle's description invites a phallic interpretation—he is short and squat, and the reference to socks carries a connotation of limpness. Since Argyle is clearly not a sexual threat, he receives kinder treatment.

One cannot fail to be impressed by the quality of the netnews discussion. For the participants, MUDding throws issues of the impact of gender on human relations into high relief. Fundamental to its impact is the fact that it allows people to experience rather than merely observe what it feels like to be the opposite gender or have no gender at all.

Male characters often expect sexual favors in return for technical assistance.

Without makeup, special clothing, or risk of social stigma, gender becomes malleable in MUDs. When gender becomes a property that can be reset with a line of code, one bit in a data structure, it becomes an "object to think with," to use Seymour Papert's terminology [6]. In public forums like rec.games.mud, people reflect the values that our society attaches to gender. In private experiences, people can explore the impact of gender on their lives and their constructions of themselves.

Conclusion

Gender is just one example of an aspect of personal identity that people explore on MUDs. Examples abound. Jack is a British student studying in America. He logs onto MUDs in the morning when it is afternoon in Britain and many British players are on. He enjoys confusing them—he tells them he is in America, but displays a detailed knowledge of Britain. On further questioning, Jack tells me he is trying to decide whether to return to Britain or continue his studies in America. What does it mean to be British or American? Jack is exploring his sense of national identity in virtual reality. MUDs are an identity workshop.

Gender swapping is an extreme example of a fundamental fact: the network is in the process of changing not just how we work, but how we think of ourselves—and ultimately, who we are.

References

[1] A. Bruckman. "Identity Workshop: Emergent Social and Psychological Phenomena in Text-Based Virtual Reality." Unpublished manuscript, 1992. Available via anonymous ftp from media.mit.edu in pub/asb/papers/identity-workshop.{ps.Z, rft.Z}

[2] A. Bruckman and M. Resnick. "Virtual Professional Community: Results from the MediaMOO Project." Presented at the Third International Conference on Cyberspace in Austin, Texas, on May 15th, 1993. Available via anonymous ftp from media.mit.edu in pub/asb/papers/MediaMOO-3cyberconf.{ps.Z,rtf.Z,txt}

[3] P. Curtis. "MUDding: Social Phenomena in Text-Based Virtual Realities." Proceedings of DIAC T92. Available via anonymous ftp from parcftp.xerox.com, pub/MOO/papers/DIAC92.{ps, txt}.

[4] P. Curtis and D. Nichols. "MUDs Grow Up: Social Virtual Reality in the Real World." Presented at the Third International Conference on Cyberspace in Austin, Texas, on May 15th, 1993. Available via anonymous ftp from parcftp.xerox.com in pub/MOO/papers/MUDsGrowUp. {ps,txt}

[5] S. Freud. *Group Psychology and Analysis of the Ego.* New York: W. W. Norton & Company, 1989.

[6] S. Papert. *Mindstorms: Children, Computers, and Powerful Ideas.* New York: Basic Books, 1980.

[7] E. Raymond. *The New Hacker's Dictionary.* Cambridge, MA: MIT Press, 1991.

[8] S. Turkle. *The Second Self: Computers and the Human Spirit.* New York: Simon & Schuster, 1984.

[9] L. Winner. *The Whale and the Reactor.* Chicago: University of Chicago Press, 1986.

Notes

1. Amy Bruckman was with the MIT Media Laboratory. Now she is a faculty member at Georgia Tech.
2. In fact, I retell this story secondhand; the details may not exactly reflect the television show.
3. I have chosen to write in the first person, because many of the ideas in this paper are based on my experiences as a participant-observer and because notions of identity are part of my topic.
4. On March 6th, 1992, there were 143 MUDs based on 13 kinds of software. This is an increase of 93 percent in number of MUDs and 54 percent in number of types of software over slightly more than a year. MUDs are constantly being created and destroyed. A current list is regularly posted to the Usenet news group rec.games.mud.announce.
5. To connect to MediaMOO, type "telnet purple-crayon.media.mit.edu 8888" from a UNIX system on the Internet. Send electronic mail to mediamoo-registration@media.mit.edu for more information.
6. The earliest multi-player games existed on stand-alone time-sharing systems. In 1977, Jim Guyton adapted a game called "mazewar" to run on the ARPAnet. Participants in mazewar could duck around corners of a maze and shoot at one another, but could not communicate in any other fashion [e-mail conversation with Jim Guyton, March 1992]. Numerous multi-user games based on the *Dungeons and Dragons* role playing game appeared in 1978–1979, including *Scepter of Goth* by Alan Klietz and MUD1 by Roy Trubshaw and Richard Bartle [e-mail conversation with Alan Klietz, March 1992].
7. MicroMUSE is at chezmoto.ai.mit.edu 4201.
8. This is an excerpt from a Usenet discussion about MUDs. Communications technologies have complex interactions. Since most MUDders have read Usenet groups about MUDding for at least some period of time, the cultures of Usenet and of MUDs are in some ways linked. Social conventions evolve in the context of the complete set of technologies in use, including e-mail, netnews, surface mail, telephones, answering machines, voice mail, television, radio, newspapers, magazines, books, and the like. E-mail, netnews, and MUDs have especially complex interactions.
9. The name of the MUD has been changed.
10. LPMUDS are a type of adventure-game-style MUD.
11. The abbreviation "r.g.m." stands for "rec.games.mud," the Usenet newsgroup on which this discussion is taking place.
12. A newbie is a new player with little experience. According to Raymond [7], the term comes from British slang for "new boy," and first became popular on the net in the group talk.bizarre. A newbie monster is a monster that a low-level player could defeat.
13. This is an abbreviation for "by the way."

 Article Review Form at end of book.

What expectations do we develop about relationships we form online? Were the charges of ethical wrongdoing in this case justified?

The Strange Case of the Electronic Lover

Lindsy Van Gelder

I "met" Joan in the late spring of 1983, shortly after I first hooked my personal computer up to a modem and entered the strange new world of on-line communications. Like me, Joan was spending a great deal of time on the "CB" channel of the national network CompuServe, where one can encounter other modem owners in what amounts to a computer version of CB radio. I was writing an article for *Ms.* about modems and doing on-line interviews with CB regulars. Joan was already a sought-after celebrity among the hundreds of users who hung out on the channel—a telecommunications media star.

Her "handle" was "Talkin' Lady." According to the conventions of the medium, people have a (usually frivolous) handle when they're on "open" channels with many users; but when two people choose to enter a private talk mode, they'll often exchange real information about themselves. I soon learned that her real name was Joan Sue Greene, and that she was a New York neuropsychologist in her late twenties, who had been severely disfigured

in a car accident that was the fault of a drunken driver. The accident had killed her boyfriend. Joan herself spent a year in the hospital, being treated for brain damage, which affected both her speech and her ability to walk. Mute, confined to a wheelchair, and frequently suffering intense back and leg pain, Joan had at first been so embittered about her disabilities that she literally didn't want to live.

Then her mentor, a former professor at Johns Hopkins, presented her with a computer, a modem, and a year's subscription to CompuServe to be used specifically doing what Joan was doing—making friends on-line. At first, her handle had been "Quiet Lady," in reference to her muteness. But Joan could type—which is, after all, how one "talks" on a computer—and she had a sassy, bright, generous personality that blossomed in a medium where physicalness doesn't count. Joan became enormously popular, and her new handle, "Talkin' Lady," was a reflection of her new sense of self. Over the next two years, she became a monumental on-line presence who served both as a

support for other disabled women and as an inspiring stereotype-smasher to the able-bodied. Through her many intense friendships and (in some cases) her on-line romances, she changed the lives of dozens of women.

Thus it was a huge shock early this year when, through a complicated series of events, Joan was revealed as being not disabled at all. More to the point, Joan, in fact, was not a woman. She was really a man we'll call Alex—a prominent New York psychiatrist in his early fifties who was engaged in a bizarre, all-consuming experiment to see what it felt like to be female, and to experience the intimacy of female friendship.

Even those who barely knew Joan felt implicated—and somehow betrayed—by Alex's deception. Many of us on-line like to believe that we're a utopian community of the future, and Alex's experiment proved to us all that technology is no shield against deceit. We lost our innocence, if not our faith.

To some of Alex's victims—including a woman who had an affair with the real-life Alex, after being introduced to him by Joan—the experiment was a "mind rape," pure and simple. (Several people, in fact, have tentatively explored the possibility of bringing charges against Alex as a psychiatrist, although the case is without precedent, to put it mildly.) To some other victims, Alex was not so much an imposter as a seeker whose search went out of control. (Several of these are attempting to continue a friendship with Alex—and, as one woman put it, "to relate to the soul, not the sex of the person. The soul is the same as before.") Either way, this is a peculiarly modern story about a man who used some of our most up-to-date technology to play out some of our oldest assumptions about gender roles.

More than most stories, it requires a bit of background. A modem, of course, is the device that connects a computer to the phone and from there to any other similarly equipped computer. CompuServe is the largest of a number of modem networks; it charges its subscribers an initial small fee to open an account with a special ID number and then charges hourly fees for access to its hundreds of services, from stock reports to airline information. In addition to its business services, the network also offers a number of "social" services (including numerous Special Interest Groups—SIGs—and the CB channels) where users can mingle.

The unfolding of an on-line relationship is unique, combining the thrill of ultrafuturistic technology with the veneration of the written word that informed nineteenth-century friendships and romances. Most people who haven't used the medium have trouble imagining what it's like to connect with other people whose words are wafting across your computer screen. For starters, it's dizzyingly egalitarian, since the most important thing about oneself isn't age, appearance, career success, health, race, gender, sexual preference, accent, or any of the other categories by which we normally judge each other, but one's mind. My personal experience has been that I often respond to the minds of people whom, because of my own prejudices (or theirs), I might otherwise not meet. (For example, my best friend on-line is from Appalachia, which I once thought was inhabited only by Li'l Abner and the Dukes of Hazzard. My friend, in turn, had never had a gay friend before.)

But such mind-to-mind encounters presume that the people at both keyboards are committed to getting past labels and into some new, truer way of relating. In the wake of the Alex/Joan scandal, some on-line habitués have soberly concluded that perhaps there's a thin line between getting out of one's skin and getting into a completely false identity—and that the medium may even encourage impersonation. (One network, for example, has a brochure showing a man dressed up as Indiana Jones, Michael Jackson, and an Olympic athlete; the copy reads, "Be anything you want on American PEOPLE/LINK.") Still, when it works, it works. Disabled people are especially well represented on-line, and most of them say that it's a medium where they can make a first impression on their own terms.

Another positive consequence of the medium's mind-to-mind potential—and this is germane to Joan's story—is that it's powerfully conducive to intimacy. Thoughts and emotions are the coin of this realm, and people tend to share them sooner than they would in "real life" (what CBers refer to as "off-line"). Some people, in fact, become addicted to computer relationships, per se. But most use the modem merely as a way to start relationships that may, in time, continue off-line. After several on-line conversations with someone who seems especially compatible, people commonly arrange to speak on the telephone, to exchange photographs, and eventually, to meet in person, either by themselves or at one of the regular "CB parties" held around the country. (Several marriages have resulted from on-line meetings on CompuServe CB alone.) I've met four good computer friends in person, and found them all much the same off-line as on. For me, the only odd thing about these relationships has been their chronology. It's a little surreal to know intimate details about someone's childhood before you've ever been out to dinner together.

One of the reasons that Joan's real identity went undetected for so long was that her supposed disability prevented her from speaking on the phone. (Several people did communicate with Joan on the phone, in one case because Joan had said that she wanted to hear the sound of the other woman's voice. Joan in turn "would make horrible noises into the receiver—little yelps and moans.") There was also the matter of Joan's disfigurement; she supposedly drooled and had a "smashed up" face, untreatable by plastic surgery. She was, she said, embarrassed to meet her computer friends in person. Those who wanted to be sensitive to disabled concerns naturally didn't push. It was an ingenious cover.

Alex supposedly began his dual identity by mistake.

One of the social realities of the computing world is that the majority of its inhabitants are male; women usually get a lot of attention from all the men on-line. (Women who don't want to be continually pestered by requests from strange males to go into private talk mode often use androgynous handles.) Female handles also get attention from other women, since many women on-line are pioneering females in their fields and feminists. Alex apparently came on-line sometime in late 1982 or early 1983 and adopted the handle "Shrink, Inc." His epiphany came one evening when he was in private talk mode with a woman who for some reason mistook him for a female shrink. "The person was open with him in a way that stunned him," according to one of the women—let's call her Laura—who has maintained a friendship with Alex. "What he really found as Joan was that most women opened up to him in a way he had never seen before in all his years of practice. And he realized he could help them."

"He later told me that his female patients had trouble relating to him—they always seemed to be leaving something out," said Janis Goodall, a Berkeley, California software firm employee who also knew both Joan and Alex. "Now he could see what it was." (Despite their similar recollections, Goodall is in the opposite camp from Laura, and says: "For someone supposedly dedicated to helping people, I think he rampaged through all of our feelings with despicable disregard.") At some point after Shrink, Inc.'s inadvertent plunge into sisterhood, Joan was born.

According to both Goodall and Laura (both of whom are disabled themselves), Alex has a

back condition, "arthritis of the spine or a calcium deposit of some kind," according to Goodall," which causes him discomfort, and has the potential, but not the probability of putting him in a wheelchair someday." Goodall added that Alex later defended his choice of a disabled persona by claiming that he "wanted to find out how disabled people deal with it." Others online believe that Joan's handicaps were a way both to shroud her real identity and aggrandize her heroic stature.

If Joan began spontaneously, she soon became a far more conscious creation, complete with electronic mail drop, special telephone line, and almost novelistically detailed biography (although she sometimes told different versions to different people). She was, by my own recollection and by the accounts of everyone interviewed, an exquisitely wrought character. For starters, she had guts. (She had once, before the accident, driven alone across the interior of Iceland as a way to cure her agoraphobia.) She had traveled everywhere, thanks to money left to her by her family's textile mill fortune. She lived alone (although neighbors checked on her and helped her with errands) and was a model independent female. In fact, Joan was quite a feminist. It was she who suggested the formation of a women's issues group within CompuServe, and she actively recruited members. Several women had relationships with Joan in which they referred to each other as "sister."

Joan was earthy, too, and spoke easily about sex. One woman remembers hearing at length about Joan's abortion at age sixteen; another recalls having a long conversation about Joan's decision not to embark on

a particular course of spinal surgery that might relieve her leg pain, but "would also affect her clitoral nerve, and she wouldn't do that." She was bisexual. Although her family had been religious (she told some people that her parents were ministers), she herself was an ardent atheist who liked to engage religious people in debate. She was also a grass-smoker who frequently confessed to being a little stoned if you encountered her late at night. Her usual greeting was a flashy, flamboyant "Hi!!!!!!!!!!!!"

Interestingly, the two people who knew Joan and also met Alex in person say that their surface personalities were opposite. Alex is Jewish. He almost never drinks or smokes pot (although one of his medical specialties is pharmacology). He is a workaholic whose American Psychiatric Association biography reports wide publication in his field. "Joan was wild and zingy and flamboyant and would do anything you dared her to," notes Laura. "A part of Alex wanted to be like that, but he's actually quite intellectual and shy." Adds Janis Goodall: "Alex has a great deal of trouble expressing his emotions. There are long silences, and then he'll say, 'uh-huh, uh-huh'—just like a shrink."

Above all, Joan was a larger-than-life exemplary disabled person. At the time of her accident, she had been scheduled to teach a course at a major New York medical school (in fact, the teaching hospital that Alex is affiliated with as a psychiatrist). Ironically, Joan noted, the course dealt with many of the same neurological impairments that she herself now suffered. One of Joan's goals was eventually to resume her career as if the accident had never happened—and when I first knew her, she was embarked on an ambitious plan to employ a computer in the classroom to help her teach. The idea was that Joan would type her lecture into a computer, which would then be either magnified on a classroom screen or fed into student terminals. To all of us techno-fans and believers in better living through computers, it was a thrilling concept.

Joan was also a militant activist against the dangers of drunken drivers. Early in her convalescence, when she was frequently half out of her mind with anger, she had on several occasions wheeled herself out of her apartment and onto the streets of Manhattan, where she would shout at passing motorists. On one such occasion, police officers in her precinct, upon learning her story, suggested that she put her rage and her talent to more productive use. Joan then began to go out on patrol with a group of traffic cops whose job it was to catch drunken drivers. Joan's role in the project was twofold: (1) as a highly credentialed neuropsychologist, she was better trained than most to detect cars whose drivers had reflex problems caused by too much drinking; and (2) she was willing to serve as an example to drunken drivers of what could befall them if they didn't shape up.

On one of Joan's forays, she met a young police officer named Jack Carr. As he and Joan spent more time together, he came to appreciate her spirit in much the same way the rest of us had. They fell in love—much to the distress of Jack's mother, who thought he was throwing his life away. (Joan's on-line friends were heartened to learn much later that Mrs. Carr had softened after Joan bought her a lap-top computer, and the two of them learned to communicate in the on-line world where Joan shone so brightly.) Jack occasionally came on-line with Joan, although I remember him as being shy and far less verbal than Joan.

Shortly after I met Joan, she and Jack got married. Joan sent an elaborate and joyous announcement to all her CB pals via electronic mail, and the couple held an on-line reception, attended by more than 30 CompuServe regulars. (On-line parties are not unusual. People just type in all the festive sound effects, from the clink of champagne glasses to the tossing of confetti.) Joan and Jack honeymooned in Cyprus, which, according to Pamela Bowen, a Huntington, West Virginia newspaper editor, Joan said "was one of the few places she'd never been." Bowen and many of Joan's other on-line friends received postcards from Cyprus. The following year Joan and Jack returned to Cyprus and sent out another batch of cards.

"I remember asking Joan how she would get around on her vacation," recalls Sheila Deitz, associate professor of law and psychology at the University of Virginia. "Joan simply replied that if need be, he'd carry her. He was the quintessential caring, nurturing, loving, sensitive human being"—a Mr. Right who, Deitz adds, exerted enormous pull on the imaginations of all Joan's on-line female friends. In hindsight, Deitz feels, "he was the man Alex would have loved to be"—but in fact could only be in the persona of a woman.

Joan was extraordinarily generous. On one occasion, when Laura was confined to her bed because of her disability and couldn't use her regular computer, Joan sent her a lap-top model—a gift worth hundreds of dollars. On another occasion, when Laura mentioned that no one had ever sent her roses, Joan had two dozen delivered. Marti Cloutier, a 42-year-old Massachusetts woman with grown children, claims that it was Joan who inspired her to start college. "She made me feel I could do it at my age." When it came time for Cloutier to write her first term paper, she was terrified, but Joan helped her through it, both in terms of moral support and in the practical sense of sending her a long list of sources. (Ironically, Cloutier's assignment was a psychology paper on multiple personalities. She got an "A" in the course.) On another occasion, Joan told Cloutier that she was going out to hear the "Messiah" performed. When Cloutier enviously mentioned that she loved the music, Joan mailed her the tape. On still another occasion, when Cloutier and her husband were having difficulties over the amount of time she spent on-line, Joan volunteered to "talk" to him. Cloutier's husband is also a part-time police officer, as Jack ostensibly was, and he and Joan easily developed a rapport. According to Marti Cloutier, Joan was able to persuade him that if his wife had her own friends and interests, it would ultimately be good for their marriage. "She was always doing good things," Cloutier recalls, "and never asking anything in return."

My personal recollections are similar. Once, when Joan and I were chatting on-line late at night, I realized to my great disbelief that a bat had somehow gotten into my apartment and was flapping wildly about, with my cats in crazed pursuit. I got off the computer, managed to catch the bat and get it back out the window—but in the attendant confusion, the windowpane fell out of the window and onto my arm, slicing my wrist and palm. Needless to say, I ended up in the emergency room. Joan dropped me several extremely solicitous notes over the next few weeks, making sure that my stitches were healing properly and that I was over the scare of the accident. Even earlier, around the time I first met Joan, the child of two of my oldest friends was hit by a car and knocked into a coma that was to last for several weeks. Joan had a lot of thoughts about the physiology of comas, as well as about how to deal with hospital staffs, insurance companies, and one's own unraveling psyche in the midst of such a crisis. She offered to set up an on-line meeting with the child's mother. I later heard that Joan had also helped several women who had suicidal tendencies or problems with alcohol.

Still another way that Joan nurtured her friends—hilarious as it sounds in hindsight—was to try to keep CB free of impostors. Although Joan was probably the slickest and most long-lived impostor around, she was hardly the only one; they are a continuing phenomenon on CompuServe and on every other network. Some lie about their ages, others about their accomplishments. Some appropriate the handles of established CB personae and impersonate them. (Unlike ID numbers, handles can be whatever you choose them to be.) There are also numerous other gender benders, some of them gay or bisexual men who come on in female guise to straight men. Most aren't hard to spot. Joan herself told several friends she had been fooled by a man pretending to be a gay woman, and she was furious. "One of the first things she ever told me," recalls Janis

Goodall, "was to be terribly careful of the people you meet on CB—that things were not always as they seemed."

Sheila Deitz remembers meeting a man on-line who said he was single, but turned out to be not only married in real life, but romancing numerous women on-line. Deitz met the man off-line and realized that his story was full of holes. "Joan was very sympathetic when I told her about it, and we agreed that we didn't want this guy to have the chance to pull this on other women." At some later point, according to Deitz, "Joan created a group called the Silent Circle. It was sort of an on-line vigilante group. She'd ferret out other impostors and confront them and tell them they'd better get their act together."

All of Joan's helping and nurturing and gift-giving, in Deitz's opinion, "goes beyond what any professional would want to do. Alex fostered dependency, really." But at the time, especially among those of us who are able-bodied, there was a certain feeling that here was a person who needed all the support we could give her. Numerous disabled women have since rightly pointed out that our Take-a-Negro-to-Lunch-like attitudes were in fact incredibly patronizing.

The truth is that there was always another side to Joan's need to be needed. She could be obnoxiously grabby of one's time. Because she and I both lived in New York, she once suggested that we talk directly, modem to modem, over our phone lines— thus paying only the cost of a local call instead of Compu-Serve's $6 an hour connect charges. But as soon as I gave Joan my phone number, I was

sorry. She called constantly—the phone would ring, and there would be her modem tone—and she refused to take the hint that I might be busy with work, lover, or children. "Everybody else had the same experience," according to Bob Walter, a New York publisher who also runs Compu-Serve's Health SIG, where Joan (and later Alex, too) frequently hung out. "She would bombard people with calls." Finally, I had to get blunt—and I felt guilty about it, since Joan, after all, was a disabled woman whose aggressive personality was probably the best thing she had going for her. (My first somewhat sexist thought, when I found out that Joan was really a man, was Of course! Who else would be so pushy?)

Joan was sexually aggressive. Every woman I interviewed reported—and was troubled by— Joan's pressuring to have "compusex." This is on-line sex, similar to phone sex, in which people type out their hottest fantasies while they masturbate. (In the age of herpes and AIDS, it has become increasingly popular.) According to one woman, "one time she said she and Jack had been smoking pot and then he'd gone off to work, but she was still high. She told me she had sexual feelings toward me and asked if I felt the same." (Joan's husband, who was conveniently off on undercover detail most nights, supposedly knew about these experiments and wasn't threatened by them, since Joan's partners were "only" other women.) Her MO, at least with friends, was to establish an intense nonsexual intimacy, and then to come on to them, usually with the argument that compusex was a natural extension of their friendship. In one case, cited by several sources, a woman became so involved as Joan's compusex lover that she was on the verge of leaving her husband.

Interestingly, Joan never came on to me—or, to my knowledge, to any bisexual or gay women. Sheila Deitz is of the opinion that Alex only wanted to have "lesbian" compusex with heterosexual women, those whom he might actually be attracted to in real life. Some straight women apparently cooperated sexually not out of physical desire, but out of supportiveness or even pity—and this too might have been part of Alex's game. But it would be misleading to overemphasize Joan's sexual relationships, since compusex in general tends to be a more casual enterprise on-line than affairs of the heart and mind. Deitz estimates that at least fifteen people were "badly burned" by the revelation that Joan was Alex, and that only a few were compusex partners. Lovers or not, most were caught in Joan's emotional web.

Janis Goodall was in a category all her own. Now thirty-seven and cheerfully describing herself as "a semiretired hippie from 'Berserkeley,' California," Goodall met Joan at a time in her life "when I was a real sick cookie—an open raw wound." Goodall was herself coping with the emotional and physical aftermath of an automobile accident. (Although she can walk, Goodall's legs are badly scarred and she suffers from both arthritis and problems of the sciatic nerve.) Beyond her injuries, Goodall was also dealing with a recent separation from her husband and her brother's death. "It was Joan who helped me to deal with those things and to make the transition into the life of a dis-

abled person who accepts that she's disabled."

Joan and Goodall were "fixed up" by other CompuServ regulars after Goodall attended an on-line conference on pain management. When she and Joan arranged via electronic mail to meet in CB, "it was love at first sight. By the end of that first discussion, which lasted a couple of hours, we were honorary sisters. Later, I went around profusely thanking everyone who had told me to contact her."

The fact that Joan's disability was more severe than her own gave her an authority in Goodall's eyes, and her humor was especially therapeutic. "We used to make jokes about gimps who climb mountains. At the time, just to get through the day was a major accomplishment for me, and my attitude was screw the mountains, let me go to the grocery store." The two never became lovers, despite strenuous lobbying on Joan's part. ("I often found myself apologizing for being straight," said Goodall.) But they did become intense, close friends. "I loved her. She could finish my sentences and read my mind."

About a year ago, Joan began telling Goodall about "this great guy" who was also on-line. His name was Alex. He was a psychiatrist, very respected in his field, and an old friend of Joan's, an associate at the hospital. Largely on the strength of Joan's enthusiastic recommendation, Goodall responded with pleasure when Alex invited her into private talk mode. "During our second or third conversation, he began to get almost romantic. He clearly thought I was the greatest thing since sliced bread. I couldn't understand why an established Manhattan psychiatrist his age

could be falling so quickly for a retired hippie—although of course I was very flattered. Hey, if a shrink thought I was okay, I was okay!"

Alex told Goodall that he was married, but that his marriage was in trouble. Last winter he invited her to come visit him in New York, and when she said she couldn't afford it, he sent her a round-trip ticket. "He treated me like a queen for the four days I was there," Goodall remembers. "He put me up at a Fifth Avenue hotel—the American Stanhope, right across the street from the Metropolitan Museum. He took me to the Russian Tea Room for dinner, the Carnegie Deli for breakfast, Serendipity for ice cream, museums, everywhere—he even introduced me to his daughters." The two became lovers, although, Goodall says, his back problems apparently affected his ability and their sex life was less than satisfactory. Still, it seems to have been a minor off note in a fabulously romantic weekend. There were also many gifts. Once, Goodall says, "he went out to the corner drugstore to get cigarettes and came back with caviar. I went to Berkeley on Cloud Nine."

Naturally, Goodall had also hoped that she might meet Joan during her New York holiday. None of Joan's other women friends had. Some of the able-bodied women, especially, were hurt that Joan still felt shame about her appearance after so many protestations of love and friendship. According to Sheila Deitz, several people were reported to have arranged rendezvous with Joan and were stood up at the last minute—"although you just know Alex had to be lurking about somewhere, checking them out." Joan would, in each case, claim to have gotten cold feet.

Marie Cloutier says that Joan told her that she had promised her husband that she would never meet any of her on-line friends, but "that if she ever changed her mind and decided to meet any of her on-line friends, I would be one of them." In fact, the only CB person who had ever seen Joan was her hospital colleague—Alex. Over the course of Goodall's four days in the city, she and Alex both tried to reach Joan by phone, but without success. Goodall had brought Joan a gift—a stylized, enameled mask of a smiling face. Alex promised to deliver it. Back in Berkeley, Goodall resumed her on-line relationship with Joan, who had been out of town for the weekend. Joan, however, was anxious to hear every detail of Goodall's trip. Did she think she was in love with Alex? Was the sex good?

It was the disabled women on-line who figured it out first. "Some things about her condition were very farfetched," says one. Says another woman: "The husband, the accomplishments—it just didn't ring true from the beginning." But her own hunch wasn't that Joan was a male or able-bodied; she suspected that she was in fact a disabled woman who was pretending to have a life of dazzling romance and success.

Although such theories, however, ultimately ran up against the real postcards from Cyprus, people began to share their misgivings. "There were too many contradictions," says Bob Walter. "Here was this person who ran off to conferences and to vacations and did all these phenomenal things, but she wouldn't let her friends on-line even see her. After a while, it just didn't compute."

In hindsight, I wonder why I didn't question some of Joan's exploits more closely. As a journalist, I've dealt with the public relations representatives of both the New York City Police Department and the hospital where Joan supposedly taught—and it now seems strange to me that her exploits as drunk-spotter and handicapped professor weren't seized on and publicized. Pamela Bowen says she once proposed Joan's story to another editor, but urged him "to have somebody interview her in person because her story was too good to be true. So my instincts were right from the beginning, but I felt guilty about not believing a handicapped person. I mean, the story could have been true." It's possible that many of us able-bodied were playing out our own need to see members of minority groups as "exceptional." The more exceptional a person is, the less the person in the majority group has to confront fears of disability and pain.

Even with the contradictions, the game might have continued much longer if Joan hadn't brought Alex into the picture. According to both Goodall and Laura, Alex has, since his unmasking, said that he realized at some point that he had gotten in over his head and he concocted a plan to kill Joan off. But after seeing how upset people were on one occasion when Joan was off-line for several weeks, supposedly ill, he apparently couldn't go through with it. "It would have been a lot less risky for him to let Joan die," according to Laura, "but he knew it would be cruel." (Meanwhile, someone had called the hospital where Joan was thought to be a patient and had been told that no such person was registered.)

What Alex seems to have done instead of commit compu-murder was to buy a new ID number and begin his dual on-line identity. Joan increasingly introduced people to her friend Alex, always with great fanfare. We may never know what Alex intended to do with Joan eventually, but there's certainly strong evidence that he was now trying to form attachments as Alex, both off-line (with Goodall) and on.

One might imagine that The Revelation came with a big bang and mass gasps, but this was not the case. According to Walter, months and months went by between the time that some of Joan's more casual acquaintances (he among them) put it together and the time that those of her victims whom they knew heeded their warnings. "People were so invested in their relationships with the female persona that they often just didn't want to know," Walter said. And Joan was also a brilliant manipulator who always had an explanation of why a particular person might be trashing her. "If you ever questioned her about anything," Goodall recalls, "she would get very defensive and turn the topic into an argument about whether you really loved her."

Goodall now acknowledges that she and others ignored plenty of clues, but, as she says, "Let's remember one thing—it was a pro doing this." Deitz, whose off-line work sometimes involves counseling rape victims, agrees that Alex's victims were caught in an intolerable psychological bind. Alex zeroed in on good people," she says, "although they were often good women at vulnerable stages of their lives." To admit that Joan was a phantom was, in many cases, also to assault the genuine support and self-esteem that they had derived from the relationship. In fact, with only two exceptions—pressuring for compusex and, in Goodall's case, using the man persona to pump "girl talk" confidences about Alex—there seems to have been absolutely nothing that Joan did to inspire anyone's rancor. What makes people angry is simply that Joan doesn't exist. "And a lot of what a lot of people were feeling," Deitz adds, "is mourning."

Laura ultimately confronted Joan on-line. She had already "cooled off" her relationship with Joan because of all the inconsistencies in her persona, but while she was suspicious, she had failed to suspect the enormity of the imposture. In February, however, she called another woman close to Joan, who told her she was convinced that Joan was a man. When Laura found Joan on-line later that night, she immediately asked Joan about the charge. Joan at first denied it. It was only after Laura made it clear that "I believed that we're all created after the image of God, and that I loved the person, not the sex, and would continue to do so" that Alex came out. Laura, who is Catholic and says that her decision to stick with Alex is partially motivated by principles of Christian love, admits that it took her several weeks to "make the transition." Since then, however, she's met Alex in person and come to love him "as my adopted brother instead of my adopted sister."

Marti Cloutier to this day hasn't confronted Alex, although she has talked with him by CB and phone. "I just haven't the courage. Once, when we were talking, he mentioned something about going for a walk that day,

and I wrote back that it would be a lovely day for Joan to go for a walk. I was instantly sorry." Cloutier adds: "Joan was a very special person and I loved Joan. I feel as if she died. I can't really say that I love Alex, although maybe I could, in time. Maybe I wouldn't have given him a chance if I'd known from the beginning he was a male. I've tried to sort out my feelings, but it's hard. I know I don't feel like a victim, and I don't understand why some of these other women have gone off the deep end. I don't think he was malicious. What I can't get out of my mind was that he's the same person I've spent hours and hours with."

Sheila Deitz had been introduced on-line to Alex by Joan, but found him not all that interesting" and never became close to him. But as a visible on-line person known to many as a psychologist, she heard from many of the victims—some of whom formed their own circle of support, and in Goodall's words, "sort of held each other together with bubble gum." Some victims, according to Deitz, were so upset by the chain of events that they stopped using their modems temporarily.

Janis Goodall heard it first over the telephone, from Alex himself who mistakenly assumed that Goodall already knew. "I had just come home from the doctor, and was incredibly frustrated at having just spent $155 to have some asshole neurosurgeon tell me I would have to live with what was bothering me. The phone rang, and it was Alex. The first words out of his mouth were 'yep—it's me.' I didn't know what he was talking about. Then he said: 'Joan and I are the same person.' I went into shock. I mean, I really freaked out—I wanted to jump off a bridge."

Since then, she has communicated with Alex by letter but has refused to see him. She emphatically resents those on-line who have spent efforts trying to "understand" him. She agreed to speak for this interview in part because "although I think this is a wonderful medium, it's a dangerous one, and it poses more danger to women than men. Men in this society are more predisposed to pulling these kinds of con games, and women are predisposed to giving people the benefit of the doubt."

Laura thinks that CompuServe and other networks ought to post warnings to newcomers that they might, in fact, encounter impostors. Others believe that the fault doesn't lie with the medium or the network, but with human frailty. "Blaming CompuServe for impostors makes about as much sense as blaming the phone company for obscene calls," says Bob Walter. CompuServe itself has no official position on the subject, although CompuServe spokesman Richard Baker notes: "Our experience has been that electronic impersonators are found out about as quickly as are face-to-face impersonators. While face-to-face impersonators are found out due to appearance, on-line impersonators are found out due to the use of phrases, the way they turn words, and the uncharacteristic thought processes that go into conversing electronically. I also believe that people are angrier when they've been betrayed by an electronic impersonator."

It would have been nice to hear Alex's side of the story. The first time I called his office, I gave only my name (which Alex knows)—not my magazine affiliation or the information that I was working on an article about "our mutual friend Joan." The receptionist asked if I was a patient. Did I want to make an appointment? I had a giddy vision of impersonating one but decided against it. Although I telephoned twice more and identified myself as a journalist, Alex never returned my calls. He has continued his presence on-line, however, even telling Deitz that he planned to form a SIG—on another network—for psychologists and mental health professionals.

Meanwhile, in the aftermath of the Joan/Alex case, soul-searching has run rampant on CompuServe's CB and in certain SIGs. One common thread was that of Eden betrayed. As one man wrote: "I guess I figured the folks here [on-line] were special . . . but this has certainly ruptured the 'pink cloud' of CompuServe." A woman wrote back: "The feelings remind me of the ending of my first love relationship. Before that, I didn't realize fully how much hurt could result from loving."

Some of the reactions were frankly conservative—people who were sickened simply by the notion of a man who wanted to feel like a woman. There was much talk of "latency." Others seemed completely threatened by the idea that they might ever have an "inappropriate" response

to someone of the "wrong" gender on-line. One message left by a male gravely informed other users that he and his girlfriend had nearly been conned by a male pretending to be a swinging female—until the girlfriend was tipped off by the impersonator's "claiming to be wearing panty hose with jeans." The message prompted an indignant reply by someone who insisted: "I always wear heels with my jeans, and when I wear heels I wear panty hose, and I don't think that is odd, and I am all female!"

But Alex's story raises some other questions that have special resonance for feminists. Chief among them, for me, is why a man has to put on electronic drag to experience intimacy, trust, and sharing. Some women have suggested that the fault is partly ours as women—that if Alex had approached us as a male, with all of Joan's personality traits, we wouldn't have been open to him. I for one reject that notion—not only because I have several terrific male friends on-line but also because it presumes that men are too fragile to break down stereotypes about themselves. (After all, we've spent the last fifteen years struggling to prove that we can be strong, independent, and capa-

ble.) On the other hand, in Alex's defense, I can't help but appreciate the temptation to experience life in the actual world from the point of view of the other sex. Think of "Tootsie" and "Yentl." Annie Lennox and Boy George. What Alex did was alien, taboo, weird . . . and yet the stuff of cosmic cultural fantasy. Haven't you ever wanted to be a fly on the locker room (or powder room) wall?

Sheila Deitz comments that some on-line transsexualism may be essentially harmless. Where she draws the line—and where I would also—is at the point that such experimentation starts impinging on other people's trust. Joan clearly stepped over that line years ago.

Maybe one of the things to be learned from Alex and Joan is that we have a way to go before gender stops being a major, volatile, human organizing principle—even in a medium dedicated to the primacy of the spirit.

I personally applaud those souls on CB who, when asked "R u m or f?" [Are you male or female?], simply answer "yes."

 Article Review Form at end of book.

Can words assault a victim as much as action? Should perpetrators of cyber-rape suffer criminal penalties?

Cyber-Rape:
How virtual is it?

Debra Michals

Debra Michals specializes in writing about women's entrepreneurship.

On a summer night in 1995 I witnessed my first gang rape. I stumbled across it while exploring America Online's (AOL) "chat rooms" (areas in which Internet users converse with each other on specific subjects in real time). Having heard so much about the potential for human interaction in this burgeoning communications medium known as cyberspace, I decided to check it out. That's when I began my nocturnal forays on AOL. In my initial searches, I discovered that there was lots of chatter, lots of flirting, and lots of sex—most of it banal reflections of barroom culture. Then, one night, as I scrolled through the list of rooms, among those created by individual members rather than AOL, I saw one titled "Rape Fantasy." Couldn't be, I said to myself, but finally decided that I had to know. So I called it up on-screen and, to my shock, entered a room where a gang rape was taking place. There, on my screen, five men were writing about brutally violating a woman who seemed to be encouraging them.

Here's what appeared on my screen (although the names of the participants have been changed, they closely parallel the ones they used online):

Greg0987: Hold her down, guys.

Panther: I got her legs.

Robodude: I got her pinned.

Greg0987: She wants it bad. Don't ya, bitch?

Brenda: Give it to me. Give it to me good.

Panther: I'll fuck you so hard, it'll tear you open.

Bigcock: Like it rough, stupid cunt? Hit her in the face, Greg. Smash her.

Pussyeater: Don't move or I'll cut you with this knife.

Greg0987: Me first, then the rest of you go. Stop moving or I'll hit you, bitch.

Barely a minute passed—though it felt like hours—before I broke my silence.

Me: What the hell is going on in here?

Greg0987: We're raping her, what do you think?

Me: I think this is really sick.

Greg0987: Chill out. We're just playing.

Me: Playing? Women are raped and beaten every day, and it isn't play.

Greg0987: If you don't like it, get out of here. You don't have to stay.

Before I could respond, I was assaulted by so many private messages telling me to shut up or get lost that my machine jammed and I had to reboot. I sat there in front of my computer, feeling shocked and enraged.

Was this some unusual occurrence? Hardly. After the skirmish over the passage of the Communications Decency Act in 1995, many of these overtly violent spaces seemed to have disappeared from the AOL chat room roster. But their disappearance is an illusion. Although AOL no longer allows words like "rape" or "sex" to be used in naming public spaces, anything goes when it comes to user-created private rooms, and Internet users also skirt the ban by coming up with inventive names. The result is that anyone seeking a "gang bang," or a host of other sexually graphic and often violent scenarios, including "incest," can either find it easily online, or create their own room.

It hardly takes a rocket scientist to guess what may be going on in rooms with titles like "daughterblowsdad," "Unusual-Desires," and "Torture Females." When I checked out "Torture Females" last October, a man threatened to burn my hand and hang a 19-pound weight from the inside of my vagina with sharp pins. All this to get him hard. And in one incest room, on more than one occasion, participants who claimed to be teenage boys described acts of sexual violence against female siblings that seemed all too real. But my experiences on AOL were pretty tame compared to what goes on in unsupervised Internet Relay Chats, MUDs (multiuser dimensions/dungeons), or similar interactive spaces that have few boundaries or controls imposed by any online service.

The often violent nature of many of the sexual "fantasies" played out in these interactive chat rooms raises important questions about the dark side of human sexuality and the way in which the Internet permits its free and unquestioned expression in easily accessible public spaces. Despite the disclaimers of many of the participants that what occurs on the Net is pure fantasy, questions abound. If "words *are* deeds," as Sherry Turkle, a sociology of science professor at the Massachusetts Institute of Technology, notes in her book *Life on the Screen: Identity in the Age of the Internet* (Simon & Schuster), what exactly are the deeds being carried out in these spaces? Do they belong merely to the realm of fantasy role-play or do they transform the sexual psyches of the participants? Are fantasies being explored or are past deeds

being recounted? Do these games ultimately blur the distinction between fantasy and the reality of women's sexual desires? Or, since men are so often at the helm of these games, do they merely reinscribe male domination of female sexuality in both realms—the real and the imagined? While participants will tell you they understand the difference between fantasy and reality, what of the lurker who never participates but avidly takes it all in? How can we measure the impact on him or on the woman who consents to an erotic scenario and finds it spiraling out of control?

Given the number of actual rapes that are committed in our society, this online behavior obviously mimics real life. But what effect does it have on us in both our real and virtual lives? Clearly, "virtual rape" is not the same as the rape a woman experiences in the physical world. But something as yet unnameable is going on in chat rooms where an erotic scenario can shift to a gang bang with a few keystrokes from an observing male who jumps in with, "Let's skull-fuck the bitch." It is not that all, or even most, Internet sex is violent; rather, that the potential for violent intrusions hovers around any exchange, be it sexual or not.

Women on the receiving end of this graphic sexual violence on the Net have indeed reported being traumatized by the experience. While many may turn off their computers or leave a chat area if they feel attacked, they often have trouble shaking the memory that a stranger at a far-off computer terminal wanted to hurt them. Vonnie Cesar, a 27-year-old nurse and regular Internet user from Albany, Georgia, is still troubled by an early experience. "I went into a

chat room pretending to be a 15-year-old girl, just to see how people would respond to me," she explains. "One of the men asked me to go into a private room with him, and when I did, seven or eight other guys came in and started sending me pictures of women who had been beaten and raped. The pictures looked real—not like some studio shot or makeup job. They said they wanted to rape me, spank me until I bled. What made it especially scary is that, as far as they knew, I was just a young girl, a virgin in fact."

Cesar's story has disturbing implications. What if she had actually been a 15-year-old girl? Or what if one of the male participants, some of whom may be teenagers, themselves, decided to act his sick fantasies out on a real girl? While most Internet providers allow parents to restrict children's access to sexually explicit areas online, the reality is that not all parents become so involved. Consequently, there are many young people frequenting Internet chat rooms and being influenced by what they encounter. For young people still learning the difference between fantasy and reality, the lessons may well be that violence is a normal part of male behavior, that for men sexual domination is erotic, and that for women passivity and a willingness to be victimized are the rule.

Because the Internet is still fairly new, it remains to be seen how such violent role-playing will affect our sexual relationships and our larger goals of ensuring male respect for women. "The question is, are we desensitizing people about how they can relate to each other, rather than helping them move toward more compassionate relationships?" asks Patti

Britton, Ph.D., a clinical sexologist and a spokeswoman for Feminists for Free Expression, an anti-censorship group. Regardless of the risks, Britton remains opposed to stifling free speech. "I don't think we can draw a causal link at this point, but what I do know is that what we suppress, expresses. If we keep our fantasies in darkness, they grow stronger. So maybe we'll find that through the Internet, we're 'Gestalting' out the demons that keep us from having healthy relationships." Perhaps. But isn't it more likely that airing such violent inclinations freely and without reproach will merely normalize these tendencies, inuring society to the viciousness and inequality at its core?

No doubt, the Internet makes it easier for disturbed people to find each other or to identify unwitting victims. Participants' risk of being victimized is heightened by the fact that the Internet also encourages a false sense of trust and of what's real and what's make-believe. There is no eye contact in cyberspace, no opportunity to hear the inflection in a person's voice. A person can omit certain facts about themselves, or accentuate the qualities that might be more socially acceptable—so even the most unbalanced person might appear sane online.

Two cases late last year seem to indicate that for some Internet users, there is a dangerous link between online fantasy and real-world behavior. In October, a Maryland woman was found murdered in a shallow grave behind the home of a man she had met on the Internet, to whom she had allegedly expressed a desire to be sexually tortured and killed. Slightly more than a month later, a 20-year-old student at Barnard College in New York City claimed that she had been held captive and sexually assaulted by a Columbia University graduate student she had met on the Internet and agreed to meet in real life. While one of the grad student's attorneys has cited the woman's sexually graphic e-mail to him in claiming that he "didn't force anybody to do anything," the case points up the essential dilemma about where or whether fantasy and reality intersect. If, as many users assert, what is said online should be taken as fantasy, then the young woman's explicit e-mail should not be taken as evidence of her real-life desires. Or should it?

Given that more and more women are going online, the prevalence of graphic depictions of sexual violence will bring pornography into an increasing number of women's lives. "Up to now, pornography has been somewhat avoidable," says Gloria Steinem. "You can't avoid the newsstands, but you don't have to open the magazines." Steinem sees some slight benefit to this. "Now, the Internet brings it into your home, and there's the chance for an important education for people who think it's rare or harmless, or who don't realize how sadistic pornography really is." A woman seeking anything from an erotic online encounter to professional networking could find herself being accosted by some Internet junkie seeking to impose his twisted fantasies. Women in offices also report that pornographic images and fantasies are becoming an increasingly common workplace reality, as male coworkers gather around each other's computer terminals to check out sex sites online.

As of August 1996, there were approximately 36 million Internet users, a figure that is growing rapidly, according to Nielsen Media Research, a polling and tracking group. But although more women are online today than a few years ago, most estimates still hold the ratio of males to females at two to one. For the moment, some of the most flagrant forms of male domination seem to flourish on the Internet because men, by sheer force of their numbers, dictate the tone and content of what occurs. Perhaps the pervasiveness of violent role-playing online is a reflection of male angst in an era of changing gender norms. Perhaps virtual rapists represent patriarchy's storm troops, who hope to hold the forces of history at bay by engaging in this last stand on the edge of a new frontier. If this is the case, sexual violence online may function as both an assertion of dominance and a means of chasing women away from the Internet. The experience of Susan Racer, a student at New York University, who reports being accosted upon entering some chat rooms by messages such as "I've just smacked you, and you're lying on the floor" is an all too familiar one. It's as if she is being immediately reminded of her place in the virtual world before she has a chance to assert herself there.

That many Internet providers guarantee users anonymity adds to the sense of license. People can choose screen names that disguise their identities and gender. Providers also allow users to cre-

Given that more women are going online, the prevalence of graphic depictions of sexual violence will bring pornography into an increasing number of women's lives.

ate a profile of themselves—a brief and publicly accessible résumé indicating age, sex, hobbies, and hometown—at their own discretion. Some users never submit any information, others stay close to the truth, and still others choose to alter their profiles to reflect whatever role or identity they wish to take on.

While anonymity makes sense in online support groups for survivors of abuse or incest, it also enables would-be aggressors to act without repercussions. "People experiment online with identities and actions they would never actually adopt in real life," says Claudia Springer, an English and film studies professor at Rhode Island College and author of *Electronic Eros: Bodies and Desire in the Postindustrial Age* (University of Texas Press). "The Internet offers an opportunity to be radically other than oneself without suffering the consequences."

Disguising one's gender can provide some protection from online abuse. Nikki Douglas, the editor of the Web 'zine *RiotGrrl*, says she sometimes goes online posing as a man to avoid the harassing messages and rape photos she receives when she signs on as herself. But gender cloaking can also take a number of bizarre turns. Consider, for example, that "Brenda," the woman being gang-raped in the chat room I entered, may have been a man posing as a woman. In such cases, these female impersonators are representing their fiction of what women want as though it were the real thing. "If men are playing the role of the rape victim, they are playing out their fantasies of women responding to rape so they can have this text out there," says Catharine MacKinnon, law professor at the University of

Michigan and coauthor, with Andrea Dworkin, of proposed civil rights ordinances recognizing pornography as sex discrimination. "It normalizes the violence for them by making it seem as if the woman likes it."

Certainly some women do consent not only to cybersex but also to violent scenarios. In fact, many techno-feminists argue that this medium represents a kind of sexual revolution for women in which they can act out their wildest desires with complete safety. Women who enjoy cybersex say it has enabled them to explore their sexual fantasies; they can go online and engage in an evening of anonymous sex without the fear they would experience from a similar scene in real life. But as in the case of that Barnard student, the world is not so tidy. Users often forget that across the miles, at another computer, is a real person who may not be trustworthy or emotionally balanced.

Because women can log off whenever things get too violent, Carla Sinclair, author of *Net Chick: A Smart Girl Guide to the Wired World* (Henry Holt), denies that women can be sexually violated online. "You're not going to get on the Internet and end up attacked in some dark alley," says Sinclair, who posed for the April 1996 "Women of the Internet" spread in *Playboy*. "All this talk perpetuates the idea that women are weak and that they have to be protected. You're only a victim if you say you are. You can empower yourself by getting out of a chat room when it gets uncomfortable. People have a right to choose where they go, just as they need to take responsibility for the consequences their choices produce."

The problem with the way babe feminists like Sinclair define control and consent is that these words become synonymous with female compliance or retreat. Women either play the game or leave, which is hardly empowering. "In some cases, turning off the machine is a copout and could be damaging to a woman's perception of herself and her sense of control," argues Laurel Gilbert, coauthor of *SurferGrrrls* (Seal Press), a women's guide to the Internet. "It could be analogous to the ways in which women shut down after being sexually abused and are left feeling awful about themselves and what happened to them."

But notions of power or freedom are at best an illusion in cases of online violence in which women are submitting to their own violation. Regardless of how "powerful" they may feel, they are still following a patriarchal cultural script that reaffirms gender hierarchy and validates the assumption that *all* women really want to be treated this way. "I would not call it a feminist triumph because we can choose to have our lovers beat us silly in this or any realm," says Elizabeth Reba Weise, coeditor of *Wired Women: Gender and New Realities in Cyberspace* (Seal Press). However, "I would draw the distinction between cheerfully play-acting with your partner and having someone sew your labia shut. Having your partner call you a slut or a whore online hardly subverts the patriarchal order."

Worse, as MacKinnon argues, is that the consequences of these games may extend beyond the individual woman herself. "The word 'consent' can cover up some very important issues. If it's truly a woman being violated, seeming to go along with it, we don't know if she was sexually abused as a child and is therefore feeling this form of assault as being loved. We do know that most women used in pornography were sexually abused as children. But a lot of other women stand to be harmed by her appearing to welcome abuse. Whatever her experience, she isn't the only woman in the world. As all these men enjoy her purported consent to being violated, she gives sexual credibility to a male fantasy that can get other women hurt."

What does all this bode for the future? There have already been cases where sexual violence online has reached beyond the keyboard. It seems inevitable that more such cases will occur. And there is no doubt that new technology will also reshape online interactions. New sites under the CUSeeMe banner have sprung up on the World Wide Web, where users employ standard video cameras to watch each other act out fantasies in real time. According to Donna Hoffman, associate professor of management at Vanderbilt University in Nashville, video-conferencing of this nature, though offering only slow and grainy pictures at present, will likely become more refined in the next few years. In addition to the plethora of interactive CD-ROM sex games available, experts also expect we'll be seeing sensory devices that let users feel what they envision. Bill LeFurgy, editor of the weekly newsletter "Culture in Cyberspace," predicts that "in five to ten years it will probably be possible for people to hook up sensory devices to themselves that let them feel as they would if they were actually doing what they imagine online."

Meanwhile, women are starting to assert themselves online, and a new generation of Internet feminists is emerging with full claims on cyberspace. Some women are posting erotica on the Web, and others are standing up to those who, with violent messages, try to chase them out of chat rooms. One woman has launched her own campaign to seize control of sexually violent chat rooms and turn them into loving spaces. She claims that "this medium has tremendous potential to teach, and I want these guys to learn how they should treat the women in their lives when it comes to sex."

The shortage of women online may give women who choose to engage these men in their playpens more control, since many of them seem willing to consent to any scenario just to have cybersex with a real woman. And some women do see this as an opportunity to assert themselves by creating a woman-friendly climate that provides a more accurate representation of women's sexuality and humanity. Techno-feminists like Douglas and Weise argue that, rather than fleeing violent spaces, women should turn the tables and hold their ground.

But many of us have no desire to engage the sexually violent Internet user or to play sex games online. So what do we do when they invade our turf? Groups of women together can chase violators out of chat rooms by simply barraging the interloper with "get lost" messages. We can also insist that Internet providers prevent users from changing their online names and profiles at will. While users could remain anonymous, by making them stick to one name, a degree of accountability would be instituted. You wouldn't be able to behave abusively under one name and then take another one to hide behind. Some providers, like The WELL, a small California-based bulletin board, already employ this policy, and users report few problems with sexual violence.

With computers and the Internet becoming an increasing presence in the lives of children, it is important to educate them early about the prevalence of sexual violence online, and about the difference between fantasy and reality. Children should come to the Internet knowing that what exists in the recesses of people's imaginations is not necessarily the truth about what they as individuals, or what women and men collectively, may want to experience in real life. Young people should know what kind of people may lurk online, and be warned not to trust everyone they meet, not to give out personal information, and not to yield their right to this space to cyberspace bullies, or anyone else who tries to manipulate them.

If there's a moral to all this, it's don't just sit back and take the abuse. The most powerful thing women can do is refuse to collaborate.

 **Article Review Form at end of book.**

Is life online a mirror of real life, or a different world? What differences does Herring observe in the communication styles of men and women?

Gender and Democracy in Computer-Mediated Communication

Susan C. Herring

The Democratization Claim

Despite a substantial body of research demonstrating sex differences in face-to-face communication (see, e.g., Coates, 1986), the question of sex differences in computer-mediated communication has only recently begun to be raised. The lag is due in large part to a climate of general optimism surrounding the new technology: specifically, the belief that computer-mediated communication (hereafter, CMC) is inherently more democratic than other communication media. Thus philosophers and social theorists see in CMC a more equal access to information, empowering those who might otherwise be denied such information, and leading ultimately to a greater democratization of society (Ess,

1994; Landow, 1992; Nelson, 1974). Educators evoke the potential of computer networks to foster creativity and cooperation among students, and to help break down traditional barriers to communication between students and instructors (Kahn and Brookshire, 1991; Kiesler, Siegel, and McGuire, 1984; McCormick and McCormick, 1992). Even feminists are encouraged by evidence of more equal communication between women and men in the absence of status- and gender-marked cues (Graddol and Swann, 1989), and by the opportunities for women to establish grass roots electronic communication networks of their own (Smith and Balka, 1991).

The notion of democracy as it emerges through these claims has two essential components: access to a means of communication, and the right to communicate equally, free from status constraints. These components are in-

herent in the formal "rules of reason" proposed by the German philosopher Habermas (1983, p. 89; discussed in Ess, 1994) as criteria that must be observed in order for a discourse to be truly democratic:

1. Every subject with the competence to speak and act is allowed to take part in the discourse.

2a. Everyone is allowed to question any assertion whatever.

2b. Everyone is allowed to introduce any assertion whatever into the discourse.

2c. Everyone is allowed to express his [sic] attitudes, desires, and needs.

3. No speaker may be prevented, by internal or external coercion, from exercising his [sic] rights as laid down in (1) and (2).

This article appeared originally in *The Electronic Journal of Communication*/La revue electroniquede communication, Vol. 3, No. 2, 1993.

Habermas's third rule provides for an important social dimension: in a truly democratic discourse, there can be no censorship. To the extent that computer technology facilitates open, egalitarian communication of this sort, it is held to be democratizing (Ess, 1994).

A number of specific characteristics of CMC have been claimed by researchers and users to facilitate communication that is democratic in nature. The first of these is *accessibility*. Through universities and other institutions, increasing numbers of people are able to gain access to computer networks at little or no cost. This access in turn makes available to them a variety of benefits, the most widely touted of which is information, in the form of on-line library catalogs, public domain databases, and the like. Less commonly mentioned, but equally if not more important, are the opportunities provided by electronic networks to connect and communicate, to express one's views and be recognized in a public forum, potentially even by large numbers of people (including, now that President Clinton has a public access e-mail address, highly influential people) around the world. In theory, anyone with access to a network can take equal advantage of these opportunities.

A second potentially democratizing characteristic of CMC is its *social decontextualization*. As noted by Graddol and Swann (1989) and Kiesler *et al.* (1984), the identity of contributors need not be revealed, especially given login "names" and return addresses that bear no transparent relationship to a person's actual name, sex, or geographical location.[1] Further, CMC neutralizes social status cues (accent, handwriting/voice quality, sex, appearance, etc.) that might otherwise be transmitted by the form of the message. Although on one hand these characteristics render the medium less personal, they also provide for the possibility that traditionally lower-status individuals can participate on the same terms as others—that is, more or less anonymously, with the emphasis being on the content, rather than on the form of the message or the identity of the sender. As one member of an academic discussion list wrote in a recent posting to another:

"One of the greatest strengths of e[lectronic]-mail is its ability to break down socio-economic, racial, and other traditional barriers to the sharing and production of knowledge. You, for example, have no way of knowing if I am a janitor or a university president or an illegal alien—we can simply communicate on the basis of our ideas, not on any preconceived notions of what should be expected (or not expected) from one another."

Although one might question the assumption that the posts of anonymous janitors, university presidents, and illegal aliens would not reveal their status (via differences in, e.g., grammatical usage, stylistic register, and familiarity with conventions of CMC and academic discourse), the idealism expressed by this writer is typical of that of many network users.

Third, as a relatively new discourse type, CMC lacks a set of consensually agreed-upon and established *conventions of use* (Ferrara, Brunner, and Whittemore, 1991; Kiesler *et al.*, 1984). As a result, users may be less inhibited, leading to "flaming" and outrageous behavior on one hand, and to greater openness on the other. This feature has led hypertext theorists such as Bolter (1991), Landow (1992), and Nelson (1974) to characterize CMC as "anarchic" as well as "democratic," with the potential to contribute to the breakdown of traditional hierarchical patterns of communication.

Finally, overt *censorship* on the electronic networks is as yet rare; what censorship exists is typically more concerned with selectively blocking the use of vulgar language than with blocking message content.[2] Even moderated discussion lists tend to accept virtually all contributions and post them in the order in which they are received. Thus each and every contributor to a discussion theoretically has the same opportunity to have his or her messages read and responded to by other members of the group (Habermas's third "rule of reason").

Taken together, these four characteristics would appear to constitute a strong a priori case for the democratic nature of CMC. But how democratic is the communication that is actually taking place currently via electronic networks? Specifically, does it show evidence of increased gender equality, as Graddol and Swann (1989) claim?

Summary of Investigative Results

The research reported on in this article is based primarily on investigations carried out over the past year on male and female participation in two academic electronic lists (also known as "bulletin boards" or "discussion groups"): LINGUIST, devoted to the discussion of linguistics-related issues; and Megabyte University (MBU), informally organized around the discussion of computers and writing. What follows is a summary of findings analyzed in detail in three recent articles (Herring, 1992; Herring, 1993; Herring, Johnson, and DiBenedetto, 1992); much of the data and analysis on which the earlier studies were based has of necessity been omitted here.

Three types of methods were employed in investigating participation on LINGUIST and MBU. The first was *ethnographic observation* of discussions as they occurred: I subscribed to and saved contributions to both lists over a period of one year, in the process assimilating information about contributors, current issues in the field, and other relevant background information. (CMC is especially amenable to data collection of this type, in that observers can easily remain invisible, thus avoiding the "observer's paradox" of altering by their presence the nature of the phenomenon they seek to observe.) Second, I subjected the texts of two extended discussions from each list to a *discourse analysis* in which patterns of grammatical and stylistic usage were identified. Observed patterns of usage were then correlated with participant sex, which was determined either from contributors' names when available (i.e., because they signed their message, or their mailer program included it in tracing the path of the message), or else by matching electronic addresses to names from a publicly available list of subscribers to each list.[3] Finally, I prepared and distributed two electronic surveys, one each for LINGUIST and MBU, in which I asked for participants' reactions to a particular discussion that had taken place on the list to which they subscribed, and solicited background information regarding their sex, professional status, and familiarity/competence with computers. The data collected by these three methods were subjected to quantitative as well as qualitative analysis. The combined results reveal significant differences between male and female participants. The principal differences are discussed below.

Amount of Participation

The most striking sex-based disparity in academic CMC is the extent to which men participate more than women. Women constitute 36% of LINGUIST and 42% of MBU subscribers.[4] However, they participate at a rate that is significantly lower than that corresponding to their numerical representation. Two extended discussions were analyzed from each list, one in which sexism was an issue, and the other on a broadly theoretical topic. Although the "sexism" discussions were more popular with women than discussions on other topics, women constitute only 30% of the participants in these discussions on both lists; in the "theoretical" discussions, only 16% of the participants were women. Furthermore, the messages contributed by women are shorter, averaging a single screen or less, while those of men average one and a half times longer in the sexism discussions, and twice as long in the theoretical discussions, with some messages ten screens or more in length. Thus, although a short message does not necessarily indicate the sex of the sender, a very long message invariably indicates that the sender is male.

What accounts for this disparity? It does not appear on the surface as though men are preventing women from participating—at least, on one of the lists (MBU), male participants actively encourage more women to contribute. There is evidence to suggest, however, that women are discouraged from participating or intimidated on the basis of the reactions with which their posts are met when they do contribute. In a medium that permits multiple contributors to post messages more or less simultaneously to the group, gaining the focus of the group's attention or the "conversational floor" depends entirely on the extent to which other participants acknowledge and respond to one's postings. In the CMC analyzed here, messages posted by women consistently received fewer average responses than those posted by men. In the MBU sexism discussion, 89% of male postings received an explicit response, as compared with only 70% of those by women; on LINGUIST, the disparity is even greater. Of interest is the fact that it is not only men who respond more often to men, but women as well; postings from women acknowledging the postings of other women constitute the smallest portion of total responses, an implicit recognition, perhaps, of the more powerful status of men in the groups. In keeping with the unequal rate of response, topics initiated by women are less often taken up as topics of discussion by the group as a whole, and thus women may experience difficulty and frustration in getting the group to talk about topics that are of interest to them.

On those rare occasions when, out of special interest or a strong commitment to a particular point of view, women persist in posting on a given topic despite relative lack of response, the outcome may be even more discouraging. During the period of this investigation, women participated actively three times: once during the MBU sexism debate, in which men and women became polarized regarding the legitimacy of offering a special course on "Men's Literature," and twice on LINGUIST, the first in a discussion of the interpretation of Sister Souljah's remarks on the Rodney King beating, and the second in a sexism discussion on the question of whether the label "dog" refers primarily to women, or to unattractive persons of either sex. In all three discussions, women's rate of posting increased gradually to where it equaled 50% of the contributions for a period of one or two days. The reaction to this increase was virtually identical in all three cases: a handful of men wrote in to decry the discussion, and several threatened to cancel their subscription to the list. Various reasons were given, none of them citing women's participation directly: in the MBU discussion, the tone was too "vituperative";[5] in the LINGUIST discussions, the topics were "inappropriate." Although the LINGUIST list moderators (one male, one female) intervened to defend the appropriateness of the Sister Souljah threat, the discussion died out almost immediately thereafter, as did the others. Of course, the possibility cannot be ruled out that the men who protested were responding to the content rather than (or in addition) to the frequency of women's posts. Nevertheless, the coincidence is striking, since at no other time during the period of observation did women participate as much as men, and at no other time did any subscriber, male or female, threaten publicly to unsubscribe from either list. Reactions such as these are consistent with Spender's (1979) claim that women cannot contribute half of the talk in a discussion without making men feel

uncomfortable or threatened. She found that men (and to a lesser degree, women) perceive women as talking more than men when women talk only 30% of the time. This phenomenon is not limited to Spender's academic seminar data or to CMC, but rather is a feature of mixed-sex conversation in public settings more generally (Holmes, 1992).

This interpretation is further supported by the results of a survey conducted on MBU several months after the Men's Literature discussion. All available external evidence points to the conclusion that, despite the temporary increase in women's participation, men were more successful than women overall in the Men's Literature debate—men posted more, were responded to more, and introduced more successful topics in the discussion; further, the real-world course of action they advocated was ultimately followed (that is, a Men's Literature course was offered). However, when MBU subscribers were surveyed later regarding their reactions to the discussion, male respondents indicated a higher degree of dissatisfaction than women, and were more likely to say that women had "won" the debate; women, in contrast, were more likely to say that neither side had won (Herring, Johnson, and DiBenedetto, 1992). When women's attempts at equal participation are the cause of (male) dissatisfaction—even if voiced publicly by only a few— and disruption of list functioning, a message is communicated to the effect that it is more appropriate for women to participate less. And so they do: the day after the MBU protests, women's contributions dropped back to 15% of the total, and the discussion continued apace. The rather depressing

conclusion to be drawn from this is that it is "normal" for women to participate less than men, such that an increase in the direction of true equality is perceived as deviant, even in liberal, academic settings.

Topic

The above observations indicate that although women contribute less than men overall, they contribute relatively more on certain topics of discussion, specifically those that involve real-world consequences as opposed to abstract theorizing. Herring (1993) describes a ranking of preferences based on participation in different topic types during a random two-week period on LINGUIST. Men were found to contribute most often to discussions of issues, followed by information postings (i.e., where they provided information, solicited or otherwise), followed by queries and personal discussions. Women, on the other hand, contributed most to personal discussions (talk about linguists, as opposed to talk about linguistics), followed by queries soliciting advice or information from others, with issues and information postings least frequent. The ranking of preferred topic types is represented schematically below:

MEN: issues > information > queries > personal

WOMEN: personal > queries > issues > information

A tendency for women to contribute less to discussions of theoretical issues than to other types of exchanges is evident on MBU as well.

Independent support for these observations comes from the Women's Studies List (WMST), devoted to issues involved in the organization and administration of women's studies programs. WMST, which is owned by a woman and has a subscribership that is currently 88% female, constitutes a context in which women post almost exclusively for and among themselves. Personal discussions are avoided on WMST, presumably in the interest of greater academic professionalism. Instead, the overwhelming majority of messages posted to WMST are queries for advice and/or information. Answers to queries, however, are required (according to posted list protocol) to be sent privately to the asker—although summaries of answers thus collected may be publicly posted—and issues discussions are explicitly prohibited by the list owner, who sees the list as "serving as a source of information" rather than "as a place to hold discussions about that information." Although on one hand participants might simply be following WMST protocol in formulating their contributions as queries rather than as messages of other types, as an active list with a steadily increasing membership (currently approaching 2000 members). WMST is proof that many women are comfortable with CMC that consists primarily in asking advice and information of others.

At the same time, there are indications that women do not avoid discussion of issues entirely by choice. Issues discussions arise periodically on WMST, only to be cut short by reminders from the list owner and other self-appointed list vigilantes; more than a few subscribers have written in to complain that the most interesting threads are invariably censored. The list owner feels, however, that it is important to avoid such exchanges in the inter-

Table I	Features of Women's and Men's Language
Women's Language	**Men's Language**
Attenuated assertions	Strong assertions
Apologies	Self-promotion
Explicit justifications	Presuppositions
Questions	Rhetorical questions
Personal orientation	Authoritative orientation
Supports others	Challenges others
	Humor/sarcasm

ests of limiting message volume, and out of a fear that "discussion about highly-charged societal issues . . . would attract all sorts of unpleasant, acrimonious people who are just looking for a fight."[6] As the following section shows, this fear is not entirely unfounded.

Manner of Participation

The stylistic register of all of the CMC analyzed here is that of academic discourse. Nevertheless, there are significant sex-based differences to be noted, such that it is often possible to tell whether a given message was written by a man or a woman, solely on the basis of the rhetorical and linguistic strategies employed.[7]

In Herring (1992), I identify a set of features hypothesized to characterize a stylistic variety conventionally recognizable as "women's language" as opposed to "men's language" on the LINGUIST list. These features are summarized in Table 1.

The examples below, taken from messages posted during the LINGUIST "issues" discussion, illustrate some of the features of each style.

[female contributor]
I am intrigued by your comment that work such as that represented in WFDT may not be as widely represented in LSA as other work because its argumentation style doesn't lend itself to falsification à la Popper. Could you say a bit more about what you mean here? I am interested because I think similar mismatches in argumentation are at stake in other areas of cognitive science, as well as because I study argumentation as a key (social and cognitive) tool for human knowledge construction.
[personal orientation, attenuation, questions, justification]

[male contributor]
It is obvious that there are two (and only two) paradigms for the conduct of scientific inquiry into an issue on which there is no consensus. One is [. . .]. But, deplorable as that may be, note that either paradigm (if pursued honestly) will lead to truth anyway. That is, whichever side is wrong will sooner or later discover that fact on its own. If, God forbid, autonomy and/or modularity should turn out to be His truth, then those who have other ideas will sooner or later find this out.
[authoritative orientation, strong assertions, sarcasm]

In order to quantify the distribution of these features according to sex, I then analyzed 261 messages in two extended LINGUIST discussions, coding each message for the occurrence or nonoccurrence of each of the features in Table 1. The results show that women's language features are indeed used more often by women, and men's language features more often by men. Sixty-eight percent of the messages produced by women contained one or more features of women's language, as compared with only 31% of those produced by men. In contrast, 48% of the messages produced by men contained features of only men's language, as compared with 18% of women's messages. Although the majority of women's messages (46%) combined a mixture of male and female rhetorical features, the fewest men's messages (14%) combined features. This finding supports the view that it is easier for men to maintain a distinct style (masculine, feminine, or neutral) than it is for women, who must employ some features of men's language in order to be taken seriously as academics, and some features of women's language in order not to be considered unpleasant or aggressive.

These observations on gender-marked styles lead to a second finding regarding manner of participation. Discussion on each of the lists investigated tends to be dominated by a small minority of participants who abuse features of men's language to focus attention on themselves, often at the expense of others. Such abuse, which I term "adversarial" rhetoric, ranges from gratuitous displays of knowledge to forceful assertions of one's views to elaborate put-downs of others with whom one disagrees. In the two LINGUIST discussions analyzed, 4% and 6% of the participants, respectively (all but one of them male), were responsible for the majority of adversarial

rhetoric. This same 4% and 6% also posted the most words (33% and 53% of the total, respectively, or more than eight times the participant average), and thus dominated in amount as well as in manner of participation.[8]

A similar pattern is found in a different kind of CMC—electronic mail exchanges between undergraduates (75% male) on a local network, as investigated by McCormick and McCormick (1992). The authors report that 4.7% of the undergraduates used the network "a great deal," and "may have been responsible for generating most of the electronic mail." Although the content and purpose of communication in this setting is quite different from that on professional academic discussion lists, the minority also seems to have imposed its style on the discourse overall, turning the computer lab into "an adolescent subculture" complete with crude jokes, threats, and put-downs.

The extent to which other participants are negatively affected by the behavior of a dominant minority may depend, at least partly, on their sex. A survey of LINGUIST subscribers distributed after the "issue" discussion took place revealed that 73% of respondent's of both sexes felt intimidated and/or irritated by the adversarial tone of the discussion (Herring, 1992). Men and women appear to behave differently on the basis of this reaction, however. Male respondents indicated that they take it in stride as part of academic interaction; as one man remarked: "Actually, the barbs and arrows were entertaining, because of course they weren't aimed at me." Many women, in contrast, expressed a deep aversion and a concern to avoid interactions of this type. Comments included: "I was terri-

bly turned off by this exchange, which went on and on forever. I nearly dropped myself from the list of subscribers," and "I was disgusted. It's the same old arguments, the same old intentions of defending theoretical territory, the same old inabilities of open and creative thinking, all of which make me ambivalent about academics in general." The concern expressed by the owner of the WMST list to avoid acrimonious exchanges is fully consistent with the comments of the female LINGUIST survey respondents. Why do women react with greater aversion than men to adversarial exchanges? Sheldon (1992) suggests that this aversion can be traced to cultural norms of sex-appropriate behavior with which children are indoctrinated from an early age: while boys are encouraged to compete and engage in direct confrontation, girls are taught to "be nice" and to appease others, a distinction internalized in the play behavior of children as young as three years of age. As a consequence, verbal aggressiveness comes to have a different significance for women than for men; as Coates (1986) observes, women are apt to take personal offense at what men may view as part of the conventional structure of conversation.

Discussion of Results

The results of this research can be summarized as follows. Despite the democratizing potential described in the first section of this article, male and female academic professionals do not participate equally in academic CMC. Rather, a small male minority dominates the discourse both in terms of amount of talk, and rhetorically, through self-promotional and adversarial strategies. Moreover, when women do attempt to participate on a more equal basis, they risk being actively censored by the reactions of men who either ignore them or attempt to delegitimize their contributions. Because of social conditioning that makes women uncomfortable with direct conflict, women tend to be more intimidated by these practices and to avoid participating as a result. Thus Habermas's conditions for a democratic discourse are not met: although the medium theoretically allows for everyone with access to a network to take part and to express their concerns and desires equally, a very large community of potential participants is effectively prevented by censorship, both overt and covert, from availing itself of this possibility. Rather than being democratic, academic CMC is power-based and hierarchical. This state of affairs cannot, however, be attributed to the influence of computer communication technology; rather, it continues preexisting patterns of hierarchy and male dominance in academia more generally, and in society as a whole.

How can we reconcile these findings with the more encouraging reports of democratization based on earlier research? The claim of status-free communication hinges in large part on the condition of anonymity (Graddol and Swann, 1989; Kiesler et al., 1984), a condition that is not met in the discourse analyzed here, since most messages were signed, or else the sender's identity is transparently derivable from his or her electronic address.[9] In a very few cases could there have been any doubt upon receipt of a message as to the sex of the sender, and thus sex-based discrimination could freely apply. However, given the existence of

"genderlects" of the sort identified here, it is doubtful that such discrimination would disappear even if everyone were to contribute anonymously. Just as a university president or a janitor's social status is communicated through their unconscious choices of style and diction, CMC contains subtle indications of participants' gender.

Second, CMC is claimed to be more uninhibited (disorganized, anarchic), because of lack of established conventions of use (Kiesler et al., 1984; Nelson, 1974). It is important, however, to distinguish between the adversarial behavior observed on academic lists and "flaming," which is defined as "excessive informality, insensitivity, the expression of extreme or opinionated views, and vulgar behavior (including swearing, insults, name calling, and hostile comments)" by McCormick and McCormick (1992, p. 381). While flaming may well result from spontaneously venting one's emotion, adversariality is a conventionalized and accepted (indeed, rewarded) pattern of behavior in academic discourse, and characterizes postings that otherwise show evidence of careful planning and preparation. Rather than being at a loss for a set of discourse conventions, the members of these lists appear to have simply transferred the conventions of academic discourse, as they might be observed, for example, in face-to-face interaction at a professional conference, to the electronic medium, with some modifications for the written nature of the message.

Another factor claimed to lead to decreased inhibition is the supposedly depersonalized nature of CMC. However, this assumption too can be challenged.

From my observations, academic list subscribers do not view the activity of posting as targeted at disembodied strangers. Their addresses are people with whom they either have a professional relationship, or could potentially develop such a relationship in the future. This is likely to increase (rather than decrease) inhibition, since one's professional reputation is at stake. In this respect, the CMC discussed here differs from the experimental CMC described by Kiesler et al., where subjects risked nothing beyond the confines of the experimental setting. Three factors in Kiesler et al.'s (1984, p. 1129) experimental design were found to correlate with less inhibited verbal behavior: anonymity, simultaneity (as opposed to linear sequencing of messages), and simultaneous computer conferencing (as opposed to electronic mail). None of these conditions obtained in the CMC investigated in this study, since discussion lists, in addition to not meeting the anonymity condition, present postings linearly, and typically after some delay.

In concluding, we return to the question of censorship, freedom from which is an essential condition for democracy. Although it is true that no external censorship was exercised by the moderators or owners of LINGUIST or MBU, women participating in CMC are nevertheless constrained by censorship both external and internal. Externally, they are censored by male participants who dominate and control the discourse through intimidation tactics, and who ignore or undermine women's contributions when they attempt to participate on a more equal basis. To a lesser extent, nonadversarial men suffer the same treatment, and in and of itself, it need not prevent anyone who is determined to participate from doing so. Where adversariality becomes a devastating form of censorship, however, is in conjunction with the internalized cultural expectations that we bring to the formula: that women will talk less, on less controversial topics, and in a less assertive manner. Finally, although it was not a focus of the present investigation, women are further discouraged from participating in CMC by the expectation—effectively internalized as well—that computer technology is primarily a male domain (McCormick and McCormick, 1991; Turkle, 1991). This expectation is reflected in the responses of female survey respondents on both LINGUIST and MBU to the question: "How comfortable/competent do you feel with computer technology?" Female respondents overwhelmingly indicated less confidence in their ability to use computers, despite the fact that they had had the same number of years of computer experience as male respondents.[10] Internalized censorship of this sort reflects deeper social ills, and it is naive to expect that technology alone will heal them.

References

Bolter, J. D. (1991). *Writing Space: The Computer, Hypertext, and the History of Writing*. Lawrence Erlbaum, Hillsdale, NJ.

Coates, J. (1986). *Women, Men, and Language*. Longman, New York.

Ess, C. (1994). "The Political Computer: Hypertext, Democracy, and Habermas," in George Landow (ed.), *Hypertext and Literary Theory*. Johns Hopkins University Press, Baltimore, MD.

Ferrara, K., H. Brunner, and G. Whittemore (1991). "Interactive Written Discourse as an Emergent Register." *Written Communication*, 8, 8–34.

Graddol, D., and J. Swann (1989). *Gender Voices*. Basil Blackwell, Oxford.

Habermas, J. (1983). "Diskursethik: Notizen zu einem Begruendungsprogram," in Moralbewusstsein und kommunikatives Handeln (Frankfurt: Suhrkamp). Translated as "Discourse Ethics: Notes on Philosophical Justification," in Christian Lenhardt and Shierry Weber Nicholsen (trans.), *Moral Consciousness and Communicative Action* (43–115). MIT Press, Cambridge (1990).

Herring, S. (1992). "Gender and Participation in Computer-Mediated Linguistic Discourse." Washington, DC: ERIC Clearinghouse on Languages and Linguistics, Document no. ED345552.

Herring, S. (1993). "Men's Language: A Study of the Discourse of the LINGUIST List." in A. Crochetihre, J. C. Boulanger, and C. Ouellon (eds.), *Les Langues Menacies: Actes du XVe Congres International des Linguistes*, Vol. 3, pp. 347–350. Quibec Les Presses de l'Universiti Laval.

Herring, S. (forthcoming). "Two Variants of an Electronic Message Schema." in S. Herring (ed.), *Computer-Mediated Communication: Linguistic, Social, and Cross-Cultural Perspectives*. John Benjamins, Amsterdam/Philadelphia.

Herring, S. C., D. Johnson, and T. DiBenedetto (1992). "Participation in Electronic Discourse in a 'Feminist' Field," in *Locating Power: Proceedings of the 1992 Berkeley Women and Language Conference*. Berkeley Linguistic Society.

Herring, S., D. Johnson, and T. DiBenedetto (in press). " 'This Discussion Is Going Too Far!' Male Resistance to Female Participation on the Internet." in M. Bucholtz and K. Hall (eds.), *Gender Articulated: Language and the Socially-Constructed Self*. Routledge, New York.

Holmes, J. (1992). "Women's Talk in Public Contexts." *Discourse and Society*, 3(2), 131–150.

Kahn, A. S., and R. G. Brookshire (1991). "Using a Computer Bulletin Board in a Social Psychology Course." *Teaching of Psychology*, 18(4), 245–249.

Kiesler, S., J. Siegel, and T. W. McGuire (1984). "Social Psychological Aspects of Computer-Mediated Communication." *American Psychologist*, 39, 1123–1134.

Landow, G. P. (1992). *Hypertext: The Convergence of Contemporary Critical Theory and Technology*. Johns Hopkins University Press, Baltimore, MD.

McCormick, N. B., and J. W. McCormick (1991). "Not for Men Only: Why So Few Women Major in Computer Science." *College Student Journal*, 85(3), 345–350.

McCormick, N. B., and J. W. McCormick (1992). "Computer Friends and Foes: Content of Undergraduates' Electronic Mail." *Computers in Human Behavior*, 8, 379–405.

Nelson, T. H. (1974). "Dream Machines: New Freedoms through Computer Screens—A Minority Report." *Computer Lib: You Can and Must Understand Computers Now*. Hugo's Book Service, Chicago. (rev. ed.). Microsoft Press, Redmond, WA (1987).

Sheldon, A. (1992). "Conflict Talk: Sociolinguistic Challenges to Self-Assertion and How Young Girls Meet Them." *Merrill-Palmer Quarterly*, 38(1), 95–117.

Smith, J., and E. Balka (1991). "Chatting on a Feminist Computer Network," in C. Kramarae (ed.), *Technology and Women's Voices* (pp. 82–97). Routledge and Kegan Paul, New York.

Spender, D. (1979). "Language and Sex Differences," in *Osnabrueker Beitraege zur Sprach-theorie: Sprache und Geschlect* II, 38–59.

Turkle, S. (1991). "Computational Reticence: Why Women Fear the Intimate Machine," in C. Kramarae (ed.), *Technology and Women's Voices* (pp. 41–61). Routledge and Kegan Paul, New York.

Notes

1. Examples of opaque electronic addresses drawn from the data reported on in this study include 'f24030@barilvm,' 'T52@ dhdurz1,' 'SNU00169@krsnucc1,' and the like.

2. An example of such censorship is the Defense Communications Agency's periodic screening of messages on the government-sponsored network ARPANET "to weed out those deemed in bad taste" (Kiesler *et al.*, 1984, p. 1130).

3. With sex-neutral first names such as Chris or Robin, or with foreign names that I did not recognize, I contacted individuals by e-mail, identified the nature of my

research, and asked whether they were male or female. By employing a combination of methods, I was able to determine with a reasonable degree of certainty the sex of approximately 95% of contributors on both lists.

4. These percentages were calculated from lists of subscribers as of September 1992, on the basis of names from which sex could reliably be inferred.

5. Although it is difficult to evaluate objectively what might count as evidence of a "vituperative" tone, the only postings to contain personal criticism of other participants (excluding the messages of protest) were those contributed by the man who originally proposed the "Men's Literature" course.

6. Korenman, Joan (KORENMAN@UMBC.BITNET), Women's Studies List, June 9 11:08 PDT, 1992. In the only instance I observed where an issues discussion on WMST was allowed to take place, the discussion—concerned with media bias in reporting research on sex differences in the brain—was one in which all participants were

essentially in agreement. (See Herring, in press.)

7. There are also differences in character between the two lists. The overall level of formality is higher, and differences in sex-based styles greater, for LINGUIST than for MBU. Perhaps because of the rhetorical practices that currently characterize the two fields (formal argumentation in linguistics vs. creative collaboration in composition), discourse in the former tends to be more adversarial, or "masculine," while discourse in the latter is more personal, or "feminine." (For example, both men and women reveal information about their feelings and their nonacademic lives on MBU, whereas postings of this sort are virtually nonexistent on LINGUIST.)

8. The tendency for a small minority to dominate the discourse is evident on MBU as well. Eight percent of participants (all but one of them male) produced 35% of the words in the sexism discussion. This minority dominated rhetorically by posting long-winded and often obscure

postings, on MBU an abuse more common than overt adversarial attacks.

9. As far as I was able to ascertain, surprisingly few participants took advantage of the anonymity potential of the medium. Fewer than 2% of contributors attempted to disguise their identity, and when they did so, it was for humorous effect.

10. In the MBU survey, 30% of female respondents reported feeling "somewhat hesitant" about using computers, as compared with 5% of the men (the rest of whom rated themselves as "competent" or "extremely competent"). In the LINGUIST survey, 13% of the women responded "somewhat hesitant" as compared with none of the men. The average length of computer use for both sexes was nine years on MBU and eleven years on LINGUIST.

 Article Review Form at end of book.

How much time online is too much? Are relationships formed online an acceptable substitute for those formed in the physical world?

Sad, Lonely World Discovered in Cyberspace

Amy Harmon

In the first concentrated study of the social and psychological effects of Internet use at home, researchers at Carnegie Mellon University have found that people who spend even a few hours a week on line experience higher levels of depression and loneliness than if they used the computer network less frequently.

Participants who were lonelier and more depressed, as determined by standard questionnaires at the start of the two-year study, were no more drawn to the Internet than those who were originally happier and more socially engaged. Instead, Internet use itself appeared to cause a decline in psychological well-being, the researchers said.

The results of the $1.5 million project ran completely contrary to expectations of the social scientists who designed it and to many of the organizations that financed the study. These included technology companies like the Intel Corporation, Hewlett Packard, AT&T Research and Apple Computer, as well as the National Science Foundation.

"We were shocked by the findings, because they are coun-terintuitive to what we know about how socially the Internet is being used," said Robert Kraut, a social psychology professor at Carnegie Mellon's Human Computer Interaction Institute. "We are not talking here about the extremes. These were normal adults and their families, and on average, for those who used the Internet most, things got worse."

The Internet has been praised as superior to television and other "passive" media because it allows users to choose the kind of information they want to receive, and often, to respond actively to it in the form of E-mail exchanges with other users, chat rooms or electronic bulletin board postings.

Research on the effects of watching television indicates that it tends to reduce social involvement. But the new study, titled "HomeNet," suggests that the interactive medium may be no more socially healthy than older mass media. It also raises troubling questions about "virtual" communication and the disembodied relationships that are often formed in the vacuum of cyberspace.

Participants in the study used inherently social features like E-mail and Internet chat more than they used passive information gathering like reading or watching videos. But they reported a decline in interaction with family members and a reduction in their circles of friends that directly corresponded to the amount of time they spent on line.

At the beginning and end of the two-year study, the subjects were asked to agree or disagree with statements like "I felt everything I did was an effort," and "I enjoyed life" and "I can find companionship when I want it." They were also asked to estimate how many minutes each day they spent with each member of their family and to quantify their social circle. The subjects were given standard questionnaires used to determine psychological health.

For the duration of the study, the subjects' use of the Internet was recorded. For the purposes of this study, depression and loneliness were measured independently, and each subject was rated on a subjective scale. In measuring depression, the responses were plotted on a scale of 0 to 3, with 0 being the least depressed and 3 being the most depressed. Loneliness was plotted on a scale of 1 to 5.

By the end of the study, the researchers found that one hour a week on the Internet led, on average, to an increase of .03, or 1 percent, on the depression scale, a loss of 2.7 members of the subject's social circle, which averaged 66 people, and an increase of .02, or four-tenths of 1 percent, on the loneliness scale.

The subjects exhibited wide variations in all three measured effects, and while the net effects were not large, they were statistically significant in demonstrating deterioration of social and psychological life, Professor Kraut said.

Based on these data, the researchers hypothesize that relationships maintained over long distances without face-to-face contact ultimately do not provide the kind of support and reciprocity that typically contribute to a sense of psychological security and happiness, like being available to baby-sit in a pinch for a friend, or to grab a cup of coffee.

"Our hypothesis is there are more cases where you're building shallow relationships, leading to an overall decline in feeling of connection to other people," Professor Kraut said.

The study tracked the behavior of 169 participants in the Pittsburgh area who were selected from four schools and community groups. Half the group was measured through two years of Internet use, and the other half for one year. The findings will be published this week by *The American Psychologist,* the peer-reviewed monthly journal of the American Psychological Association.

Because the study participants were not randomly selected, it is unclear how the findings apply to the general population. It is also conceivable that some unmeasured factor caused simultaneous increases in use of the Internet and decline in normal levels of social involvement. Moreover, the effect of Internet use varied depending on an individual's life patterns and type of use. Researchers said that people who were isolated because of their geography or work shifts might have benefited socially from Internet use.

Even so, several social scientists familiar with the study vouched for its credibility and predicted that the findings would probably touch off a national debate over how public policy on the Internet should evolve and how the technology might be shaped to yield more beneficial effects.

"They did an extremely careful scientific study, and it's not a result that's easily ignored," said Tora Bikson, a senior scientist at Rand, the research institution. Based in part on previous studies that focused on how local communities like Santa Monica, Calif., used computer networks to enhance civic participation, Rand has recommended that the Federal Government provide E-mail access to all Americans.

"It's not clear what the underlying psychological explanation is," Ms. Bikson said of the study. "Is it because people give up day-to-day contact and then find themselves depressed? Or are they exposed to the broader world of Internet and then wonder, 'What am I doing here in Pittsburgh?' Maybe your comparison standard changes. I'd like to see this replicated on larger scale. Then I'd really worry."

Christine Riley, a psychologist at the Intel Corporation, the giant chip manufacturer that was among the sponsors of the study, said she was surprised by the results but did not consider the research definitive.

"For us, the point is there was really no information on this before," Ms. Riley said. "But it's important to remember this is not about the technology, per se; it's about how it is used. It really points to the need for considering social factors in terms of how you design applications and services for technology."

The Carnegie Mellon team—which included Sara Kiesler, a social psychologist who helped pioneer the study of human interaction over computer networks; Tridas Mukophadhyay, a professor at the graduate business school who has examined computer mediated communication in the workplace, and William Scherlis, a research scientist in computer science—stressed that the negative effects of Internet use that they found were not inevitable.

For example, the main focus of Internet use in schools has been gathering information and getting in touch with people from far-away places. But the research suggests that maintaining social ties with people in close physical proximity could be more psychologically healthy.

"More intense development and deployment of services that support pre-existing communities and strong relationships should be encouraged," the researchers write in their forthcoming article. "Government efforts to wire the nation's schools, for example, should consider on-line homework sessions for students rather than just on-line reference works."

At a time when Internet use is expanding—nearly 70 million adult Americans are on line, according to Nielsen Media Research—social critics say that the technology could exacerbate the fragmentation of American society or help to fuse it, depending on how it is used.

"There are two things the Internet can turn out to be, and we don't know yet which it's going to be," said Robert Putnam, a political scientist at Harvard University whose forthcoming book, *Bowling Alone,* which is to be published next year by Simon & Schuster, chronicles the alienation of Americans from each other since the 1960's. "The fact that I'm able to communicate daily with my collaborators in Germany and Japan makes me more efficient, but there are a lot of things it can't do, like bring me chicken soup."

Professor Putnam added, "The question is how can you push computer mediated communication in a direction that would make it more community friendly."

Perhaps paradoxically, several participants in the Internet study expressed surprise when they were informed of the study's conclusions.

"For me it's been the opposite of depression; it's been a way of being connected," said Rabbi Alvin Berkun, who used the Internet for a few hours a week to read *The Jerusalem Post* and communicate with other rabbis across the country.

But Rabbi Berkun said his wife did not share his enthusiasm for the medium. "She does sometimes resent when I go and hook up," he said, adding after a pause, "I guess I am away from where my family is while I'm on the computer." Another possibility is that the natural human preference for face-to-face communication may provide a self-correcting mechanism to the technology.

The rabbi's daughter, Rebecca, 17, said she had spent a fair amount of time in teen-age chat rooms at the beginning of the survey in 1995.

"I can see how people would get depressed," Ms. Berkun said. "When we first got it, I would be on for an hour a day or more. But I found it was the same type of people, the same type of things being said. It got kind of old."

 **Article Review Form at end of book.**

Why was the methodology of the Carnegie Mellon study criticized?
What kind of methodological approach might satisfy the critics?

Technology:

Critics are picking apart a professor's study that linked Internet use to loneliness and depression

Denise Caruso

Robert Kraut, a co-author of a new study linking depression with Internet use, sounded a bit depressed himself last week.

"I thought I was finished with this," Mr. Kraut, a professor of social psychology and human-computer interaction at Carnegie Mellon University, said with a sigh. He was alluding to the flood of attention—and criticism—that his study, titled "Home Net," had received since it was published two weeks ago.

Starting in 1995, "Home Net" researchers gave PC's and free Internet accounts to 169 people in 73 families in the Pittsburgh area. After monitoring their on-line behavior, in some cases for more than two years, the researchers concluded that spending time on the Internet was associated with statistically significant increases in depression and loneliness.

Critics assert that the study has fatal flaws that neutralize its findings and that they are appalled at the authors' far-reaching conclusions about the impact the findings might have on Internet policy and technology development.

Donna L. Hoffman, a Vanderbilt University professor and outspoken critic of Internet research design, was unequivocal about the "Home Net" study.

"Speaking as an editor, if this had crossed my desk, I would have rejected it," said Ms. Hoffman, who edits the journal *Marketing Science*. "The mistakes are so bad that they render the results fairly close to meaningless."

Among those mistakes, she said, were the absence of two standard safeguards: a control group and random selection of subjects.

"With 'Home Net,' we don't know for sure what led to their results," Ms. Hoffman said of the lack of a control group, "because

we don't know what happened to people who weren't using the Internet."

In addition, the study recruited people from high schools and community service organizations, instead of selecting people randomly from a large area. Random selection is crucial to building a truly representative sample of a population—in this case, residents of the United States.

The study found that one hour a week on line led to small but measurable increases in depression and loneliness and loss of friendships. While those measurements might well be statistically significant, critics assert that without a random sample, they are meaningless outside the group that was studied.

"The assertions have no statistical relevance to any population of Internet users beyond those in the study population—even in principle," declared Charles Brownstein, a former director at the National Science Foundation, now an executive director at the Corporation for National Research Initiatives in Reston, Va.

Although research studies do not always have to use control groups or randomly chosen participants to be valid, Ms. Hoffman said, those safeguards become imperative "when you're doing a study that claims causal relationships and that these relationships hold in the larger population."

The "Home Net" team clearly made such claims. For example, the news release stated that "Carnegie Mellon Study Reveals Negative Potential of Heavy Internet Use on Emotional Well Being," and even suggested that parents move PC's out of teen-agers' bedrooms and into shared family rooms.

Mr. Kraut was quoted extensively in the release, with such statements as, "We were surprised to find that what is a social technology has such anti-social consequences." Also: "Our results have clear implications for further research on personal Internet use. As we understand the reasons for the declines in social involvement, there will be implications for social policies and for the design of Internet technology."

Last week, Mr. Kraut wearily defended his study. "In 1995, we did start with a control group, but it was very hard to keep it, with little in the way of incentives for them to continue to fill out questionnaires," he said. "And we couldn't use a random sample because of the nature of the study's design—we wanted to be able to include groups who already had social connections with each other so we could observe some shifting, if it was going to occur, between existing social relationships."

And despite criticism of the researchers' methods, he said that the study was widely applicable.

"We have changes big enough that they aren't likely to have occurred on the basis of chance," Mr. Kraut said. "There is something here to explain."

But critics like Ms. Hoffman look askance at such results, given her experience debunking other Internet studies, including one from Neilsen Media Research in which she participated in 1996 and another in 1995 in which Marty Rimm, a graduate student in Carnegie Mellon's College of Engineering, published a study purporting to show that the Internet was overrun with pornography.

The impact of Mr. Rimm's study, though based on false premises and quickly discredited, was profound. The resulting furor in the media and in Congress helped bring about the Communications Decency Act, which the Supreme Court ruled was a violation of the First Amendment.

Critics fear that the "Home Net" study might end up having a similar effect.

"It's easy to imagine the results of this study being used to influence policy decisions about Internet access, especially in controversial funding decisions for schools and libraries," Ms. Hoffman said.

But in the end, Ms. Hoffman said, protecting the Internet itself is not the point.

"We're trying to protect the standard of research," she said. "This isn't obscure ivory-tower stuff that never sees the light of day. It has an impact on people's lives. If we're going to the trouble to study the Internet, at least we should make sure we're doing it right."

 Article Review Form at end of book.

WiseGuide Wrap-Up

Computer-mediated communication affects notions of self and identity in unexpected ways, as the experience of gender-swapping illustrates. Intense experience in virtual worlds may lead to increased feelings of loneliness and depression, raising questions about the emotional quality of computer-mediated social relationships. To further explore the issues in this section, interview a frequent chat room participant about why he or she participates in this forum, or explore your own reasons for doing so. If you are new to chat, or to MUDs and MOOs, spend some time lurking in a chat room or a MOO. What strikes you as interesting or strange? Why do you think people enjoy participating in these forums?

R.E.A.L. Sites

This list provides a print preview of typical **Coursewise** R.E.A.L. sites. There are over 100 such sites at the **Courselinks**™ site. The danger in printing URLs is that web sites can change overnight. As we went to press, these sites were functional using the URLs provided. If you come across one that isn't, please let us know via email to: webmaster@coursewise.com. Use your Passport to access the most current list of R.E.A.L. sites at the **Courselinks**™ site.

Site name: Loebner Prize Home Page

URL: http://www.loebner.net/Prizef/loebner-prize.html

Why is it R.E.A.L.? The Loebner Prize is awarded every year to the world's most human computer, based on the results of the Turing Test, which evaluates the ability of a computer to think like a human. This site includes fascinating "conversation" transcripts of past prize winners, including the program PC Therapist and the "Chatterbot" Albert One.

Key topics: human-computer interaction, ethics

Try this: Visit the site to read the conversation transcript for PC Therapist or another prize winner. How might such programs be useful? What ethical issues might come into play when a computer is designed to imitate a human?

Site name: Sexuality and Cyberspace

URL: http://www.echonyc.com/~women/Issue17/index.html

Why is it R.E.A.L.? This special issue of *Women and Performance: A Journal of Feminist Theory* presents a collection of interesting articles about identity, gender, and sexuality in cyberspace. Many esoteric titles, including "Phone Sex Is Cool: Chatlines as Superconductors" and "Modem Butterfly, Reconsidered."

Key topics: gender, identity, cyberculture

Try this: Visit the site to review one of the articles on cyberculture. What is the author's thesis? Does the thesis have merit? Why or why not?

Site name: Texts by Julian Dibbell

URL: http://www.levity.com/julian/indexvanilla.html

Why is it R.E.A.L.? This site contains a collection of Dibbell's articles on cyberculture—for example, "MUD Money: A Talk on Virtual Value."

Key topics: gender, identity, cyberculture

Try this: Visit the site to review one of Dibbell's articles on cyberculture. Identify and evaluate his main point or points.

section 5

Censorship, Privacy, and Security in Cyberspace: Is Big Brother Watching You?

Suppose you are sitting next to another student in a college computer lab. You glance at your neighbor's screen and notice an image depicting a violent and pornographic act. Quickly, you look away, but you can't put the image out of your mind. You're upset, unable to concentrate, and no longer feel comfortable working in the lab. After a few minutes, you decide to leave.

Are you a victim of sexual harassment? Or are you guilty of invading another student's privacy? Should you report the incident to the computer lab monitor or to a college administrator? Should the college take action against the student and adopt a policy that prohibits students from viewing such images in public places? Or should it place "privacy screens" on each computer, so that no one can accidentally view another student's monitor?

At universities, schools, and libraries today, policy makers are struggling to deal with these questions and others. Where is the line between the First Amendment and sexual harassment and other forms of intimidation? How do we shield children from unsavory images while protecting constitutional rights to free speech and privacy? Who has the right to control the information and images to which the public has access?

Communities, schools, and libraries have been dealing with these issues from the day that the U.S. Constitution was drafted. But, with print resources, unofficial "filtering" mechanisms work to reduce the number of occasions when controversy might be generated. Libraries cannot afford to purchase every book published. Teachers select the materials that students will read in class. The federal government controls broadcast media in the way it regulates the broadcast bandwidth. Even cable television is regulated by the market, with decisions about what programs to produce based on how many potential viewer-consumers will tune in.

But the Internet operates outside of these formal and informal systems of regulation, providing easy and immediate access to unlimited quantities of text and images. Furthermore, it provides opportunities for anyone to self-publish whatever they choose. The circulation of ever larger quantities of unfiltered material almost guarantees controversy as people deem some of it offensive.

Advocates for protecting civil liberties on the Internet emphasize that the basis of democracy is the free and unfettered flow of information. Attempts to regulate, filter, or limit what people can publish or access on the Internet, they argue, is the beginning of the descent down the slippery slope to abridgement of the First Amendment.

Learning Objectives

- Describe the problems associated with filtering software in public libraries.

- Describe O'Neil's position on the Jake Baker case.

- Summarize the methods used by some governments to control the Internet.

- Describe the reasons for the Supreme Court's decision to strike down the Communications Decency Act (CDA).

- Outline three provisions of the CDA for which employers remain liable.

- Describe how privacy invasion affects our lives.

- Summarize why Obser contends that "privacy is the problem, not the solution."

133

If the issue of Internet censorship hasn't hit your community library, it will. The first article in this section, "Sex, Kids, and the Public Library" gives you one librarian's perspective on why libraries should screen Internet access for minors.

Colleges also have been challenged by similar concerns. In 1995, a student at the University of Michigan was suspended and charged with criminal threatening after circulating a fantasy story about another student on the Internet. Robert O'Neil's article, "Free Speech on the Electronic Frontier," an opinion piece from *The Chronicle of Higher Education*, examines that situation.

"Two-Edged Sword: Asian Regimes on the Internet" reports on how and why government officials in such countries as China and Singapore are attempting to control the flow of information over the Internet. It suggests how governments can use Internet censorship to contain dissidents and other sources of opposition. Could such scenarios ever occur in your country?

The next piece, "On the Net, Anything Goes," reports on the U.S. Supreme Court decision to strike down large parts of the Communications Decency Act, which Congress passed in 1996 in an attempt to regulate the flow of information on the Internet. "What's Left of the Communications Decency Act?"—originally published in *HR Magazine*—explains which parts of this law were upheld by the Court and how the law affects employers.

An issue related to censorship is that of privacy and security. The unfettered flow of electronic information also means that our personal information increasingly becomes public. Every time we use an ATM machine, shop with a credit card, or provide some information over the Internet, we are making private information public. Once the information becomes public, we lose control over how it is used.

Is the collection of private information innocuous and even helpful, allowing merchants and other service providers to tailor their services to our needs? Or can this information be used in harmful ways, especially when it is recorded erroneously? An error in a credit rating report may result in the denial of a mortgage or car loan. A transposed social security number may reinvent its holder as a criminal from another state.

What's most disturbing about these scenarios is that often you don't know how electronic information has been used and circulated until it creates a problem. If you do find out that your electronic identity has been misrepresented, setting the record straight often involves time, expense, and lots of perseverance.

Privacy is the main concern of David Linowes in the article "Your Personal Information Has Gone Public," which describes how computers access, store, and use personal information. But, in the final selection, Jeffrey Obser contends that "Privacy Is the Problem, Not the Solution." Obser presents a somewhat complex argument about modern life to illustrate why concerns about privacy in electronic environments may be exaggerated.

The companion web sites at the end of the section provide you with additional resources for investigating issues related to censorship, privacy, and security. If you want to find out the latest information on legislation and court decisions in this area, check out the sites for the Center for Democracy and Technology; for EPIC, the Electronic Privacy Information Center, and for the Electronic Frontier Foundation.

As you review the articles in this section, remember that decisions are being made every day at your school, in your community, and in the political arena that will determine how and if the Internet is to be regulated. This era may be unsurpassed for the amount of public attention focused on constitutional questions being played out in forums around the United States. Could the Founding Fathers have envisioned the Internet? Probably not—but it's exciting that a document dating back more than 200 years still serves as the foundation for policy in the Information Age.

? Questions ?

Reading 22. For librarians, does intellectual freedom mean providing unlimited information to everyone all the time? What are some potential consequences if libraries filter access to the Internet, or if they refuse to do so?

Reading 23. Was the University of Michigan justified in suspending Mr. Baker? Should colleges and universities regulate student use of the Internet?

Reading 24. What do governments' attempts to control the Internet suggest about the power of this medium? What do they suggest about the powers of government?

Reading 25. Why did Congress pass the Communications Decency Act? Why did the Supreme Court reject it?

Reading 26. How are employers liable for employees' use of telecommunications equipment? Why did the Supreme Court allow parts of the Communications Decency Act to stand?

Reading 27. What happens when our personal information becomes public? What steps can we take to protect private information?

Reading 28. How does the "collapse of trust" relate to contemporary concerns about privacy? What is the role of the "portable reputation" in today's society?

For librarians, does intellectual freedom mean providing unlimited information to everyone all the time? What are some potential consequences if libraries filter access to the Internet, or if they refuse to do so?

Sex, Kids, and the Public Library

New issues of censorship and selection raised by the Internet speak to the very role of the public library.

Marilyn Gell Mason

Marilyn Gell Mason is director of the Cleveland (Ohio) Public Library

"Sex at the library. News at eleven." Television, talk shows, and newspapers are shouting the message in community after community across the country from Orange County to Boston, from Oklahoma City to Medina, Ohio, from Houston to New York.

They say that public libraries are no longer safe havens for children. They say that ALA has libraries peddling pornography. They say that librarians are unresponsive to the public's concern. They say that something must be done.

The problem is a knotty one. How does a library provide free and open access to the 34 million sites now available worldwide through the Internet without inflaming parents and others in the community concerned about children viewing pictures that most believe are pornographic? It is one thing to fight the Communications Decency Act in court for its obvious legal failings

and quite another to confront a room full of enraged parents and elected officials armed with pictures printed off the Internet in a public library.

The legal aspects of pornography on the Internet are outside the purview of this article. I believe that the current position of ALA in its suit challenging the Communication Decency Act is appropriate. What I fear, however, is that we may win in court and lose in the court of public opinion. The very real issues arising from pornography on the Internet are not going to be resolved by the courts; they are going to be resolved by public libraries and public library users. How they are resolved will determine whether public libraries continue to be the most respected (perhaps the only respected) public institution in the country.

In spite of the official ALA position outlined in the Library Bill of Rights and its interpretation on electronic information (AL, Mar. 1996, insert*) that there

*Refers to the March 1996 issue of *American Libraries*.

should be free and open access to all library materials for everyone, regardless of age, including material on the Internet, libraries across the country are experimenting with some mechanism for limiting children's access, at least to the seamier sites. Some are using the technological solution of filtering software; others have sought legal sanction by requiring parental approval for children to use the Internet; still others rely on behavioral responses such as making the computer screen public, making the computer screen private, or asking users to desist when viewing offensive images.

The problem with all of the solutions currently available is that none of them work all that well, and many of them are creating additional, unanticipated problems. Current filtering software screens out some material we want left in and leaves in material we want screened out, and suggests to the public that the problem is solved when it is not. Even so, and whatever the official position of ALA on this subject, there is no question in my mind that were filtering software available that reliably filtered out the "adults only" sites without screening out information on sexually transmitted diseases and breast cancer, libraries would leap at the chance to install it.

As for the parental-approval approach, it doesn't take children without their parents' permission long to borrow someone else's card. And having to monitor screens may put library staff in an awkward position.

In the absence of a technological silver bullet, we are struggling to solve a radically new problem with old paradigms. With the Internet we are now offering the public material we have not, and in some instances would not, select. What does censorship mean in this context? What is our real responsibility to children? What is the purpose of the public library—from the public's point of view?

Intellectual freedom is a bedrock issue for libraries. Most of us at one time or another have been called upon to defend a selection decision and are proud of our ability to defend the retention of Judy Blume, J. D. Salinger, or Salman Rushdie. Some of us make and defend more-controversial purchases, like Madonna's *Sex*. Most libraries make these decisions and defend them on the basis of a well-thought-out, carefully crafted selection policy. Our selection policies and the library profession's strong defense of intellectual freedom are grounded in our conviction that libraries serve individuals not groups, and that our communities have a wide spectrum of social, political, and religious belief. Moreover, access to a broad spectrum of ideas is fundamental to a democracy.

Nevertheless, there has always been material that most libraries don't buy. (Much of what can be found in an adult bookstore falls into this category.) When we make these judgments we call it selection. When we choose to exclude material we call it censorship. Evidence suggests that the distinction lacks meaning in an electronic environment.

Consider the following: Public Library A decides to handle the furor over a child's access to pornographic material by selecting several hundred sites out of the 34 million available as appropriate to children and making those, and only those, available in its children's room. Public Library B decides to install filtering software that blocks access to several thousand questionable sites. Which library is providing better access to more information? The one that selects or the one that censors? Is it any less valid to "select out" material than it is to "select in" material?

Many have argued that selection is cost-driven, that no library can afford to buy everything and selection policies codify priorities. Many claim that there is no marginal cost involved in providing access to everything on the Internet because once a library is wired there is no separate charge for each site accessed. Yet consider the following: A representative of one large urban library that has recently installed banks of computers privately acknowledges that at any given time as many as half of the public-access PCs are being used to view pornography. Is this the library's purpose in installing the computer system? Can we say that access is free? What about costs for hardware, software, and space? The cost for the material

itself is only a small part of the total costs.

Purists argue that if we "select out" some material we are opening the door for would-be censors to impose even greater constraints on our collections. This argument sounds very much like the "domino theory," a diplomatic posture that has become obsolete in our post-Cold War era. In truth, many feel that by casting our protective net wide enough to cover material that would be illegal in many communities we are losing our credibility in defending other selection decisions.

Unresolved Issues

The issues here are far from being resolved. The ACLU is threatening to sue libraries for use of blocking software, for asking library users to remove offending image from screens, for failure to provide private viewing places, for almost anything that doesn't ensure full access to everything by everyone. Some library users have asked if public viewing of pornography constitutes a new form of sexual harassment. Some political jurisdictions are tying library funding to the use of filtering software, while others have discussed imposing fines on anyone providing children access to pornography.

At the heart of this debate is nothing less than the definition of the role of the public library. We must never forget that public libraries belong to the public. We hold them in trust for present and future generations, and ultimately public libraries will be what the public wants them to be. If we want the community to hear and understand our position on these issues, we must hear and understand theirs. We must search together for a solution that will enable parents to continue to send their children to the public library with confidence without eroding our ability to meet the information needs of adults with vastly different opinions and orientations.

Within the profession we must treat each other with respect as well and avoid saying—as one prominent ALA representative said to a librarian in a public meeting in Ohio last year—that the librarian should "look for an-other career" because he dared to disagree with the Association's position on this topic. We need the best thinking of everyone, even—maybe especially—those who are not repeating conventional wisdom.

What is censorship in this environment? Censorship is what happens if we are forced to pull the plug on the Internet because legal or financial constraints make it impossible for us to do anything else. Censorship occurs if we deny citizens who are unable to afford computers access to a world of information now found on those 34 million Web sites (a number that is doubling every three months), thereby effectively redlining people because of their economic condition. Censorship is providing nothing to anyone because we are unwilling or unable to search for new solutions appropriate to an electronic age.

 Article Review Form at end of book.

Was the University of Michigan justified in suspending Mr. Baker?
Should colleges and universities regulate student use of the Internet?

Free Speech on the Electronic Frontier

Robert M. O'Neil

*Robert M. O'Neil is founding director of
the Thomas Jefferson Center for the
Protection of Free Expression.*

Apparently the most dangerous desperado on an American campus earlier this year was armed not with a gun or a knife or a bomb but with a keyboard. The University of Michigan's response—summary suspension of Jake Baker, an unusually imaginative undergraduate—began a new era in academic life.

Mr. Baker's offense was writing a bizarre and twisted tale in which he fantasized the rape and torture of a female classmate, whom he named. Had his story appeared in an underground magazine, little more would have been heard of it. What made his story different was that he had posted it on the Internet.

The posting attracted scant attention on campus or elsewhere in the United States. Only when a Michigan alumnus in Moscow came upon the story while surfing the Net one night, and notified campus officials in Ann Arbor, did anyone seem to care. But then they cared deeply and acted accordingly.

Not only was Mr. Baker summarily suspended from the university—a process usually reserved for students so dangerous to life and limb that the formal hearings normally provided as part of due process must be preempted; criminal charges also were filed in federal court by the local U.S. Attorney. Mr. Baker was charged under a law that makes it a crime to transmit threats across state lines (in his case, to a friend in Canada). When Mr. Baker's lawyer sought his release pending trial, arguing that the student apparently did not know and had never contacted the coed he named in his story, a magistrate denied bail. He said that, as the father of a 13-year-old girl, he felt that Mr. Baker was "somebody who probably should not be walking the streets."

The criminal charges eventually were dismissed by a judge, who held that any punishment due Mr. Baker should be handed out by the university, not by the court. The judge also pointed out that the charges against the student were quite vague, adding that to "infer an intention to act upon the thoughts and dreams of this language would stray far be-

yond the bounds of the First Amendment and would amount to punishing Baker for his thoughts and desires."

Mr. Baker's Internet fantasy was not the first time his electronic prose had evoked concern on campus. Late in 1994, he had attracted attention because of sexual fantasies contained in e-mail messages that he had sent to Canada. At the urging of university officials, he underwent two psychological examinations, which subsequently declared him no threat to himself or to others. Yet when "Pamela's Ordeal" surfaced on the Internet, Mr. Baker's electronic fantasy about torturing a fellow student with a hot curling iron suddenly made him and his keyboard dangerous to "the health, diligence and order among . . . students" (the standard set in the university's rules for summary suspension).

Not only was there no clear evidence that Mr. Baker posed a risk to the physical safety of other people on campus; the fellow student who was the object of the fantasy had been unaware of the whole event, until a reporter contacted her after Mr. Baker's arrest. Under our laws, mere verbal

The Chronicle of Higher Education, November 11, 1995. Copyright 1995 Robert M. O'Neil.

threats, save those against the life of the President of the United States, are treated as free speech, unless the target seems in imminent peril.

However, the university's handling of Mr. Baker's case implies that electronic threats are profoundly different from threats made in more familiar ways. Although the federal judge who dismissed the criminal charges against Mr. Baker rejected the view that electronic threats are different, the nature and legal status of such threats are sure to be explored and tested in other litigation. Electronic communication does seem to inspire excess, hyperbole, and incivility among users to a degree seldom found in print. Anonymous electronic messages may evoke a degree of fear that is not aroused by the spoken or written word; if only because the recipient may not know whether the sender is halfway around the world or in the next room. Especially in this relatively early phase of digital communication, a higher degree of apprehension may be warranted. Institutions also may fear that courts will hold them liable for failing to anticipate the effects of electronic threats.

On the other hand, Internet threats may, in some respects, actually be less ominous. There is no electronic analogue of "fighting words"—the face-to-face verbal assaults likely to provoke a fight that underlie many a campus speech code. No amount of electronic "flaming" will create the incendiary condition that in real life would permit the arrest of a person for hurling slurs and insults in someone's face. Further, the recipient of a digital message

is less likely to be a "captive audience," unable to escape verbal assaults, as one might be in a campus or neighborhood setting.

So the differences between the new and the old media actually could cut both ways. Surely, the evidence to date would not seem to justify treating Jake Baker's keyboard like the moral equivalent of a gun or knife, possession of which might legitimately trigger the summary suspension of a student.

The University of Michigan is hardly alone in taking a fearful view of the digital world. A few months before the Baker case, Carnegie Mellon University took the extraordinary step of making inaccessible through the campus computer network the "alt.sex" newsgroups on the Internet. These groups, among the most popular on the Internet, include discussions of a variety of sex-oriented topics. Some groups provide only text; others also provide graphic material, ranging from soft- to hard-core pornography. After a storm of protest on and off campus, Carnegie Mellon officials a few days later altered the ban to apply only to graphic sexual material; they permitted continued access to sexually explicit text. The university also created a committee to study the issue.

Carnegie Mellon was not the first university to impose such a ban; Stanford had briefly imposed a similar one several years earlier, but soon revoked it. Officials at other institutions have said they are studying the issue, perhaps wishing to deflect unwelcome criticism from parents, legislators, and others who take a dim view of allowing students—

"Electronic communication does seem to inspire excess, hyperbole, and incivility among users to a degree seldom found in print."

or anyone else—to use campus equipment to gain access to sexually explicit material.

In the meantime, other courts, as well as lawmakers, are addressing issues related to electronic communication. In Congress, the House of Representatives and the Senate soon must reconcile starkly different versions of bills concerning content on the Internet. The Senate's bill would impose severe sanctions on anyone initiating "indecent" material. In the House, where Speaker Newt Gingrich has opposed constraints of the Senate's type, the basic provision on digital content is hortatory rather than regulatory, and keeps the Federal Communications Commission from policing Internet communications. The House bill would, however, make it a crime to use offensive terms about "sexual or excretory activities or organs" in communicating by computer with anyone believed to be under 18.

At least five states already have enacted laws restricting, in various ways, the sexually explicit material that may be sent in electronic form. At least as many other states have such bills under consideration.

In the courts, the U.S. Court of Appeals for the Sixth Circuit has just heard an appeal of the first federal conviction for computer obscenity. The judge treated the case just as though the material had been physically sent in print or video form. The digital material in question consisted of sexually explicit graphic images, which a postal inspector in Memphis had downloaded after joining a California-based bulletin board under a pseudonym.

A second major computer-libel case, with a $200-million claim at stake, was dropped recently after Prodigy—a commercial computer network—agreed to apologize for a comment posted by a subscriber on the Internet. The posting charged a Long Island investment company and its president with fraudulent, even criminal, activity. In a preliminary ruling last May, the judge refused to dismiss the case, treating Prodigy essentially as the publisher of the statements rather than as an innocent distributor.

Another case filed recently raises the issue of whether a person who has been defamed electronically may force the electronic network or server to identify the source of the message.

Even though it is still early in the electronic age, we should be able to establish principles and guidelines for handling such cases. The only novelty these cases present is the medium used, not the content conveyed. Thus the basic precept would appear to be simple: The principles of free speech and a free press developed for written and oral communication should apply fully to electronic material, save to the ex-

tent that we eventually find that unique features of the digital medium require different treatment. No such special circumstance would seem to justify either criminal or civil sanctions against, say, a Jake Baker, unless he could be punished if the same material appeared in print.

Many complex issues, such as whether the network or the bulletin boards will be held liable in cases of defamation, will turn on what model the courts use in deciding the case; the conveyors of digital information could be seen as publishers or as distributors or as something in between.

Valid concerns exist about the issues of access to sexually explicit material—the Carnegie Mellon case—and the appropriate use of institutional resources. But such factors have no bearing on content. Thus restrictions on access to sexually explicit material in digital form would be valid only when access to such material in more traditional form could be denied to, say, library users. Since few universities would deny or limit the access of students and

faculty members to sexually explicit materials in their library collections, there seems to be no basis for comparable constraints on digital access. The university need not, of course, subscribe to every sex magazine that appears on the newsstand, but that obvious point in no way justifies denying access to material that someone has posted on a bulletin board and that is available at little additional cost.

Unless and until we have evidence that electronic communication is somehow more dangerous than communication in more familiar modes, we should apply standard First Amendment principles, which countenance few and only narrowly defined exceptions to the right of free expression. If we shape our policies on new media in accordance with our traditional rules, we may find the electronic age a bit less frightening than the early skirmishes might suggest.

 **Article Review Form at end of book.**

What do governments' attempts to control the Internet suggest about the power of this medium? What do they suggest about the powers of government?

Two-Edged Sword:

Asian regimes on the Internet

Philip Shenon

Hanoi, Vietnam—Tran Ba Thai sits among tangles of computer wire in his dingy Hanoi office, hoping that he can continue to connect this long-isolated nation to the distant reaches of cyberspace.

So far, the aging Communists who run Vietnam have gone along with Mr. Thai's plans for Net Nam, the first commercial service plugging Vietnam into the global web of computer networks known as the Internet. But Mr. Thai, a 44-year-old computer scientist with Vietnam's Institute of Information Technology, worries that as Vietnam's electronic postmaster, he may be walking a line as thin as a strand of computer wire.

While the Internet holds the promise of bolstering Vietnam's economy by connecting this impoverished nation to the information superhighway, it also means that Vietnam might soon be deluged with the sort of information that the Government has long sought to keep out of the public's hands: the writings of Vietnamese dissidents, reports by human rights groups, pornography.

"I'm sure the Government is concerned about this," Mr. Thai said. "But the Government knows that the advantages of this system are bigger than the disadvantages. Vietnam has been totally isolated, and the Internet is the fastest, cheapest way to reintegrate Vietnam into the world."

The cyberspace revolution may have been born in the computer labs of the West, but its impact will be felt most intensely in the authoritarian nations of Asia, the continent that is home to two-thirds of the world's population and its fastest-growing economies.

And Asian governments are vowing to do what they can to control the Internet. Last week, the iron-fisted Government of Singapore announced that it would prosecute anyone who posted defamatory or obscene material on the Internet. China is expected to restrict access by keeping the cost of local Internet service artifically high.

But it will be impossible to shut off the Internet completely, short of cutting telephone lines and confiscating computers—solutions that are not feasible in countries that are trying to build modern, technologically advanced economies. Information moves over the Internet so rapidly and uncontrollably that in many countries, censorship could be a thing of the past.

While most Asian governments have no affection for the concept of freedom of speech, their disdain for the free flow of information is tempered by the understanding that the future of the world's economy will depend on computers—and the transfer of information, including financial data and mail, over computer networks. Their economic vitality may depend on having a population that is computer literate and, more specifically, Internet literate.

And so China, Vietnam, Indonesia, Singapore and Malaysia, which strictly censor every other form of information available to the public, have been forced to open the information floodgates with the Internet, even though that means allowing everything from political dissent to pornography to go on line.

"For authoritarian governments, it's going to be a losing game to try to control this," said Anthony M. Rutkowski, executive director of the Internet Society, a nonprofit organization in Reston, Va. An estimated 200,000 computers in Asia are now connected to the Internet, a number that is expected to grow exponentially over the next several years. According to the Internet Society, there are now more than 15,000 computers hooked up to the Internet in Hong Kong, more than 8,000 in Singapore, more than 3,000 in Thailand and more than 500 in China.

Most computers are found at universities, government offices and in the offices of large corporations, although increasingly—especially in prosperous areas of Hong Kong and Singapore—computers are found at home, used for everything from word processing to computer games. But given the shortage of reliable telephone lines outside major cities, the Internet is largely an urban phenomenon in Asia.

Among Asia's authoritarian nations, only North Korea and Myanmar, formerly Burma, are sitting out the communications revolution for now, if only because they are too poor to afford computers and the telephone equipment needed to reach the network.

Internet service made its debut in China only two years ago, but there are already at least eight Internet servers there, including a commercial service available to the general public that was established in cooperation with Sprint, the American telecommunications company. The servers allow a computer hookup to the Internet through a local telephone number.

In January, Beijing announced that it would create a nationwide computer network linking more than 100 college campuses to the Internet, even though students at those same campuses were the center of political dissent before the violent 1989 crackdown in Tiananmen Square.

The Communist Government of Vietnam is allowing Internet servers to open for business, even though it has already had difficulty controlling the deluge of electronic mail from dissidents living abroad.

Some fervently anti-Communist Vietnamese dissidents in Southern California have tried to flood the personal electronic mail box of the Prime Minister of Vietnam, Vo Van Kiet, an early advocate of the Internet. That has alarmed the operators of Net Nam, which is urging its subscribers, most of them businesses and private organizations, to avoid transmitting "antisocial" information over the Internet.

No country seems to be more aware of the opportunity and the threat posed by the Internet than Singapore, the wealthy authoritarian city-state that has some of the strictest censorship laws in Asia.

In Singapore, the Government is struck by a contradictory impulse as it tries to establish Singapore as the communications and financial hub of Southeast Asia. The Government talks of making Singapore "an intelligent island," and so it not only allows the public access to the Internet, it encourages it.

The Singapore Government offers two services connecting computer users to the Internet, and a third, private service is being formed. "The choice is either we master the technology or it will master us," said George Yeo, the Minister of Information and the Arts.

But what that means is that a budding Singaporean dissident need only sit down at a computer, dial a local telephone number and type a simple instruction on the keyboard: "soc.culture.singapore," to find a plethora of mostly anonymous invective about the Government, along with some spirited defenses of it.

The free-wheeling criticism —which might well have prompted a knock on the door from the police if it had appeared in a newspaper—is now freely available to tens of thousands of computer users in Singapore— and millions around the world— through the Internet. *Playboy* may be banned in Singapore, but the magazine's centerfold can be viewed, in full color, on the World Wide Web, an area of the Internet devoted to individually designed collections of text, graphics and sound, ("sites" or "home pages") which are loosely linked together.

China is reportedly planning to limit access by setting high fees for Internet use. At a seminar in Hong Kong last week, a researcher for China's Ministry of Posts and Telecommunications, Jiang Lintao, said that China was looking for other ways of controlling access—"for putting a brake on certain information when the networks become popular." He did not elaborate.

Singapore is calling for self-policing of the system and has warned that it will take legal action against anyone who uses the Internet to transmit pornographic or seditious material. "We should never allow Singapore to be a source of pornographic or incendiary broadcasts," Mr. Yeo said.

Last year, the Singapore Government acknowledged it rifled through the files of users of Technet, one of the two Government-financed Internet providers, in search of pornography. The search turned up a few pornographic images, leading the Government to post a computerized warning to Technet users about "countersocial activity."

But the sweep also alarmed foreign corporations operating in Singapore that use the Internet for electronic mail. The companies feared that the Government might eventually begin snooping into confidential corporate information. The Singapore Government has since assured the companies that it has no intention of conducting more unannounced searchers.

Stewart A. Baker, the former general counsel of the National Security Council who is now a Washington lawyer and a specialist in international telecommunications law, said he suspected that Singapore and other governments would crack down on the Internet through litigation against the large companies that provide access to the system—say, a defamation suit against a large multinational corporation with assets in Singapore, whose employees place rude messages about Singapore on the Internet.

"I would think there would be difficulty enforcing this against the little guys—the message senders—but they will go after the big companies that carry the messages," he said.

 **Article Review Form at end of book.**

Why did Congress pass the Communications Decency Act? Why did the Supreme Court reject it?

On the Net, Anything Goes

The Supreme Court rules that online speech, sexually explicit or not, is protected. So now what?

Steven Levy and Karen Breslau

Born of a hysteria triggered by a genuine problem—the ease with which wired-up teenagers can get hold of nasty pictures on the Internet—the Communications Decency Act (CDA) was never really destined to be a companion piece to the Bill of Rights. Last week the Supreme Court officially deleted the CDA on constitutional grounds, concluding that the act endangers free speech and "threatens to torch a large segment of the Internet community."

The decision had resonance far beyond dirty pictures. This was the first time that the highest court had contemplated the status of the key medium of the next century. Instead of regarding the Net with the caution the court usually shows while exploring new frontiers, the justices went out of their way to assure that this most democratic of mediums (where "any person . . . can become a town crier . . . [or] pamphleteer," the court gushed) would receive the highest level of protection. Internet speakers will not be shackled with the regulations that limit content on television and radio; instead, they will

enjoy the freedom granted to printed matter. And it will be up to parents, not the government, to keep kids from accessing smut. "This represents the legal birth certificate for the Internet," said Bruce Ennis, who argued the case before the court, representing a group of plaintiffs ranging from the American Library Association to Human Rights Watch.

In contrast, the CDA was a virtual death sentence. Introduced by (now retired) Sen. James Exon, without hearings or formal debate, the amendment to the 1996 Telecommunications Bill not only outlawed the electronic circulation to minors of "indecent" material (in the legal sense, this includes everything from nude photos of Pamela Lee Anderson to a stray four-letter epithet); it also ordained big fines and two years upriver to those who spoke out of turn. Opponents insisted that this trespassed on the First Amendment, and a year ago they convinced a three-judge panel in Philadelphia that the lawmakers had overstepped their bounds. As ACLU lead attorney Chris Hansen sees it, the key was requesting that the judges hear expert witnesses on

the issues. By the end of the hearings the judges had attained near-ninja Internet knowledge—which taught them the impossibility of keeping smut from minors without infringing on all speech.

The highest court proved equally adept students. John Paul Stevens's opinion reads like a cyberspace primer, providing the Lexis crowd with crisp definitions of e-mail, chat rooms, mail exploders and the World Wide Web. Reading this must have set the plaintiffs' hearts aflutter, because in order to see how the CDA steps on the First Amendment, it is crucial to understand how the Internet works. Congress proceeded on the reasonable premise that it should be wrong to send smut to minors. But it is impossible to fully control who sees information posted on the Net. And in the Philadelphia hearings, witnesses proved that material outlawed went far beyond smut: it included AIDS information, Pulitzer Prize-winning plays, museum exhibits and, according to a government witness, the Vanity Fair cover showing a pregnant Demi Moore.

If there was alarm in the court's response, it was not at the prospect of pimply adolescents exposed to *Hustler's* Web site, but at other sorts of scenarios, like a parent going to jail for sending birth-control information to a 17-year-old son or daughter away at college. Even the partial dissent, written by Justice Sandra Day O'Connor and endorsed by Chief Justice William Rehnquist, shared the majority's disdain for the CDA's excesses. Unlike the majority, they felt that it was possible to sanction indecency knowingly sent by adults to minors.

"The court did its homework," said Ennis. "In Congress, they should have done theirs." While some legislators accepted the rap—"Our law was like a bull in a china shop," admits GOP Rep. Rick White—others felt that the justices blew it. "I'm at a loss to see how the court makes the distinction between a TV and a computer screen," said Republican Sen. Dan Coats. Read the decision, Senator: "The Internet is not as 'invasive' as radio or television," writes Stevens, citing the lower court's finding that for Net users the "odds are slim" of accidentally encountering porn. (Especially since most commer-

cial online pornographers require credit cards, and even those who don't do so generally ask browsers to affirm that they are over 18.)

And if the kid wants to see the hot stuff? That's where parents must come in. The CDA's opponents have long contended that the solution to the problem is having Mom and Dad utilize the growing family of Internet filters to prevent Junior from surfing in the flesh zone. These products are constantly improving, but the fact is that the Internet makes it easier for a motivated youngster to access salacious material. That, the court decided, was the trade-off to preserving free speech.

While the court feels comfortable with this, the forces in Congress that wrought the CDA can't accept that trade-off—and they are already vowing to try again. "Given the court's decision, I don't know what we can craft, short of a constitutional amendment," says Coats, who does not rule out such a movement. Others advise against knee-jerk tactics. "Congress should take a deep breath, read the decision and think," says White.

"Passing a law may not be the solution to the problem."

The Clinton administration has its own ideas: in mid-July it will unveil a plan to make the filtering technologies ubiquitous. (Currently fewer than 40 percent of parents use them.) "We're going to get the V-chip for the Internet," says White House senior adviser Rahm Emanuel. "Same goal, different means."

Cyberspace will surely discuss all of this in its own unrestrained, long-winded manner. Last week, though, it was celebration time, not only online but at in-the-flesh rallies in Austin, Texas, and San Francisco. Mike Godwin, a lawyer for the Electronic Frontier Foundation, spoke for Netheads everywhere. After citing the likes of Thomas Jefferson, he quoted a more up-to-date authority, Martha and The Vandellas: "Summer's here and the time is right," he said of the day when the Supreme Court went cyberpunk.

 Article Review Form at end of book.

How are employers liable for employees' use of telecommunications equipment? Why did the Supreme Court allow parts of the Communications Decency Act to stand?

What's Left of the Communications Decency Act?

Anthony M. Townsend, Michael E. Whitman, and Robert J. Alberts

Anthony M. Townsend, Ph.D., is an assistant professor of management at the University of Nevada-Las Vegas. Michael E. Whitman is an assistant professor of management information systems at Kennesaw State University. Robert J. Alberts, J.D., is a professor of finance at the University of Nevada-Las Vegas

The Communications Decency Act may have been shredded by the U.S. Supreme Court, but the remnants of the act can still cause problems for unaware employers and HR professionals.

When the Supreme Court last July issued its controversial ruling in *Reno vs. American Civil Liberties Union No.* (96-511, 1997), many news outlets were quick to proclaim the demise of the Communications Decency Act of 1996 (CDA). Consider, for example, the headline that *Newsweek* chose for its story: "On the Net, Anything Goes."

Yet most of the articles failed to note that the ruling, while striking down key portions of the law, left intact several provisions with potentially significant ramifications for employers.

Still in effect are prohibitions on the use of various telecommunications media that are widely available in the workplace—including e-mail and faxes—to harass and annoy. Human resource professionals would be remiss if they expected their information systems (IS) departments to bear the brunt of ensuring that these prohibitions are followed.

Unfortunately, many companies view telecommunications policies as being solely within the purview of the IS staff. Although the IS department should have substantial input into the policies' technical considerations, the final responsibility for publication and compliance should probably rest with HR. Ultimately, any telecommunications policy is an employment policy that will require training, monitoring and enforcement.

The CDA Still Has Teeth

The better-known portions of the CDA sought to ban indecent and obscene material from the Internet and other telecommunications devices if there was a possibility that a minor might receive the mater-

ial. The Supreme Court struck down those provisions as violations of the First Amendment protections of free speech.

What most observers fail to note, however, is that the CDA also extended the Communications Act of 1934 to cover all telecommunications equipment, not just the telephone, and made it a federal crime to use this equipment in ways designed to harass or annoy another party.

The average employee's access to a wide range of telecommunications equipment creates the potential for a liability disaster.

What the post-Reno CDA specifically prohibits is the following:

- Using telecommunications equipment to send a comment, request, proposal or image (i.e., a picture file) that is obscene, lewd or lascivious with the intent to annoy, abuse, threaten, or harass the recipient or a third party, such as a co-worker.

- Knowingly sending obscene images, communications, requests, etc., to a minor. Employers have a concern here because employees may seek to engage in this type of contact from office machines.

Reprinted with permission of *HR Magazine* published by the Society for Human Resource Management, Alexandria, Virginia.

- Using any telecommunications device to anonymously contact an individual with the intent to threaten, annoy or abuse the party that is contacted. This is an extension of an old prohibition against anonymous threatening phone calls. In the computer age, this includes anonymous faxes and e-mail messages.

- Repeatedly calling an individual and hanging up (or letting the phone ring indefinitely) with the intent to harass the person receiving the call. This still only applies to the telephone. One may reasonably assume, however, that courts will read the act broadly and apply it to beepers or other evolving technologies that "ring."

- Repeatedly using telecommunications equipment to contact another individual solely to harass that person. This prohibition extends protection from non-anonymous threatening calls to include faxes and e-mail, as well as any other system that could be used for this purpose.

The "remaining" CDA provides for fines and jail time for those who knowingly permit the use of equipment under their control for any of the above activities. Fortunately, the act provides a broad indemnification from liability for employers who proactively develop and enforce proper policies.

Dodging the Bullet

For organizations—and, in particular, for their HR staffs—a careful response to the CDA is warranted. A well-developed and properly handled response will diminish the likelihood that violations will occur and will reduce the organization's liability for infractions beyond its control.

Most CDA-prohibited activities can be prevented by developing

- A training and indoctrination program for telecommunications system use.

- Policies that clearly articulate the banned actions and stipulate that employees will be disciplined or terminated for violations.

A good training program reaffirms the values espoused in the telecommunications policy and encourages users to work with equipment in appropriate ways.

Some firms may want to consider developing a monitoring system for their telecommunications equipment. While this may have a certain appeal for some organizations, many will consider such a system to be an inappropriate invasion of their employees' privacy. Keep in mind that there are varying degrees of system monitoring.

Unprepared Employers

We have found that only a handful of companies nationwide have comprehensive policies governing the use of telecommunications equipment. While the causes of this problem are unclear, both the HR and IS staffs believed either that policy development was the responsibility of the other party, or that it was unnecessary.

To ensure that your organization has an appropriate policy in place, you may wish to consider the following procedures:

- Audit the current policy. If your organization has a telecommunications policy as part of either a computer use policy or a general employee handbook or policy statement—read the policy carefully. Is it up to date in its reference to covered equipment? Does it clearly articulate both prohibited uses of telecommunications equipment, and penalties and disciplinary procedures if the policy is violated?

- Talk to employees. How do your employees use the telecommunications equipment? What do they need to be able to do with the equipment to do their jobs well? Whether your contact is informal or done through focus groups or questionnaires, the feedback you receive will help you better understand what types of issues a policy may have to address. Feedback also may alert you to developing problems.

- Develop (or rework) a policy. If you have done the preliminary groundwork, drafting a policy will be simple. Good policy codifies the permissible things that people are doing and eliminates the impermissible. Work with your IS staff and relevant employee groups to develop both a sound policy and "buy-in" from all employees.

- When the policy portion is complete, develop an implementation plan that may include memos, training sessions or any other programs that may be necessary to achieve successful compliance.

Although some employees balk at restrictions on how they may use e-mail, faxes, phones or Internet access, most will understand that the organization's policy was developed to comply with federal law. While new policies may seem restrictive to some, the vast majority of employees will see little change in how they use telecommunications systems.

By following these procedures and developing a sound telecommunications use policy, you and your staff will help to indemnify your organization from substantial exposure to liability arising from system misuse. As a bonus, you will have developed a great deal of knowledge about telecommunications and computer systems use that will serve you well in future employee development programs.

 Article Review Form at end of book.

What happens when our personal information becomes public? What steps can we take to protect private information?

Your Personal Information Has Gone Public

David F. Linowes

Privacy invaders are all around us. We live in a social environment comprised of organizations that have an insatiable appetite for personal information. These massive information bases have developed into new and disturbing forms of potential social controls, the ramifications of which society is just beginning to understand. Computer technology makes mass surveillance efficient. Never before in the history of man has it been possible to surreptitiously monitor the personal affairs of millions of individuals. Today it is done with little or no oversight. The objectives are legitimate in most instances, but will they always be so?

Data on individuals are held by business organizations, banks, insurance companies, government organizations, schools, political and even religious organizations. People are being surprised constantly at how easy it is for others to obtain information they assume is confidential.

A New York City woman received a telephone call from a salesman offering her long-distance services. She told him she didn't make many out-of-town calls, hoping to dissuade him. He persisted, saying that was surprising since he noted that her telephone records showed frequent calls to New Jersey, Delaware, and Connecticut. When the woman demanded to know where the salesman had obtained her telephone records, he quickly hung up.

A person's telephone bill, bank checking account, and credit card records are a reflection of one's lifestyle, personal interests, and political beliefs. They reveal the books and magazines read, the political party supported, things bought, and places traveled. Computers track customers' shopping and banking habits. Cable companies, advertisers, and direct marketing firms are just some of the users.

Investigative firms offer services to many organizations, especially business corporations. When information is not readily available through legitimate channels, they routinely turn to covert and even illegal means.

One private investigative agency trained its operatives to pose as physicians on the telephone. File cards were kept on hospitals all over the country with specific instructions for soliciting information. Suggestions included items such as to call after midnight, talk with a black accent, and so on. At times, interns or nurses were paid as informants. The agency claimed a 99% success rate in obtaining the information it went after. In flyers produced for its insurance company clients, the firm boasted that it could secure medical record information without patient authorization.

Telephone taps, both legal and illegal, have been used for years to eavesdrop on personal conversations. Now computer technology makes it possible for electronic listening devices to pick out a single voice from among an entire telephone system without the targeted person ever knowing about the monitoring.

The use of electronic bugging devices is becoming increasingly common, even though it is illegal. New monitoring equipment is both inexpensive and easy to operate. For an investment of $695, anyone can purchase an Infinity Transmitter that allows for monitoring someone's home or office. After the miniature transmitter is attached to the target telephone, the eavesdropper just dials that telephone's number from any other telephone. The phone does not ring, but any sound in the room up to thirty feet away can be overheard by the caller. Other devices are attached to the phone line outside the home or business, making surveillance of telephone conversations even easier.

Sounds monitored on inexpensive baby-room monitors sold in many stores are easily adapted for listening in on a variety of radio communication frequencies. Some scanners can pick up conversations a mile or two away, making one observer comment that it was like having an open microphone in an adult bedroom.

Uses of Personal Information

Just last year, an extensive network of "information brokers" known as the Nationwide Electronic Tracing Company (NET) was uncovered. These brokers traded in stolen computer files from the Social Security Administration by bribing Social Security employees $25 for an individual's Social Security information. The information was then sold to insurance companies, employers, and attorneys.

The company's brochure said that if provided with a home address, it could find a Social Security number in two hours. With a subject's name and address, the telephone numbers and addresses of up to nine current neighbors were available in two hours. A name and Social Security number were all that were needed to obtain a subject's earnings for the last ten years. An individual's complete credit history costs just $10. Driving records and criminal histories also were available.

Ironically, it was the sales brochure that tipped off authorities. NET pleaded guilty in Florida to conspiracy charges in connection with this illegal work, but the practice still continues. Some of these "information brokers" have learned from investigative firms. Its operatives simply call the Social Security Service Center pretending to be government officials and request the information, which is readily furnished. A total information base is thus created, which is a valuable resource to third parties, to be used for many unintended purposes in unexpected places.

Employee Monitoring

Privacy continues to be a fundamental workplace issue as managers are increasingly using new surveillance technology to control worker behavior. It has been estimated that employers eavesdrop on 400 million telephone conversations between workers and consumers every year. Eavesdropping is especially prevalent in the telecommunications, insurance, and banking industries where as many as 80% of the workers are subjected to telephone or computer-based monitoring. Employer eavesdropping on electronic mail messages is also widespread and currently not prohibited by federal wiretapping laws.

Two Nissan employees who trained dealers, sales staff, and mechanics on using the company's electronic mail system were fired for making disparaging e-mail remarks about a supervisor.

In 1991, two male employees of Boston's Sheraton Hotel were videotaped without their knowledge while changing clothes in their locker room. The taping was part of a drug investigation. Authorities later admitted the two men were never suspects.

The Olivetti Corporation has developed electronic ID cards called "smart badges," which track employees as they move from location to location within a building or complex. The system is designed to route telephone calls to a phone near the wearer, but such technology can also tell managers where an employee is at any given moment.

How Privacy Invasions Affect Our Lives

When personal information is taken out of context, hardships often result. Where the information is inaccurate, it can cost the individual a job, promotion, or result in denial of credit or insurance. The cases of hardship resulting from such mishandling of information are limitless.

Many of the ways information gets into a record are strange, indeed, and help create the broad concerns about privacy. In one case, a free-lance artist in southern California discovered that his doctor had erroneously written on his file that he had AIDS. The doctor explained his mistake by saying a radiologist had referred to the man as being HIV positive on a report of a CT scan.

A Roxbury, Massachusetts man was told he had to pay a 25% surcharge for disability insurance because he was an alcoholic. The man was startled because he hadn't had a drink in seven years. His medical record, however, said he had a drinking problem and had attended Alcoholics Anonymous. The man then realized that years earlier he had mentioned on an insurance application that he had gone to some AA meetings while trying to quit smoking.

Personal vulnerability when seeking insurance coverage is extensive. The general authorization form that is signed when one applies for a policy has been characterized as a "search warrant without due process." Unless specifically limited, it gives the holder the right to obtain data from any organization having information about the individual.

In addition, the agent receives information from outside investigators and centralized industry data banks. The Medical Information Bureau furnishes personal information, not just medical information, from 800 insurance companies throughout the country. Much of it is not verified, and some of it may not always be true.

The consumer credit industry is another area where mistakes in personal information can have serious consequences for individuals and families. The industry is the No. 1 source of consumer complaints in America, according to the Federal Trade Commission.

Free-lance, Washington, D.C. journalist Stephen Shaw was surprised by a call from his local bank when he applied for low-interest credit. The loan processor said Shaw had many loans on his credit report he hadn't listed on his application. In addition, the report said Shaw had moved from Washington to Winter Park, Florida where he was working as a car salesman. Among his recent credit purchases were a new $19,000 car, $3000 in Visa charges, a $2000 IBM computer, electronic items worth more than $1300, and $7500 worth of home furnishings.

Shaw was the victim of credit-card fraud on a massive scale. In all, nearly thirty accounts under his name had been established with balances totaling nearly $100,000. Apparently someone in the Orlando area had circulated his Social Security

number and it had been used to retrieve his file from a credit bureau database. Even though it has been more than a year since Shaw first discovered the problem, the phony accounts keep popping up and his credit bureau file still lists a Winter Park address.

When Consumers Union surveyed 161 credit reports, they found that one-half contained inaccuracies. Based on a sampling of 1500 reports from Equifax, Trans Union, and TRW Credit Data, a credit bureau official in New York City found that there were mistakes in as many as 43% of the credit reports they issue.

A Norwich, Connecticut doctor's car loan was held up because his credit report said he owed thousands in back taxes. The doctor was surprised to say the least since his financial condition had been first-rate. When the bank checked with TRW, the credit-reporting firm, it discovered that the doctor wasn't the only one with a problem. In fact, every taxpayer in Norwich was listed as a deadbeat.

TRW, it turned out, had made a huge mistake. A young investigator had obtained a list of taxpayers and thought they were delinquent. As a result, 1500 residents of the town were listed as tax evaders. Tax-lien data was also falsely reported in TRW files from other Vermont towns and in New Hampshire, Rhode Island, and Maine.

What Can Be Done to Help

There is a need today for a national public policy on individual information privacy protection. Most of the democracies in the world have such a policy. We do not. Such a policy would establish relationships between individuals

and organizations that are essentially fair business practices.

Until such protection is enacted, we can try to help prevent abuse by following some fundamental guidelines:

1. Give out information only that is relevant to the decision at hand. And ask that it be used only for that purpose.

2. If the organization must transfer data about you to a third person, ask them to get your approval first.

3. Ask what sources the organization might contact to get additional information and how the data will be used.

4. Ask to see the records about you the organization has.

5. If a government official wants access to records about you, ask the organization to require proper authorization and then ask to be notified.

Over the last several years, the United States has lagged behind the European nations in privacy protection. Other countries have enacted wide-ranging laws that restrict the use of personal information without one's knowledge or consent. Canada and most European nations have established privacy commissions or data-protection agencies to regulate the use of personal data by the government and private companies. Even though almost all fifty states have enacted some pieces of privacy legislation, it is wholly inadequate. We need and should have federal legislation providing for a broad public policy on information privacy protections.

 Article Review Form at end of book.

How does the "collapse of trust" relate to contemporary concerns about privacy? What is the role of the "portable reputation" in today's society?

Privacy Is the Problem, Not the Solution

Jeffrey Obser

I wonder what Richard Nixon would have thought of the recently concluded [June 1997] Federal Trade Commission (FTC) hearings on privacy in the datasphere. After all, Nixon suffered the most humiliating privacy loss ever. Surely he could empathize with all the people who are upset that strangers can find dossiers about them on the World Wide Web, or that their personal information has become an unregulated commodity floating through distant databases. He was as shocked and confused as we are that a convenient new communications technology—in his case, audiotape—would turn around and tattle on him. And, just like us, he reacted by demanding more privacy.

It mystifies us that the man thought he could have it both ways—record everything, and get away with everything. But curiously, it mystifies nobody that we all expect to talk freely and shop with convenience through electronic networks with-

out establishing some sort of reputation for ourselves. In conditions of the utmost anonymity, living in "communities" where neighbors don't talk to one another, we expect, as Nixon did, to be trusted. And we are outraged to find that it's not possible, and they're subpoenaing our tapes on Capitol Hill. Why, we ask, does anyone need to know all this stuff about me?

Privacy May Be a Problem

The exploitation of personal data that the FTC hearings took up is plainly a serious problem. But nobody wants to admit that privacy itself may really be that problem's root cause rather than its antidote.

Modern life allows us an unprecedented level of physical privacy in real time and space. This isolated existence not only feeds our paranoia but necessitates the electronic record keeping that enables us to deal all day with total strangers. As the scale of interactions and commerce

> "Simple loss of privacy is not the real problem underlying all the tossing and turning we're going through over the openness the Internet has thrust upon us."

broadens across the Web, the complexity of that record keeping promises only to deepen.

Want to buy gas on credit? Easy? Even easier than the times when the mechanic down the street knew you personally. The difference is that now, the pump will know your name, a distant computer will make a record and the fellow behind the bulletproof glass won't give a damn. He has privacy, you have privacy. Everyone happy?

It's no coincidence that the jurist Louis Brandeis wrote his often-cited, groundbreaking "right to be let alone" privacy screed in 1890, just when the close-knit scrutiny of real villages began to give way to the anonymity of urban life. People took privacy for granted until then; in the days before databases, it was not an abstract quality. One's bedroom or backyard were either private or they weren't—and one's reputation was rarely more permanent or widespread then the memory banks of the people one dealt with personally.

Over the last 50 years, our journey into suburbs and cars and flickering TV nighttimes behind barred windows has given us extraordinary seclusion in our personal and home lives. And yet we've only felt more insecure. Only 34 percent of Americans polled by the Louis Harris firm expressed concern about personal privacy in 1970. By 1995, the figure was up to 80 percent.

What happened? This growing concern doesn't indicate a simple increase in how much we value privacy, any more than the soaring number of lawyers in the U.S. means we value justice more. Instead, it's a fearful reaction to the collapse of trust in our culture.

Technological Innovations and the Loss of Privacy

In *The Naked Society* (1964), Vance Packard trembled at the 20th century innovations that were draining American life of privacy and autonomy: social control by large, impersonal employers; pressure on companies to scrutinize customer choices in a sophisticated manner in order to compete for market share; galloping advances in electronic technology; and the McCarthy-era adoption of a pervasive top-security mentality in both government and business.

Nearly a decade later, at the dawn of computerized record keeping, James B. Rule pointed out in *Private Lives and Public Surveillance* (1973) that the transition to a society of mobile strangers didn't necessarily increase surveillance—the prying eyes of small-town neighbors are, he felt, in most cases worse. But it did lead to more *centralized* surveillance—out of sight and, for practical purposes, beyond the control of the individual.

By 1993, in the book *The Costs of Privacy*, Steven L. Nock

attacked privacy itself as the problematic result of systemic social separation. "Privacy grows as the number of strangers grows," Nock wrote. "And since strangers tend to not have reputations, there will be more surveillance when there are more strangers. Privacy is one consequence, or cost, of growing numbers of strangers. Surveillance is one consequence, or cost, of privacy."

Nock called credit cards, those handy generators of much of the personal data we've lost control over, "portable reputations." In the era of the Internet, cheap computing and an increasingly global economy, those portable reputations record more and more of our activities, and more and more strangers and institutions demand them from us. The trends toward economic consolidation, less face-to-face accountability in our public lives and faster computing will exert great pressure for ever more elaborate identification and credentialing schemes. The spread of the use of the social security number to 60 government agencies is one result of this pressure. Retina and thumbprint scans, already in pilot testing, will be the next.

We can complain all we want about Big Brother, but when we wrested our reputations from human memory and turned them over to far less judgmental computer circuits and phone lines—vanquishing those nasty old village snoops who might keep us from living out our hearts' desires—reputation remained as important as ever. The difference is that even as we have downplayed its significance—whether out of honest egalitarianism or excessive individualism—we have consigned it to the banal, impersonal testing ground of su-

permarket checkout stands and pre-employment background checks.

Are Privacy Laws Needed?

The only thing a computer ever asks is: Are you approved, or not? And everyone from medical insurers to prospective employers to creditors views us as a potential threat until our data prove otherwise. Setting up new privacy regulations isn't going to alleviate this pressure; it may only lead to more elaborate credentials and invasive identifiers for individuals, and increased secrecy for the institutions that manage our reputations.

Privacy, particularly when enshrined in law, can protect the corrupt and malign as well as the good and upstanding. But the bulk of breathless newspaper reports issuing forth on this issue since 1996 have almost universally ignored this, instead focusing on the hypothetical risks of baddies out there finding out where Joe Consumer lives and (gasp!) what his children's names are. Most have taken the same grave, utterly simplistic angle: Privacy good. Stalkers bad. Internet dangerous. Call Congressman. All have invariably repeated the same shopworn Top 10 privacy-violation horror stories, mostly hypothetical and mostly based on the absurdity of having to hide out from one's Health Maintenance Organization (HMO), spoon-fed to hungry reporters by a small group of widely quoted privacy activists. James Wheaton, senior counsel of the First Amendment Project, an Oakland, Calif., group trying to protect and expand the Freedom of Information Act, laments "enormous imprecision" in the concerns raised by some of these activists.

By giving government officials the power to deny public-records access to anyone without credentials (i.e. the little guy), Wheaton says, "the privacy activists may inadvertently be helping the moneyed interests and doing nothing for greater security." Even with their good intentions and a laudable commitment to civil liberties, the professional privacy advocates have little besides fear as a selling point—fear of the stalker, the fraud perpetrator, the government agency run amok. But the fear and paranoia that have become so entrenched in the public mind are the primary cause of all this high-tech surveillance in the first place, because nobody wants to deal with anybody in person any more.

Sure, there are legitimate issues of informational privacy, and at their best, the FTC hearings constructively aired them. Businesses that collect personal information from Web browsing should have some regulation against selling it, and anyone can see that companies compiling dossiers on every American are a threat to—well, let's not bring up Hitler again. But the drumbeat of scare stories has focused too much attention on the Internet, even though nobody has explained how the Internet causes the problems in any direct or unique way. Credit-card fraud, costing literally billions of dollars in losses in recent years, was a problem as soon as credit cards were invented—and the Secret Service, which investigates computer crime, has no evidence to date that the resourceful credit-fraud rings have sought or needed help from the Internet.

Collection of Information by the Government

It's ironic that Americans are asking for privacy protection from the same government that has in the last few years expanded electronic surveillance beyond Richard Nixon's wildest dreams— always with an appeal to public fear and mistrust. Federal agencies are creating centralized databases to track every new job hire in the country (to catch illegal immigrants and deadbeat dads), to make sure that welfare recipients don't overstay their five years by changing states and to provide instant "terrorist" profiling to airport security agents. The country has not hesitated in the last few years to wipe out the civil liberties of whole swaths of the population in futile gropes for greater public security that's never attained.

But as soon as the most minute interest of upper-income people is threatened, Congress is shut down with phone calls, as it was during the Lexis-Nexis fiasco in the summer of 1995 and the Social Security Web site controversy in April 1996. Privacy is a vastly different issue to those whose names aren't on anyone's direct-mail list. Ask a homeless person what "privacy" means and the answer might involve a large appliance box. Once you're on the street, you're a reputation refugee—and no computer is ever going to approve your e-cash transaction.

The Need to Reevaluate Trust

Simple loss of privacy is not the real problem underlying all the tossing and turning we're going through over the openness the Internet has thrust upon us. The entire experience of Internet use has total privacy as its point of departure—"meatspace" privacy, real-time anonymity, the kind that keeps anyone from knowing you're surfing the Web in your partner's underwear.

No, privacy is only part of the equation. The other part is the basic question of trust, that elusive property that we've all, in our hearts, given up on. This wide-ranging loss of our electronic virginity was well under way 20 years ago, but remained invisible until the Web forced us to confront it. We should be grateful for that. The arrival of the Global Village could be an opportunity to reevaluate our notions of trust and strangerhood. Maybe it will force us to.

Nixon's demands for privacy were ultimately fruitless and pathetic because there was no longer any trust to base that privacy on. He never understood that—and as privacy-loss hysteria begins to push laws through Congress that may do more harm than good, sadly, neither do we.

 Article Review Form at end of book.

WiseGuide Wrap-Up

Issues surrounding censorship, privacy, and security in cyberspace likely will remain in the public eye for many years to come. In George Orwell's novel *1984*, the dictator Big Brother used technology as a surveillance tool to control people's thoughts and actions. Are we heading toward the world of *1984*? Or will technology provide solutions to many of the problems it creates in the areas of free speech, privacy, and security? To further explore these issues, examine your college's computer use policy. What values are promoted in the policy?

R.E.A.L. Sites

This list provides a print preview of typical **Coursewise** R.E.A.L. sites. There are over 100 such sites at the **Courselinks**™ site. The danger in printing URLs is that web sites can change overnight. As we went to press, these sites were functional using the URLs provided. If you come across one that isn't, please let us know via email to: webmaster@coursewise.com. Use your Passport to access the most current list of R.E.A.L. sites at the **Courselinks**™ site.

Site name: Center for Democracy & Technology

URL: http://www.cdt.org/

Why is it R.E.A.L.? CDT is a nonprofit organization that promotes the advancement of civil liberties and democratic values in emerging information technologies. Site includes updates and information on new and proposed legislation related to privacy, censorship, and other civil liberties issues.

Key topics: censorship and privacy, cyberdemocracy

Try this: Take the "Privacy Quiz: Privacy on Trial" and record your score. What answer surprised you the most? Why?

Site name: Electronic Privacy Information Center

URL: http://www.epic.org/

Why is it R.E.A.L.? EPIC is a nonprofit organization dedicated to public education on emerging civil liberties issues and to the protection of privacy, the First Amendment, and other constitutional rights. The site includes a searchable archive.

Key topics: censorship and privacy

Try this: Explore EPIC's Online Guide to Practical Privacy Tools. Would you use any of these tools to protect your privacy? Why or why not?

Site name: Electronic Frontier Foundation

URL: http://www.eff.org/

Why is it R.E.A.L.? EFF is a nonprofit organization working to protect civil liberties on computers and the Internet. Site includes information on recent and past legislation related to Internet censorship and regulation.

Key topics: censorship and privacy

Try this: Visit EFF to learn about a recent development in the area of cyberspace and civil liberties. What are the specifics of the issue? Can you relate it to any readings in the text?

section 6

Learning Objectives

- Analyze Salinger's use of Internet sources to report the friendly-fire missile theory.

- Evaluate the impact of hate groups on the Internet.

- Describe why assumptions used in simulations might narrow the scope of inquiry.

- Summarize the critique of courtroom simulations.

- Imagine how other news providers or governments might use the methods of journalist Stephen Glass.

- Evaluate Rosen's concerns about the use of digital technology in photography.

Truth, Lies, and the Creation of Knowledge

WiseGuide Intro

How do we know if something is true? Philosophers have discussed this question for centuries. Epistemology is the branch of philosophy that investigates the origin, nature, methods, and limits of human knowledge. Though the term *epistemology* is rarely used outside of academic circles, questions related to epistemology figure prominently in the Information Age.

In his book *Technopoly,* Neil Postman points out that, all too often, computers are accepted as infallible purveyors of truth: if the computer says the information is correct, then it must be so. What's often forgotten is that computers are only as reliable as the imperfect humans who enter data or develop software programs.

Postman probably would not deny that computers can be efficient processors of information. His point, however, is that computers often present illusions that we are all too willing to accept as truth. For example, computer-generated simulations increasingly are used to represent past events or envision future ones. Simulations may be useful, but can any simulation ever account for the complexity of human behavior? Is a simulation for a driving test the same experience as driving a car? Is the simulation of a physics experiment or a surgical procedure sufficient training for budding physicists or doctors? Is the simulation of an automobile accident an adequate basis for determining who was at fault?

The Internet also raises provocative questions about the creation of knowledge, because it provides a forum by which people can spread information that confirms our beliefs about what is true. The easy availability of information makes the Net a very useful tool, but much of what passes as "information" is twisted, outdated, or just plain wrong. In extreme instances, the Internet can provide revisionists with the opportunity to rewrite history. For example, the World Wide Web has proven to be a popular forum for "Holocaust denial"—for people and groups who deny that the genocide of 6 million Jews actually occurred during World War II. This phenomenon existed prior to the web, but the use of web pages and forums such as Usenet News groups allows proponents of this "history" to reach a wider audience. As adherents to this belief become more numerous, the overall impact in society could be a normalization of the idea that the Holocaust never happened, or of the notion that the effects of this tragedy have been exaggerated.

This example is extreme, but others abound. Recently, a story about gang initiation rites circulated on the Internet, with readers warned not to flash their headlights, lest they become the unwitting victim of a newly initiated gang member. An emerging field of Internet folklore studies how such myths are created and transmitted over the Internet.

The articles in this section explore different ways in which the Internet and other forms of digital media can distort events or can otherwise create "truth" and "history." The first selection, "How a Quack Becomes a Canard," by Jonathan Vankin and John Whalen, examines the evolution of conspiracy theories on the Internet about TWA Flight 800. Major news organizations relied on these Internet sources to report that the flight had been downed by a friendly-fire U.S. Navy missile.

The next article, "As Hate Spills onto the Web, a Struggle over Whether, and How, to Control It," examines the rise of hate groups on the Internet. This *New York Times* article by Elizabeth Olson also raises questions about censorship, but it is included here because it illustrates how hate groups use technology to attract converts to their ideologies and beliefs.

The next two articles investigate questions surrounding the use of computer simulations. In "Seductions of Sim: Policy as a Simulation Game," Paul Starr uses the example of the children's game "Sim City" to discuss how simulations can limit the way we view a given situation. In "Simulations on Trial," Arielle Emmett reviews how simulations have been used in trials to convince juries to choose one version of truth over another.

Journalism also has been affected by technologies that can distort or fabricate the facts. In "New Media Caveat: The Truth May Not Be Out There," *Newsday* columnist Clive Thompson discusses the case of disgraced journalist Stephen Glass, who created web sites and then used them as sources for stories reported as truth. In "What Is Truth?" Sheri Rosen examines the idea of truth in photography in an era when digital technology makes it easy to alter photos and other images.

The companion web sites provide resources for more in-depth investigations of the ideas presented in this unit. At HateWatch, you can review web sites posted by hate groups and learn more about how such groups use Internet technology. The site Thinking Critically About World Wide Web Resources provides guidelines for evaluating information on the Internet. The National Budget Simulation site provides an opportunity to test some of the criticisms about the use of simulations in policy making.

Knowing that technology makes it cheap and easy to alter or fabricate the truth, sometimes we may feel paralyzed in our ability to make a judgment about what constitutes the "truth." Ultimately, we all make decisions based on our conclusions and judgments, and sometimes we're compelled to accept one version of truth over another at a given moment. By making you more aware of these issues, this section, I hope, will sharpen your critical thinking, so that you feel confident about making conclusions and judgments, both about technology and about other issues important to you.

If enough people believe something, does that make it true? What criteria come into play in evaluating the reliability of Internet sources?

How a Quack Becomes a Canard

Could "friendly fire" have brought down T.W.A. 800? No way. But thanks to the Internet—where conspiracy theories are born, mutate and spread at a cyber-clip—the idea just won't go away.

Jonathan Vankin and John Whalen

Jonathan Vankin and John Whalen are the authors of The 60 Greatest Conspiracies of All Time.

On the night of July 17, T.W.A. Flight 800 exploded and crashed off the coast of Long Island, killing everyone on board. For months, investigators have focused on three possible causes—a bomb, mechanical failure or a terrorist missile—but what really happened remains a mystery.

That's the formal line, anyway. Barely 36 hours after the disaster, a message posted on an Internet discussion site called "rec.aviation.piloting" suggested a darker possibility. "Did the Navy do it?" wrote someone from New York who identified himself as Evan B. Gillespie. "It is interesting how much evidence there is that it was hit by a missile."

Actually, there wasn't any weightier "evidence" for this than for the other two theories. Reports from eyewitnesses—who said they saw a streak of light approaching the jet before it crashed—prompted investigators to entertain the idea that someone shot it down. This still hasn't been ruled out, though it's now considered the least likely possibility. Within days of the crash, however, numerous Net writers mulled over the witness reports and made a startling leap: they speculated that the jet was downed by accidental "friendly fire" from a United States Navy ship on a training cruise. Such a horrifying blunder, according to the evolving theory, was quickly covered up by a conspiracy involving Federal investigators, the military and President Clinton.

Even by conspiracy standards, this one was pretty weak. But as a study in how conspiracy theories mutate in the age of easy global communication, the friendly fire story is a gem. On the Internet, conspiracy theories gestate almost instantly, and spread with dizzying speed. The theorists seize on and often distort mainstream media reports, make gross assumptions about the Government's allegedly boundless capacity for malevolence and, occasionally, fabricate reports outright.

In the case of Flight 800, the process happened so fast and with such intensity that the conspiracy theory, which once might have bounced around harmlessly on the fringe, briefly elbowed its way into mainstream coverage. In September and again in October, prompted largely by the Internet's conspiratorial buzz, journalists felt compelled to ask officials about the possibility of friendly fire. The authorities labeled it "an outrageous allegation."

News organizations, which subsequently took a closer look, agreed. But the fact that friendly fire came up at all says a lot about the power of the Internet. Here is a chronological review of how a theory catapulted to 15 minutes of fame.

July 17–23: A Penny for Your Plots

In the immediate aftermath of the crash, unhinged speculation was cheap. Some theorists suggested that the true target of the T.W.A.

"attack" was Henry Kissinger, who was supposedly on board. (He wasn't.) Over time, the theories included such notions as the jet being zapped by a death ray possibly operated by a consortium of Russians, North Koreans, and the Japanese Aum Shinrikyo cult. Predictably, some asserted that a U.F.O. was responsible.

But only the friendly fire theory developed real legs, thanks largely to a July 21 *Jerusalem Post* story in which unnamed "French Defense Ministry experts" asserted that "the infrastructure needed to fire a missile powerful enough to hit a plane at that altitude is only possessed by Army units."

The story was clearly presented as "what if" speculation, but many conspiracy theorists took it as confirmation that the U.S. Government had shot down Flight 800. The *Post* is available on the World Wide Web, and the story spread rapidly all over the planet. "I think it's pretty obvious," stated one contributor to the "talk.politics.guns" news group, "that T.W.A. 800 was taken down by a SAM. . . . Friendly fire, as it were."

July 24–29: Troopergate

A posting in the news group "alt.conspiracy" made a more startling claim: Clinton was probably involved. "Two of the passengers were former Arkansas state troopers that were on Bill Clinton's security detail," it read, explaining that the men were on their way to Paris to tell all to *Le Monde*. The "source" for this shocker? The *Miami Herald*.

The "Troopergate" message generated excitement among Net conspiracy theorists, many of

whom believe Clinton to be capable of anything, from drug dealing to multiple homicide. "Suddenly the T.W.A. 800 explosion got a whole lot less mysterious," wrote one correspondent in "misc.survivalism." Over in "alt.politics.org.batf," an American Online subscriber wondered, "How many (total) does that make now of people who have previously known our Komrad Klinton who are now pushing up daisies?"

Aug. 2: Cyberhoax

The *Miami Herald* quickly exposed the trooper message as a hoax. The *Herald* traced it to the Net address of one Gene Hilsheimer, a Florida resident. The *Herald* said "Hilsheimer denied creating it," though he did opine later that the posting was probably designed to bait "conspiracy nuts." Despite this particular debunking, friendly fire kept on going. Other writers surged ahead with the unsupported claim that "there is a report of sailors at sea routinely locking on to airliners during mock missile practice."

Aug. 22: Russell Takes Charge

Friendly fire might have stalled were it not for an anonymous message that began circulating in late August. "T.W.A. Flight 800 was shot down," one version stated, "by a U.S. Navy guided missile ship which was in area W-105 . . . a Warning Area off the southeast coast of Long Island."

The message was attributed to "a man who was Safety Chairman for the Airline Pilots Association for many years and

he is considered an expert on safety." In fact, it was written on America Online by Richard Russell, a 66-year-old Floridian and former United Airlines pilot. Russell later told reporters that he never intended his message—originally a private E-mail communication sent to about a dozen friends who were aviation accident investigators—to be widely distributed. Nonetheless, replicated countless times by unknown Net-izens, it spread like a viral contagion.

"Hey, those who want the truth. This is no joke!!!" wrote one fan. "Just read on and watch the papers, knowing where you heard it first. Pretty shocking."

Aug. 28–Sept. 1: Friendly Fire Skyrockets

As the crash investigation of T.W.A. 800 entered its second month, friendly fire talk began to move beyond the Internet. It was helped along, inadvertently, by news reports of more eyewitness anomalies, including the murky snapshot taken by Linda Kabot, a Long Island secretary. Blown up and distributed on the Net, it showed a blip, supposedly a long cylinder streaking through the night sky, allegedly in the vicinity of the doomed jet.

About this time, multiple copies of the hijacked Russell opinion began arriving in newsrooms via fax and E-mail. With populist speculation about friendly fire becoming a roar, major media outlets decided to take a closer look. On Sept. 1, *Newsday* launched a pre-emptive strike on the friendly fire theory, quoting a "senior Federal source" who advised, perhaps wishfully, "You can put that to bed."

Sept. 5–7: Going Up, Up, Up. . . .

Another mainstream report—this one by a local TV reporter—helped amplify the Net buzz about friendly fire. On Sept. 5, Marcia Kramer of WCBS-TV in New York broadcast that investigators were examining whether a missile from "a U.S. military plane" might have torn through the jet without exploding. Her sources? Unnamed officials close to the investigation. Kramer's report was ignored by most of her colleagues, a fact that itself inflamed Net suspicion. "This news item did not show up anywhere else on radio or TV during the following day," one Net surfer wrote. "Shades of censorship?"

Sept. 8–17: Pffft! Russell Fizzles

In the next several days *Newsday, Newsweek,* the Associated Press, Reuters and CNN decided they had to take a hard look at friendly fire. "Because so many people were talking about it we felt it was the responsible thing to do, to revisit this question," says Ron Dunsky, a CNN producer whose network investigated friendly fire in July, found no evidence to support it and didn't run a story.

Why did it come to the fore again, since there was no new evidence?

"The Internet was part of the reason," he says, "one of the factors that tipped the scales."

At a Sept. 16 news briefing on Long Island, Federal Bureau of Investigation and National Transportation Safety Board officials found themselves under unfriendly fire from a fixated press corps. The investigators responded to at least four straight questions about the theory—including one from CNN, which later that day ran a serious report on friendly fire. It mentioned the Russell-authored message and conveyed emphatic denials from the Government.

Russell can't be accused of courting publicity. He says he has been contacted by several major television shows, but they've all lost interest because he won't give up his source. Unless Russell decides to say more, or his claimed source comes forward, his now-notorious E-mail message has to remain filed under "Rumors: Unsubstantiated."

Aftermath: It Lives!

Though the Russell-gram seemed at a dead end, the Net has made it immortal. On Sept. 27 Tom Snyder, on his "Late Late Show,"

announced that he'd just found the message on the Net and wondered aloud—albeit skeptically—about a Government cover-up.

Then on Nov. 8, friendly fire made headlines again. This time it was Pierre Salinger—the noted journalist and Kennedy Administration press secretary—who went public with the theory. Salinger, according to news accounts, said his source was a document given to him by "someone in French intelligence in Paris," written by an American who "was tied to the U.S. Secret Service, and has important contacts in the U.S. Navy."

Apparently, though, the document was the Russell message, or at least a clone of it. CNN showed Salinger a copy of the message, and he said: "Yes. That's it. That's the document. Where did you get it?" He also told other reporters that he learned only after he went public on Nov. 7 (U.S. media ran the story the next day) that the same document had been on the Net for weeks. He said the message was dated Aug. 22—the same day Russell sent his famous E-mail.

As Net writers might say: "Interesting!!!"

 Article Review Form at end of book.

Should hate groups on the Internet be controlled? How does the Anti-defamation League propose to do so?

As Hate Spills onto the Web, a Struggle Over Whether, and How, to Control It

Elizabeth G. Olson

The World Wide Web site of a group called the Charlemagne Hammerskins opens with an image of a man in a ski mask, carrying a gun and standing by a swastika. A click on a button below labeled, in French, "Access for sub-humans," yields a picture of what appears to be a concentration camp, accompanied by a not-so-veiled threat: "Be assured, we still have many one-way tickets for Auschwitz."

The site—one of a number created by groups with similar names and agendas—was carried by America Online's French service until this month, when it was closed by administrators who decided its content was offensive, said Michelle Gilbert, a spokesman for the on-line service.

"Putting a Nazi site on line is illegal in France," she noted, because the country's laws prohibit material that incites racial

hatred. The site, however, soon reappeared on an Internet server in Canada.

The skinhead site is hardly the only one vilifying various ethnic groups—most often, but not exclusively, blacks and Jews. One site, based on a computer in Sweden and purporting to belong to a group called Radio Islam, is devoted to questions about the reality of the Holocaust and features caricatures of evil-looking figures with black beards and exaggerated noses, wearing Stars of David.

The hatred that drips from these and other such Web sites, of course, exists independent of any technology and occurs in all media. Indeed, the photographs, monographs and cartoons on many sites are taken from other media, mostly print.

But for a group of conferees meeting in Geneva earlier in November under the sponsorship of the United Nations Human Rights Center, the question was

how to apply European countries' legal prohibitions against hate speech to this new medium.

Michael Schneider, head of the Electronic Commerce Forum in Bonn, which represents German Internet service providers, said there had been several cases in which German authorities had demanded that providers eliminate sites or face prosecution. But he argued that Internet Service providers cannot control content, saying "They are nothing more than carriers."

Still, Debra Guzman, director of an American organization, the Human Rights Information Network, called the Internet "a utopia for all kinds of hate groups, from neo-Nazis to anarchists," who are "targeting teenage males with this propaganda."

Agha Shahi of Pakistan, the meeting's chairman, said sites that promote racism violate a global treaty against racial discrimination. The 148 countries that signed the pact "are under obligation to enact measures to eliminate it," he said.

The United States has signed the document, but has said it will not pass laws infringing on free speech.

Conference members seemed at a loss as to how to balance what one speaker called "the two most powerful revolutions of the 20th century, those of human rights and information technology."

Opponents of regulation answered pleas for controls with descriptions of the practical, technological and legal difficulties of regulation.

The Internet "enables the instant marketing of hate and mayhem," said Marc Knobel, a Paris-based researcher who monitors Web sites for the Simon Wiesenthal Center in Los Angeles. The number of hate sites has nearly doubled to 600 in the last year, he said; he has catalogued 300.

There are at least 94 sites promoting a racial hierarchy that would classify Europeans by skin color, religion, ethnicity and even preferred language, he said. He counts 87 neo-Nazi sites, 35 white supremacist sites and 51 sites espousing terrorism.

It is often impossible to determine who is responsible for hate sites, most of which are based on computer servers in the United States. Among the sites is the White Aryan Resistance Hate Page. It caricatures a black youth, with a greatly distended mouth and protruding teeth.

The divergent histories of the United States, with its tradition of free-speech guarantees, and of Europe, with its World War II legacy of genocide and its recent history of ethnic strife in the Balkans, were evident at the conference. United States representatives argued that the Internet cannot be regulated; others sought ways to ban offensive sites and punish their sponsors.

A World Wide Web page, "even one advocating the supposed benefits of achieving racial purity, lacks the potential for imminent incitement," to violence, Philip Reitinger, a United States Justice Department attorney, said at the conference, adding that it is "not through government censor-ship that equality is well served; that principle—one which accords freedom of expression the highest respect—applies with equal force to the Internet."

With European laws varying country to country, border-jumping is one way to avoid accountability for hate messages. Hate site sponsors also can change service providers or take other routes to reopen their sites.

That appears to have happened with Robert Faurisson of Vichy, France. Mr. Knobel said that Mr. Faurisson was behind a Holocaust revisionist site that was shut down earlier this year. It then popped up on the Radio Islam site.

Mr. Faurisson, 68, denies having a Web site. Fined $20,000 in October by a French court for printed statements denying the Holocaust, Mr. Faurisson now denies his denial; in sarcastic tones, he said in a telephone interview, "I do believe in the gas chambers that I used to call magic."

 Article Review Form at end of book.

Are simulations always an appropriate tool for developing public policy? What lessons can we learn from "Sim City"?

Seductions of Sim:

Policy as a simulation game

Paul Starr

Standing around the computer, my two older daughters, nine and eleven years old, scan the picture of the city we're creating and debate whether it needs more commercial or residential development. My six-year-old son suggests we look at the city budget. In just a few weeks he has learned enough to ask the critical question: "What's the cash flow?"

This is SimCity, one of a series of computer simulations that turn public policy and ideas into popular entertainment. With the advent of dramatically improved graphics and powerful, low-cost multimedia computers, a new generation of "edutainment" software has finally begun to fulfill the long-touted promise of computers in education. Most of the new programs use interactive multimedia to make games out of traditional subjects such as arithmetic or geography. In MathBlasters, for example, children solve math problems in order to fuel up a rocket and find a villain in outer space.

However, the Sim series, produced by California-based Maxis, goes a step further: it makes games out of simulations

of complex natural and social systems, based on advanced and sometimes controversial areas of science and decision making, such as climatology and environmental science, genetics, and sociobiology. Those who think designing cities is prosaic can move on to simulating the development of planetary ecosystems (SimEarth) or the evolution of new life forms (SimLife). Other programs make games out of the management of railroads (A-Train), and farms (SimFarm), and even national health policy (SimHealth). These are unlikely ever to challenge Nintendo's SuperMario World in sales. Still, it isn't only policy wonks who are buying the games for themselves and their kids. Sim City has sold two million copies since its release in 1989 and has probably introduced more people to urban planning than any book ever has.

When my family first began playing SimCity and others like it not long ago, my initial reaction was a mixture of excitement and skepticism. The new simulations are certainly a lot more fun than most textbooks. Rather than present information, they provide tools for inventing worlds, exploring hypotheses, and stretch-

ing imaginations. Several have a public viewpoint. In SimCity—unlike Monopoly—the player builds a community. One of the "scenarios" in the latest version of SimCity puts the player in Flint, Michigan in 1974 with the task of rebuilding the local job base and community. In SimEarth and SimLife, the object is to create sustainable environments and avoid extinctions.

But I worried whether the games might not be too seductive. What assumptions were buried in the underlying models? What was their "hidden curriculum"? Did a conservative or a liberal determine the response to changes in tax rates in SimCity? While playing SimCity with my eleven-year-old daughter, I railed against what I thought was a built-in bias of the program against mixed-use development. "It's just the way the game works," she said a bit impatiently.

My daughter's words seemed oddly familiar. A few months earlier someone had said virtually the same thing to me, but where? It suddenly flashed back: the earlier conversation had taken place while I was working at the White House on the development of the Clinton health plan. We were discussing the simulation model likely to be used by the Congressional Budget Office (CBO) to "score" proposals for health care reform. When I criticized one assumption, a colleague said to me, "Don't waste your breath," warning that it was hopeless to get CBO to change. Policy would have to adjust.

There are, of course, important differences between computer simulation games and the simulations used to assess policy options. The games are designed to be entertaining; fidelity to empirical reality is not foremost. But simplification is inherent in any simulation. Even "real" simulations (if that is not an oxymoron) inevitably rely on imperfect models and simplifying assumptions that the media, the public, and even policy makers themselves generally don't understand. Both types of simulation are examples of what might be called a *crossover intellectual technology*, one that has only recently moved from academic and technical fields into popular and public use. The crossover of simulation holds out the promise of an enriched understanding of the world, particularly of complex systems. But there is a danger too: forgetting that simulations depend on the models on which they are built.

The danger is particularly worrisome when simulations are used to make predictions and evaluate policies. And when policymakers depend on simulations to guide present choices—especially when legislators put government on "automatic pilot," binding policy to numerical indicators of projected trends—they cede power to those who define the models that generate the forecasts. This is happening in America today, most notably with

the rise of the CBO as a power center in national policy. In a sense, Washington is already SimCity.

Original Sim

Although it has taken three decades for them to come of age, simulation games—and SimCity in particular—are really children of the '60s. Indeed, their development follows a classic pattern of our time. In their infancy, simulations and related advances in computer technology were nurtured by government grants for both military and domestic policy purposes. In their maturity, they are being turned by private initiative and investment into a phenomenon of popular culture.

To be sure, the genealogy of simulation can be traced back to a varied history preceding the 1960s. At least since their use by the Prussian army in the eighteenth century, simulations of combat have been a staple of military training. War games were, so to speak, the cradle of simulation. By the post-World War II era, engineers and corporate managers were using simulations to design and run power grids, telecommunications networks, factories, and businesses. Business simulations, which began primarily as training exercises, evolved into a routine management tool. And as researchers gained access to computers in the 1950s and '60s, simulations came into wide use for scientific purposes to understand complex systems such as climates, economies, ecosystems, and international relations.

As these examples suggest, simulations referred to at least two types of activity. One kind of simulation created a role-playing game and engaged participants in working out a scenario under

prescribed conditions and rules. The other kind projected the behavior of a complex system on the basis of a quantitative model. The new computer simulations create games based on models of complex systems and, in that sense, they combine the two.

The forerunners of these games were developed in the 1960s. "Social simulation" took off during the '60s in several independent forms. At Johns Hopkins, the sociologist James S. Coleman and his colleagues worked on simulations as a means of both advancing social theory and improving education, particularly for minority youth. Role-playing simulations and games, they argued, would enliven the teaching of subjects as diverse as mathematics and social studies. One of the games, called Ghetto, sought to expose the logic of inner-city life. The hope was that as a tool of research, simulations and games would enable the theorist to define and grasp the underlying rules of social systems. (Economics, of all the social sciences, has most used games this way.) As a tool of school reform, simulations would provide a more accessible, participatory method of education for children who did not respond well to traditional instruction. John Dewey's educational ideals would finally be realized—or at least simulated.

Advanced training programs and consensus-building for professionals and decision makers also made increasing use of role-playing simulation games, sometimes involving large groups working under a trained facilitator. Some of the earliest games simulated urban conflicts over resource allocation. In 1964, one of the founders of the field, Richard Duke, designed a game called

Metropolis for the city council in Lansing, Michigan. The game used role-playing to work through policy decisions and employed computers to track the effects, as the group went through one cycle of decision making after another. By the mid-1970s, a later version of the game, Metro-Apex, gave computer simulation a central role.

During the 1950s and 1960s, a variety of planners and social scientists concerned with urban problems had been developing large-scale computer models of cities to simulate and predict their development under varying policies. These models were first designed primarily for transportation and land-use planning. The federal highway program provided a major impetus. Modeling burgeoned in both academic and professional city-planning departments and displaced older traditions that conceived of planning as "architecture writ large."

Large-scale urban simulation models first caught the public eye through the work of an outsider to the field. In 1969, Jay W. Forrester, an electrical engineering professor at MIT with no background in urban research, published *Urban Dynamics*, a book purporting to disprove common intuitions about urban policy. Forrester's next work, *World Dynamics*, proposed a model for the entire planet. A group based at MIT and led by his protégés prepared the 1972 report *The Limits to Growth* sponsored by the Club of Rome, which claimed to show that the world was reaching the end of its ecological tether.

Because of their dramatic conclusions, Forrester and the Club of Rome report captured the public imagination, but the reception accorded their work by re-searchers and professionals was much cooler. Forrester's urban model was not based on empirical evidence and had no spatial dimension. According to Britton Harris, a leading exponent of modeling and emeritus professor of planning, transportation, and public policy at the University of Pennsylvania, Forrester's model had little influence on urban planning. The Club of Rome report did incorporate data and had real influence, though it too had no spatial dimension. From the vantage of the Club of Rome, the world consisted only of aggregates and averages. While undoubtedly contributing to public awareness of global environmental problems (and better subsequent research), the report itself has not withstood the passage of time. For example, nearly all the resources that it predicted would be in short supply at escalating prices in the 1990s now have larger known reserves and are available at lower prices than they were in 1972.

Professional disillusionment with large-scale models was already setting in at the time of the Club of Rome report. In 1973, a leading journal in urban planning published a "requiem" for large-scale models. The emerging consensus was that the models had overreached; both the theory underlying the models and the available data were inadequate to make the kind of predictions the modelers were attempting. The modelers' "loss of faith," as one of the leading urban modelers, William Alonso, calls it, became part of a broader collapse of confidence in planning in the 1970s and 1980s. In the same era, efforts to apply simulation and games to the education of minority youth were also proving a disappointment. Critics questioned whether the educational payoff was worth the effort.

But while social simulation flagged, work on simulation models and games did not actually disappear. Rather, it retreated into more specialized circles. Role-playing simulations have become a standard technique for professional training and conflict resolution. During the next two decades, the development of computers, software, and data resources transformed both the scientific and popular potential of computer simulation. By the late 1980s, there was talk of a "renaissance" of large-scale models in urban planning, even though many in the field are still as wary as ever about the models' predictive powers.

The spread of desktop computers and advance of visualization techniques have been particularly important for the revival and popular crossover of simulation. Early computer simulations and games required access to mainframe computers and skills that were, to most people, esoteric. Improved graphics made simulations and games not only more accessible and absorbing, but also more "playable."

Much of the research behind advances in computer graphics was originally sponsored by the Department of Defense and space programs and grew out of work on flight simulation, which in the 1960s and '70s was centered at the University of Utah. The defense and space programs had a similar catalytic role in the development of the Internet. Virtual reality has followed the same route.

Improved graphics hit the home market with the growth of video games and the advent of the Macintosh. Even flight simulation has crossed over to become home entertainment.

It was while working on a video game for bombing islands that Will Wright, a Macintosh programmer, came up with the idea for SimCity. Wright told me recently that while designing a "terrain editor" to create the landscape, he discovered that he had "more fun building the islands than bombing them."

Wright had never studied urban planning—his background was in robotics and computer games—but on his own he found his way to the planning literature, including Forrester and Jane Jacobs. The subject became interesting to him only after he began simulating urban development. (Many people who have since played SimCity have probably had the same experience.) Draw-ing on research begun decades earlier, Wright fashioned the models of land use, traffic, power systems, and other aspects of urban development that underlie SimCity. He says he conceived of SimCity not as a game but rather as a "toy" because at least in its standard use there is no preset goal or contest. The player decides what kind of city to build—whether to emphasize its size, wealth, beauty, or harmony with the environment. In 1987, unable to find a software publisher who thought there was a market for such a toy, Wright joined with a businessman, Jeff Braun, to start Maxis and develop SimCity. The company now has more than 20 titles on the market and has spun off a separate firm to create business and public policy applications.

Inside SimCity

The seductive power of computer simulation games lies partly in their extraordinary variety and intricacy. Generating complex variation is one thing that computers do especially well. But interest in such games was limited as long as the "user interface" was text. Adding stereo sound and three-dimensional graphics enables people to handle greater complexity at a faster pace. This is what makes multimedia simulation such a powerful communication medium. SimCity shows why.

Like several other programs in the Sim series, SimCity offers a choice between two types of play: building a system from scratch or solving the problems in a specific scenario. (All references here are to SimCity 2000, the more elaborate, three-dimensional version of the game released in 1993.) The player who builds a city de novo receives a starting fund and a randomly generated, five-square-mile terrain whose features can be chosen and modified at no cost prior to the start of play. For example, the player can decide whether to locate the city on a coast or river and how much area will be covered by water, hills, and forests. The terrain will be different every time. Once play begins, the development of the city is open-ended, with no fixed objectives or time limits, except as the player defines them. In contrast, in the second type of play, the player loads a scenario with a given map and limited time to accomplish a specific task, such as revitalizing Flint, rebuilding Charleston, South Carolina after a hurricane, or turning "Dullsville, U.S.A.," into an exciting community.

As mayor of SimCity, the player has extraordinary powers; there is no city council, state government, or public employee union to worry about. (Weep, Rudolph Giuliani, weep.) The mayor can set local tax rates and locate and build various community facilities and services, such as power plants, water systems, roads, highways, rails, airports, police and fire stations, schools, and hospitals. The mayor can also control annual spending on city services, adopt ordinances on matters ranging from pollution control to the promotion of tourism, and zone areas for industrial, commercial, or residential use.

SimCity operates on a "field of dreams" principle. If as mayor the player creates the right environment, the Sims—the imaginary inhabitants of the city—will come and build factories, shops, and homes. When they do, buildings and factories pop up on the land and change as the city develops. But if things turn sour—if unemployment rises or high crime rates in a neighborhood drive people away—the icons on the screen change or go dark to indicate population losses or building abandonment. All this takes place in vaguely historical time (the player can set the starting data at 1900, 1950, 2000, or 2050), which primarily affects the available technology and rate of energy consumption.

To help make decisions about zoning, taxes, expenditures, bond issues, and other policies, the program provides a wealth of constantly changing data in maps and graphs showing the city's population growth and density, demand for residential, commercial, and industrial land, unemployment, power and water supply, crime, traffic congestion, pollution, and various other aspects of the city's development. The same sources report changes in interest rates and the growth of the national economy and neighboring cities. Newspapers periodically deliver reports of local sentiment, including the latest public opinion polls and inane, jumbled stories about local and made-up international events. A hallmark of the Sim games is a light touch. (My favorite example: In SimAnt, which translates the sociobiology of ant behavior into game form, one ant curses a group from another colony, "Your queen mates with termites.")

The key to SimCity is the interaction of private land values with the public budget. As the player constructs a city, the value of property zoned for development is continually changing. These changing values are critical, for they affect property tax receipts and determine—as my six-year-old quickly discovered—whether the cash flow in the city budget is positive or negative and therefore whether the player has to raise taxes, cut spending on city services, and skimp on public investments.

Will Wright aptly refers to the basic conceptual framework of SimCity as a "capitalistic land value ecology" and argues that it fits the development of American cities in the twentieth century but would not account for the development, for example, of St. Petersburg. In fact, SimCity is somewhat more constraining; the game seems to require a particular type of American city built on an industrial base.

The model in SimCity, as Wright describes it, consists of a series of "concentric rings." At the core is a so-called "basic/nonbasic" or "export/import" model, borrowed from the traditional urban development literature, that describes the evolving relationship of the industrial, commercial, and residential sectors. SimCity assumes that while 70 percent of industrial production is exported outside of a city, 70 percent of commercial produc-

tion is consumed internally. Thus in the early stages of a city's development, while its internal market is small, the industrial sector must predominate. As the city and its internal market grow, commerce begins to expand, ultimately overtaking industry as the main source of employment. The demand for residential space depends on the growth of other sectors. If jobs outnumber potential participants in the labor force, people will move to the city and demand for residential development will increase. If the local economy is doing badly and there are fewer jobs than workers, unemployment will rise and people will leave the city.

According to Wright, SimCity uses a "bid rent" model to determine land valuations. Property carries different values depending on its use; for example, proximity to the urban center is valued most for commercial and residential purposes and least for industry. The actual numbers used in SimCity for land values, city investments, and other items bear no relation to the real world. However, the overall valuation of SimCity and thus its tax base will depend on how the player distributes and locates different zones and allocates resources among roads, schools, and other public services.

Wright says SimCity is built "from the inside out." In the outer rings are models for traffic, energy, water, and other systems, which react back upon and modify the land-use model at the core. The hardest problem, according to Wright, is not what to put in but what to leave out. He is disarming about the game's limits. Inevitably, SimCity is a "caricature" of reality. The models deliberately exaggerate effects to provide feedback to the player; in

real life, the effects of many decisions would be imperceptible. The purpose of SimCity is not accuracy or prediction but communication. "Unless it's entertaining, the educational value is irrelevant." Asked how he handles controversial choices, like the effects of tax rates on development, Wright dodges the question and says, "We go for game play"—whatever is most fun.

Still, when players make decisions in SimCity, the game generates effects on employment, crime, population growth, tax revenues. I would be more worried about too easy an acceptance of the validity of those effects if SimCity worked with real data. Games of that kind may well be on the market not long from now, enabling players to download real maps and data into a game with a visual interface like SimCity. But, as now designed, SimCity is clearly a fictional world and the effects seem only as real as points scored in a video game. This is even true of the Flint scenario because of the patently fictional quality of all the numbers used in the game.

SimCity's players learn not from any particular aspect of the model but from the process of being forced to make choices and face the consequences. Most immediately, they confront choices of spatial design in distributing land among potential uses and locating community resources like schools and NIMBY's like power plants. These choices have a temporal as well as spatial dimension. Players who overinvest too early in costly capital projects like an airport or stadium will quickly find themselves in fiscal trouble.

The important payoff comes from struggling to master complexity. Wright observes, "Playing the game is the process of discovering how the model works." Of course, few players will be able to give any formal expression to the model. But much of it is implicit in the manual that comes with the game, and many players will be able to figure out critical relationships from the signals that the game provides. To keep up with a city's changing size and demands, the game requires constant monitoring of the city's power, water, transportation, budget, and other systems.

If there is a "hidden curriculum" in SimCity and other Sim games, it lies here. Shoshana Zuboff's 1988 book *In the Age of the Smart Machine* describes the confusion and alienation of workers in factories and offices as computers were first introduced over the previous decade. Physical contact with the production process had been an important source of practical knowledge; for example, workers at pulp mills that Zuboff studied had been able to tell whether anything was wrong merely from the color and odor of the pulp. Now the workers were asked to make decisions based on information flashing on a computer screen. This shift deemphasized sensory knowledge and put a premium on more abstract, "intellective" capacities. This is exactly what SimCity teaches: the management of complex systems based on "intelligent scanning" of streams of constantly changing information.

As SimCity has evolved, it has incorporated increasing levels of complexity. For example, in the original SimCity, the fiscal options were limited. There was one tax rate that players could raise or lower, no possibility of floating bonds, and just three types of operating expenditure—transportation, police, and fire protection. In SimCity 2000, the

player can vary property tax rates by class (residential, commercial, industrial); offer tax incentives to specific industries; impose a sales or income tax; borrow funds; refinance bonds; budget a wider variety of programs now including education, health, and welfare; and vary expenditures within each budget category (for example, primary and secondary schools versus higher education) and even by neighborhood.

This degree of complexity may seem astonishing in a game for children. But when children play SuperMario World and other popular adventure games, they must learn the most intricate facts about the many imaginary places they navigate. These worlds are typically filled with strange creatures, hidden passageways, and special treasures. Going from one level of the game to the next demands an extraordinary mastery of detail. Compared with these demands, managing SimCity is surprisingly straightforward.

SimCity makes complexity manageable partly by enabling players to ignore much of it when they are first learning the game. For example, players can turn on "auto-budget" and let the program follow its default options until they are ready to take up fiscal alternatives. When they do, they will find that SimCity allows the mayor to get advice from various city council members—or are they consultants?—who appear at the click of a mouse. Their recommendations may not, however, always be consistent. As I was playing, one adviser urged me to raise taxes to cut the city's deficit, while another said I should cut taxes to stimulate growth. This difference seemed to me a truly real-world touch.

Wright says that the next stage in SimCity's development

may enable the player to dive into a city to run a business inside it. He also wants to give players the ability to modify the model's assumptions. "We want the user to be able to define more and more of the model." Ultimately, he says, the game could allow players to build the models themselves. Whether many people would use this opportunity is unclear. But the option would permit mastery of a simulation in the more fundamental sense of being able to manipulate the assumptions and relationships behind it. In its current version, the model is an unreachable black box. A new Sim game, SimHealth, does allow players to modify assumptions and define the governing values. But in practice, SimHealth shows some of the limitations of the genre.

A Simulation Muddle

The premise of SimHealth is that you have been elected to Congress in 1992 and seek to get reelected by choosing policies for health care. The game and the voters then rate your performance not against an independent standard but rather against your own—the values you have selected at the outset. This is an attractive concept. However, the framework for "clarifying" values adopted by SimHealth is based on hackneyed and misleading premises. SimHealth asks players to define their values in terms of two dualities—liberty and equality, and community and efficiency—on the premise that more of one value in a pair necessarily means less of the other.

But is this the case? Historically, many societies that have denied basic liberties have also had extreme inequalities. When we talk about rights, we generally mean equal rights; thus the two concepts overlap, often reinforcing one another. For example, does the right to assemble peaceably for redress of grievances express the value of liberty or equality? What about equal educational opportunity? Compared to the U.S. system today, is Canadian-style national health insurance an expression of equality (since everyone is covered) or of liberty (since all are guaranteed individual choice of physician and no one suffers from job lock)?

To assume a zero-sum relation between liberty and equality, and community and efficiency, obscures a central challenge of policy—how to achieve progress on more than one value at a time. For example, few would disagree that by eliminating administrative sources of inefficiency, we are better able to carry out aims benefiting the community as a whole. But in SimHealth, efficiency and community are counterposed. Perhaps even more fundamental, SimHealth's framework fails to appreciate that the main political differences in health policy, as in other areas of American politics, concern conflicting interpretations of widely shared values. Those who take different positions do not necessarily differ in the value they place, for example, on liberty; they often disagree about what liberty means in relation to health care (freedom to change jobs without fear of losing coverage, freedom to pick a health plan, freedom to pick a doctor, freedom to consult alternative healers, and so on).

SimHealth's philosophical muddle is inadvertently apparent from the arbitrary connections it asserts between values and particular statements that are supposed to embody them. The value of community supposedly calls for "restructur[ing] health insurance to provide the highest quality care." But it is obscure to me why "community" should mean an emphasis on quality of care rather than, say, careful stewardship of resources, priority for public health measures, or universal coverage.

SimHealth does no better a job of explaining health care policies and proposals. Indeed, the game is littered with crude simplifications and outright errors of fact. It mixes up the concepts of managed care and managed competition, confuses an individual's share of premiums with the coinsurance rate (the individuals' share of payments for covered services), and misstates the basic arrangements proposed in the Clinton and other proposed health plans in Congress. The effects of particular policies on public opinion seemed entirely arbitrary and capricious. I did not detect any particular political bias. But SimHealth contains so much misinformation that no one could possibly understand competing proposals and policies, much less evaluate them, on the basis of the program. And although SimHealth enables users to modify some assumptions, the model is never clearly explained and the basic architecture is beyond reach.

The oversimplified values framework and misinformation in SimHealth could be fixed, but the bigger problem is false pretensions. Unlike the plainly fictional SimCity, SimHealth claims to simulate the effects of different real-world proposals, which it cannot do. I suspect that if SimCity purported to help evaluate policies toward the homeless, it would seem equally inadequate.

SimHealth is a case of overshoot. The Sim games generally achieve their impact by engaging players in concrete tasks. SimHealth, however, seeks to engage players in formulating policy, which is entirely different. A child can start playing SimCity without any conceptual understanding of urban development. But to choose among various policy options in SimHealth, the player needs to understand their relation to one another. The conceptual threshold is too high, and it is not clear that a game can overcome it. On the other hand, for those who are familiar with the elements of health policy, playing SimHealth quickly becomes repetitive; it lacks the complex variation and intricacy of SimCity and other Sim games. Once the novelty of making health policy into a game has worn off, I doubt SimHealth will hold much interest. It certainly has no value in assessing health care reform.

Simulation in Reality

The critical problem raised by simulation is the black-box nature of the models. In the "real world" of policy simulation, the models are subject to criticism and debate, at least among professionals. Opposing sides in policy disputes often come armed with their own simulations, ready to fight numbers with numbers. However outrageously biased some of these may be, there is nothing remarkable or offensive about the practice—it is simply one aspect of today's pursuit of politics by other means.

The troubling questions, in my view, concern the use of simulation as an element of statecraft. In principle, models used for official purposes are more open to scrutiny than are those in the private sector, and that is enormously important. Within and across the branches of the federal government, the validity of the models and assumptions is subject to intense scrutiny, and a strong sense of professionalism limits political manipulation. However, to most participants in policy debates as well as the public at large, the models are opaque. Only a few can penetrate the black box and understand what is inside. This has two opposite effects. At a conscious level, many people are distrustful of official projections, like much else about government. In practice, however, the numbers take on immense importance. As a result, those who have technical authority over the black boxes acquire an extraordinary degree of influence in the political process. And technical authority matters because the outcome of simulations often depends on what is assumed in the first place.

There is no obvious remedy to the black-box problem, and it affects conservatives as much as liberals. Conservatives who are wary of planning still depend on large-scale models for budgetary projections. Indeed, the most recent version of the balanced-budget amendment would require Congress to balance not actual outlays and receipts but projections of future streams. Since those projections would be produced through computer simulations, the amendment would give unprecedented authority to whoever served as official simulator—a role that sounds like the modern equivalent of court magician, and perhaps is.

The official simulator today, CBO director Robert Reischauer, may now be as powerful a figure as any member of Congress. The CBO has no veto over legislation, but it has a power that is nearly as great—the power to "score"

legislation to determine compliance with budget rules and future effects on the deficit. When someone in Washington today claims savings for a proposed change in national policy, people ask not whether the savings are real but rather, "Are they scoreable?" This aspect of national policy has all the features of a game with arcane rules and assumptions. (One of the staff economists at the Council of Economic Advisers joked last year that after leaving he would write a kiss-and-tell book called *How to Score in Washington*.)

From the formative stages of policymaking, the effects are substantial. For the past several years, the CBO has cast a broad shadow over the debate about health care reform. Among the cognoscenti, cost-containment proposals have been classified in two ways—"scoreable" and "unscoreable"—depending on whether the CBO was likely to smile or frown. The prospect that the CBO would frown on a policy and deem it "unscoreable" has been a grave, sometimes fatal strike against it.

When the CBO finally made its report on the Clinton health plan, it was front-page news, and again the black-box problem was apparent. Now it was time to hear the score, though few understood what went into it. The president's critics heralded Reischauer for saying that premiums paid to health alliances should be counted in federal receipts (albeit as an "off-budget" item) and that the plan would raise the federal deficit by $70 billion in the years prior to 2004 before reducing it. It almost did not matter that the CBO estimated a near-term increase in the federal deficit in part because it projected larger savings to state and local

government (indeed, recapturing those savings for the Treasury would make the plan virtually budget-neutral). Nor did conservatives who were praising Reischauer seem to appreciate the implications of CBO's general view of cost containment. While casting a skeptical eye on the market-oriented measures generally favored by conservatives, CBO has endorsed the effectiveness of regulatory measures that conservatives dislike. CBO accepted the Clinton premium caps as 100 percent effective. It has favorably assessed the impact of single-payer plans, particularly on administrative costs. This is by no means to say that CBO's judgments will be decisive, only that they have come to hold unprecedented influence.

CBO has emerged as a power center as the influence of Congress has grown relative to the executive branch over the past two decades. But CBO has also become a force in its own right, apart from the Congress, because of the predominance and persistence of budgetary issues in national politics and the search by the Congress to find ways to bind itself, like Ulysses to the mast, to resist strong impulses within. The official simulator is now called upon to provide not just clairvoyance but collective self-discipline. The discipline will hold only if the simulations do—only if there is one authoritative mechanism for defining the future in the present. The power of CBO has become an institutional necessity.

In the wider world, there is no comparable imperative to find a single mechanism for simulating alternative policies and theories. If there must be black boxes, at least we should have many of them to discourage faith in any one. Even better, we need to open up the boxes by making the models more transparent.

Transparency ought to become both the objective of simulation designers and a critical basis for judging their success. Richard Duke—the pioneer who first introduced computers into urban simulation games in the 1960s—is now deeply skeptical about models embedded in computers that oblige the user simply to accept an outcome as valid. Currently a professor at the University of Michigan and president of the International Simulation and Gaming Association, Duke says, "If a simulation hides the model, it's of little interest to me. If a simulation exposes the model, I'm much more interested." His own work now emphasizes role-playing policy simulation exercises that allow different players to engage each other, not just a black-box model. Besides allowing participants to practice skills in negotiation and group problem solving, the role-playing approach is much less deterministic: it introduces an unpredictable element of human choice into simulation games.

Computer simulation games with many simultaneous players linked through the Internet may also introduce more unpredictability. Moreover, as computer games become more elaborate and widely used, their sheer multiplication and increasing plasticity may promote a healthy skepticism about their predictive power. Playing with simulation is one way to see its limits as well as its possibilities.

For better or worse, simulation is no mere fad. Indeed, to think of simulation games as mere entertainment or even as teaching tools is to underestimate them. They represent a major addition to the intellectual repertoire that will increasingly shape how we communicate ideas and think through problems. The advent of this new medium has escaped the attention of cultural critics because it has come in the form of children's games. But the computer simulation game is an art form; when combined with three-dimensional graphics and sound, it is an extraordinarily powerful one. We shall be working and thinking in SimCity for a long time.

 **Article Review Form at end of book.**

Can simulations of crimes or accidents construct a reliable version of actual events? When and how are they most compelling?

Simulations on Trial

Arielle Emmett

Arielle Emmett is a freelance writer based in Wallingford, Pa.

Computer-generated animations are helping judges and juries visualize the final moments of an air crash, the ballistics of an unsolved murder, even botched medical care. But should viewers believe what they see?

During the last few seconds of an otherwise routine descent into Dallas/Fort Worth airport one sultry August night in 1985, Delta Flight 191 flew suddenly into a killer thunderstorm. Windshear forces quickly dashed the craft to the ground, where it rolled violently across the airfield into some reservoir tanks, killing all 137 people on board. Two years later, Delta sued both the Federal Aviation Administration and the National Weather Service for failing to warn the pilots that a storm of such severity had developed.

Preparing to do battle with Delta's lawyers before a lone federal judge, Kathlynn Fadely, a young attorney with the U.S. Department of Justice, commissioned a series of computer-generated animations to simulate the Lockheed Tristar's performance and explain critical instrument readings in the last moments of flight. It soon became clear from the aircraft's maneuvers that the pilots knew at least as much about the weather as ground control did. "They were playing Russian roulette by flying into that storm," she says. "The judge said the animations were both helpful and powerful," Fadely recalls.

By translating digital data from the aircraft's "black box" into striking images of the pilots' actions, and superimposing the cockpit soundtrack, she was able to weave a convincing narrative of pilot overconfidence and horrifying errors. She won the case, exonerating the federal government.

The animations in the Delta case are not unique. According to estimates by Forensic Technologies International (FTI), a San Francisco-based animation firm, computer animations are becoming powerful evidentiary tools in 10 percent of all U.S. trials. These animations translate data into intelligible images, illustrate expert testimony, and teach courtroom juries complex facts in record time. Though embryonic just a few years ago, the courtroom-animation industry, ranging from tiny startups to sophisticated engineering firms, exceeds $30 million in annual billings.

In a sense, forensic animations are a natural evolution of the video technology now used to capture scenes of violent crime, such as in the recent Rodney King and Reginald Denny cases in Los Angeles. A chief difference between live video and computer animation, however, is that animations create sequences of images based on information available only after the fact. Unfortunately, such information is frequently incomplete or colored by human bias. Thus, while the precise renderings of computer animations may lend an air of scientific authenticity to courtroom proceedings, they often reconstruct versions of reality that may not represent the truth.

Where Animations Shine

If a single picture is worth a thousand words, a convincing series of computer-generated moving pictures may be worth millions—in both words and dollars—in today's high-stakes courtroom trials. Indeed, forensic animations have gained a strong foothold in technically oriented cases where the dollar figures are high—such as in medical malpractice law, environmental and patent litigation, arson, and crash incidents of all kinds.

"Technical cases are where computer animations really shine," declares Alan Treibitz, president of Z-Axis, a forensic animation firm based in Englewood, Colo. For example, technical animations have illustrated dynamic forces acting on an aircraft, the human brain, or a building set on fire. Others have plotted the probable trajectory of cars involved in a crash or bullets used in a murder. "Jurors say they understand technical concepts much better with such animations than they could have with verbal testimony alone," says Treibitz.

Although the impact of animations varies considerably—depending on the case, the quality of the animation, and, in some instances, the willingness of the judge to accept the animation as evidence—attorneys may spend tens, if not hundreds, of thousands of dollars on them to support technical arguments and settle questions of time, place, and human activity. For example:

- In March 1991, Edward Walsh, a personal injury attorney in Wheaton, Ill., spent $24,000 on computer animations to support a malpractice claim involving a baby girl whose congenital brain-stem defect prevented her from breathing normally at night. After being placed on a home-ventilator system, the girl suffered a stroke at the age of 15 months that debilitated her for the rest of her life. The computer-drawn images helped Walsh's medical experts explain how the human respiratory system normally works and how a slowdown in bloodflow from improper ventilation, not her abnormal physiology, was responsible for the damage. Walsh believes the animation was one of the most important pieces of evidence in educating the jury during the trial. He won the case and $10 million for his client.

- In a contentious four-month trial that ended in January 1992, Honeywell paid computer animators at FTI $150,000 to help prove that Minolta infringed on Honeywell's patented autofocus camera technology. Minolta in turn hired FTI's rival, Z-Axis, to create similarly sophisticated animations for its defense.

  Jurors viewed dozens of competing tutorial animations featuring material on optics, camera focusing, and patent-protection regulations. Honeywell used one video to carefully disassemble Minolta's focusing apparatus and expose it as virtually identical to Honeywell's autofocus technology. That approach paid off. Honeywell won the case and received $127 million in damages from Minolta.

- In 1993, Alexander Jason, a San Francisco-based ballistics consultant, made history when his computer-generated animation of a murder became the first one admitted into a criminal trial. Using physical evidence such as bullet casings, autopsy reports, 911 recordings, and the angles of bullet holes in the doors and walls, Jason reconstructed the shooting of San Francisco businessman Artie Mitchell by his older brother, Jim. The four-minute simulation showed that the murder was not, as the defendant claimed, the result of a panic shooting committed in self-defense. Instead, by illustrating the sequence of shots, where they were fired from, and the location of the victim throughout the incident, the animation showed that the bullets were fired at regular intervals and therefore that the shooting was a deliberate murder.

Jim Mitchell was found guilty of voluntary manslaughter, though some jurors thought the verdict should have been first-degree murder. He was sentenced to seven years in prison.

Potential for Distortion

Despite these successes, the use of computer animation in the courtroom has come under intense scrutiny. Although most participants in the legal system believe that it is fully prepared to handle the visual complexity of such animations, many judges, attorneys, and even some forensic animators wonder whether the industry is adequately monitored.

"The potential for distortion of computer animations is enormous," notes Terry Day, president of Engineering Dynamics Corp., makers of "Edcrash," a program for reconstructing car accidents. "Software can be manipulated and images digitally enhanced or doctored so that something that isn't true can appear to be true," he says. For example, in a recent Louisiana football-injury case, the defendant, a helmet manufacturer, wanted to prove that a player, the plaintiff in the case, broke his neck and was rendered quadriplegic not because of a faulty helmet but because he had lowered his head into a vulnerable position before making the injury-inducing tackle. Defense attorneys asked Litigation Sciences, a Los Angeles-based forensic-animation firm, to digitally enhance a video taken of the critical impact to determine the position of the tackler's head.

"The video was taken at a wide angle, and the players were hard to see," says Robert Seltzer, executive director of graphic evidence at Litigation Sciences. "But after we sharpened the video picture to get a better understanding of the motion and zoomed in on the tackler in slow motion, it was clear that he had put his head down."

The plaintiff's "enhanced" version of the video, however, was entirely different, showing that the tackler kept his head up. Ten days before the trial, defense attorneys who had received the plaintiff's video for review asked Litigation Sciences to account for the discrepancy. To create the false image, Seltzer explains, the plaintiff's animation company isolated six critical frames from the video and used a computer painting system to create a digital copy of another player's helmet and paste it on the tackler's shoulders in the head-up position. The player suddenly had two heads, but the head that was up appeared more prominently.

"When it was the defendant's turn to testify, we rolled the original video in slow motion to show the head-down position," says Seltzer. "We then showed the doctored video and how two heads were painted onto one." In effect, the tampering was perjury, and the defense won the case.

Matters of Opinion

A more subtle problem arises when animations present an ex-pert's theories about what may have happened rather than the pure facts of the case. Although federal regulations mandate that a judge must carefully weigh the factual value and relevance of any piece of evidence before allowing it in the courtroom, many judges acknowledge that animations of what-if scenarios can be difficult to evaluate.

One example is the series of animations used in the 1989 trial to decide whether Northwest Airlines or McDonnell-Douglas was responsible for the crash of Northwest Flight 255, which killed 156 people on take-off in Detroit in August 1987. During the 18-month legal slugfest, the longest aviation trial in history, the adversaries presented dueling reconstructions of the accident.

McDonnell-Douglas, maker of the MD-80 aircraft in question, decided to present a literal reconstruction. Jeffrey Morof, an attorney with Bryan Cave, a Los Angeles law firm representing McDonnell-Douglas, showed animations based on the aircraft's black-box data, as well as on cockpit voice-recorder data and eyewitness reports, arguing that pilot error was responsible for the fatal crash. In particular, he demonstrated that the crew ignored a stall warning and improperly set the aircraft's flaps and slats.

Northwest, by contrast, presented a series of videos that reconstructed hypothetical situations for which there was no hard evidence—for instance, that the crash was caused by the failure of a critical circuit-breaker warning system, not the incompetence of the pilots. The video showed what the crew would have done if the warning system had worked properly during the flight.

Northwest's approach proved unsuccessful. Chief Judge Julian Cook of the Third District Court in Detroit accepted most of McDonnell-Douglas's animations into evidence but dismissed Northwest's "what-if" approach as "speculative and argumentative." McDonnell-Douglas won the case, expected to exceed $10 million in liability damages. (Northwest was granted an appeal, now pending, after its attorneys claimed they had inadequate time to determine the accuracy of the McDonnell-Douglas animations.)

Still, judges often waver when walking the astonishingly fine line between computer animations purporting to tell the facts and those that make speculative claims. For example, judges may allow animations that go beyond simply illustrating what is or what was, according to the Department of Justice's Kathlynn Fadely, because they may want to understand "not only why an accident happened but alternate scenarios of how the accident could have been avoided in an attempt to answer who or what was responsible."

When judges are besieged by thousands of conflicting pieces of evidence, bias is almost impossible to weed out, argues Michael Seltzer of Graham & James, attorneys for Northwest. In fact, Judge Cook himself admitted a McDonnell-Douglas video that may have made equally speculative arguments about the infamous circuit-breaker warning system, according to Northwest attorneys. The video attempted to show that, contrary to Northwest's claims, particle contaminants could not have blocked current to the circuit breaker.

"That video was clearly misleading," says Selter. "The video purported to be general and tutorial in nature, yet it clearly implied that particle contamination could not possibly have affected the circuit breaker on that flight. It left the jury with the impression that the video was an accurate and specific representation of what happened."

Judges and juries should be crystal clear about the subjective nature of what they are seeing. But even animators wonder whether this is the case. "Juries tend to think, this is computer-generated, so it must be objective; it must be reality," says Z-Axis's Treibitz. But computer animations combine artistry and facts to make clear one side's position, he says. "It's telling a story, but it's a story from an advocate's point of view."

Questionable Programs

Perhaps even more worrisome is the question of whether software programs designed to analyze data are adequately peer reviewed and tested. In the growing field of car-accident reconstruction, for example, they aren't. At least that's the conclusion of some forensic experts regarding a crop of untested personal-computer analysis tools routinely used by local police departments and engineering organizations reporting on collisions.

The programs typically ask users to provide information about which vehicles were hit, their position at impact and at rest, their probable trajectories, and the amount of damage. Often using algorithms constructed from staged collisions, the programs create animated versions of the speeds and crash trajectories of the vehicles that indicate which party is responsible.

"These programs, where you put crash data in and the computer does an analysis and draws a nice picture, are far more dangerous than a graphic that simply illustrates one person's conclusion," notes Thomas Bohan, an attorney and technical consultant from Portland, Maine. The problem is that "the authors say the programs are proprietary, and they're not going to tell you how they work."

Bohan's colleague, Arthur Damask, a physicist who in 1984 made the first computer animation of a fatal car accident, has similar reservations. "None of these PC-based crash-reconstruction programs have won widespread acceptance in the scientific community," he says. Although presumably based on crash-analysis algorithms developed several years ago for mainframes at Calspan, a highway safety research institute at Cornell University, "not a single one of the newer programs has undergone the kind of peer testing and review that has become the sine qua non for scientific acceptance."

"You don't know whether the program is being accurate or just playing with numbers," notes David Muir, senior vice president of FTI. "There are a lot of ways of analyzing the physics of a car crash."

Terry Day of Engineering Dynamics argues that the leading collision-reconstruction programs, some of them developed for the more powerful engineering workstations, are in fact rigorously tested by comparing calculated results with actual test crashes. "But there's a fly in the ointment," he admits. "It must still use data gathered by people watching the crash or measuring

it many minutes or hours later. If the input is incomplete, the accuracy of the program's result is anyone's guess."

Despite these caveats, some judges seem to be snowed by any kind of computer-analysis program. "It's frustrating when somebody on the other side has a program that has not been peer reviewed," says Muir, "and you get a judge who lets it in, despite the fact that you make arguments against it."

To Use the Power Wisely

The legal and engineering communities are actively seeking ways to resolve these issues. In fact, a growing number of forensic animators and attorneys with experience in the area have been writing articles and putting on seminars that explain how to evaluate computer animations in court.

For example, to address some of the potential abuses, the Detroit-based Society of Automotive Engineers is drawing up guidelines to help attorneys, judges, juries, and engineers decide when animations contain misleading or inaccurate elements. Wesley Grimes, chair of the task force, wants attorneys and judges to ask more probing questions about the pictures jurists are about to see, including where the information comes from and the basis for the "environment" of the video.

For example, says Grimes, if forensic animators are depicting a visibility problem during an aircraft accident, attorneys should ask how they determined the visibility shown in the simulation and what the visibility should have been. In many cases, elements are put into videos that can be purposefully distracting. "We are trying to classify every pictorial element in an animation as primary or secondary," he says. "Primary elements are critical; secondary elements can be removed completely with no adverse effect on the presentation."

Grimes also worries that in many states, attorneys have inadequate time at depositions to question the opposing side or to consult with experts regarding the reliability of the underlying data and assumptions. "Some states require advanced notification that one side or the other will be presenting an animation, but others don't," he says. And while federal law requires notification, many attorneys complain that the time allotted for analyzing computer animations and, if necessary, for preparing "defensive" videos is insufficient. Northwest's attorneys used this argument to appeal their case against McDonnell-Douglas.

The most important caveat for judges and juries is to treat skeptically the arguments by forensic animators that the flat lighting, smooth surfaces, and cartoonish unreality of computer animations provide a "cooler," more detached environment in which to review crimes of passion, accidents, and other upsetting events. "Computer animations are powerful emotional instruments because they appeal to all the senses, including sight and hearing," notes Judge Julian Cook.

Simply watching a computer-generated video of an air acci-dent coupled with a soundtrack of dying pilots is enough to prove that animations can be as painful as they are persuasive: the so-called "sanitized medium" never obviates the horror of reliving the moment. Indeed, it may amplify it. No matter how much denial is in the air, attorneys and forensic animators are banking on the emotional impact of animations to keep juries believing in their case. The challenge now is to use that tool's power wisely, to ensure that animations tell the truth, the whole truth, and nothing but the truth—just like any good witness.

 **Article Review Form at end of book.**

Why did Glass get away with manufacturing so many stories? What does his story suggest about the authority we often allocate to technology?

New Media Caveat:

The truth may not be out there

Clive Thompson

By now, most media-watchers have heard of Stephen Glass—the journalist who sounded too good to be true, and who, in fact, was.

Last month, the 25-year-old wunderscribe of *The New Republic* published a colorful article about a teen computer hacker who was coercing a software company into hiring him as an anti-hacker security specialist. After some simple fact checking, the online edition of *Forbes* magazine, *Forbes Digital Tool,* disclosed that neither the kid nor the company existed. The entire story, in fact, had been made up.

Nor is that all. Last week, an abashed *New Republic* published an editorial apology to its readers, rehearsing the in-house tale of Glass' prompt dismissal and reasserting the magazine's devotion to its "stringent tradition" of hard-nosed, factual political discourse. It also announced that it was going back over the Glass oeuvre to detect further lapses from accuracy. Alas, two other pieces—an account of a convention of political novelty vendors,

and a dispatch from a gathering of anti-Clinton activists—now appear to be fictional, as does the lead anecdote of a piece on the investment community's worship of Federal Reserve chairman Alan Greenspan. One can't help but suspect that these are just the initial foundations to be shaken loose in the Glass edifice: The magazine has published 41 pieces by Glass since he came on board in 1995.

Predictably, Glass' tale has provided fodder for endless coffee-break conversations and Journalism 101 ethics classes, although analysis of the ethical problems here is rather like shooting fish in a barrel. Add your favorite gloomy, apocalyptic pronouncement about the state of journalism here: Reporters these days are getting too cocky, too young; nobody's learning the old basics of news gathering; Glass was egged on to his gruesome fate by a magazine mafia more concerned with sexy stories than hard issues. Historic comparisons are invoked, grimly. Glass' debacle parallels the furor in 1981 around Janet Cook, the

Washington Post reporter who won a Pulitzer Prize for a story about "Jimmy," an 8-year-old heroin addict who also, unfortunately, didn't exist.

What's unique here, though, is the peculiarly digital nature of Glass' hoax. Here was a scam assisted, and even created, by the singularly do-it-yourself vibe of the Web.

Glass went to some incredible lengths to fool the fact-checkers at *The New Republic.* He created a fake website for Jukt Micronics, the fictitious company in the piece, and set up fake e-mail accounts for the company's executives. He created a voice-mail message on a cell phone number, purporting to be Jukt's head office. He even posted a heated condemnation of his own *New Republic* article on the fake website, to make it look like he had angered the company with his reporting.

This is subterfuge for the '90s. Who cares if that company you want to profile doesn't actually exist? A 12-year-old with a $99 piece of software can create a professional-looking Internet site

Clive Thompson is a technology columnist based in New York.

in about an hour and a half. Better yet, most journalists and fact checkers are still highly Net-illiterate, so your forgery will likely never even be suspected, let alone detected. Sadly, editors remain generally unsure of the Net's epistemology; you'd expect them to be hard-bitten cynics, but all too often the reverse is true—if it's on-line, it must be true.

There's an old joke about this phenomenon: "On the Internet, nobody knows you're a dog." Today, we could usefully update that aphorism. On the Internet, it seems, nobody knows you're Stephen Glass.

Indeed, Glass is really only the tip of the iceberg. As our information becomes increasingly digital, this question of online reality is beginning to plague mainstream media. As the Web becomes a medium not only for news gathering but news publishing, the peculiarities of the medium are creating brand-new ethical dilemmas. It is, indeed, one of the defining problems of the 20th Century: Our tools are once again evolving faster than we are.

Consider, for example, the issue of printing retractions and corrections. It's a journalistic issue you rarely see discussed, but it's one that has undergone a fascinating devolution on-line.

Historically, when newspapers or TV stations made an error, they'd print or broadcast a correction as soon as possible. It was considered an essential part of publishing: Admitting your mistakes was central to maintaining credibility. Even if the admission was initially humiliating, it was even worse to leave the printed error sitting around, unaddressed.

Online, though, things have begun to work differently, in some disturbing ways. These days, media have found that, when they make an error, it's easier simply to go back and rewrite the story—rewriting history, as it were.

For example, in late January, the *Dallas Morning News* published a story on their Web site claiming that a Secret Service agent was prepared to talk with independent counsel Kenneth Starr about seeing the president and infamous White House intern Monica Lewinsky in a "compromising situation." Within hours, however, the story's main source recanted. Panicked, the *Morning News* editors pulled the story offline entirely. The next day, they ran a story explaining the error—but they didn't put the original story back up. It had vanished forever, as if it never existed.

The Wall Street Journal performed the exact same flip-flop after it published a story about the original *Dallas Morning News* story (a piece of information-age autoeroticism typical of today's media-eating media.)

After a bit of hunting, I discovered dozens of quietly hidden similar cases. In March, the *San Francisco Bay Guardian* published a piece on its site alleging improprieties in an advertisement for an online brokerage house. The story contained some factual errors, and after the brokerage house complained to the *Guardian* editor, he pulled the article off the site. Later in the day, a "fixed" version went back online, with no reference to the former story—and no notice of a correction or error.

The word "Orwellian," to be sure, gets thrown around far too much for its own good. But in this case, you could argue that it's precisely what George Orwell was talking about in *1984*: rewriting history to suit your self-image. Or, in Glass' case, creating documents to support an elaborate lie.

Should we be surprised at this stuff? Probably not. Ten years ago, newspapers and magazines began digitizing their photos and using software to subtly alter them. At the time, there was a fair bit of concern for how this might affect news gathering. A few media-ethics psychics wondered, for example, whether digitally processed photos would be admissible in court.

With online publishing, those very same issues are now affecting words and print. Yet this time around, journalists have pretty much ceased to inquire into the ethical impact of new technologies. Possibly, the deterioration of journalistic standards overall is so advanced that there seems to be little point in complaining. After all, it's not as if traditional media—newspapers, TV and magazines—are paragons of news gathering and publishing ethics. It's been years since newspapers demanded that reporters regularly double-source facts. And the loopy, conservative biases of organs like *The Washington Times* or *The American Spectator* are quite enough to distort the news, without recourse to digital means. Ideology, after all, is a hell of a powerful technology.

Meanwhile, damage control surrounding the Glass affair is breeding publishing irony upon publishing irony. Doubtless figuring that it had suffered enough public humiliation, *The New Republic* quietly yanked Glass' ill-fated hacker piece off its website shortly after it had bounced Glass off its masthead. The Web, however, has a way of enacting its own revenge. A media-criticism group made a digital copy of the Glass story, and posted it on their own website, along with the rest of Glass' now-dubious ouevre. Anyone interested in the infamous hacker piece can read it at http://www.nihidyll.com/glass/glass051898.htm.

At least, I think it's an exact copy of the original story. With these online sites, you never can tell.

 Article Review Form at end of book.

Is a photograph an accurate depiction of reality? How do digital technologies destabilize ideas about truth in photography?

What Is Truth?

Sheri Rosen

Sheri Rosen is senior employee communication specialist at USAA in San Antonio.

Quotation marks are handy symbols. Writers conveniently and clearly tell readers when a statement reflects exactly what was said.

Well, most of the time, that is. It's a practice of some organizational publications to correct grammatical errors in a quote, for example. But if a writer changes words or summarizes a speaker's statement, out go the quote marks.

The truth gets fuzzy in photographs.

Photojournalists freeze a moment in truth. Their prints once became halftones, and that was that; now they become digital images that can be manipulated without anyone knowing.

There are no quote marks.

The code of the American Society of Media Photographers places the responsibility on the photojournalist to never alter the content or meaning of a news photograph.

But in reality, long-standing darkroom techniques as tame as burning and dodging can hedge

the visual truth. Then, once an art director gets hold of the image, digital alteration and manipulation go a step further. It's easy to take out a person in the crowd, for example. You'd never really know by just looking at a photograph that it wasn't what the photographer saw through the viewfinder.

What are we dealing with here? Ethical questions? Or legal issues?

Attorneys at Weyerhaeuser Co. (Washington state) advised editors of *Weyerhaeuser Today* that alterations that were not misleading shouldn't present legal problems. But there was that one photo that already had appeared in a company publication; a strategically placed, computer generated bush covered the fact that one person was wearing the wrong kind of safety boots. It won't happen again.

"Safety is our top priority at Weyerhaeuser. For us to correct an unsafe situation with a computer probably would put us at risk if someone in that situation had gotten hurt and we had falsified the way things were," said Dan Berglund, *Weyerhaeuser Today* graphic designer.

After those conversations with the lawyers a couple of years ago, Weyerhaeuser developed guidelines for digitized photos. It's OK to:

- darken overexposed areas and lighten underexposed areas or make minor improvements that previously would have been done in a darkroom,

- improve the appearance of people, such as removing blemishes,

- remove elements that would distract from the main message of the photo (you know, the telephone pole growing from someone's head), and

- correct optical illusions created by the camera.

On the flip side, nothing can be added, removed, or changed that would:

- alter the main message of the photo,

- create an image that would look different from the way those present remember it, or

- make subjects appear to be working in a safer manner than they actually were when the photo was taken.

Communication World, March 3, 1995. Reprinted with permission.

For Berglund, the message is clear: "We don't try to tell a story other than what's in the photograph." On the other hand, he's had good results with digital manipulation. "We've salvaged poor or underexposed shots. We're using it to give us better photos, not different photos," he said.

At the Interactive Telecommunications Program at New York University, the concern is ethical. Does the manipulation of a photograph unfairly influence the reader?

If text can carry a symbol of truth like quote marks, why can't photos carry a similar symbol? That's exactly what the school's Committee for New Standards for Photographic Reproduction in the Media calls for. "We are suggesting that a label be placed next to every image that has been significantly manipulated while still appearing to have been created by photographic processes," reports the committee.

The committee proposes two icons. Unaltered images earn a boxed circle icon, with the circle representing a camera lens. Altered photos get a similar icon, only this one has a slash through it. Either way, the icon should appear just outside the bottom perimeter—left or right—of the image, says the committee.

And just what qualifies as altering? Just about anything that goes beyond those traditional darkroom techniques.

Icons are a convention of computer screen graphics, and in fact, the committee suggests using the not-a-lens icon for interactive media or television news, not just printed publications.

This committee is serious: "What is at stake is the photographic document's credibility, the authority of the news media, and the ability of citizens in a democracy to be informed as to the nature of the world in which they live."

In truth, these lofty ideals are not so far removed from organizational communication.

 Article Review Form at end of book.

WiseGuide Wrap-Up

Technology makes it easy for anyone to create and disseminate multiple versions of events, news, and history. As information becomes more abundant, sometimes it threatens to overwhelm us. We may become susceptible to accepting what's presented to us without making the effort to ask critical questions. What criteria do you use to decide if something is true? How do you make judgments about the material you find on the World Wide Web?

R.E.A.L. Sites

This list provides a print preview of typical **Coursewise** R.E.A.L. sites. There are over 100 such sites at the **Courselinks**™ site. The danger in printing URLs is that web sites can change overnight. As we went to press, these sites were functional using the URLs provided. If you come across one that isn't, please let us know via email to: webmaster@coursewise.com. Use your Passport to access the most current list of R.E.A.L. sites at the **Courselinks**™ site.

Site name: HateWatch

URL: http://www.hatewatch.org/

Why is it R.E.A.L.? This web-based organization monitors hate group activity on the Internet. The site includes RealAudio interviews with hate group members and organizers and with activists campaigning against them. The site is excellent for conducting research on how hate groups are using the Internet to recruit members and spread their message.

Key topics: hate groups

Try this: What is the primary strategy offered by HateWatch to contain hate groups on the Internet? Is the strategy necessary? Will it be effective?

Site name: Thinking Critically About World Wide Web Resources

URL: http://www.library.ucla.edu/libraries/college/instruct/web/critical.htm

Why is it R.E.A.L.? This site, authored by Esther Grassian of the UCLA College Library, provides guidelines for critically evaluating information resources on the web.

Key topics: evaluating Internet resources

Try this: Save or print out the guidelines from this site and use them to evaluate a web site in this book, or at the **Courselinks** web site. Write a critical review of the site that incorporates the evaluation guidelines.

Site name: National Budget Simulation

URL: http://garnet.berkeley.edu:3333/budget/budget.html

Why is it R.E.A.L.? The National Budget Simulator is a simulation game intended to help people achieve a better understanding of the trade-offs required to balance the federal budget. Participants can complete a short or long version of the simulation.

Key topics: simulation, cyberdemocracy

Try this: Work with a small group to play the short version of the National Budget Simulator until you have balanced the budget. Consider the ideas raised by Paul Starr in his article about simulations. How do the assumptions influence the results in this simulation?

section 7

The Internet, Democracy, and the Silent Majority

Learning Objectives

- Analyze how Dibbell's tale is relevant to the discussion of cyberdemocracy.

- Summarize the advantages and disadvantages of cyberdemocracy.

- Evaluate the impact of information technology on citizen empowerment.

WiseGuide Intro

Imagine an Election Day on which, instead of voting for candidates, you fire up your computer to check off your positions on the federal budget. You approve more funds for technology research and decide that, instead of a tax cut, you want the surplus used to trim the national debt. Because you enjoyed your stay at the Grand Canyon, you generously vote to increase the allocation for the Park Service.

Such electronic voting offers the potential for quickly taking the nation's pulse on an issue or for making the process of voting easier and more convenient. The Internet, enthusiasts avow, presents the possibility of "cyberdemocracy," because it promotes both the open and free exchange of ideas and more active citizen participation in the democratic process. With e-mail, for example, citizens can immediately make their views known to their representatives and even can communicate with the president, or at least with a member of the White House staff.

The Monica Lewinsky scandal presents a somewhat bizarre example of electronic democracy in action. When Special Prosecutor Kenneth Starr released his report on the Lewinsky affair via the Internet, the lurid details of President Clinton's relationship with Ms. Lewinsky were immediately available to a worldwide audience. Voters could access, read, and make up their own minds about the report and many did.

The World Wide Web already offers a plethora of information resources for voters. At sites such as those sponsored by Project Vote Smart, the Center for Responsive Politics, and the Federal Election Commission, citizens can access information about a candidate's positions, promises, finances, and voting records. These resources surely will grow in number and in quality.

But is information truly a means to power? Does information alone promote participation in the democratic process? Will voters choose to access information, evaluate it, and use it to make informed choices about their candidates? Will the availability of information on the Internet lead to increased voter registration?

Critics of cyberdemocracy contend that its potential is overhyped. Furthermore, they say, the Internet easily could become a tool of tyranny as well as that of democracy. E-mail petitions mailed to congressional representatives, for example, may represent only a tiny fraction of citizen views, but, because those citizens use the Internet to mobilize like-minded thinkers, their collective voice has a greater impact than their actual numbers might suggest. Electronic voting also presents the prospect of large numbers of citizens voting on issues without truly understanding them, and it shuts out the many Americans not connected to the Information Highway.

As with censorship and privacy, such concerns are not new and not relevant only to the Internet. Politicians always have used emotional appeals to influence voter decisions. Television advertising allows candidates to misrepresent the positions of opposing candidates. But the Internet is different in that it provides immediate access to unlimited quantities of information presented by whoever chooses to post a web page.

This section opens with Julian Dibbell's piece, "A Rape in Cyberspace: Or How an Evil Clown, a Haitian Trickster Spirit, Two Wizards, and a Cast of Dozens Turned a Database into a Society," which addresses several issues already discussed in this book, including social relationships, identity, and censorship. Its bizarre title may lead you to wonder why I've chosen to include it here. Dibbell presents his story about an online rape as a tale of democracy in action. The rape required the citizens of LambdaMOO to develop consensus about appropriate behavior in the MOO. As Dibbell relates, developing such a consensus was no easy task. His story points to the struggles and compromises inherent in the democratic process—difficulties made more obvious today as communities and governments attempt to craft policy about the public use of the Internet.

The next two selections, "Cyberdemocracy: Tip O'Neill, Meet Alvin Toffler" by Rick Henderson, and "The Promise and Perils of Cyberdemocracy," by Norman Ornstein and Amy Schenkenberg, present contemporary anecdotes and examples, along with imaginary scenarios, to examine the advantages and disadvantages posed by cyberdemocracy.

The article by social activist Ralph Nader, "Digital Democracy in Action," provides a contemporary example of how information available via the Internet empowers ordinary citizens.

The companion web sites, all sponsored by nonprofit organizations, offer resources for continued research in this area. At the sites sponsored by the Center for Responsive Politics and by Project Vote Smart, citizens can access information about congressional spending, voting records, and campaign finance. The Center for Civic Networking site is an excellent one to explore if you are interested in how the Internet can promote democracy in local communities.

How will the Internet ultimately impact the democratic process? For now, we can only speculate and watch as the story evolves.

Questions

Reading 35. How does a community develop rules to police itself? When is it necessary to introduce laws as a means of regulating social norms and expectations?

Reading 36. Does the availability of information promote citizen participation in government?

Reading 37. How might the Internet influence the political process?

Reading 38. When is information power? How can citizens use the Internet to effect social change?

How does a community develop rules to police itself? When is it necessary to introduce laws as a means of regulating social norms and expectations?

A Rape in Cyberspace:

Or how an evil clown, a Haitian trickster spirit, two wizards, and a cast of dozens turned a database into a society

Julian Dibbell

They say he raped them that night. They say he did it with a cunning little doll, fashioned in their image and imbued with the power to make them do whatever he desired. They say that by manipulating the doll he forced them to have sex with him, and with each other, and to do horrible, brutal things to their own bodies. And though I wasn't there that night, I think I can assure you that what they say is true, because it all happened right in the living room—right there amid the well-stocked bookcases and the sofas and the fireplace—of a house I've come to think of as my second home.

Call me Dr. Bombay. Some months ago—let's say about halfway between the first time

you heard the words *information superhighway* and the first time you wished you never had—I found myself tripping with compulsive regularity down the well-traveled information lane that leads to LambdaMOO, a very large and very busy rustic chateau built entirely of words. Nightly, I typed the commands that called those words onto my computer screen, dropping me with what seemed a warm electric thud inside the mansion's darkened coat closet, where I checked my quotidian identity, stepped into the persona and appearance of a minor character from a long-gone television sitcom, and stepped out into the glaring chatter of the crowded living room. Sometimes, when the mood struck me, I emerged as a dolphin instead.

I won't say why I chose to masquerade as Samantha Stevens's outlandish cousin, or as the dolphin, or what exactly led to my mild but so-far incurable addiction to the semifictional digital otherwords known around the Internet as multi-user dimensions, or MUDs. This isn't my story, after all. It's the story of a man named Mr. Bungle, and of the ghostly sexual violence he committed in the halls of LambdaMOO, and most importantly of the ways his violence and his victims challenged the 1000 and more residents of that surreal, magic-infested mansion to become, finally, the community so many of them already believed they were.

That I was myself one of those residents has little direct bearing on the story's events. I mention it only as a warning that my own perspective is perhaps too steeped in the surreality and magic of the place to serve as an entirely appropriate guide. For the Bungle Affair raises questions that—here on the brink of a future in which human life may find itself as tightly enveloped in digital environments as it is today in the architectural kind—demand a clear-eyed, sober, and unmystified consideration. It asks us to shut our ears momentarily to the techno-utopian ecstasies of West Coast cyberhippies and look without illusion upon the present possibilities for building, in the on-line spaces of this world, societies more decent and free than those mapped onto dirt and concrete and capital. It asks us to behold the new bodies awaiting us in virtual space undazzled by their phantom powers, and to get to the crucial work of sorting out the socially meaningful differences between those bodies and our physical ones. And most forthrightly it asks us to wrap our late-modern ontologies, epistemologies, sexual ethics, and common sense around the curious notion of rape by voodoo doll—and to try not to warp them beyond recognition in the process.

In short, the Bungle Affair dares me to explain it to you without resort to dime-store mysticisms, and I fear I may have shape-shifted by the digital moonlight one too many times to be quite up to the task. But I will do what I can, and can do no better I suppose than to lead with the facts. For if nothing else about Mr. Bungle's case is unambiguous, the facts at least are crystal clear.

The facts begin (as they often do) with a time and a place. This time was a Monday night in March, and the place, as I've said,

was the living room—which, due to the inviting warmth of its decor, is so invariably packed with chitchatters as to be roughly synonymous among LambdaMOOers with a party. So strong, indeed, is the sense of convivial common ground invested in the living room that a cruel mind could hardly imagine a better place in which to stage a violation of LambdaMOO's communal spirit. And there was cruelty enough lurking in the appearance Mr. Bungle presented to the virtual world—he was at the time a fat, oleaginous, Bisquick-faced clown dressed in cum-stained harlequin garb and girdled with a mistletoe-and-hemlock belt whose buckle bore the quaint inscription "KISS ME UNDER THIS, BITCH!" But whether cruelty motivated his choice of crime scene is not among the established facts of the case. It is a fact only that he did choose the living room.

The remaining facts tell us a bit more about the inner world of Mr. Bungle, though only perhaps that it couldn't have been a very comfortable place. They tell us that he commenced his assault, entirely unprovoked, at or about 10 P.M. Pacific Standard Time. That he began by using his voodoo doll to force one of the room's occupants to sexually service him in a variety of more or less conventional ways. That this victim was legba, a Haitian trickster spirit of indeterminate gender, brown-skinned and wearing an expensive pearl gray suit, top hat, and dark glasses. That legba heaped vicious imprecations on him all the while and that he was soon ejected bodily from the room. That he hid himself away then in his private chambers somewhere on the mansion grounds and continued the at-

tacks without interruption, since the voodoo doll worked just as well at a distance as in proximity. That he turned his attentions now to Starsinger, a rather pointedly nondescript female character, tall, stout, and brown-haired, forcing her into unwanted liaisons with other individuals present in the room, among them legba, Bakunin (the well-known radical), and Juniper (the squirrel). That his actions grew progressively violent. That he made legba eat his/her own pubic hair. That he caused Starsinger to violate herself with a piece of kitchen cutlery. That his distant laughter echoed evilly in the living room with every successive outrage. That he could not be stopped until at last someone summoned Zippy, a wise and trusted oldtimer who brought with him a gun of near wizardly powers, a gun that didn't kill but enveloped its targets in a cage impermeable even to a voodoo doll's powers. That Zippy fired this gun at Mr. Bungle, thwarting the doll at last and silencing the evil, distant laughter.

These particulars, as I said, are unambiguous. But they are far from simple, for the simple reason that every set of facts in virtual reality (or VR, as the locals abbreviate it) is shadowed by a second, complicating set: the "real-life" facts. And although a certain tension invariably buzzes in the gap between the hard, prosaic RL facts and their more fluid, dreamy VR counterparts, the dissonance in the Bungle case is striking. No hideous clowns or trickster spirits appear in the RL version of the incident, no voodoo dolls or wizard guns, indeed no rape at all as any RL court of law has yet defined it. The actors in the drama were university students for the most part, and they sat rather undramatically before computer screens the entire time, their only actions a spidery flitting of fingers across standard QWERTY keyboards. No bodies touched. Whatever physical interaction occurred consisted of a mingling of electronic signals sent from sites spread out between New York City and Sydney, Australia. Those signals met in LambdaMOO, certainly, just as the hideous clown and the living room party did, but what was LambdaMOO after all? Not an enchanted mansion or anything of the sort—just a middlingly complex database, maintained for experimental purposes inside a Xerox Corporation research computer in Palo Alto and open to public access via the Internet.

To be more precise about it, LambdaMOO was a MUD. Or to be yet more precise, it was a subspecies of MUD known as a MOO, which is short for "MUD, Object-Oriented." All of which means that it was a kind of database especially designed to give users the vivid impression of moving through a physical space that in reality exists only as descriptive data filed away on a hard drive. When users dial into LambdaMOO, for instance, the program immediately presents them with a brief textual description of one of the rooms of the database's fictional mansion (the coat closet, say). If the user wants to leave this room, she can enter a command to move in a particular direction and the database will replace the original description with a new one corresponding to the room located in the direction she chose. When the new description scrolls across the user's screen it lists not only the fixed features of

the room but all its contents at that moment—including things (tools, toys, weapons) and other users (each represented as a "character" over which he or she has sole control).

As far as the database program is concerned, all of these entities—rooms, things, characters—are just different subprograms that the program allows to interact according to rules very roughly mimicking the laws of the physical world. Characters may not leave a room in a given direction, for instance, unless the room subprogram contains an "exit" at that compass point. And if a character "says" or "does" something (as directed by its user-owner), then only the users whose characters are also located in that room will see the output describing the statement or action. Aside from such basic constraints, however, LambdaMOOers are allowed a broad freedom to create—they can describe their characters any way they like, they can make rooms of their own and decorate them to taste, and they can build new objects almost at will. The combination of all this busy user activity with the hard physics of the database can certainly induce a lucid illusion of presence—but when all is said and done the only thing you *really* see when you visit LambdaMOO is a kind of slow-crawling script, lines of dialogue and stage direction creeping steadily up your computer screen.

Which is all just to say that, to the extent that Mr. Bungle's assault happened in real life at all, it happened as a sort of Punch-and-Judy show, in which the puppets and the scenery were made of nothing more substantial than digital code and snippets of creative writing. The puppeteer

behind Bungle, as it happened, was a young man logging in to the MOO from a New York University computer. He could have been Al Gore for all any of the others knew, however, and he could have written Bungle's script that night any way he chose. He could have sent a command to print the message "Mr. Bungle, smiling a saintly smile, floats angelic near the ceiling of the living room, showering joy and candy kisses down upon the heads of all below"—and everyone then receiving output from the database's subprogram #17 (a/k/a the "living room") would have seen that sentence on their screens.

Instead, he entered sadistic fantasies into the "voodoo doll," a subprogram that served the not-exactly kosher purpose of attributing actions to other characters that their users did not actually write. And thus a woman in Haverford, Pennsylvania, whose account on the MOO attached her to a character she called Starsinger, was given the unasked-for opportunity to read the words "As if against her will, Starsinger jabs a steak knife up her ass, causing immense joy. You hear Mr. Bungle laughing evilly in the distance." And thus the woman in Seattle who had written herself the character called legba, with a view perhaps to tasting in imagination a deity's freedom from the burdens of the gendered flesh, got to read similarly constructed sentences in which legba, messenger of the gods, lord of crossroads and communications, suffered a brand of degradation all-too-customarily reserved for the embodied female.

"Mostly voodoo dolls are amusing," wrote legba on the evening after Bungle's rampage, posting a public statement to the widely read in-MOO mailing list called *social-issues, a forum for debate on matters of import to the entire populace. "And mostly I tend to think that restrictive measures around here cause more trouble than they prevent. But I also think that Mr. Bungle was being a vicious, vile fuckhead, and I . . . want his sorry ass scattered from #17 to the Cinder Pile. I'm not calling for policies, trials, or better jails. I'm not sure what I'm calling for. Virtual castration, if I could manage it. Mostly, [this type of thing] doesn't happen here. Mostly, perhaps I thought it wouldn't happen to me. Mostly, I trust people to conduct themselves with some veneer of civility. Mostly, I want his ass."

Months later, the woman in Seattle would confide to me that as she wrote those words posttraumatic tears were streaming down her face—a real-life fact that should suffice to prove that the words' emotional content was no mere playacting. The precise tenor of that content, however, its mingling of murderous rage and eyeball-rolling annoyance, was a curious amalgam that neither the RL nor the VR facts alone can quite account for. Where virtual reality and its conventions would have us believe that legba and Starsinger were brutally raped in their own living room, here was the victim legba scolding Mr. Bungle for a breach of "civility." Where real life, on the other hand, insists the incident was only an episode in a free-form version of Dungeons and Dragons, confined to the realm of the symbolic and at no point threatening any player's life, limb, or material well-being, here now was the player legba issuing aggrieved and heartfelt calls for Mr. Bungle's dismemberment.

Ludicrously excessive by RL's lights, woefully understated by VR's, the tone of legba's response made sense only in the buzzing, dissonant gap between them.

Which is to say it made the only kind of sense that *can* be made of MUDly phenomena. For while the *facts* attached to any event born of a MUD's strange, ethereal universe may march in straight, tandem lines separated neatly into the virtual and the real, its meaning lies always in that gap. You learn this axiom early in your life as a player, and it's of no small relevance to the Bungle case that you usually learn it between the sheets, so to speak. Netsex, tinysex, virtual sex—however you name it, in real-life reality it's nothing more than a 900-line encounter stripped of even the vestigial physicality of the voice. And yet as any but the most inhibited of newbies can tell you, it's possibly the headiest experience the very heady world of MUDs has to offer. Amid flurries of even the most cursorily described caresses, sighs, and penetrations, the glands do engage, and often as throbbingly as they would in a real-life assignation—sometimes even more so, given the combined power of anonymity and textual suggestiveness to unshackle deep-seated fantasies. And if the virtual setting and the interplayer vibe are right, who knows? The heart may engage as well, stirring up passions as strong as many that bind lovers who observe the formality of trysting in the flesh.

To participate, therefore, in this disembodied enactment of life's most body-centered activity is to risk the realization that when it comes to sex, perhaps the body in question is not the physical one

at all, but its psychic double, the bodylike self-representation we carry around in our heads. I know, I know, you've read Foucault and your mind is not quite blown by the notion that sex is never so much an exchange of fluids as it is an exchange of signs. But trust your friend Dr. Bombay, it's one thing to grasp the notion intellectually and quite another to feel it coursing through your veins amid the virtual steam of hot netnookie. And it's a whole other mind-blowing trip altogether to encounter it thus as a college frosh, new to the net and still in the grip of hormonal hurricanes and highschool sexual mythologies. The shock can easily reverberate throughout an entire young worldview. Small wonder, then, that a newbie's first taste of MUD sex is often also the first time she or he surrenders wholly to the slippery terms of MUDish ontology, recognizing in a full-bodied way that what happens inside a MUD-made world is neither exactly real nor exactly makebelieve, but profoundly, compellingly, and emotionally meaningful.

And small wonder indeed that the sexual nature of Mr. Bungle's crime provoked such powerful feelings, and not just in legba (who, be it noted, was in real life a theory-savvy doctoral candidate and a longtime MOOer, but just as baffled and overwhelmed by the force of her own reaction, she later would attest, as any panting undergrad might have been). Even players who had never experienced MUD rape (the vast majority of male-presenting characters, but not as large a majority of the female-presenting as might be hoped) immediately appreciated its gravity and were moved to condemnation of the perp. legba's missive to *social-issues followed a strongly worded one from Zippy ("Well, well," it began, "no matter what else happens on Lambda, I can always be sure that some jerk is going to reinforce my low opinion of humanity") and was itself followed by others from Moriah, Raccoon, Crawfish, and evangeline. Starsinger also let her feelings ("pissed") be known. And even Jander, the Clueless Samaritan who had responded to Bungle's cries for help and uncaged him shortly after the incident, expressed his regret once apprised of Bungle's deeds, which he allowed to be "despicable."

A sense was brewing that something needed to be done—done soon and in something like an organized fashion—about Mr. Bungle, in particular, and about MUD rape, in general. Regarding the general problem, evangeline, who identified herself as a survivor of both virtual rape ("many times over") and real-life sexual assault, floated a cautious proposal for a MOO-wide powwow on the subject of virtual sex offenses and what mechanisms if any might be put in place to deal with their future occurrence. As for the specific problem, the answer no doubt seemed obvious to many. But it wasn't until the evening of the second day after the incident that legba, finally and rather solemnly, gave it voice:

"I am requesting that Mr. Bungle be toaded for raping Starsinger and I. I have never done this before, and have thought about it for days. He hurt us both."

That was all. Three simple sentences posted to *social. Reading them, an outsider might never guess that they were an application for a death warrant.

Even an outsider familiar with other MUDs might not guess it, since in many of them "toading" still refers to a command that, true to the gameworlds' sword-and-sorcery origins, simply turns a player into a toad, wiping the player's description and attributes and replacing them with those of the slimy amphibian. Bad luck for sure, but not quite as bad a what happens when the same command is invoked in the MOOish strains of MUD: not only are the description and attributes of the toaded player erased, but the account itself goes too. The annihilation of the character, thus, is total.

And nothing less than total annihilation, it seemed, would do to settle LambdaMOO's accounts with Mr. Bungle. Within minutes of the posting of legba's appeal, SamIAm, the Australian Deleuzean, who had witnessed much of the attack from the back room of his suburban Sydney home, seconded the motion with a brief message crisply entitled "Toad the fukr." SamIAm's posting was seconded almost as quickly by that of Bakunin, covictim of Mr. Bungle and well-known radical, who in real life happened also to be married to the real-life legba. And over the course of the next twenty-four hours as many as fifty players made it known, on *social and in a variety of other forms and forums, that they would be pleased to see Mr. Bungle erased from the face of the MOO. And with dissent so far confined to a dozen or so antitoading hardliners, the numbers suggested that the citizenry was indeed moving toward a resolve to have Bungle's virtual head.

There was one small but stubborn obstacle in the way of this resolve, however, and that was a curious state of social affairs known in some quarters of

the MOO as the New Direction. It was all very fine, you see, for the LambdaMOO rabble to get it in their heads to liquidate one of their peers, but when the time came to actually do the deed it would require the services of a nobler class of character. It would require a wizard. Master-programmers of the MOO, spelunkers of the database's deepest code-structures and custodians of its day-to-day administrative trivia, wizards are also the only players empowered to issue the toad command, a feature maintained on nearly all MUDs as a quick-and-dirty means of social control. But the wizards of LambdaMOO, after years of adjudicating all manner of interplayer disputes with little to show for it but their own weariness and the smoldering resentment of the general populace, had decided they'd had enough of the social sphere. And so, four months before the Bungle incident, the arch-wizard Haakon (known in RL as Pavel Curtis, Xerox researcher and LambdaMOO's principal architect) formalized this decision in a document called "LambdaMOO Takes a New Direction," which he placed in the living room for all to see. In it, Haakon announced that the wizards from that day forth were pure technicians. From then on, they would make no decisions affecting the social life of the MOO, but only implement whatever decisions the community as a whole directed them to. From then on, it was decreed, LambdaMOO would just have to grow up and solve its problems on its own.

Faced with the task of inventing its own self-governance from scratch, the LambdaMOO population had so far done what any other loose, amorphous agglomeration of individuals would have done: they'd let it slide. But now the task took on new urgency. Since getting the wizards to toad Mr. Bungle (or to toad the likes of him in the future) required a convincing case that the cry for his head came from the community at large, then the community itself would have to be defined; and if the community was to be convincingly defined, then some form of social organizations, no matter how rudimentary, would have to be settled on. And thus, as if against its will, the question of what to do about Mr. Bungle began to shape itself into a sort of referendum on the political future of the MOO. Arguments broke out on *social and elsewhere that had only superficially to do with Bungle (since everyone agreed he was a cad) and everything to do with where the participants stood on LambdaMOO's crazy-quilty political map. Parliamentarian legalist types argued that unfortunately Bungle could not legitimately be toaded at all, since there were no explicit MOO rules against rape, or against just about anything else—and the sooner such rules were established, they added, and maybe even a full-blown judiciary system complete with elected officials and prisons to enforce those rules, the better. Others, with a royalist streak in them, seemed to feel that Bungle's as-yet-unpunished outrage only proved this New Direction silliness had gone on long enough, and that it was high time the wizardocracy returned to the position of swift and decisive leadership their player class was born to.

And then there was what I'll call the technolibertarians. For them, MUD rapists were of course assholes, but the presence of assholes on the system was a technical inevitability, like noise on a phone line, and best dealt with not through repressive social disciplinary mechanisms but through the timely deployment of defensive software tools. Some asshole blasting violent, graphic language at you? Don't whine to authorities about it—hit the @gag command and the asshole's statements will be blocked from your screen (and only yours). It's simple, it's effective, and it censors no one.

But the Bungle case was rather hard on such arguments. For one thing, the extremely public nature of the living room meant that gagging would spare the victims only from witnessing their own violation, but not from having others witness it. You might want to argue that what those victims didn't directly experience couldn't hurt them, but consider how that wisdom would sound to a woman who'd been, say, fondled by strangers while passed out drunk and you have a rough idea how it might go over with a crowd of hard-core MOOers. Consider, for another thing, that many of the biologically female participants in the Bungle debate had been around long enough to grow lethally weary of the gag-and-get-over-it school of virtual-rape counseling, with its fine line between empowering victims and holding them responsible for their own suffering, and its shrugging indifference to the window of pain between the moment the rape-text starts flowing and the moment a gag shuts it off. From the outset it was clear that the technolibertarians were going to have to tiptoe through this issue with care, and for the most part they did.

Yet no position was trickier to maintain than that of the MOO's resident anarchists. Like the technolibbers, the anarchists didn't care much for punishments or policies or power elites. Like them, they hoped the MOO could be a place where people interacted fulfillingly without the need for such things. But their high hopes were complicated, in general, by a somewhat less thoroughgoing faith in technology ("Even if you can't tear down the master's house with the master's tools"—read a slogan written into one anarchist player's self-description—"it is a damned good place to start"). And at present they were additionally complicated by the fact that the most vocal anarchists in the discussion were none other than legba, Bakunin, and SamIAm, who wanted to see Mr. Bungle toaded as badly as anyone did.

Needless to say, a pro death penalty platform is not an especially comfortable one for an anarchist to sit on, so these particular anarchists were now at great pains to sever the conceptual ties between toading and capital punishment. Toading, they insisted (almost convincingly), was much more closely analogous to banishment; it was a kind of turning of the communal back on the offending party, a collective action which, if carried out properly, was entirely consistent with anarchist models of community. And carrying it out properly meant first and foremost building a consensus around it—a messy process for which there were no easy technocratic substitutes. It was going to take plenty of good old-fashioned, jawbone-intensive grassroots organizing.

So that when the time came, at 7 P.M. PST on the evening of the third day after the occurrence in the living room, to gather in evangeline's room for her proposed real-time open conclave, Bakunin and legba were among the first to arrive. But this was hardly to be an anarchist-dominated affair, for the room was crowding rapidly with representatives of all the MOO's political stripes, and even a few wizards. Hagbard showed up, and Autumn and Quastro, Puff, JoeFeedback, L-dopa and Bloaf, HerkieCosmo, Silver Rocket, Karl Porcupine, Matchstick—the names piled up and the discussion gathered momentum under their weight. Arguments multiplied and mingled, players talked past and through each other, the textual clutter of utterances and gestures filled up the screen like thick cigar smoke. Peaking in number at around thirty, this was one of the largest crowds that ever gathered in a single LambdaMOO chamber, and while evangeline had given her place a description that made it "infinite in expanse and fluid in form," it now seemed anything but roomy. You could almost feel the claustrophobic air of the place, dank and overheated by virtual bodies, pressing against your skin.

I know you could because I too was there, making my lone and insignificant appearance in this story. Completely ignorant of any of the goings-on that had led to the meeting, I wandered in purely to see what the crowd was about, and though I observed the proceedings for a good while, I confess I found it hard to grasp what was going on. I was still the rankest of newbies then, my MOO legs still too unsteady to make the leaps of faith, logic, and empathy required to meet the spectacle on its own terms. I was fascinated by the concept of virtual rape, but I couldn't quite take it seriously.

In this, though, I was in a small and mostly silent minority,

for the discussion that raged around me was of an almost unrelieved earnestness, bent it seemed on examining every last aspect and implication of Mr. Bungle's crime. There were the central questions, of course: thumbs up or down on Bungle's virtual existence? And if down, how then to ensure that his toading was not just some isolated lynching but a first step toward shaping LambdaMOO into a legitimate community? Surrounding these, however, a tangle of weighty side issues proliferated. What, some wondered, was the real-life legal status of the offense? Could Bungle's university administrators punish him for sexual harassment? Could he be prosecuted under California state laws against obscene phone calls? Little enthusiasm was shown for pursuing either of these lines of action, which testifies both to the uniqueness of the crime and to the nimbleness with which the discussants were negotiating its idiosyncracies. Many were the casual references to Bungle's deed as simply "rape," but these in no way implied that the players had lost sight of all distinctions between the virtual and physical versions, or that they believed Bungle should be dealt with in the same way a real-life criminal would. He had committed a MOO crime, and his punishment, if any, would be meted out via the MOO.

On the other hand, little patience was shown toward any attempts to downplay the seriousness of what Mr. Bungle had done. When the affable HerkieCosmo proposed, more in the way of an hypothesis than an assertion, that "perhaps it's better to release . . . violent tendencies in a virtual environment rather than in real life," he was tut-

tutted so swiftly and relentlessly that he withdrew the hypothesis altogether, apologizing humbly as he did so. Not that the assembly was averse to putting matters into a more philosophical perspective. "Where does the body end and the mind begin?" young Quastro asked, amid recurring attempts to fine-tune the differences between real and virtual violence. "Is not the mind a part of the body?" "In MOO, the body IS the mind," offered HerkieCosmo gamely, and not at all implausibly, demonstrating the ease with which very knotty metaphysical conundrums come undone in VR. The not-so-aptly named Obvious seemed to agree, arriving after deep consideration of the nature of Bungle's crime at the hardly novel yet now somehow newly resonant conjecture "all reality might consist of ideas, who knows."

On these and other matters the anarchists, the libertarians, the legalists, the wizardists—and the wizards—all had their thoughtful say. But as the evening wore on and the talk grew more heated and more heady, it seemed increasingly clear that the vigorous intelligence being brought to bear on this swarm of issues wasn't going to result in anything remotely like resolution. The perspectives were just too varied, the memescape just too slippery. Again and again, arguments that looked at first to be heading in a decisive direction ended up chasing their own tails; and slowly, depressingly, a dusty haze of irrelevance gathered over the proceedings.

It was almost a relief, therefore, when midway through the evening Mr. Bungle himself, the living, breathing cause of all this talk, teleported into the room.

Not that it was much of a surprise. Oddly enough, in the three days since his release from Zippy's cage, Bungle had returned more than once to wander the public spaces of LambdaMOO, walking willingly into one of the fiercest storms of ill will and invective ever to rain down on a player. He'd been taking it all with a curious and mostly silent passivity, and when challenged face to virtual face by both legba and the genderless elder statescharacter PatGently to defend himself on *social, he'd demurred, mumbling something about Christ and expiation. He was equally quiet now, and his reception was still uniformly cool. Legba fixed an arctic stare on him—"no hate, no anger, no interest at all. Just . . . watching." Others were more actively unfriendly. "Asshole," spat Karl Porcupine, "creep." But the harshest of the MOO's hostility toward him had already been vented, and the attention he drew now was motivated more, it seemed, by the opportunity to probe the rapist's mind, to find out what made it tick and if possible how to get it to tick differently. In short, they wanted to know why he'd done it. So they asked him.

And Mr. Bungle thought about it. And as eddies of discussion and debate continued to swirl around him, he thought about it some more. And then he said this:

"I engaged in a bit of a psychological device that is called thought-polarization, the fact that this is not RL simply added to heighten the affect of the device. It was purely a sequence of events with no consequence on my RL existence."

They might have known. Stilted though its diction was, the gist of the answer was simple, and something many in the room had probably already surmised: Mr. Bungle was a psycho. Not, perhaps, in real life—but then in real life it's possible for reasonable people to assume, as Bungle clearly did, that what transpires between word-costumed characters within the boundaries of a make-believe world is, if not mere play, then at most some kind of emotional laboratory experiment. Inside the MOO, however, such thinking marked a person as one of two basically subcompetent types. The first was the newbie, in which case the confusion was understandable, since there were few MOOers who had not, upon their first visits as anonymous "guest" characters, mistaken the place for a vast playpen in which they might act out their wildest fantasies without fear of censure. Only with time and the acquisition of a fixed character do players tend to make the critical passage from anonymity to pseudonymity, developing the concern for their character's reputation that marks the attainment of virtual adulthood. But while Mr. Bungle hadn't been around as long as most MOOers, he'd been around long enough to leave his newbie status behind, and his delusional statement therefore placed him among the second type: the sociopath.

And as there is but small percentage in arguing with a head case, the room's attention gradually abandoned Mr. Bungle and returned to the discussion that had previously occupied it. But if the debate had been edging toward ineffectuality before, Bungle's anticlimactic appearance had evidently robbed it of any forward motion whatsoever. What's more, from his lonely corner of the room Mr. Bungle kept issuing periodic expressions of a prickly sort of remorse, interlaced with sarcasm and belligerence, and though it was hard to tell if he wasn't still just conducting his experiments, some people thought his regret genuine enough that maybe he didn't deserve to be toaded after all. Logically, of course, discussion of the principal issues at hand didn't require unanimous belief that Bungle was an irredeemable bastard, but now that cracks were showing in that unanimity, the last of the meeting's fervor seemed to be draining out through them.

People started drifting away. Mr. Bungle left first, then others followed—one by one, in twos and threes, hugging friends and waving goodnight. By 9:45 only a handful remained, and the great debate had wound down into casual conversation, the melancholy remains of another fruitless good idea. The arguments had been well-honed, certainly, and perhaps might prove useful in some as-yet-unclear long run. But at this point what seemed clear was that evangeline's meeting had died, at last, and without any practical results to mark its passing.

It was also at this point, most likely, that JoeFeedback reached his decision. JoeFeedback was a wizard, a taciturn sort of fellow who'd sat brooding on the sidelines all evening. He hadn't said a lot, but what he had said indicated that he took the crime committed against legba and Starsinger very seriously, and that he felt no particular compassion toward the character who had committed it. But on the other hand he had made it equally plain that he took the elimination of a fellow player just as seriously, and moreover that he had no desire to return to the days of wizardly fiat. It must have been difficult, therefore, to reconcile the conflicting impulses churning within him at that moment. In fact, it was probably impossible, for as much as he would have liked to make himself an instrument of LambdaMOO's collective will, he surely realized that under the present order of things he must in the final analysis either act alone or not act at all.

So JoeFeedback acted alone.

He told the lingering few players in the room that he had to go, and then he went. It was a minute or two before ten. He did it quietly and he did it privately, but all anyone had to do to know he'd done it was to type the @who command, which was normally what you typed if you wanted to know a player's present location and the time he last logged in. But if you had run an @who on Mr. Bungle not too long after JoeFeedback left evangeline's room, the database would have told you something different.

"Mr. Bungle," it would have said, "is not the name of any player."

The date, as it happened, was April Fool's Day, and it would still be April Fool's Day for another two hours. But this was no joke: Mr. Bungle was truly dead and truly gone.

They say that LambdaMOO has never been the same since Mr. Bungle's toading. They say as well that nothing's really changed. And though it skirts the fuzziest of dream-logics to say that both these statements are true, the MOO is just the sort of fuzzy, dreamlike place in which such contradictions thrive.

Certainly whatever civil society now informs LambdaMOO owes its existence to the Bungle Affair. The archwizard Haakon made sure of that. Away on business for the duration of the episode, Haakon returned to find its wreckage strewn across the tiny universe he'd set in motion. The death of a player, the trauma of several others, and the angst-ridden conscience of his colleague JoeFeedback presented themselves to his concerned and astonished attention, and he resolved to see if he couldn't learn some lesson from it all. For the better part of a day he brooded over the record of events and arguments left in *social, then he sat pondering the chaotically evolving shape of his creation, and at the day's end he descended once again into the social arena of the MOO with another history-altering proclamation.

It was probably his last, for what he now decreed was the final, missing piece of the New Direction. In a few days, Haakon announced, he would build into the database a system of petitions and ballots whereby anyone could put to popular vote any social scheme requiring wizardly powers for its implementation, with the results of the vote to be binding on the wizards. At last and for good, the awkward gap between the will of the players and the efficacy of the technicians would be closed. And though some anarchists grumbled about the irony of Haakon's dictatorially imposing universal suffrage on an unconsulted populace, in general the citizens of LambdaMOO seemed to find it hard to fault a system more purely democratic than any that could ever exist in real life. Eight months and a dozen ballot measures later, widespread participation in the new regime has produced a small arsenal of mechanisms for dealing with the types of violence that called the system into being. MOO residents now have access to an @boot command, for instance, with which to summarily eject berserker "guest" characters. And players can bring suit against one another through an ad hoc arbitration system in which mutually agreed-upon judges have at their disposition the full range of wizardly punishments—up to and including the capital.

Yet the continued dependence on death as the ultimate keeper of the peace suggests that this new MOO order may not be built on the most solid of foundations. For if life on LambdaMOO began to acquire more coherence in the wake of the toading, death retained all the fuzziness of pre-Bungle days. This truth was rather dramatically borne out, not too many days after Bungle departed, by the arrival of a strange new character named Dr. Jest. There was a forceful eccentricity to the newcomer's manner, but the oddest thing about his style was its striking yet unnameable familiarity. And when he developed the annoying habit of stuffing fellow players into a jar containing a tiny simulacrum of a certain deceased rapist, the source of this familiarity became obvious:

Mr. Bungle had risen from the grave.

In itself, Bungle's reincarnation as Dr. Jest was a remarkable turn of events, but perhaps even more remarkable was the utter lack of amazement with which the LambdaMOO public took note of it. To be sure, many residents were appalled by the brazenness of Bungle's return. In fact, one of the first petitions circulated under the new voting system was a request for Dr. Jest's toading that almost immediately gathered fifty-two signatures (but has failed so far to reach ballot status). Yet few were unaware of the ease with which the toad proscription could be circumvented—all the toadee had to do (all the ur-Bungle at NYU presumably had done) was to go to the minor hassle of acquiring a new Internet account, and LambdaMOO's character registration program would then simply treat the known felon as an entirely new and innocent person. Nor was this ease generally understood to represent a failure of toading's social disciplinary function. On the contrary, it only underlined the truism (repeated many times throughout the debate over Mr. Bungle's fate) that his punishment, ultimately, had been no more or less symbolic than his crime.

What *was* surprising, however, was that Mr. Bungle/Dr. Jest seemed to have taken the symbolism to heart. Dark themes still obsessed him—the objects he created gave off wafts of Nazi imagery and medical torture—but he no longer radiated the aggressively antisocial vibes he had before. He was a lot less unpleasant to look at (the outrageously seedy clown description had been replaced by that of a mildly creepy but actually rather natty young man, with "blue eyes . . . suggestive of conspiracy, untamed eroticism and perhaps a sense of understanding of the future"), and aside from the occasional jar-stuffing incident, he was also a lot less dangerous to be around. It was obvious he'd undergone some sort of personal transformation in the days since I'd first glimpsed him back in evangeline's crowded room—nothing radical maybe, but powerful

nonetheless, and resonant enough with my own experience, I felt, that it might be more than professionally interesting to talk with him, and perhaps compare notes.

For I too was undergoing a transformation in the aftermath of that night in evangeline's, and I'm still not entirely sure what to make of it. As I pursued my runaway fascination with the discussion I had heard there, as I pored over the *social debate and got to know legba and some of the other victims and witnesses, I could feel my newbie consciousness falling away from me. Where before I'd found it hard to take virtual rape seriously, I now was finding it difficult to remember how I could ever *not* have taken it seriously. I was proud to have arrived at this perspective—it felt like an exotic sort of achievement, and it definitely made my ongoing experience of the MOO a richer one.

But it was also having some unsettling effects on the way I looked at the rest of the world. Sometimes, for instance, it was hard for me to understand why RL society classifies RL rape alongside crimes against person or property. Since rape can occur without any physical pain or damage, I found myself reasoning, then it must be classed as a crime against the mind—more intimately and deeply hurtful, to be sure, than cross burnings, wolf whistles, and virtual rape, but undeniably located on the same conceptual continuum. I did not, however, conclude as a result that rapists were protected in any fashion by the First Amendment. Quite the opposite, in fact: the more seriously I took the notion of virtual rape, the less seriously I was able to take the notion of freedom of speech, with its tidy

division of the world into the symbolic and the real.

Let me assure you, though, that I am not presenting these thoughts as arguments. I offer them, rather, as a picture of the sort of mind-set that deep immersion in a virtual world has inspired in me. I offer them also, therefore, as a kind of prophecy. For whatever else these thoughts tell me, I have come to believe that they announce the final stages of our decades-long passage into the Information Age, a paradigm shift that the classic liberal firewall between word and deed (itself a product of an earlier paradigm shift commonly known as the Enlightenment) is not likely to survive intact. After all, anyone the least bit familiar with the workings of the new era's definitive technology, the computer, knows that it operates on a principle impracticably difficult to distinguish from the pre-Enlightenment principle of the magic word: the commands you type into a computer are a kind of speech that doesn't so much communicate as *make things happen*, directly and ineluctably, the same way pulling a trigger does. They are incantations, in other words, and anyone at all attuned to the technosocial megatrends of the moment—from the growing dependence of economies on the global flow of intensely fetishized words and numbers to the burgeoning ability of bioengineers to speak the spells written in the four-letter text of DNA—knows that the logic of the incantation is rapidly permeating the fabric of our lives.

And it's precisely this logic that provides the real magic in a place like LambdaMOO—not the fictive trappings of voodoo and shapeshifting and wizardry, but the conflation of speech and act that's inevitable in any computer-mediated world, be it Lambda or the increasingly wired world at large. This is dangerous magic, to be sure, a potential threat—if misconstrued or misapplied—to our always precarious freedoms of expression, and as someone who lives by his words I do not take the threat lightly. And yet, on the other hand, I can no longer convince myself that our wishful insulation of language from the realm of action has ever been anything but a valuable kludge, a philosophically damaged stopgap against oppression that would just have to do till something truer and more elegant came along.

Am I wrong to think this truer, more elegant thing can be found on LambdaMOO? Perhaps, but I continue to seek it there, sensing its presence just beneath the surface of every interaction. I have even thought, as I said, that discussing with Dr. Jest our shared experience of the workings of the MOO might help me in my search. But when that notion first occurred to me, I still felt somewhat intimidated by his lingering criminal aura, and I hemmed and hawed a good long time before finally resolving to drop him MOO-mail requesting an interview. By then it was too late. For reasons known only to himself, Dr. Jest had stopped logging in. Maybe he'd grown bored with the MOO. Maybe the loneliness of ostracism had gotten to him. Maybe a psycho whim had carried him far away or maybe he'd quietly acquired a third character and started life over with a cleaner slate.

Wherever he'd gone, though, he left behind the room he'd created for himself—a treehouse "tastefully decorated" with rare-book shelves, an operating table, and a life-size William S. Burroughs doll—and he left it unlocked. So I took to checking in there occasionally, and I still do from time to time. I head out of my own cozy nook (inside a TV set inside the little red hotel inside the Monopoly board inside the dining room of LambdaMOO), and I teleport on over to the treehouse, where the room description always tells me Dr. Jest is present but asleep, in the conventional depiction for disconnected characters. The not-quite-emptiness of the abandoned room invariably instills in me an uncomfortable mix of melancholy and the creeps, and I stick around only on the off chance that Dr. Jest will wake up, say hello, and share his understanding of the future with me.

He won't, of course, but this is no great loss. Increasingly, the complex magic of the MOO interests me more as a way to live the present than to understand the future. And it's usually not long before I leave Dr. Jest's lonely treehouse and head back to the mansion, to see some friends.

 Article Review Form at end of book.

Does the availability of information promote citizen participation in government?

Cyberdemocracy:

Tip O'Neill, meet Alvin Toffler

Rick Henderson

Rick Henderson is Washington editor of REASON.

Richard Hartman's business card is informative and symbolic. It informs you that Hartman is co-founder of Reform Congress 94, described as "America's First CyberSpace PAC." It provides the political action committee's telephone number and fax number, along with Internet and Compu-Serve addresses. It also tells you that Hartman is one of the principals of the De-Foley-ate Project, which had one purpose: to help defeat Rep. Tom Foley (D-Wash.), who until the November election was speaker of the House of Representatives.

The card is symbolic because it doesn't list a physical address. Reform Congress 94 was a "virtual PAC" that used faxes and a computer bulletin-board service to get out its message rather than relying upon legions of volunteers to operate telephone banks and stuff envelopes. Hartman, a software engineer from Spokane, did rent an office, but he says that was "a waste of time and money. We went there twice." Along with one other person, Hartman and his wife Mary ran a political action committee from their home.

The Hartmans officially launched their effort in late August, a few weeks before the Washington primary. They hoped to raise $500,000, but fell a bit short: They received only about $26,000. But they faxed press releases to local radio talk shows, reminding the hosts that Foley had sued his own constituents in an attempt to overturn Washington's term-limit referendum and that he had voted to ban "assault weapons" in the crime bill. They set up an electronic BBS, to which Richard says hundreds of thousands of respondents dialed in.

And when participants in a September gun show in Florida wanted to distribute anti-Foley literature, Richard placed the literature on-line, including the software that would let the folks in Florida produce camera-ready posters. "We could have sent the information by Federal Express overnight," he says. Electronic media, however, "let us tailor the message to this precise audience instantly."

The Hartmans' circumstances were certainly unusual: They weren't political pros trying to run a national operation but rather ordinary citizens determined to defeat their local con-

gressman. Because the local congressman was speaker of the House and a political lightning rod, it was certainly more likely that they would get attention (and contributions) from across the country. And they did know how to use the latest technologies, or as Richard says, "We had the right tools in our tool kit" to run a shoestring operation. But their unusual story demonstrates the unintended ways in which new technologies have let normal people gain access to the political process.

A new form of activism is shaking the political establishment, and it may crumble congressional and regulatory fiefdoms more thoroughly than last November's election. By using broadcast faxes, satellite television programs, radio talk shows, and electronic forums like those on CompuServe and the Internet, grassroots activists like the Hartmans can bypass traditional media outlets. The rather anarchic nature of computer culture suggests that the infomedia revolution will tend to erode the statist foundations of the political establishment. While this outbreak of cyberpolitics is not universally appreciated, there's little the Beltway powerbrokers can do to stop it.

The explosion of cyber-democracy doesn't please everybody. "Some of the information technologies that so pervade Washington life have not only failed to cure our ills but actually seem to have made them worse," writes Robert Wright in the January 23 *Time*. "Intensely felt public opinion leads to the impulsive passage of dubious laws," though the only one Wright comes up with is the "three strikes, you're out" component of last year's crime bill.

In part, Wright's criticism resembles the gripes made by political bosses when sunshine laws opened government meetings to the public and made documents more accessible to average citizens. The explosion of information technologies has revoked the near monopoly on access to policy makers that high-priced lobbyists and prestige journalists once held. Quips American Conservative Union chairman David Keene, politicians "don't like to be lobbied by people who don't take them to play golf."

More substantively, Wright argues that floods of e-mail messages, faxes, and calls from talk-show listeners drown out the deliberation that is necessary for sound policy making. "Politics is pandering in a hyperdemocracy," he writes.

Three lengthy, high-profile policy battles of the Clinton presidency belie Wright's assertion. Two major trade bills, the North American Free Trade Agreement and the General Agreement on Tariffs and Trade, each passed Congress though leaders of the president's party opposed them and populists left (Ralph Nader), right (Pat Buchanan), and center (Ross Perot) ginned up their info-media networks to denounce them. In both cases, advocates of the trade deals had to defend them publicly, and on principle—a process that might not have taken place had the deals been negotiated entirely behind closed doors. And the Clinton administration made its most public case for NAFTA by circumventing traditional broadcast networks and having Vice president Al Gore debate Perot on a talk show—CNN's Larry King Live.

The failure of the president's Health Security Act again shows how information-age technologies can enhance deliberative debate. ClintonCare was formulated in a series of secret meetings by 500 experts hand-picked by the White House. In the first weeks after the Clinton plan was introduced, Republicans were on the defensive, seriously considering accommodation with the White House. Then-Senate minority leader Bob Dole and the Heritage Foundation were each pushing variations of universal health-care entitlements. Yet as details of the Clinton plan became available, they were dissected on talk shows and electronic bulletin boards, as well as on op-ed pages, in opinion magazines, and in the famous "Harry and Louise" series of television commercials. The Health Security Act, conceived in secrecy, could not survive when exposed to the light of public scrutiny.

Some Washington pundits have also expressed concerns about cyberdemocracy. *Washington Post* columnist David Broder worries that the "mobilization [of public opinion] has fallen into the hands of private interests, pursuing very specific and narrow agendas. . . . In such struggles against private groups," Broder continues, "money will be important, not just in spreading the message but in hiring the people who know how to engineer quick responses." In the world of info-media, *Demosclerosis* author Jonathan Rauch says, "narrowly focused groups are favored more than those [supporting] broad-reaching reforms. Ordinary people don't organize," he says. "Pros use this stuff."

But the Hartmans aren't political pros. And the backbone of the property-rights movement is the thousands of small landowners who attend zoning meetings, write their legislators, and communicate by fax. Communications technologies turn individuals into a supportive, quick-response network. An advocacy group may still have an advantage if it has a D.C. representative who can take a member of Congress to lunch; but that same legislator can't ignore hundreds of faxes and telephone messages from his or her own constituents.

"There are two prerequisites for a free society," says Jim Warren, one of the organizers of the first Computers, Freedom, and Privacy conference. "Citizens must have timely access to adequate information on which to base informed decisions. And they must have timely and economical access to the body politic. The [Internet] provides both of these. No longer do you have to buy newsprint by the ton or own a television license or a radio license in order to be able to conduct effective community outreach that is pervasive." With the Internet, he says, "You can instantly penetrate the full fabric of the community."

Without question, modern technologies make it easy for a few individuals to inexpensively form a single-interest organization. Unlike the large, successful lobbies of the past, such as the American Association of Retired Persons, which often sought to protect federal perks, many of the successful newcomers have had a different, more-sweeping agenda: Rein in government power one program at a time.

C-SPAN, radio talk shows, e-mail, and broadcast faxes have provided massive amounts of information to anyone who wants it. They have also created a new generation of political activists. "Fifty percent of our contributors listen to talk radio at least two hours a week," says the ACU's David Keene. "Ten years ago, our [typical] member would send us $15 and say, 'Do a good job.' Now, he says, 'Tell me what I can do.' "

An early indication of the speed and power of cyberdemocracy occurred last February, during the reauthorization of the Elementary and Secondary Education Act. A provision in the bill would have required every school district in the nation to certify all full-time teachers in the subjects they instruct. Home-schoolers—parents of the one million children who receive all their schooling at home—believed this requirement would force them to put their kids in more traditional schools. Communicating on the Internet, home-schoolers flooded Capitol Hill with hundreds of thousands of telephone calls and faxes. The onslaught of outrage forced the House to move the vote up by two weeks; by a vote of 424 to 1, it voted to strip the certification requirement from the bill.

Other cyber-battles were fought in the 103rd Congress. A barrage of letters, faxes, and telephone calls from the members of wise-use and property-rights groups prevented the National Biological Survey from being considered for a vote and the Endangered Species Act, the Clean Water Act, and the Safe Drinking Water Act from being reauthorized by the 103rd Congress. (See "Bill Killers," August/September 1994.*) And in September, when Congress threatened to force advocacy groups to disclose their donor lists to the Internal Revenue Service, hundreds of thousands of telephone calls and faxes from activists and trade-association members shut down the Capitol Hill switchboards and killed the lobbying bill.

Grassroots organizations have shown they can work the phone lines and fax machines to clog the Capitol Hill switchboard. But these activities represent a minuscule sample of the ways individuals and groups use infomedia. For instance:

- The National Taxpayers Union has placed its two congressional rating guides, BillTally and VoteTally, on the CompuServe electronic service. Anyone with an IBM-compatible computer can download the programs and get a detailed voting record of any member of Congress.

  The BillTally guide estimates whether individual pieces of legislation will increase or decrease federal spending. VoteTally ranks members of Congress according to the net amount of spending increases or cuts they proposed during an entire session of Congress. When NTU first started tracking for BillTally in 1991, over the first nine months, members of the 102nd Congress introduced 57 bills that would reduce spending. By the end of the 103rd Congress, 638 bills that would reduce spending were pending.

  Until this information went on-line, NTU promoted

  *Refers to the August/September 1994 issue of *Reason*.

  its ratings through direct contacts with news outlets in every congressional district. Now with CompuServe, individuals can download the entire programs or simply call up an individual legislator's rating at any time. "Incentives matter in the legislative process," says NTU Vice-President Paul Hewitt. "This cold, hard data has changed the incentives for legislators and empowered the general public to [demand] spending cuts."

- Americans for Tax Reform is another active, creative user of infomedia to promote its anti-tax, anti-regulation message. It sponsors regular conference calls with members of Congress, governors, and other elected officials to explain items on the legislative agenda. ATR faxes an invitation to listen to the call to its supporters, along with leaders of other grassroots organizations and political reporters. Over the past few months, for instance, by calling an 800 number, you could hear Reps. Tim Penny (D-Minn.) and John Kasich (R-Ohio) explain the Penny-Kasich budget-cutting plan or listen to school-choice activists from Arizona and New Jersey discuss proposals in their states.

  ATR President Grover Norquist appears on a weekly National Empowerment Television program, informing viewers how to contact members of Congress or talk-show hosts about different bills. The group regularly faxes notices about national and state issues to local activists, talk-show hosts, and journalists. Commercial broadcast-fax services can send a one-page document to thousands of locations, each for about the cost of a first-class stamp. As ATR's Jim Lucier points out, batch-faxing information is not only faster than relying on the Postal Service; you don't have to recruit people to stuff envelopes and lick stamps.

And ATR has begun targeting op-eds and fax notices to community newspapers that would be too small to justify traditional mail campaigns. "These are the places that print coupons for the local supermarket and write about high-school football games and the prom," Lucier says. "It's an important audience to reach."

- Activists inside the computer community have worked to make government documents available at low cost on-line. Jim Warren worked with legislative staffers to place California's public records on the Internet rather than on a separate computer system that would have cost millions of dollars to construct and maintain and would have been costly for individuals to dial up.

And individuals can now reach the Library of Congress's "Thomas" program on the Internet and download the legislative language of any bill before Congress within seconds of its being filed. New speaker [1995] Newt Gingrich believes "Thomas" will weaken Washington lobbyists and make it tougher to pass bills that benefit narrow interests. At a January 10 conference sponsored by the Progress & Freedom Foundation, Gingrich said disseminating information in "real time" will give everyone, not just well-paid lobbyists with research staffs, access to the same information. "There's no longer an advantage to being an insider," he said, "because everyone's an

insider" who's willing to get the data. ATR's Lucier says "'Thomas' lets anyone play 'Find the Pork' with their home computers."

Before "Thomas" was up and running, unless you could walk over to Capitol Hill (or pay someone to do it), it would take days to get the text of bills pending in Congress by mail. And unless you had solid contacts on Capitol Hill, forget about quickly obtaining copies of committee reports, the staff-prepared briefs that outline the projected costs and regulatory impacts of pending bills.

Organizations across the political spectrum form "working groups" to respond to legislation affecting areas as disparate as immigration, criminal sentencing, and gun laws. A few hours after a meeting ends, thousands of activists can learn by fax or e-mail what's happening in Washington and what they can do to assist in legislative battles.

And they have an impact. By raising a ruckus on the Internet, for instance, civil-liberties groups have derailed proposals to make digital telephone communications easier for governments to wiretap. They have also caused an indefinite delay in the introduction of the Clipper Chip encryption device. Says Jim Warren, "The Net is a potent tool for enhancing citizen control over state and federal legislative activity."

But Rauch argues that technologies aren't the problem; lobbies are. He admits that the grassroots infomedia groups have been most effective in stopping intrusive legislation. But he wonders if new "veto" groups won't spring up that stop laws that roll back existing entitlements and regulations.

Such groups may emerge. Indeed, greens use electronic communications (the ECO-NET news service, for instance) extensively. But their main thrust has been extending regulation, which has recently become a legislative nonstarter. And as Paul Hewitt of the NTU points out, the latest technologies are in the hand of younger people who are more suspicious of government entitlements than their parents. Warren agrees. "On the Net," he says, "Generation X has an equal voice to the AARP."

The coalitions that fought the Clipper Chip, the 1993 tax hikes, ClintonCare, teacher certification, and the lobbying bill were part of what ATR's Lucier calls "the leave us alone coalition." These technologies provide fast and flexible responses to government attempts to micromanage peoples' lives. Working on many fronts, individuals and groups can chip away at the center of power in Washington.

Richard Hartman thought his family's life would return to normal after the election. Now political consultants and grassroots activists across the country want to hear how they ran an effective political-action committee out of a couple of rooms. He's planning to sponsor a seminar in Spokane in late spring or early summer to explain how they did it. "We had no long-range agenda," he says. "Everything we did was focused on getting rid of Mr. Foley." Now that Foley has become a D.C. lobbyist, the Hartmans may be able to show other activists how to give their local legislators early retirements.

 Article Review Form at end of book.

How might the Internet influence the political process?

The Promise and Perils of Cyberdemocracy

Norman Ornstein and Amy Schenkenberg

Norman Ornstein is a resident scholar at the American Enterprise Institute, where Amy Schenkenberg is a research associate.

In 1992, Ross Perot promised that if elected president he would use electronic town hall meetings to guide national decisions. Perot lost the election (and never made clear how those meetings would operate), but the idea of "cyberdemocracy" aroused much interest and is spreading quickly as technology advances. Every U.S. senator and 190 representatives currently have World Wide Web pages, as do all eight major Republican presidential contenders. In 1995, the Library of Congress, under the leadership of Newt Gingrich, established an on-line system offering all legislation considered and passed by Congress.

On the local level, the city government of Colorado Springs has a non-commercial electronic bulletin board called Citylink. Established in 1990 to allow citizens to communicate with city managers and city council members, it's available free of charge. In 1994, the Minnesota Electronic Democracy Project conducted on-line debates among candidates in the gubernatorial and senate races.

States have begun fashioning their governmental processes around this direct-democracy ideal. Twenty-four states permit citizen initiatives that place legislation or constitutional amendments on the ballot. Oregon has held local vote-by-mail elections since 1981, and in 1995 initiated its first statewide mail ballot to replace Senator Bob Packwood. North Dakotas 1996 presidential primary will be by mail ballot.

All this may be just the beginning. As new technologies emerge, many futurists paint rosy scenarios of more direct roles for individuals in law-making. Some prophesy that legislators will vote and debate from their home state through computers and televisions, eliminating the need for the actual houses of Congress in Washington. Lawrence Grossman, former president of PBS and NBC, imagines Congress evolving into a body that discusses issues and disseminates information, but only makes decisions after being instructed by the public. Futurist Christine Slaton questions the need for elected legislators at all. She envisions using technology to create a participatory democracy where representatives are selected by lot and rotated regularly. Alvin and Heidi Toffler of "third wave" fame predict that today's political parties will disappear, replaced by fluid coalitions that vary according to changing legislative interests. The Tofflers also envision representatives chosen by lot, or at a minimum, elected officials casting 50 percent of a vote and a random sampling of the public casting the other 50 percent. In this scenario, individuals will not only vote on more things than they do now, they'll vote on more complex questions, as simple yes/no votes are replaced by if-then referenda. Nor will voters have to inconvenience themselves by traveling to the local polling station. They probably won't even have to lick a stamp. Instead, voters will simply punch in their vote from their TV remote control, never leaving the house, never having to speak with another individual, not even having to spend more than a few seconds thinking about their choice.

Enchanting as these innovations may sound to Americans grown weary of Washington ways, several questions arise: Would cyberdemocracy in fact be more representative? Would voters take seriously their new responsibilities? Would they even be interested? Who will determine the exact questions the public will decide? And most importantly, what sort of deliberation, if any, will exist under this new regime?

A cyberdemocracy based on personal computers and upscale television systems will not be equally open to all citizens. Twenty-two percent of college graduates go on line at least weekly, while only 1 percent of those with a high school diploma do, a recent Times Mirror survey reports. Men are twice as likely as women to be daily on-line users. Twenty-seven percent of families with incomes of $50,000 or greater have gone on line, but only 6 percent of those with incomes under $20,000 have. Indeed, the Colorado Springs information systems manager reported that in 1995 there were only 250 active Citylink users in a city of over 300,000. No doubt the popularity of comparable information systems will increase substantially over time, and costs will come down, but a skew toward the highly educated and well-to-do is inevitable.

Even if the technology were made available to everyone equally, how would interest be sustained? Lloyd Morrisett, president of the Markle Foundation, recently wrote that he envisions the early fascination with cyberdemocracy ebbing until cybervoting falls into the same predicament as current voting rights: treasured but not necessarily used. Studying California's experience with referenda, Morrisett found that "the ballot has become so loaded with complex initiatives that it seems to discourage people from going to the polls, rather than motivating them to express their judgment." If the average voter tuned out complex items flashing across his screen, "voting" would be much less representative than it is today.

Cyberdemocracy's greatest danger lies in the way it would diminish deliberation in government. Everyone applauds technology's capacity to inform voters and to improve communications between them and their representatives. But we must also recall that the Founders expressly rejected "pure" democracies where citizens "assemble and administer the government in person," because they usually end in the tyranny of the majority. The Constitution instead establishes a republic where voters select representatives to make and execute the laws. The Founders designed this process to produce a public judgment, enlarging upon and refining popular opinions. That judgment, as opposed to public emotions, can only arise through deliberation. In the slow process of debate, give-and-take, and face-to-face contact among representatives, all perspectives and interests can be considered. The need to persuade an informed group of representatives with diverse concerns should, the Founders thought, result in decisions that are more just and more likely to meet the test of time with citizens.

Deliberation even figures in our political campaigns. Over weeks and months, campaigns provide a larger deliberative canvas, an opportunity for voters to consider issues, governing philosophies, and questions of leadership, resulting in a greater appreciation of the choices that will face Congress and the President. Of course, our governing system does not always live up to the challenge of serious deliberation, but it still remains our foundation.

What happens to deliberation with the ascent of cyberdemocracy? Consider elections. For all the understandable criticism of never-ending campaigns, negative advertising, and demagoguery, campaigns still work, at least sometimes, as deliberative processes. Voters' initial inclination, not to mention their priorities on issues, often change as they receive more information. Early polls rarely reflect the actual voting. Citizens striving for informed judgments usually make them in the final, most intense days of a campaign. Instantaneous electronic voting would destroy whatever is left of this deliberative process. In Oregon most voters return their mail ballots within five days, casting their votes well before the final days (or even weeks) of intense campaigning.

Mail or electronic balloting also removes the symbolic quality of voting as an act where voters make a private judgment in a public place, surrounded by their fellow citizens, acknowledging simultaneously our individuality and our collective responsibility and common purpose. Compare standing in line at a polling place, going into a private booth, and making individual choices with the alternatives of vote-by-mail—the political equivalent of filling out a Publishers Clearing House ballot—or electronic voting, where elections would resemble the Home Shopping Network.

Voting by mail or electronically is only one challenge cyberpolitics presents to deliberative democracy: Consider the difference between laws passed by referenda and laws passed in legislatures. Legislative deliberation encourages informed debate among some-what-informed individuals with different interests. It allows a proposal to change, often dramatically, as it goes through the gauntlet of hearings, floor debate, and amendment in both houses of Congress.

To be sure, some debate can occur during a state referendum campaign, through ads and media analysis, but that is no substitute for face-to-face debate involving not just two sides, but sometimes dozens or hundreds, reflected in representatives from various areas and constituencies. Mail or electronic balloting would short-circuit campaigns even further. And referenda have no amendment process, no matter how complex the issue. Their outcome relies on voters who have many other things to do besides study the issues, much less read the bills or provisions.

Could electronic town meetings provide a popular equivalent to traditional legislating? Theoretically, a broad mass of voters could be part of a different deliberative process. That's the thesis of political scientist James Fishkin, whose "deliberative poll" brought a random sample of 600 citizens together in late January at considerable expense for three days of expert-guided discussion in Austin, Texas. Even if the Fishkin experiment were scrupulously fair, such enterprises generally seem susceptible to undemocratic manipulation by "experts" and agenda-setters. And "deliberative polls" are unlikely to win out over the allure of a quick, trigger-like vote on the TV or computer. Cyberdemocratic meetings would likely turn into fancier versions of "Talk Back Live." And most deliberation would be reduced—as now in California and other initiative-prone states—to high-tech public relations campaigns by powerful interests with the resources to put their issues on the ballot—making for more special interest influence, not more democracy.

Cyberspace offers wonderful possibilities for citizens to discuss issues. New electronic alliances based on similar interests can be enjoyed. And every day, citizens and legislators can download more information. But the combination of cynical distrust of political institutions, a rising tide of populism glorifying "pure" democracy, and the increased speed of information technology, is a highly dangerous one. While Newt Gingrich has benefited from the political cynicism and populism that drove voters in 1994, he knows the dangers facing deliberative democracy. As he told one of his college classes, "Direct democracy says, Okay, how do we feel this week? We all raise our hand. Let's rush off and do it. The concept of republican representation, which is very clear in the Founding Fathers, is you hire somebody who you send to a central place. . . . They, by definition, learn things you don't learn, because you don't want to—you want to be able to live your life. They are supposed to use their judgment to represent you. . . . [The Founders] feared the passion of the moment."

Newt is right. But preserving the Founders' vision as the "third wave" of cybertechnology approaches won't be easy.

 Article Review Form at end of book.

When is information power? How can citizens use the Internet to effect social change?

Digital Democracy in Action

Ralph Nader

Ralph Nader rose to prominence in the 1960s and has remained an influential social critic and self-styled consumer advocate. He ran as the Green Party candidate for president of the United States in the 1996 election.

Information is the currency of democracy, and information age technologies can make information current, accurate, and inexpensive for people to use to create a more just and prosperous society.

But technology does not have its own imperative. It reflects the distribution and the concentration of power and wealth that shape its quality, quantity, and accessibility. Right after World War II, two high technologies were touted by their boosters to the point of euphoria. One was television and the other was atomic power.

I recall my seventh-grade schoolteacher regaling us with the coming benefits of atomic power—oh, so cheap ("too cheap to meter," said one of its prominent promoters), so safe, and so adaptable. Why, just a little atomic power gadget installed in our cars, she said, would replace gasoline for the lifetime of the car.

She was citing the leading scientific projections at that time. What a difference reality makes! Troubled and risky, nuclear power is in a de facto moratorium in this country—not a single reactor has been ordered by the cost-conscious utilities for more than two decades. And gasoline stations are still flourishing.

Then there was television. My first-year high school teachers told us that an age of enlightenment was awaiting us. Whole new worlds of information, geography, debate, and mobilization would come from this living room technology. What was now controlled by the few would soon be accessible by the many. The parochial world of youngsters, they forecast, would disappear and be replaced by a young generation that would be aware and have an understanding of worldwide events. This was before Tony the Tiger, Chester Cheetah, and Mortal Kombat.

To be sure, the information age has produced much information. We are inundated with data and information, less so with knowledge, even less with judgment, and almost not at all with wisdom. Millions of information specialists never get past the in-

formation stage, and the few who deal with the next stages of knowledge and judgment are called gurus. Wisdom, alas, is left for philosophers who probably use manual Underwood typewriters.

Also, there's this sense of incompleteness about the development and application of computers. Used mostly by businesses and government, computers still seem exotic to most consumers, who usually limit their personal computer use to entertainment and modest record-keeping purposes. Computers, however, could usher in an age of consumer information that would drive competitors to offer products with higher levels of health, safety, and quality for shoppers. But, except for consumers push to compare auto insurance premiums online, the future is not here.

Even on the business side, computers have not fulfilled their promise of greater productivity in the service sector, other than in the telecommunications industry. Computer design pioneer Thomas K. Landauer in his new book, *The Trouble with Computers: Usefulness, Usability, and Productivity* (MIT Press), explains why, despite enormous investments in computers over the last twenty years, productivity in the very service industries they were built for has virtually stagnated everywhere in the world.

Because of their speed and productivity, however, when technology is driven by fundamental values of democracy and justice, these same machines can produce highly useful knowledge to change conditions for the better. Our current project on banks and mortgage redlining is a case in point.

The project demonstrates that the rapid advances in computer technology have provided a valuable and powerful tool to fight lending discrimination. To the chagrin of banks and other financial corporations, public interest groups and community activists are using the new technology to plow through mountains of aggregate data, in order to detect, with great precision, who gets mortgage loans and who gets shut out.

For the first time, the new technology has put some truly sharp teeth in the long-standing, but often futile, effort to prevent banks from adopting lending practices that deprive minority and low- and moderate-income neighborhoods of credit—a practice commonly referred to as "redlining."

These efforts have led to significant improvements. Aware that many community activists have computer-generated data, compiled from government reports, quite a few banks have cleaned up their act rather than risk public exposure. In the process, they have discovered that there is profit to be made in lending to the residents in underserved neighborhoods.

The information age is young. It has an opportunity to mature into a responsible, contributing force in our democratic society. But it requires civic engagement by many Americans for this prospect to be realized.

 Article Review Form at end of book.

WiseGuide Wrap-Up

E-mail makes it easy for voters to communicate with their political representatives, and the web quickly is becoming an incredible resource for information on political issues and candidates. The availability of these technologies, however, may or may not be sufficient for the realization of "cyberdemocracy" and could promote "the rule of the minority." What motivates people to participate in the political process? Are you an active participant? Why or why not?

R.E.A.L. Sites

This list provides a print preview of typical **Coursewise** R.E.A.L. sites. There are over 100 such sites at the **Courselinks**™ site. The danger in printing URLs is that web sites can change overnight. As we went to press, these sites were functional using the URLs provided. If you come across one that isn't, please let us know via email to: webmaster@coursewise.com. Use your Passport to access the most current list of R.E.A.L. sites at the **Courselinks**™ site.

Site name: Center for Responsive Politics

URL: http://www.crp.org/

Why is it R.E.A.L.? The CRP is a nonprofit organization that studies the role of money in congressional elections and decisions. The site includes information on how much money each congressional candidate spent on campaign expenses in the last election, as well as databases on congressional travel, lobbyists, and PACs.

Key topics: cyberdemocracy

Try this: Use the CRP database to learn how much money your congressional representative spent in the last election. Compare the figure with the amount spent by his or her opponent, or by a candidate in a neighboring state. Is this information useful to you as a voter? Why or why not?

Site name: Project Vote Smart

URL: http://www.vote-smart.org/

Why is it R.E.A.L.? This is a nonpartisan nonprofit organization that researches and distributes a wide range of information about candidates and elected officials, including voting records, campaign finances and promises, and performance evaluations from special interest groups.

Key topics: cyberdemocracy

Try this: Click on the "Issue Positions" icon to review the National Political Awareness Test completed by one of your congressional representatives. Did you learn anything new or surprising? Would you visit this site again to gather information on a candidate? Why or why not?

Site name: Center for Civic Networking

URL: http://www.civicnet.org/

Why is it R.E.A.L.? CCN advocates the public use of the information infrastructure for such purposes as community development, delivery of services, and participation in government.

Key topics: cyberdemocracy

Try this: Explore the CCN site to find an example of civic networking. What's the purpose of this network? What concerns or problems does the network present or address? Does it enhance democracy in ways similar to those discussed in the readings?

Future Trends: Computers, Information, and Society

Where will you be in the year 2020? How will you earn a living? What will you do for entertainment? What will you eat for dinner? Perhaps a computerized cooking device will prepare it for you.

Today the microwave oven, the videocassette recorder, and the answering machine are standard appliances in most American homes, yet all of these home appliances entered the mainstream less than twenty years ago. Each of these technologies contains a unique message. They have already changed the way we think and live. The constant stream of new technologies promises that more changes are on the way.

In the 1990s, computers and the Internet rapidly entered the mainstream. The number of Internet users has doubled every year since 1988, and statistics suggest that this trend will continue. By 2020, personal computers and Internet browsers probably will be as ubiquitous as television sets, at least in affluent countries. Anyone born prior to 1980 nostalgically will refer back to "LBC"—"Life Before Computers." The world will shrink in size, on a psychological level, to become the "global village" envisioned by Marshall McLuhan in 1964.

McLuhan reminds us that we can never fully anticipate the impact of a new technology or medium and the changes it generates in the ways we live, think, and act. The only certainty is that change will occur as computers, the Internet, and other technologies become fully integrated into our homes, schools, businesses, and institutions.

The articles in this section are speculative, inviting you to consider how technology may impact society in the years to come. "Inventing the Future," by Thomas and Darby Frey, presents an array of technologies and inventions that they predict will become reality. While some of their ideas may seem far-fetched, others already are near at hand. If you are interested in exploring the reliability of such futurist predictions, visit the World Future Society web site. The WFS publishes *The Futurist*, the periodical that published the Freys' article, and the organization's web site offers a list of similar predictions from the past that have come to fruition.

Technology critic Howard Besser presents a bleaker future scenario for the Information Highway in his essay "From Internet to Information Superhighway." As you read this essay, think about how recent innovations related to the Internet support his pessimism, or refute it.

Another set of interviews, "Seven Thinkers in Search of an Information Highway," presents a broader perspective on the future of the Information Highway. It was originally published in *Technology Review,* a periodical devoted to innovations in technology. The web site for *Technology Review* is an excellent resource for exploring the cutting edge of technology and its impact on society and culture.

Learning Objectives

- Imagine how the inventions described by the Freys might impact the way we think and live.

- Evaluate Besser's argument about the future of the Information Highway.

- Link the ideas of the "Seven Thinkers" to current trends on the Internet.

- Identify the assumptions in Greenfield's argument.

The last section, a reflective piece by *Newsweek* columnist Meg Greenfield, considers some of the moral and ethical questions posed by developments in technology. Consider the questions she raises in light of the many issues you've read about and discussed in your class this semester.

With computers and technology, it's sometimes difficult to imagine the future, because so often we feel that we're scrambling to keep up with developments that may already be outdated by the time we think we've caught up with the present. This section provides a space for your imagination to roam amid the swirl of constant change. Enjoy the ride!

? Questions ? ? ?

Reading 39. Would you want to converse with an "on-line personality service"? What are the potential uses and abuses of "therapeutic amnesia"?

Reading 40. Are you an information consumer or producer? According to Besser, why does the difference matter?

Reading 41. Which thinker's vision of the Information Highway is most appealing to you? To what extent has the vision been realized?

Reading 42. Is it possible to forge a consensus about the ethics of technology? How do we make ethical and moral decisions about its applications?

Would you want to converse with an "on-line personality service"?
What are the potential uses and abuses of "therapeutic amnesia"?

Inventing the Future

Two technology-trend trackers describe significant inventions that may be just over the horizon.

Thomas J. Frey and Darby L. Frey

Thomas J. Frey, a former IBM engineer, is senior researcher and co-founder of the DaVinci Institute, a future-studies organization that concentrates on inventions and technology. He conducts seminars on future inventions and is currently writing a book on the subject, called Inventions of Impact.

Darby L. Frey is president and co-founder of the DaVinci Institute. He is an electrical engineering student at the Colorado School of Mines and Technology.

At the DaVinci Institute, our goal is to forecast future inventions, many of which will have a profound effect on our lives.

We do not make value judgments as to whether or not these technologies should be pursued. Our belief is that these unborn technologies will emerge someday with or without our blessing. We believe it is in society's best interest to thoroughly understand the concepts and be fore-warned of the changes that lie ahead.

High-Impact Inventions

Here are snapshots of a few highly probable inventions that our research tells us are likely to have a profound effect on the future:

Personality Services for Computers

The day is coming when we will be able to hold an intelligent conversation with our computer. But the novelty of a talking computer will quickly give way to the need for a more complicated human-like interaction. This need will give birth to a new industry: computers equipped with personality services.

Most people will subscribe to more than one online personality service, adding a new dimension to the human-computer interface. If, for example, you were to subscribe to a David Letterman personality service, suddenly your computer voice would start sounding like David Letterman, interjecting jokes and wild comments. If your choice was a political pundit personality such as Rush Limbaugh or Geraldine Ferraro, you would be able to hold a stimulating conversation about current political topics. If you wanted to ask your computer about the news of the day, you could subscribe to a Tom Brokaw or Peter Jennings personality.

Personality services will be an interesting market to watch as celebrities leverage their name recognition even further and relative newcomers offer unique personality services at bargain prices.

Controlling the Brain

When a person's liver stops working, does it stop because the liver gives out or because the person's brain tells it to stop? This question is currently being debated by theorists in the medical community. We suspect that the answer lies somewhere in the feedback loop of impulses between the brain and the liver.

Many medical researchers believe that the brain has an override capability that can keep an organ functioning in spite of a "shut down" order. Possibly this brain function could become subject to conscious human control. One can speculate about possible ways to upload the brain's version of a batch file or lines of code to force the brain to override a shut-down signal and restart a dormant body function.

In the past, controlling the brain has always been accomplished through the use of drugs. Chemicals introduced into the body produced a chemical reaction to create the desired effect. In the future, this could be accomplished with medical algorithms, which means sending direct impulses to the brain to trigger the necessary override changes to a given body function. The advantage of algorithms over drugs is that there are no chemical side effects.

Uses for medicinal algorithms could include curing physical maladies such as color blindness or hearing loss, controlling appetite or desire for sweets, controlling addictions or illicit drug use, and improving stamina, memory, or reaction time.

Meat Grown from Plants

Researchers continue trying to develop hybrid plants to serve as meat substitutes, but a more direct breakthrough could soon yield pork, chicken, and beef plants.

In Boulder, Colorado, a company called Somatogen is in a competitive race to produce the first FDA approved artificial blood product. Plants grown using this blood as the primary source of nutrition (instead of water) could begin to exhibit a mammalian type of growth. There may also be other biocloning formulations that will accomplish the same thing. And there is definitely a ready market for plant-grown beef among vegetarians and cardiac patients.

Therapeutic Amnesia

Inducing amnesia will be beneficial in certain situations. It will be accomplished through a technology that methodically reverses the memory distribution algorithm used by the part of the human brain known as the hippocampus. In effect, memory will be "overwritten" to cancel out days, months, or years of a person's life. Therapeutic amnesia will become a unique mental-health treatment.

An induced memory loss that erases a traumatic period of someone's life may be effective therapy for victims of brutal crimes or child abuse. It may even be refined to a point where regression techniques can be used to erase distant memories and dramatically shift a person's emotional base.

Births without Mothers

Imagine the sales pitch for an artificial womb:

"We offer you childbirth without pain, stretch marks, and morning sickness. We will bring your baby to term in a perfectly safe environment, with a scientifically superior diet, in an artificial womb receiving fetal stimulation that you select, ranging from music to audio books to mathematical problem solving.

Yoshinori Kuwabara, a Japanese scientist, has already developed an artificial womb capable of incubating goat fetuses for three weeks until birth. It consists of a clear plastic box filled with amniotic fluid at body temperature and connected to an array of devices to sustain vital body functions. The fetus lies submerged in a "womb" that replaces oxygen and cleans the fetus's blood with a dialysis machine connected to the umbilical cord.

Kuwabara has expressed caution about the prospects for "no pain" childbirth. His initial goal is to reduce the age of human fetal viability for premature births. Currently, premature babies reach the age of viability at about 22 weeks in the womb.

An incubator capable of preserving a 10-week-old fetus might also be capable of handling a one-week-old fetus. If so, the fetus might not need a human womb: Following fertilization in a petri dish, the growing embryo might be placed directly into the artificial womb.

Overlooked Ideas

There are also a number of significant technologies already invented but generally overlooked. Some concepts are already being developed; others may be tied up in legal or funding battles. Here are four ideas that are within the scope of current technology and have the potential to reshape the thinking in several industries:

Spherical Shaped Computer Display

Computers come in different colors and sizes, but all computer displays are limited to the same basic shape: the rectangular screen. This configuration hasn't substantially changed since Philo Farnsworth's invention of the television was commercialized in the 1950s. Some would say that operating a computer program with our present monitors is like trying to watch a baseball game through a knothole.

A spherical display will have unique applications for computer users who need to observe the surface of the earth or some other planet. Travel agents will easily plan and display complicated international itineraries by means of a true-shaped image of the earth. Meteorologists will broadcast a real-time global view of weather patterns that will appear on a globe sitting on your desk.

Disposable Money Cards

Inspired by the success of prepaid phone cards, credit-card companies may begin to market stored-value cards in various denominations as a low-tech conversion of cash to digital money. The "prepaid credit card" will be a use-once card that will be thrown away when its credit has been used. Credit-card companies can make this a profitable venture by creating a highly automated system for handling transactions and by charging higher discount rates or transaction fees for small purchases. This innovative card will make it possible for more people to have greater access to goods and services.

Web sites will be quick to accept the new prepaid cards. Many items that have been free on the Internet—such as downloads and plug-ins can then be priced at a nominal fee of $1 or $2. Consumers who are reluctant to use their credit cards online will have no fear of giving out their stored-value card number over the Internet because any potential loss will be limited to the face value of the new card—$10 or $20. Stored-value cards are destined to become the currency of cyberspace, opening up a new market to children who previously could not make Internet purchases.

Computers That Read Aloud

Systems already exist for visually tracking eye movement; at the same time, talking computers are making inroads. It won't be long before we have a device that combines these technologies in order to pronounce words as a reader reads them. Such devices will have tremendous value in teaching students to read and to understand foreign languages. They will also create a multisensory learning experience for anyone reading a book, vastly improving levels of information retention.

Underground Steam Irrigation

In traditional surface-irrigation, water soaks down into the ground. By contrast, underground steam irrigation will force a pressurized mist up to the land surface through an extensive array of high-intensity nozzles. Steam is first blasted through to the surface by a pressure pump boiler; once the steam channels have been cut, a more traditional jet-spray form of irrigation takes place.

Underground steam irrigation will have no moving parts or lines other than remotely controlled pumps and valves. Once the system is trenched into a field it should provide maintenance-free service for many years; it will also control the surface temperature of crops during freezing weather and warm the ground for earlier crop germination.

 Article Review Form at end of book.

Are you an information consumer or producer? According to Besser, why does the difference matter?

From Internet to Information Superhighway

Howard Besser

In 1994 the mass media began devoting increased coverage to the impending arrival of the information superhighway. Readers of newspapers and popular magazines were repeatedly exposed to rosy predictions of increased access to information, improvement of education and health care, and a diversity in home entertainment that would all come from the promised "500 channels" of information.

While these social and recreational benefits might be a possible result of increased channel capacity, they are certainly not the inevitable outcome that the mass media would have us believe. Technological developments do not in themselves provide widespread social benefits. Both technology and social benefits are shaped by social forces that operate on a much broader level. We need only look at similar predictions in the recent past to see that the benefits promised by a greater channel capacity may prove to be a hollow promise.

The 1967 report of the President's Task Force on Communications Policy made a series of recommendations on the role that should be served by emerging cable television systems. The industry should be structured

to cater to as wide a variety of tastes as possible, the tastes of small audiences and mass audiences, of cultural minorities and of cultural majorities. Television should serve as varied as possible an array of social functions, not only entertainment and advertising . . . but also information, education, business, culture, and political expression. . . . Television should provide an effective means of local expression and local advertising, to preserve the values of localism, and to help build a sense of community. . . . [P]olicy should guard against excessive concentration in the control of communications media. (United States 1967)

A February 1973 report on the future of cable TV by the National Science Foundation was enthusiastic about what cable TV would offer:

Public access channels available to individual citizens and community groups. . . . Churches, Boy Scouts, minority groups, high school classes, crusaders for causes—can create and show their own programs. With public access, cable can become a medium for local action instead of a distributor of prepackaged mass-consumption programs to a passive audience. New services to individual subscribers, such as televised college courses and continuing education classes in the home. Cable's capability for two-way communication between viewer and studio may in time permit doctors to participate in clinical seminars at distant hospitals, or enable viewers to register their opinions on local issues. . . . Public and private institutions might build their own two-way cable networks or lease channels to send x-rays among hospitals, exchange computer data, and hold televised conferences. (Baer 1973, 2)

They listed key features that cable would offer including: "Instruction for homebound and institutionalized persons, Preschool education, High school and post-secondary degree courses in the home, Career education and in-service training, Community information programming, Community information centers, and Municipal closed-circuit applications." (Baer 1973, 6)

The predictions made for cable television more than two decades ago sound remarkably like the predictions being made for the information superhighway today. When listening to today's predictions, we should keep in mind how empty those promises proved for cable.

The Internet vs. the Information Superhighway

Popular discourse would have us believe that the information superhighway will just be a faster, more powerful version of the Internet. But there are key differences between these two entities, and in many ways they are based on diametrically opposed models.

Flat Fee vs. Pay Per Use

Most Internet users are either not charged to access information or pay a low flat fee. The information superhighway, on the other hand, will likely be based upon a pay-per-use model. On a gross level, one might say that the payment model for the Internet is closer to that of broadcast (or perhaps cable) television while the model for the information superhighway is likely to be more like that of pay-per-view TV.

Flat-fee arrangements encourage exploration. Users in flat-fee environments navigate through webs of information and tend to make serendipitous discoveries. Pay-per-use environments give users the incentive to focus their attention on what they know they already want, or to look for well-known items previously recommended by others. In pay-per-use environments, people tend to follow more traditional paths of discovery and seldom explore unexpected avenues. Pay-per-use environments discourage browsing. Imagine how a person's reading habits would change if they had to pay for each article they looked at in a magazine or newspaper.

Yet many of the most interesting things we learn about or find come from following unknown routes, bumping into things we weren't looking for. And people who have to pay each time they use a piece of information are likely to increasingly rely upon specialists and experts. For example, in a situation where the reader will have to pay to read each paragraph of background on Bosnia, she is more likely to rely upon State Department summaries instead of paying to become more generally informed herself. And in the 1970s and 1980s the library world learned that the introduction of expensive pay-per-use databases discouraged individual exploration and introduced the need for intermediaries who specialized in searching techniques.

Privacy

The metering that will have to accompany pay-per-view on the information superhighway will need to track everything that an individual looks at (in case she wants to challenge the bill). It will also give governmental agencies the opportunity to monitor reading habits. Many times in the past the FBI has tried to view library circulation records to see who has been reading which books. In an on-line environment, service providers can track everything a user has bought, read, or even looked at.

In an age when people engage in a wide variety of activities on line, service providers will amass a wealth of demographic and consumption information on each individual. This information will be sold to other organizations that will use it in their marketing campaigns. Some organizations are already using computers and telephone messaging systems to experiment with this kind of demographic targeting. For example, in mid-1994, *Rolling Stone* magazine announced a new telephone-based ordering system for music albums. After using previous calls to build "a profile of each caller's tastes . . . custom messages will alert them to new releases by their favorite artists or recommend artists based on previous selections" (Laura Evenson, "Phone Service Previews Albums," *San Francisco Chronicle*, June 30, 1994). Some of the early experiments promoted as tests of interactive services on the information superhighway were actually designed to gather demographic data on users ("Interacting at the Jersey Shore: Future-Vision Courts Advertisers for Bell Atlantic's Test in Toms River," *Advertising Age*, May 9, 1994).

Producers vs. Consumers

On the Internet anyone can be an information provider or an information consumer. On the information superhighway most people will be relegated to the role of information consumer.

Because services like movies-on-demand will drive the technological development of the information superhighway, movies' need for high bandwidth into the home and only narrow bandwidth coming back out will likely dominate (see Howard Besser, "Movies on Demand May Significantly Change the Internet," *Bulletin of the American Association for Information Science*, October 1994). Metaphorically, this will be like a ten-lane highway coming into the home, with only a tiny path leading back out—just wide enough to take a credit card number or to answer multiple-choice questions.

This kind of asymmetrical design implies that only a limited number of sites will have the capability of outputting large volumes of bandwidth onto the information superhighway. If such a configuration becomes prevalent, this is likely to have several far-reaching results: it will inevitably lead to some form of gatekeeping. Managers of those sites will control all high-volume material that can be accessed. And for reasons of scarcity, politics, taste, or corporate preference, they will make decisions on a regular basis as to what material will be made accessible and what will not. This kind of model resembles broadcast or cable television much more than it does today's Internet.

The scarcity of outbound bandwidth will discourage individuals and small groups from becoming information producers and will further solidify their role as information consumers. "Interactivity" will be defined as responding to multiple-choice questions and entering credit card numbers on a keypad. It should come as no surprise that some of the major players trying to build the information superhighway are those who introduced televised home shopping.

Information vs. Entertainment

The telecommunications industry continues to insist that functions such as entertainment and home shopping will be the driving forces behind the construction of the information superhighway. Yet there is a growing body of evidence that suggests that consumers want more information-related services, and would be more willing to pay for these than for movies-on-demand,

video games, or home-shopping services.

Two surveys published in October 1994 had very similar findings. According to the *Wall Street Journal* (Bart Ziegler, "Interactive Options May Be Unwanted, Survey Indicates," October 5, 1994), a Lou Harris poll found that

a total of 63% of consumers surveyed said they would be interested in using their TV or PC to receive health-care information, lists of government services, phone numbers of businesses and non-profit groups, product reviews and similar information. In addition, almost three-quarters said they would like to receive a customized news report, and about half said they would like some sort of communications service, such as the ability to send messages to others. But only 40% expressed interest in movies-on-demand or in ordering sports programs, and only about a third said they want interactive shopping.

A survey commissioned by *Macworld* (Charles Piller, "Dreamnet," *Macworld*, October 1994) claims to be "one of the most extensive benchmarks of consumer demand for interactive services yet conducted"; this survey found that "consumers are much more interested in using emerging networks for information access, community involvement, self-improvement, and communication, than for entertainment." Out of a total of 26 possible on-line capabilities, respondents rated video-on-demand tenth, with only 28 percent indicating that this service was highly desirable. Much more desirable activities included on-demand access to reference materials, distance learning, interactive reports on local schools, and access to information about government services and train-

ing. Thirty-four percent of the sample was willing to pay over $10 per month for distance learning, yet only 19 percent was willing to pay that much for video-on-demand or other entertainment services.

If people say they desire informational services more than entertainment and shopping (and say that they're willing to pay for it), why does the telecommunications industry continue to focus on plans oriented toward entertainment and shopping? Because the industry believes that, in the long run, this other set of services will prove more lucrative. After all, there are numerous examples in other domains of large profits made from entertainment and shopping services but very few such examples from informational services.

It is also possible that the industry believes that popular opinion can easily be shifted from favoring informational services to favoring entertainment and shopping. For several years telecommunications industry supporters have been attempting to gain support for deregulation of that industry by citing the wealth of interesting informational services that would be available if this industry was freed from regulatory constraints. Sectors of the industry may well believe that the strength of consumer desire for the information superhighway to meet information needs (as shown in these polls) is a result of this campaign. According to this argument, if popular opinion can be swayed in one direction, it can be shifted back in the other direction.

Mass Audience

A significant amount of material placed on the Internet is designed to reach a single person, a handful of people, or a group of less than 1,000. Yet commercial distributors planning to use the information superhighway will have to reach tens (or more likely hundreds) of thousands of users merely to justify the costs of mounting multimedia servers and programs. This will inevitably result in a shifting away from the Internet's orientation towards small niche audiences; the information superhighway will be designed for a mass audience (and even niche markets will be mass markets created by joining enough small regional groups together to form a national or international mass market).

Because distributors will view their audience as a mass audience, a number of results are likely. First of all, information distributors will favor uncontroversial programs, for fear of alienating part of their audience. In recent years we have seen the extreme version of this, where controversial programs have actually been eliminated from network television and radio, cable, local broadcast stations, and even art museums due to pressure from various organizations. Perhaps less obvious is the fact that the overwhelming majority of programming focuses on elements that appeal to most people but don't offend anyone (the least common denominator); this focus is due to the orientation toward a mass audience.

For similar reasons, programs designed for mass consumption will be favored over those perceived as having a relatively narrow appeal. The result is likely to be a lack of diversity and an emphasis on whatever has mass appeal. For an example of possible long-term results from this phenomenon, we can examine the forces affecting bookstores and video stores around the country. Beginning in the late 1980s, independent book and video stores have been rapidly replaced by chain stores. Independents tend to offer a widely diverse material and in some ways use popular, mass-appeal items to subsidize more esoteric works. Chains, on the other hand, tend to carry little other than popular items. Because of the economics of scale realized by stressing mass-appeal items, chains are putting the independents out of business, and it is getting more difficult to find items that don't have mass appeal. If this carries over onto the information superhighway, we can expect that what may start out as diverse offerings will, for economic reasons, soon turn into relatively bland and homogeneous programs with mass appeal.

Other parts of the mass formula have parallels with book and video stores. Upholding a tradition they share with libraries, independent bookstores tend to take strong stands against censorship. Chain stores, on the other hand, tend to "not want to offend" and avoid carrying controversial items. (For example, after the death threat to Salman Rushdie, many independents carried both books and displays of *The Satanic Verses*, while most chains refused to even carry it.)

Chain stores tend to deal almost exclusively with major publishers and distributors who can offer them better, volume discounts and less paperwork. Independents tend to be one of the few venues for small presses or independent videos. A decade ago we saw legislative attempts to favor large studio film and video productions over independent productions in proposals to "tax" blank tapes (see, for example, "Tax on Home Videotaping Is Urged," *The New York Times*, April 22, 1982; Ernest Holsendolph, "Legislative Plan to Tax Video Recording Gear," *The New York Times*, March 12, 1982; William Raspberry, "No to the Betamax Tax," *The Washington Post*, April 29, 1983; and Lardner (1987)). While these efforts were designed to compensate major producers for illegal copying, in effect they amounted to an attempted fund transfer from independent producers (who spent a more significant percentage of their budget on blank tape) to the large studios who were to receive the "tax" distribution based upon perceived market share.

Independents tend to be close to their community and cater to particular tastes within their community. Chains, on the other hand, tend to focus on national tastes and not carry many items that may cater to primarily local or regional tastes. Some chains have been accused of trying to impose their perception of national tastes upon local communities. Blockbuster, for example, refuses to carry programs it deems controversial because of sexual or political themes, even in communities that do not find those themes offensive (see, for example, "Blockbuster to Shun Video of 'The Last Temptation,'" *The Wall Street Journal*, June 23, 1989; and "Blockbuster," *San Francisco Weekly*, March 29, 1991).

At the same time they carry movies of a violent nature even in communities that find these themes offensive. For a generation, this same mass formula allowed broadcast television to dominate the discourse over what constitutes national taste. This is likely to carry over onto the information superhighway, with video-on-demand service providers imposing their national standards upon each local community they enter. Information providers will claim that this is done for purely economic reasons—that it is not cost-justifiable to spend a fortune digitizing and mounting a program that will be of interest only to a few communities. But this amounts to censorship by economics.

Changing Access and Relationship to Culture

As discussed above, cultural options available in an on-line environment will be dominated by mass-market productions that do not offend. But as more and more people rely on on-line access to culture, this shift is also likely to have a great effect on how people view culture, as well as on the perception and internal workings of our cultural repositories (such as museums and libraries).

As it becomes more and more convenient to view high-quality representations of cultural objects (and accompanying explanatory information) on the home computer, people are likely to visit museums less frequently. As more and more people access representations of museum objects without entering the edifice, the authority of the museum (and its personnel) will rapidly erode. In libraries, we are already beginning to see that the people who have traditionally served as caretakers of on-site collections are instead becoming designers of *access* to collections that may reside either on or off site. And as people gain the ability to seek information without the direct help of museum and library personnel, we are seeing a drastic diminution of their role as intermediaries.

As individuals look at more and more cultural objects on their workstation screens, it is likely that they will begin to confuse the representations with the original objects they represent. This is part of a general leveling effect (equating abstracts of experiences for the experiences themselves) that appears to be an integral part of contemporary life. This is not unlike viewing a video and equating that experience with watching a film in a theater—or eating at McDonald's and calling it a meal. Although in an on-line system more people gain greater access to a certain range of cultural objects, this kind of access eliminates a richness and depth of experience—what Walter Benjamin, in his classic essay "The Work of Art in the Age of Mechanical Reproduction," called the "aura" of a unique work of art.

The widespread viewing of digital images poses interesting authenticity and authorship questions. Because digital images can be seamlessly altered, how can the viewer be sure that the image on view has not been manipulated? A number of magazines have placed purposely altered images on their covers (*Time*'s June 24, 1994, darkened mug shot of O. J. Simpson, *Newsday*'s February 16, 1994, photo falsely showing Tonya Harding and Nancy Kerrigan skating together, *Spy*'s February 1993 shot of Hillary Clinton in a bondage outfit, and *Mirabella*'s September 1994 composite photo of several models' faces). Although in the above examples the magazines admitted (often in tiny print) that they altered the photos, in the future we are likely to see ever more such alterations without the publishers alerting the audience.

Having images of cultural objects widely available on line in the home is likely to lead to a pro-liferation of derivative art works based upon the on-line works. The ease of altering these digital images will lead individuals to make changes to them and incorporate them into larger works in a collagelike process. What we have seen with clip art and desktop publishing is likely to significantly increase as continuous-tone images of cultural objects become widely available.

When someone alters an existing image, this raises interesting questions as to who is the creator of the new work: the creator of the original work, the person who altered it, or a combination of the two? In anticipation of the widespread availability of digital works on line, copyright holders of existing images have attempted to strongly assert their intellectual property rights over works in other domains. In recent court cases Disney made R. Crumb stop using a mouse in his comic strips, a photographer won a multimillion-dollar judgment over Jeff Koons for "copying" his photograph of a man cradling a large litter of puppies, and the copyright holders of a song won a judgment against a rap group who incorporated pieces of "Pretty Woman" into one of their recordings.

Today, ownership of intellectual property rights of digital images of cultural objects is considered a great investment opportunity. The highly inflated price paid for Paramount Communications and Bill Gates's establishment of Continuum Productions to buy up electronic reproduction rights of images were early shots in what will become an economic battle over the ownership of content.

If it continues (as is likely, given the strong economic incentives in an on-line digital domain), this strong assertion of intellectual property rights will have a chilling effect upon future artistic endeavors. Postmodern art, especially, relies upon the recycling of images from the past, and the strong assertion of intellectual property rights will keep much material out of the hands of future artists. The strong assertion of intellectual property rights also has the potential of eliminating satire and will serve to limit social, political, and artistic commentary—all of which rely on being able to represent the domain that they are reacting against.

As it becomes easier and easier to obtain images and documents on-line in the home, it is possible that people will download and copy these somewhat indiscriminately. The advent of the photocopy machine led researchers to become less discriminating and to copy articles of only marginal interest. This led to a glut of paper in researchers' homes and offices. Word processing led to the generation of paper drafts each time a slight change to the text was made. In a similar way, on-line access to full-text documents and digital images may lead people to accumulate items of only marginal interest. And the proliferation of images (both those available and those accumulated) may lead to a reduction in meaning and context for all of them. This leveling effect (floating in an infinite sea of images) is a likely result of information overload—we are already seeing traces of it as people are caught in the web of the Internet, not being able to discriminate between valuable and worthless information, and not seeing the context of any given piece of information.

In a way, the on-line environment of the future is the logical extension of postmodernism. As in previous incarnations (like MTV), most of our images come from the media. The images are reprocessed and recycled. In the postmodern tradition, all images (and viewpoints) have equal value; in an on-line world they're all ultimately bits and bytes. Everything is ahistorical and has no context.

It is interesting to examine the development of technological communications from generation to generation. From the radio generation to the television generation to the MTV generation to the coming virtual-reality generation, we can see a steady progression incorporating an ever quicker pace and relying on the stimulation of a larger number of senses.

One of the identifying characteristics of the information age is to get people directly to the information they need without exposing them to tangentially interesting or relevant material. Information science research in the 1980s and 1990s has focused on tailoring information to user profiles and techniques borrowed from the artificial-intelligence community in order to avoid subjecting the user to information overload. But this approach devalues serendipitous discovery.

And as this approach comes to dominate, it will help reinforce the nation (promoted by various forms of technology) that chance encounters should be avoided.

From the distribution of mass-produced goods to providing a choice of movies to watch and when to watch them (rather than relying upon our local cinema), technology has always promised us more predictable, controllable experiences. In an era when most people feel pressed for time and fearful of chance encounters in a hostile world, they shun public spaces and turn to experiences that involve fewer unpredictable interactions.

Over time, our experiences with technology are replacing public spaces and human interaction. Channel-surfing on a couch in front of a 500-channel television minimizes the chance and often dangerous encounters that might take place "window shopping" past inner-city movie theaters. And computer-based "virtual" experiences (including "virtual sex") will provide us with experiences that are more predictable, less serendipitous, and less interesting than human interaction.

References

Baer, Walter S. 1973. Cable Television: A Summary Overview for Local Decision Making. National Science Foundation Research Applied to National Needs Program, 134-NSF. Santa Monica: Rand (February).

Lardner, James. 1987. *Fast Forward: Hollywood, the Japanese, and the Onslaught of the VCR.* New York: Norton.

United States. 1967. President's Task Force on Communications Policy. Final Report (August 14). Washington: GPO. [Known as "the Rostow Report."]

 Article Review Form at end of book.

Which thinker's vision of the Information Highway is most appealing to you? To what extent has the vision been realized?

Seven Thinkers in Search of an Information Highway

**Amy Bruckman,
Michael Dertouzos,
Robert Domnitz,
Nathan Felde,
Mitchell Kapor,
Martyn Roetter
and Michael Schrage**

The information highway has been a godsend to politicians and journalists. The term fits in a headline, evokes endless metaphors and puns, and encompasses such a grand sweep of technologies and national policy questions that virtually everyone has a reason to be interested in it. In fact, the questions that arise on the topic cover such a span of disciplines that it is difficult to find any one person who is an "expert" on the subject.

So we found seven prominent technologist/thinkers and put them together. The panelists represented the major sectors—industry, academia, nonprofit organizations, government, the press—that are working to craft this major piece of the global soci-

ety. The discussion took place not in the cool of cyberspace but rather the old-fashioned way: elbow-to-elbow around a table, with plenty of eye contact, interruptions, and raised voices.

The conversation, moderated by senior editor Herb Brody, was spirited, often eloquent, and occasionally heated. (Had we not pulled the plug after two hours, it seemed, our seven pioneers would have talked long into the evening.) If this thoughtful group produced more questions than answers, more problems than solutions, more mysteries than clues, that result merely reflects the complexity of the endeavor before them and the richness of the choices that technology is presenting us as a society.

TR: Two different visions of an information highway seem to be emerging. There's Vice-President Al Gore's view, where we all have access to libraries and vast databases through our personal computers. Meanwhile, the cable TV and telephone companies are moving forward with

entertainment-oriented systems that offer things like video on demand, home shopping, and games. Which information highway are we going to get?

Domnitz: It's almost inevitable that the private sector is going to be doing the heavy lifting on the development of infrastructure. Since the private sector is going to respond only to economic incentives, the services offered initially will be entertainment. But to put in the infrastructure necessary for such profit-making activities, the private sector needs access to public assets. Cable TV operators and telephone companies need rights of way. Broadcasters need spectrum space. And the government, representing the public interest, will probably decide that certain benefits should be provided to the public in return. So educational and public-service kinds of uses will come into the picture.

Felde: That sounds a little too neat, and unlikely. We'll get the information infrastructure that we pay for, and it won't be all things to all people. If it is driven opportunistically by one or two big revenue sources, like movies on demand, then it will be a different network than if it is deployed more to allow people to attend college classes remotely.

Dertouzos: The information infrastructure will reflect our society the way we function today—a certain amount of private-sector activity, a certain amount of political and educational and public-service work. TV-based recreation, with movies and home shopping and so on, is where it will start. After all, there are 80-million-plus TV sets in the United States. The cable TV companies are going to come in with a system that offers very little interaction. Information like movies or the L. L. Bean catalogue will mostly flow one-way—from a central source to you. But the information market that I envision is a medium where every person and every organization would be able to buy, sell, and exchange freely information and information services.

Kapor: Michael, why do you emphasize buying and selling as the archetypal service? Noneconomic uses, like coordination of activities for political or educational purposes, are as important, if not more important, and none of them will be possible on a one-way system designed to deliver lowest-common-denominator, mass-market entertainment.

Dertouzos: The reason I say buy and sell is because 80 percent of our $6 trillion GNP is information-related. I also say "exchange freely."

Kapor: But if people don't understand that this is about more than business, and about more than the private sector making a lot of money as industry

boundaries dissolve and realign, then we're going to miss an enormous opportunity to revitalize democratic values in society. It is all too easy to substitute an economically or technically focused discussion for what ought to be first a political and cultural discussion.

Dertouzos: Actually, the political and cultural effects will transcend buying and selling. To me, the primary feature of a true information infrastructure is the shrinking of geographical distance and the elimination of political boundaries. Think about what this means for the notion of national identity. I'm Greek. There are 9 million of us in Greece, 2 million on the East Coast of the United States, 1 million in Australia, a couple of million elsewhere in the world. Maybe it's not the Greek nation anymore. Maybe it's the Greek network. This assaults head-on the national boundaries that shaped so much of our history and that led to so many wars. People talk about an NII—a national information infrastructure. I think we should drop the "N." It's very parochial to be thinking only of a U.S. infrastructure.

TR: But whether the goal is an NII or a global information highway, we don't want to end up with a system that divides into information haves and information have-nots. How can we ensure universal access?

Domnitz: We have to distinguish between two concepts here. Access to the conduit for, say, a conversation between you and me is not necessarily the same as access to information itself—which might mean, especially, a conversation between a database and me. We do want to make sure that information is available to all. But to allow unlimited con-

versation at essentially no cost—that may cost more than society can afford to pay.

Bruckman: Oh, I disagree. One of the really exciting things about what is going on is that we're moving away from the idea that truth is contained only in libraries and official databases. People are realizing that truth is created by communities of people. Here's a personal example. I keep tropical fish, and sometimes I need some information about their care and feeding. Yes, I could go to the library and pore through a book on tropical fish—but I'll probably never find the right answer to my question. Or, I can post a message on the Usenet newsgroup alt.aquaria, and someone will respond in three minutes with exactly the information that I need. The network is changing our basic notion of the nature of information. We can't think of information and community as separate concepts any more.

Felde: Sure, but just because information is posted on the Internet as an immediate answer to a question doesn't guarantee that it's true. You might be putting something toxic in the fish tank as a result of some prankster's advice. What you're talking about sounds to me more like consensus than truth. The major "truth" that I see is that the advance in telecommunications technology has led people to expect a lot more than they used to as basic service. My two-year-old daughter used to come by our laboratory and use our videoconferencing system to talk with my colleagues. We didn't have a television in our home at the time—when we finally bought one, my daughter expected it to be as responsive as the one she had been using. She has developed the expectation that television allows direct communication with people who respond directly to you.

Dertouzos: I firmly believe that without explicit, vigilant attention by society, the information infrastructure will tend to increase the gap between rich and poor. First, there will be a disparity with respect to nations—Bangladesh is not going to have as sophisticated an information highway as the United States, Japan, or Germany. And as much as we'd like to theorize about educational applications and so on, the people in the inner city will not necessarily be able to afford these services. Not only that, but many will lack the educational background that would enable them to use the network even if they could afford it.

Kapor: Cyberspace clearly needs an Andrew Carnegie. The public library system that we have today is supported by taxes, but it didn't start out that way. Carnegie endowed 2,000 libraries and gave such a jump-start to the notion that every community should have its own library that in a fairly short period of time, people accepted the idea. But even if initially the support for these information services comes philanthropically, eventually it will be supported out of a tax base. And it's not just a matter of putting in wires—software is going to have to be built that enables whatever level of free access we as a society decide to provide. The analog to Carnegie's libraries today is not to create some sort of new physical repository where there are computer terminals that you could come to. Many libraries are doing that, and that's a good thing as a transition. But it suggests that there's some level of service that is basic and ought to be available free to all citizens.

Roetter: We should keep in mind that public financing doesn't ensure equal access. Libraries, for instance, are locally funded. There are some very good libraries in Massachusetts, but some of the less wealthy towns have practically closed their libraries altogether. There's also the question of what devices people have in their homes to hook up to this network. Only about 25 percent of households now have a personal computer.

Domnitz: Look at the current public telephone network. Most people feel that telephone service is affordable, but it's not free and therefore not "universal." How can public policy deal with that?

Kapor: Maybe it doesn't have to—at least, not in terms of cost alone. In California, most people who don't have phones have made that decision for noneconomic reasons—a lot of them are illegal aliens and they're afraid if they get a phone that immigration is going to come and deport them. Meanwhile, 98 percent of U.S. households have TVs (only 93 percent have telephones) and all those people in the 98 percent paid for their TVs—television is important enough that people go out and actually spend money on it.

TR: What do people want from the information highway? The interactive TV systems now being tested by cable and telephone companies seem a lot like the "videotex" trials that bombed in the early 1980s. Have consumer demands changed significantly since then?

Schrage: Actually, those tests revealed enormous consumer demand—but for communications, not for getting your newspaper delivered to the TV set.

Dertouzos: Figuring out what people want should not be a total mystery. There are systems out there that we can look at. France's Minitel, for instance, has 5 million users and 15,000 services. Minitel's most common use is as an electronic yellow pages. Number two, surprisingly, is matching freight carriers to freight. The third most popular use is purchasing tickets—for trains, theaters, and various events. The fourth application is what they call "romance." In this country, we have Prodigy. Its top services seem to be news, weather, stock market information, a little bit of electronic shopping, and a lot of e-mail.

Felde: And let's not limit the users to typing on keyboards or punching video remote controllers. There are 25 million camcorders out there in this country. So lots of people will be able to feed their home videos onto the network. This represents an alternate form of movie making, more closely connected to family and community than to watching "Beverly Hills Cop 9." By home videos, I mean videos about life. These are the visual phone calls of the people, by the people, and for the people. Let ordinary people plug their camcorders into each other's televisions over the public network.

Roetter: But since the technology is still embryonic, it's quite possible that the real uses of an information highway will be quite different from what we are looking at today. In general, the people who invent things don't understand how they're going to be used. A century ago, some people were convinced that a major use of telephones would be listening to opera in their homes.

TR: Despite the blizzard of media coverage about the information highway, don't we really lack a vision of what the system itself should be?

Kapor: We have a vision, but it's the wrong one. Any vision of the information superhighway that focuses on video-on-demand and home shopping rather than on providing cyberspace with its equivalent of Andrew Carnegie is too narrow. The first-order issue ought to be: what are we shooting for as a society? How are we conceiving of this great project that we are engaged in? My hope is that we reach a consensus for the system to be open, inclusive, egalitarian, and decentralized, and that it be based in the private sector so that investments can be matched with the possibility of reward. Common sense suggests that if you make something too much of an entitlement before you give businesspeople a chance to recoup an investment in what they do—let's cut right to the bottom line of what capitalism worries about here—it's going to be an unhappy situation.

Dertouzos: It's all well and good to discuss how to configure the information highway so that it provides the best social value. But at this stage of the game, we should be concentrating mainly on developing fundamental technologies. Then we will have the technical means to address many of the social and political problems that arise in the future. Historically, this is how it has usually worked. Radar, for example, was developed as a weapon of war, and then, through no intention of its inventors, became the cornerstone of modern air transportation.

Felde: Yes, and in fact the metaphoric model for the information highway—the nation's interstate highway system—was conceived originally for national defense purposes. President Eisenhower didn't want to have trouble moving tanks around in tight, crooked, unpaved streets like they had in Europe. But if the interstate highway system had been built in the 1850s instead of the 1950s, it would have been eight lanes wide going west. Today we seem to be designing an information highway that has eight lanes back from out west—Hollywood—and leaves only a footpath from the home.

Bruckman: I strongly agree with Mitch that we need to develop a vision of where we want this technology to go. In that spirit, I'll tell you where we ought to start—in the schools. That's where we can develop a vision for what we as a society want.

Schrage: No! The last thing we need to do is turn innocent children into guinea pigs for the grandiloquent ambitions of technocrats. Schools would be the single worst place to experiment with the information highway. Let's have the Fortune 1000 suffer the pains of trying to apply leading-edge technology before we let thousands of inner city schools fall victim to people whose hearts are in the right place but who can't pull any of these things off.

Bruckman: Oh, Michael, come on. Do you want to hear real stories about the things that kids are doing on networks?

Schrage: I know those wonderful anecdotes. But I think they reflect a principle that's already been proven in the workplace if you pay more attention to people—any kind of attention—they perform better. So when people like you are in the schools, those kids do better, whether they're using computers or pen and paper.

Bruckman: I couldn't agree with you more. The real value is not in the technology, but in forging connections between people. All the things that are exciting right now in education involve using technology to forge connections between people.

Felde: The ability to connect with other people is especially important nowadays because of the dislocation of families. The information infrastructure must allow people to define, reconstitute, and create their own "family."

Dertouzos: We could have had a discussion like this 120 years ago about the telephone . . .

Schrage: Yeah, some visionary would be saying something crazy like, "Let's put a phone on every desk."

Dertouzos: . . . Some people would focus on education. Others would say, no, this technology is really best suited for use by doctors or in commerce. As we look at the telephone in retrospect, people talk through it about everything—about all the economic and personal things, tangible and intangible, that govern our lives. I believe that this is what is going to happen here. Education is going to pick up its societal share of somewhere between 5 and 8 percent of the uses. There's going to be commerce on this thing, there's going to be personal communication, business communication, x-rays from labs to the family doctor, orders from factories to suppliers, people buying consumer products. It will be all of what happens today in society, but a little bit faster and maybe, if we're lucky, a little easier. That's my vision—what I call the information market.

Kapor: By putting the word "market" in the title, you turn us into consumers when we're really citizens.

Dertouzos: Those things aren't mutually exclusive. You know what goes on in a flea market in Athens? You buy some things, you talk, you gossip, you have a drink.

Schrage: I agree. You know, Milton Friedman's most successful book was *Capitalism and Freedom,* not *Capitalism or Freedom.*

Kapor: But there's a fairly small window of time before we get massive deployment of whatever it is that gets deployed—it will certainly start this decade. And during this time, the meaning and ultimate form of it all is up for grabs. If you study the history of radio and television, it's full of bright promises. A bunch of idealistic but naive people talked about the great cultural opportunities inherent in each new medium. But their rhetoric wasn't connected with the kind of commercial investment that was actually going on. As a result, we wound up being disappointed in many respects.

Schrage: My basic response to that is: So what?

Kapor: Well, I'll tell you so what. We have a chance now to do something different. If we don't take the opportunity to try, I guarantee we'll wind up with some kind of vaster wasteland. One of the things that's gotten lost here is the notion of who we are as Americans. We're citizens. Our democratic tradition emphasizes the value of active participation in the shaping of one's society. If we have an information infrastructure that is highly open and decentralized and egalitarian and supports diversity, and that lets lots of people make lots of money, then it will create numerous opportunities for types of civic participation that do not

exist today. So the point is to tip the balance back in favor of those who do not have lots of money and lots of power by giving them more of an opportunity to have their voices heard—by each other, by their elected officials, by people in their community who may not share their views.

Let's put this in historical perspective. In the first decade of the republic—when the United States was a start-up—it was Alexander Hamilton versus Thomas Jefferson for the dominant vision of what kind of government we were to have. Hamilton won, and we wound up with a highly centralized society. To fuel the engine of economic growth and raise the standard of living, we had to have centralized corporations, like the railroads, U.S. Steel, and Standard Oil. But now there's an opportunity to have sort of a rematch, under very different conditions, between the principles of Jefferson and those of Hamilton. We have the ability, given the construction of a high-capacity information infrastructure, to do things in a decentralized fashion that does not require large institutions, either public or private.

TR: What's the Jeffersonian "game plan," then?

Kapor: It is to make sure that the information infrastructure that we build is a two-way, interactive network. When we get down to detail, of course, there are very legitimate questions, like, does everybody need a multi-megabit-per-second digital line going into their living room? We'll probably conclude that they could get by with less. But we can't make practical decisions like that until we share a vision for the information infrastructure and agree on its purpose.

TR: Could you tell us what kind of explicit government intervention you have in mind?

Kapor: I haven't said anything about intervention.

Schrage: "I haven't said anything about intervention," says the gentleman who sits on the panel that's advising the administration on the national information infrastructure! You are speaking as a member of a committee that is reporting to the vice-president of the United States. You're deputized! You're already intervening.

Kapor: But the committee might recommend doing nothing—it might say laissez-faire is terrific. The ends that regulators seek are, in my book, pretty admirable. But there's something about the means themselves that are troublesome. The FCC just came out with 700 pages of regulation about the cable television industry. There's something structurally wrong with that—it's as if the government has decided, without first having figured out what people really want, what the new genome is for cable television and that the industry should work it out. Look, I built a company that, when I left it as CEO, was doing $250 million a year. I'd be pretty hypocritical not to be a big supporter of the free market. The problem is that the free-market guys fall apart at exactly the same level as the regulators—that is, when things get large. My conclusion is that the real division in society is not between public and private, it's between big and little. Because when things get big, they get broken.

TR: In that case, you must be relieved that some of the big industry mergers have been called off. Bell Atlantic's plan to acquire cable giant Tele-Communications, Inc., would have taken bigness to a new level. But does the abandonment of this and other deals mean that the "convergence" between the communications and entertainment business is not as close at hand as pundits were predicting?

Schrage: It doesn't mean much that two enterprises like Bell Atlantic and TCI don't merge. The underlying trend remains that communications systems of all kinds are going digital. And since one digital bit is just like another, the phone companies and cable companies will inevitably commingle to some extent.

Roetter: Let's not confuse what we mean by convergence. Technological convergence is not the same as convergence of businesses. That [TCI chairman] John Malone and [Bell Atlantic CEO] Ray Smith don't get together proves only that common sense finally got through when they looked at the return on investment.

TR: Bell Atlantic claimed that new FCC restrictions on cable rates lowered TCI's value.

Roetter: Yes, but it seems ridiculous that these two great individualist pioneers should start blaming the government because they're not allowed to raise prices in monopoly markets whenever they want. Consumers have already shown that they're fed up with high cable prices and they're not going to pay any more. The companies are now using the government as a convenient scapegoat.

TR: Despite merger setbacks and possible regulatory problems, the United States seems to be leading the world in information highway technology.

Schrage: Yes, the Internet is a perfect example: other countries are feeding off the American investment. The tables have certainly turned. Five years ago people were holding this kind of roundtable discussion to talk about how we'd lost consumer electronics and semiconductors to Japan and were in danger of losing the computer industry. So a lot of the discussion about the information highway mirrors a general euphoria that for a change it is U.S. companies, and the kind of people who adhere to the American economic model, who are determining the global agenda in this.

TR: We've been talking about regulation of businesses that own and operate an information highway—but what about the need to restrict content?

Roetter: There are two basic models: the press, where content is traditionally unrestricted, and broadcasters, where content and ownership are regulated. I don't know what the answer is, but there has to be some melding or synthesis of those kinds of regulations.

Kapor: If you have a network with universal service, meaning everybody has the right to purchase a connection, and open access, which means everybody who wants to put information on to the system has a right to do that, then you're going to have skinheads and child pornographers doing it—it's not going to be only nice people.

Bruckman: That may be so, but I hope the government keeps entirely out of the business of regulating content. I get gigantically bored by all these articles about little Johnny seeing X-rated stuff on the network. I'm just not alarmed. People don't think they

can walk into just any old bar or cafe and feel comfortable. The same goes with information environments. The Net gives us this wonderful ability to join and create diverse communities. There are some places where you personally may not want to go.

Domnitz: The First Amendment of the Constitution has not been repealed.

Kapor: In cyberspace, it's a local ordinance. We should remember that the Bill of Rights is quite local to the United States.

TR: So maybe the answer is to make sure that all material on the information highway is properly labeled.

Kapor: As long as there's no national labeling standard.

Schrage: Why not? I think there should be a labeling standard.

Kapor: Because that's too centralized. Let there be a free market in rating services. The system should be designed so that anybody can create a rating guide according to their tastes and values.

Bruckman: Where you get conflict in today's on-line communities is when you have people playing by two different sets of rules. One person says: hey, you kicked me in the virtual face—what did you do that for? There's a real human being on the other side of this persona. But there should be places where it's OK to kick people in the face virtually and places where it's not. The question is, how do we develop shared expectations?

Felde: It's easy to create a space on a network or at your point of access to a network much like a "porch," where you carry out a semipublic, semiprivate negotiation. People can appear on this electronic porch, and discuss there whether they're going to go inside and join in, accepting the rules of conduct that apply in this setting.

Schrage: There's a danger of vigilante censorship, too. Say that somebody with access to the Net decides that certain kinds of representations are illegal or inappropriate—they might decide to release onto public bulletin boards a computer virus that would delete certain words or cover up certain images. You see police painting over graffiti—you could have that kind of thing in cyberspace as well.

TR: Many people these days complain of information overload and might say that access to every database in the world would complicate their lives even further. How are people going to be able to cope?

Dertouzos: I agree that we need to be able to control the info-junk that assaults us. There will be a billion computers in the world by the year 2010. Each computer will have 1,000 "objects" in it, however you want to define them. That's a trillion goodies floating around. So we do need defense from info-junk. But let's believe a little bit in our ability to control the amount of junk we're willing to look at. Today, you have access to every one of the world's millions of telephones. Do you call Bangladesh daily? No. You control what you do.

Schrage: You have two secretaries, don't you, Michael?

TR: And he doesn't use e-mail.

Dertouzos: That's right. I have been not using electronic mail since we invented it, in 1963. E-mail is an open duct to your central nervous system. It occu-

pies the brain and reduces productivity. Machines don't do the work, as they should. You do the work.

Domnitz: Maybe there will be a trillion "objects," but I don't think there will be any more ideas floating around nowadays than there were 10 or 20 years ago. What's proliferating is the expression of those ideas in language that shows up on an e-mail screen. But the number of ideas that we need to convey to each other in the course of a day—it's still a very low number.

Schrage: That's why the Information Age is a misnomer. The technologies involved really affect relationships. The most successful ad campaign the old Bell system ever ran was "reach out and touch someone"—not reach out and inform someone. And we all have our own media wardrobe. Some people are great at meetings, some people are great on the phone, some people relate best through e-mail, some people do well in the kinds of virtual communities that Amy runs. Michael Dertouzos has made a decision not to use e-mail. That would cripple me. That's going to be one of the interesting asynchronies that emerge. There will be some people who you lose touch with because they don't use media or interact with their media in the same way that you do with yours.

Felde: I prefer to think in terms of an information "metabolism," because we don't just process data—we use information to build something, like a community. We add value. And just like in biological metabolism, some of what gets generated in the process of building is waste. Yet even much of this waste may be used by someone else in ways that you never intended.

Bruckman: Picking up on the metaphor of metabolism, it's important to not allow it to be all-consuming—technologies are encouraging the trend for us all to drop the boundaries between our personal and work lives. I was talking with my family the other day about beepers and cellular phones. My mother said, aren't these things wonderful—what if you're an executive who is able to go to your kid's school play in the evening only because you've got a cellular phone so the office can stay in touch with you? My response was: maybe I could have just gone to the play anyway, without a cellular phone. Maybe the business decision or whatever it was could have waited until the next morning. As Miss Manners, the arbiter of all wisdom, says, true importance comes from having reached a stage at which one mustn't be disturbed. Technology is making it harder for people to sometimes just be unavailable.

Dertouzos: There's no doubt that we're going to get an infrastructure coupling people. But if that's all it does, we will not have gained anything in productivity. Look at the analogy of work machinery. Backhoes and bulldozers took over what our muscles used to do, and now we don't have to do so much digging. I haven't seen the information bulldozers or the information backhoes yet. I see my colleagues using shovels, and using them much more frantically as the e-mail comes in.

Bruckman: You all know the story of the vacuum cleaner? You'd think that a machine like that would make less work for people. Not so. In the old days, the entire family would get together once or twice a year, take the rugs outside, and beat them. After the invention of the vacuum cleaner, the standard of cleanliness went up. People bought into the notion that they needed to clean the house much more often.

Schrage: The technology became a form of obligation in the same way that e-mail can be a form of obligation.

Bruckman: The question is, are we on the verge of the same kind of situation as with the vacuum cleaner, and if so, is there anything we can do about it?

Schrage: Hire servants.

TR: What if, tomorrow, you were named information highway czar. In that position, you'd have to act on pending decisions and formulate policy. What would you do? What would your priorities be?

Kapor: Unfortunately, it's a lot easier to make good policy by preventing bad things than by enabling good things. So if you want pragmatic advice, I'd say: kill the Clipper chip. The Clipper embodies an attempt by the Clinton administration to force-feed a crippled encryption technology into the telephone network. Copies of the keys that are used to decode information are kept in escrow by the federal government, so law-enforcement agencies will still be able to tap phone calls when they get a court order. The chip uses a secret encryption algorithm developed by the National Security Agency, and there's no guarantee it doesn't have a trap door that makes it possible to listen in without the escrow keys. My second act would be to urge anybody who has a dream or vision for the global information infrastructure to get on the Internet and try to build part of it—now. Take some direct action. Because I'm becoming less and less optimistic that the private sector will, left to itself, build the kind of infrastructure that's best for the citizens of the country. So I'd say carpe diem.

Schrage: I have three suggestions. First, eliminate software patents. Intellectual property issues are going to become more and more important, but the attempts to enforce software patents create more problems than they solve. Second, in the interests of promoting accessibility, the government should make sure that any telecommunications carrier that does not provide nondiscriminatory access is disadvantaged in the marketplace—maybe through a higher tax rate, maybe through denial of government contracts. Third, forbid the proliferation of computers in the public schools, which have failed to effectively assimilate and adopt them. If there is some sort of revolution in the schools that turns them inside out and upside down, then perhaps the role of technology in the schools could be reevaluated.

Bruckman: I believe that the network should be a place that people construct, not just access. Individuals with nothing more than a personal computer and a modem should be able to create their own communities and businesses. There need to be multiple economic models to choose from—for-profit and not-for-profit, advertising-permitted and advertising-not-permitted. Governments should facilitate the network's development—not by legislating entitlements but by structuring incentives and by funding basic research. I don't know what those incentives should look like, and I don't think anyone else does either. If I were czar of the information highway, I'd fund many small research projects that would stretch our conception of what the network might be.

Felde: There are powerful forces now promoting an information highway that would be essentially one-way. That's what "500 channel" cable TV is all about. We need to make sure that it doesn't happen, and that we build instead a switched network that allows two-way interaction between everyone who connects to it. For example, I'd redesign the FCC's "video dial tone." As presently conceived, video dial tone is a way of regulating the distribution of movies from central sources. It should instead be a means of providing individuals with universal access to the public switched network with their existing camcorders, televisions, and stereos.

I would create a tariff structure that ensures that telecommunications services cost the same regardless of geographical distance. The same 29-cent stamp now gets a letter across town or across country; e-mail, video, and other new services ought to be just as distance-insensitive. We also need to study how grassroots users—those without a lobby or an organization to represent their interests—might shape the design of the network. And to anyone who is willing to relinquish their driver's license, I would issue a telecommunications card that gives them a network address, access privileges, tax credits, equipment discounts, and low-interest home improvement loans: let people trade hydrocarbons for photons/electrons.

Roetter: First, I'd repeal any restrictions on foreign ownership of common carriers or broadcasting licenses. In fact, I would create incentives to make sure that foreign television and other programming get distributed widely in the United States. Second, with regard to the new wireless personal communications services that are going to make portable telephone service cheaper and more widely available, I would try to get a third wireless operator in every area as soon as possible. You may need two to tango but you need three for real competition. I would also look at the electronic information services that government agencies provide and try to introduce some of the best commercial practices so that we can much more effectively deal with government as citizens and as consumers.

Domnitz: As my first official act I would put half my staff on furlough. The government should get out of the way of the private sector, which has done a great job of developing innovative concepts and tools for telecommunications that are responsive to the marketplace. The best and per-haps only role for government may be to ensure universal, affordable access in situations where the market fails to provide it. I would therefore initially advocate use of government's powers only to ensure competition. If the marketplace doesn't provide everything that society needs, government can easily step in later. The federal government has been effective in deregulating and enforcing competition in the long-distance telephone industry. States that emulate the federal approach will reap substantial social and economic benefits.

Dertouzos: The first thing I'd do is try to build some awareness as to what an information infrastructure—an information market—is. I would educate people that an information market requires a lot more than just shipping uninterpreted bytes. Then I'd catalyze the establishment of agreements on standards so that computers can understand each other, so they can interpret the bytes and relieve us of work. The third thing would be to ensure more open access. That means wherever there's a question, err in the direction of shrinking the radius of control, consistent with American traditions. Finally, I would set up the beginnings of a national endowment for the information have-nots.

Schrage: I'd have really been impressed if you had led off with that one.

Dertouzos: Sometimes the most important things are last.

 Article Review Form at end of book.

Is it possible to forge a consensus about the ethics of technology?
How do we make ethical and moral decisions about its applications?

Back to the Future

The science and technology of the 21st century will be different, but we won't be.

Meg Greenfield

We are about to be engulfed in futurist talk: new term, new century, new millennium—what will it all be like? Here's one provisional answer: the science/technology will be different. Its human manipulators, subjects and beneficiaries won't. Therein lies the enduring story.

Sometimes when I am working my clumsy way through the once inconceivable electronic, cordless present I think of my own long-departed parents, when they were young and (they no doubt thought) on the cutting edge of modernity. I interrupt their 1920s courtship—the poky car they considered a new-age marvel, the relatively novel telephone and telegram and radio and movie culture in which they were comfortable and their parents were not, the manner of self-presentation and dress their parents denounced as indecent, and the cockiness with which they considered themselves newly secure in their physical health on the basis of medical advances we now consider primitive. I try to tell them about space stations and the Internet and heart and liver transplants and

cell phones and laptops. I say: look, I can sit up here in this airplane, which will get me to Europe in a very few hours, and type a story and file it to an office in Washington and exchange messages and phone calls with people around the world—all right here in my airplane seat. They are agog. But then they make the same mistake social analysts and prophets and visionaries always make. They think that life will have been transformed by these blessings in ways it has not been.

Yes, there is a sense—an important one—in which life has been transformed from the past in our age, just as it was transformed from an earlier time in theirs. Illness, ignorance and want have obviously not been eliminated. But millions upon millions of people living today, who not all that long ago would have been direly afflicted by all three, will never know them in anything like their once common form, if they know them at all. Better, faster and more are the defining terms of our culture and our condition. I don't see how anyone could doubt that or fail to be awed by the way both physical and intellectual access have been

expanded so you can go anywhere and/or learn anything with a speed that only a couple of decades ago, never mind a generation back, would have seemed merely fanciful, sci-fi stuff. And if we know anything, it is that this kind of progression is certain to continue.

Such predictions have always been a pretty safe bet. There were Greeks, there were Renaissance figures (of whom Leonardo was but one) and there were 19th-century figures, such as even the poet Tennyson, whose imaginations enabled them to see well beyond the scientific confines of their times. And so of course can we. What is harder to see is a day when human nature and human life on earth will have been commensurately transformed. What I am saying is that the humanists' insights will probably always be more to the point than the imagery of technological marvels yet to be. What Shakespeare uniquely knew about the human mind and heart and the timeless human predicament will be just as apt a millennium or two from now as it is today and was 400 years ago. The uses to which actual, famously fallible people put the newfangled marvels will still be the issue.

I think of this when the lawyer-commentators are taking us through the latest permutations of the O. J. case. All the knowledge about DNA, all the supersensitive means of analyzing microscopic traces of blood and hair and all, do not get you past an ancient kind of drama and an equally familiar set of responses to it by accuser and accused. I think of the dear old Newt mess, entangled as it now is in interception technology, unencrypted cell-phone messages, arguments about which kind of cable connector to which kind of recording device from which kind of scanner went into the notoriously taped phone call.

And, above all, I think of the tremendous conflicts in this country over the uses to which the new technologies will be put. These are conflicts riding on moral choices, and the mathematical principle has not been thought of that can resolve them. We fight about who gets the good of the lifesaving device and tech-nique. This can be a fight among equally needy individuals for a scarce resource or a fight between generations about how much one person must pay to extend another's longevity. We fight about where we should put our pooled resources to get the good of the burgeoning knowledge—in space? in bombs? in basic research? We fight about who owns the new knowledge and its fruits, who has proprietary rights, who is entitled to privacy, who should be able to hook up with whom. We fight about what to do when a new scientific blessing, as is so often the case, comes accompanied by a curse—the pesticide or vehicle or energy source that saves and also, simultaneously, sickens or kills. Decked out in our ever newer skills and abilities and seemingly magical potential, facing the glowing screens of our new life, soaring above the earth, bouncing back from a long dreaded and once mortal disease, guess what? It's the same old us.

I think it is awfully important to remember this as the rhetoric ascends toward the millennial moment, starting this week and gaining verbal altitude as the turn of the century nears. There are not and never can be any scientific rules whereby we can perfect ourselves the way we can perfect certain objects and processes in the physical world. And in this limitation will always reside our potential glory and our potential shame. It will always be easier to do the scientifically impossible thing (as we contemporaneously think of it) than to do the personally possible but difficult thing—the right thing by ourselves and by others and by the technologically amazing world we have concocted to live in. I believe, in other words, that my seemingly quaint, flapper-age parents, once they got the hang of the gadgetry, would be as at home in this world as we all would be in the super-duper one about to come. So far as its human inhabitants are concerned, we would have seen it all before.

 Article Review Form at end of book.

WiseGuide Wrap-Up

The future may be the present by the time you've finished reading the articles in this section. Do you frequently shop online? How often do you use a disposable money card or a similar product? How do these innovations make your life easier? What drawbacks do they pose? What messages do they contain? If you could "invent the future," what technology would you create to improve the quality of life?

R.E.A.L. Sites

Site name: Technology Review

URL: http://www.techreview.com/

Why is it R.E.A.L.? The mission of this cutting-edge journal published by MIT is to identify and analyze innovation, emerging technologies, and major technology breakthroughs. The site has articles about the impact of technology on culture and society and provides a free on-line archive of past issues and articles.

Key topics: future trends, computers and society

Try this: Search the TR archive to locate a recent article about future trends in computing. What new perspectives or additions does the article add to the readings in the text?

Site name: World Future Society

URL: http://www.wfs.org/index.htm

Why is it R.E.A.L.? The WFS is a nonprofit educational and scientific organization whose members are interested in how social and technological developments are shaping the future. WFS publishes *The Futurist* magazine and other periodicals. The site features "Top Ten Forecasts" published by WFS that have come to fruition.

Key topics: future trends, computers and society

Try this: Review the latest forecast offered at the site. Summarize the forecast, and explain why you think it may be reasonably accurate, or not.

Index

Names and page numbers in **bold** type indicate authors and their articles. Page numbers followed by *t* indicate tables. Page numbers followed by *n* indicate notes.

Putting it in *Perspectives*
-Review Form-

Your name:_____   Date: _____

Reading title: _____

Summarize: Provide a one-sentence summary of this reading: _____

_____

_____

_____

Follow the Thinking: How does the author back the main premise of the reading? Are the facts/opinions appropriately supported by research or available data? Is the author's thinking logical?

_____

_____

_____

_____

_____

Develop a Context (answer one or both questions): How does this reading contrast or compliment your professor's lecture treatment of the subject matter? How does this reading compare to your textbook's coverage?

_____

_____

_____

_____

_____

Question Authority: Explain why you agree/disagree with the author's main premise.

_____

_____

_____

_____

_____

COPY ME! Copy this form as needed. This form is also available at http://www.coursewise.com
Click on: *Perspectives*.